THE IMAGE OF THE FUTURE

EUROPEAN ASPECTS

A COLLECTION OF STUDIES RELATING TO EUROPEAN INTEGRATION
PUBLISHED UNDER THE AUSPICES OF THE COUNCIL OF EUROPE

SERIES A: CULTURE
NO. I

FRED. L. POLAK

Professor of Sociology at the Netherlands School of Economics, Rotterdam

THE IMAGE OF THE FUTURE

ENLIGHTENING THE PAST,
ORIENTATING THE PRESENT,
FORECASTING THE FUTURE

VOLUME TWO:

Iconoclasm of the Images of the Future, Demolition of Culture

LEYDEN – A.W.SYTHOFF
NEW YORK – OCEANA PUBLICATIONS
1961

Original title:

DE TOEKOMST IS VERLEDEN TIJD

Translated from the Dutch by Elise Boulding

LIBRARY OF CONGRESS CATALOG CARD NUMBER: 61-8137
ALL RIGHTS RESERVED

© A. W. SIJTHOFF 1961 IN LEYDEN (THE NETHERLANDS)

*This study has been originally published in Dutch with
the aid of a Council of Europe fellowship*

CONTENTS

Volume two

ICONOCLASM OF THE IMAGES OF THE FUTURE, DEMOLITION OF CULTURE

Part IV

THE DISDAINED AND DEVASTATED IMAGE OF THE FUTURE

8   CONTENTS

                                 PART V

                    THE BREACH IN OUR TIME

PART IV

THE DISDAINED AND DEVASTATED IMAGE OF THE FUTURE

INTRODUCTION

In the course of our consideration of the images of the future of western civilization we become aware of two types, at first not well differentiated, which break loose from the mass of visions. They establish themselves as independent and, ultimately, mutually hostile images: eschatology and utopia. In the process of refining the concepts connected with each image the accent has fallen increasingly on the contrasts and contradictions between the images rather than on their basic similarities as visions of the future. History has little regard for our pathetic human attempts to place ideas and movements in tidy compartments, and takes a certain pleasure in overthrowing elaborate intellectual systems. Today *all* images of the future, utopian and eschatological alike, have been driven into a corner, and out of Time. Similar causes have put them both in disrepute, and similar methods have weakened and destroyed them. The implications and consequences of this common fate which they both have suffered all point in one direction, toward a possible unfavourable turn in the future course of events for our own and succeeding generations.

Eschatology and utopia appear to be the victims of a vile conspiracy. Although they have indeed been driven into a corner, the truth is that they themselves set in motion the processes of their own dissolution. The denaturing process first began *within* each of these movements, although it was certainly in part involuntary and went much further than had ever been intended by the original participants.

The similar lines of development taken by eschatology and utopia offer a remarkable and not entirely coincidental parallel. We are forced to pause and consider why this strikingly parallel development should take place. Is there a hidden factor at work which drives these images of the future to masochistic self-destruction? If so, what relationship does it have to contemporary events, or is it perhaps an agent of the future itself, coming out into the open long enough to unchain this iconoclasm of images and then concealing itself once more from our impertinent gaze?

The most remarkable aspect of this entire development is the blindness of our generation in regard to it. How is it possible that this abrupt breach in our times, occurring mid-way through the century and already challenging the future historian to find a new label for the dawning new historical period, is going unnoticed by those participating in it? We could easily find indications of the shape of coming events from the course which the dominating images of the future for the last 30 centuries have taken in this past century. We have failed to see these indications because part of the

disintegrating process lies precisely in this, that we can no longer interpret
the messages which our own images of the future give us. We thus find
ourselves caught in a vicious cycle. We do not understand and respond to
the degeneration of our images of the future because we do not understand
their function; our lack of understanding and response hastens the silent
death of our visions. We might say that the future speaks a foreign language
to us today. But the "why" of the past remains, as well as the "where to"
of the future. We may come to an understanding of what has happened to
the old images of the future, but must we accept the absence of all present
striving to build up *new* images of the future?

The rejection and destruction of old images of the future is not the basic
phenomenon with which we are concerned. This rejection and destruction
of old images is characteristic of the dynamics of the historical process, and
has always gone on. The unique aspect of our present situation is the existence of a vacuum where the images had once been. There is a literal aversion
to images of the future as such, in the sense of positive and constructive
visions, whether of a natural or supernatural order. The image of the future
has been snatched back into the present and into daily life, with all its
doubt, sorrow and suffering. This leaves man standing at the edge of a
bottomless abyss, facing death, destruction, chaos and Nothingness.

The contemporary fashion of existentialist philosophy is even when
religious in nature and interpreted theologically, but the reverse side of the
splintered coin of the image of the future. This philosophy effectively
removes both God and the power of humanistic ideals from any influence
on the course of human events, and abandons man to the miserable empti-
ness of today. It places man on earth without perspective or goal other than
that he must die, but also without recourse to premature escape through
suicide, lest there would then be no existentialist philosophers left, or people
to admire them! Existentialist philosophy is in itself a rendition of a blind
and dumb future, possibly of a future without a future.

But let us not blame all this on existential philosophy! Theology, ideology, art, science, social movements and socialism, in short the entire style
and structure of our society, breathes the spirit of this new time, this radical
change in attitude toward the future. Every part of our culture has been
touched by this mysterious fluid, flowing not from the fountain of life but
from the fountain of death, tapping and strengthening the Freudian death
instinct latent in the social organism.

Many speak of the decline of our culture, some even speak of it as self-
destruction, but no one has, to my knowledge, laid his finger on the gaping
wound from which the life-blood of the culture is draining away—there,
where the pulsing and impassioned images of the future that have always
moved man and society now lie torn and still.

CHAPTER XVI

DE-UTOPIANIZING

We are taking up the phenomenon of de-utopianizing before that of de-eschatologizing because the de-utopianizing process is a much more obvious one, written plain for any observer to see. De-eschatologizing is a much more hidden process, and is remarked only by a small circle of experts. This is not to say that the one process is of more interest or more importance than the other, although the fate of utopia has traditionally (and in my opinion erroneously) been of more concern to the cultural sociologist than the fate of eschatology. Once we understand how the forces of destruction have operated on utopia we will understand more easily what has happened to eschatology. The novelist and the theologian may seem worlds apart, but they have both participated, each in their own way, in one and the same process. They have sat at the deathbed of the image of the future.

1. *The Historical Development of the Anti-Utopian Utopia*

In one sense the anti-utopian utopia, or the utopia which deliberately undermines itself, is as old as the genuine utopia. Its intellectual origin lies in the split nature of utopian thinking, which turns in upon itself and sees its own thinking about the future in the critic's mirror. Its spatio-temporal origin lies in Greek Antiquity, right in Plato himself, spiritual father of utopism.

Plato's *Republic* is not really a utopia according to our own definition of the term [1]. One important element is lacking; Plato does not give a fictional portrayal of his scheme as if this ideal were already or had been in operation somewhere. His book is rather a program for legislation and the future establishment of a certain social structure, based on reason and justice. Nevertheless countless utopian writers since Plato's time have made use of the many fertile ideas in the *Republic*, so that it became in effect part and parcel of the utopia literature. Plato himself made explicit utopian use of these same ideas, thus becoming his own first disciple, in his *Timaeus* and *Critias*. Both these writings achieve three things: they present the future in fictional-utopian form, they give a contrasting picture of the future which

---

1. Doren, and Ruyer, *op. cit.*, also take this view.

divides it sharply from the present, and they depict an anti-utopia at the same time that they depict the utopia.

Plato deliberately relates *Timaeus* to the *Republic* by having Socrates mention the outstanding features of the latter at the very beginning of the new work [1]. Then two contrasting kingdoms are described. The one is the *Republic* come to life as something which according to this tale already existed a thousand years ago in Attica as an ideal arch-Athenian city-state with a population of ideally virtuous citizens. The other is the kingdom of Atlantis, a mighty world power ever increasing the extent of its dominions, over Asia, Africa and Europe. This is a land overflowing with plenty and luxury, a land of intoxicated desire, where all sober self-discipline is lacking. It is strongly reminiscent of the old myths and legends about the isles of the blessed, the land of the lotus-eaters and the far-off gardens of the Gods. Atlantis's thirst for power brings the two kingdoms into conflict, and Athens is victorious. Both conquerors and vanquished are destroyed by Zeus, however, who unchains the catastrophic forces of nature and causes Atlantis to be swallowed up in the sea.

In *Critias* Plato works out the lightly-sketched utopia and counter-utopia with a more detailed description of Atlantis. This was once a noble kingdom, but it gradually degenerated. [2] The *Critias* breaks off just at the point when Zeus is aroused against the kingdom. There are many hypotheses as to why this work remained in a fragmentary state. According to some, it is completed elsewhere, in the *The Laws*. For our purposes, this question is not important. We are chiefly concerned with the idea of a counter-utopia, a device which Plato uses to explode the myths of the isles of the blessed and as a foil for the true utopia which is an ideal society of wise, sober and just people.

Theopompus imitates this procedure in a fragment of his *Philippica*, preserved by Aelianus. This is one of the oldest Greek fictional utopias, and describes the fabulous fairy land of Merope. Here again we recognize the prototypes of the black and the white utopias, of *OU*-topia and *EU*-topia. We see depicted the peaceful and pious city-state of Eusebes, inhabited by wise and perfect men possessing no material technology. Opposed to it stands the war-like, power-mad city-state of Machimos, overflowing with gold and silver, bent on perfecting military techniques and striving for world domination. Beyond the outermost boundaries of this land lies a territory from which no man returns, a land without night or day, a land

1. He says, in effect: In the *Republic* we have seen how ideal beings look in a state of inaction; now we will see them in action, and see what they are physically capable of.
2. See Dudok, *op. cit.*, for a topographical comparison with More's island of Utopia, p. 33 ff. and p. 95 ff.

of two rivers, called Pleasure and Sorrow. On a bank of the river called Pleasure there is a wondrous tree. Whoever eats of the fruit of this tree grows young again, and recedes back even further to a point *before* his earthly existence—an ancient motif in eastern legends.

With the Renaissance the utopia comes to life again, including this genre of travel romances and its complement of contra-utopias. One of the oldest of these is Bishop Joseph Hall's *Mundus alter et idem* (1605). [1] He uses the description of a land called Crapulia as an occasion for penetrating social satire. As Ross [2] summarizes it: "Government is democracy gone mad, democracy by all the people, with no one obeying, government only when drunk, government whose chief virtue is anarchy. He who eats and drinks most is regarded as the most noble and at his death his corpse is donated as a great delicacy for his servants to eat at a service to his memory. To be sober, to be moderate, to be reasonable, is a crime; man is subject to woman, fatness is the only criterion of fitness for high office and the public schools are in reality public houses."

According to Ruyer, Swift's *Gulliver's Travels* (1726) is "la première utopie anti-utopiste." [3] He is thinking primarily of the description of the island Laputa with its great academy of Lagado. This work unquestionably contains anti-utopian elements, [4] even as the earlier work of Rabelais does, and the later works of Lytton, Butler, Hudson or Tarde. But these men have not intended to create contra-utopias, although they have furnished the materials for the genuine anti-utopia of recent times.

A work that is plainly intended to be a contra-utopia is the English physician Mandeville's *The Grumbling Hive or Knaves Turned Honest*, which first appeared in 1705 and became better known in later years as *The Fable of the Bees, or Private Vices Publick Benefits* [5]. Mandeville, of French origin, is strongly under the influence of the scepticism of Montaigne and Bayle. He looks at men as they are and not as they ought to be. His main point in the *Fable of the Bees* is that only man *as he is*, with all his fearful shortcomings, can build up a great civilization; if man should succeed in

1. This was published in 1643 in Utrecht, together with Bacon's *New Atlantis* and Campanella's *City of the Sun*.
2. *Op. cit.*, p. 24.
3. *Op. cit.*, p. 193.
4. This element becomes even more pronounced in the writings of Swift's earliest imitators; for example, *A Voyage to Cacklogallinia* (1727) by Samuel Brunt, and *A Trip to the Moon* (1728) by McDermott. See Dupont, *op. cit.*, p. 271 ff.
5. Surprisingly, Aalders gives him extensive treatment (*op. cit.*, p. 83 ff.) as a utopian representative of the eighteenth century; or perhaps not so surprisingly, since it is his intention to draw as sharp a contrast as possible between eschatology and utopia.

going against his own nature and becoming really virtuous, which God forbid, he would be quickly and irrevocably doomed to destruction. By giving a central place to human egoism as an indispensable prerequisite for the general welfare (private vices public benefits) he becomes, via Adam Smith, the founder of the "dismal science", classical economics, which in turn became the great enemy of the social utopia.

The Fable of the Bees, which was at first peddled in the streets for half a penny, soon covered Europe in many translations and editions. Mandeville followed this book up with *The Moral*, in which he further emphasized the point that a wealthy, powerful and technologically advanced society could not exist as a utopia, i.e. not without the aid of the human vices of greed, dishonesty, idleness, envy, and so on, except in the minds of a few foolish men. He who would make the Golden Age live again must renounce virtue. Man cannot live by goodness alone! Every now and then Mandeville makes a polite bow in the direction of the higher Power of the deity and the church, but he does this only to show that they too are powerless to change human nature. If such an unforeseen miracle should happen, it would only cause the downfall of the human race. It is absolutely essential to the welfare of society that there should be a great mass of the unintelligent poor, who are ready and willing to work hard in the service of others. These people are also in the end the most contented members of the human race.

While the utopists raise the cry, away with this civilization based on vice, Mandeville raises the counter-cry, long live vice! Ruyer correctly points out [1] that Montesquieu takes over and makes use of this same anti-utopian conclusion in his allegorical tale of the Troglodites, in the *Lettres Persanes* of 1721. According to this counter-utopia a certain minimum amount of virtue is necessary, but a well-conducted monarchy frees itself from the bonds of a too-stern virtue and only thereby makes possible a wealthier and more refined civilization.

Another work which can be reckoned among the older counter–utopias is *Rasselas* (1759), by the legendary Samuel Johnson. Although he was a withering critic of the England of his day, he was an even more withering critic of utopias and utopian optimism: "Ye who listen with credulity to the whispers of fancy, and pursue with eagerness the phantoms of hope; who expect that age will perform the promises of youth, and that the deficiencies of the present day will be supplied by the morrow, attend to the history of Rasselas, Prince of Abyssinia [2]." Rasselas becomes restless in the Happy Valley where he dwells, and sets off on a trip around the world. This gives Johnson the opportunity to pass all manner of ways of living

---

1. *Op. cit.*, p. 198.
2. Cited in Ross, *op. cit.*, p. 13.

before the reviewing stand, to subject every type of philosophy of life to his critical scorn, and to discredit in advance all utopian striving for a better world. Completely disillusioned and demoralized, the unhappy prince finally returns home to his own valley in the last chapter (The Conclusion, in which Nothing is Concluded).

A whole century elapses before any more books appear with counter-utopia tendencies. Among those that appeared in a renewed spurt in the nineteenth century, the following may be mentioned: *Two Thousand Years Hence* (1868) by Henry O'Neil and *Across the Zodiac, The Story of a Wrecked Record*, (1880) by Percy Greg. Mallock's *New Republic* (1877), which has already been mentioned, may be included with a few reservations. It was challenged as an anti-utopia by no less than G. B. Shaw, who in his younger years published *Socialism and Superior Brains; a Reply to Mr. Mallock.*

The nineteenth century was rounded off by the publication of two books, written by the utopian author H. G. Wells, but nevertheless books with anti-utopian features which cannot be ignored. In 1899 he published *When the Sleeper Wakes*,[1] and in 1901 *The First Men in the Moon*. In both these works the evils of the time are put under the magnifying glass of the future. He describes a terrible exploitation largely based on a highly developed technology, and a systematic despotism practised by a small intelligentsia on the stupid masses. In the first book society rests on an enormously developed and extended industrial capitalism with an accompanying enslaved proletariat. In the second book the advanced state of the society depends on the artificially manipulated procreation of a super-intelligent braintrust on the one hand and of an extra-stupid species of human beings on the other, who are perfectly happy doing the most menial type of work. This is reminiscent of Mandeville, for Wells' image of the future here is certainly cast in the mold of a human insect society.

In the second quarter of the twentieth century a perfect flood of anti-utopian novels appear. At first they are inspired by the first world war and the Russian experiment, then by the second world war, the dictatorships of Mussolini, Hitler and Stalin, the atomic bomb, the Cold War, and so on. By far and away the most interesting of these novels, both from the standpoint of contents and pioneering impact, is Aldous Huxley's *Brave New World* (1932), which opens up repelling and frightening vistas of the future.

Among the most original of the writers to follow and produce a flowering of this particular catastrophic genre, are: George Orwell, with his *Animal Farm* (1946) and *Nineteen Eighty-Four* (1949), Arthur Koestler, with *Darkness at Noon* (1940) and *The Age of Longing* (1951); John Palmer, *The*

1. The revised edition published in 1911 is entitled *The Sleeper Awakes*.

Hesperides (1936), Virgil Gheorghiu, *The Twenty-Fifth Hour* (1949), Walter Jens, *Nein, Die Welt der Angeklagten* (1950), Curzio Malaparte, *La Peau* (1950), Evelyn Waugh, *Love Among the Ruins* (1953) and once again Aldous Huxley, *Ape and Essence* (1949).

So great is the popularity of this type of book today that probably every reader will have read one or more of the above-mentioned dozen. Since they are given intensive treatment in a more popular book on the modern counter-utopia which I have already started work on [1] they will not be further discussed here.

Suffice it to remark that the swelling ranks of anti-utopian novelists form a solid front against the two remaining utopists of this century, Wells and Stapledon. As far as I know, there have been no genuine utopias written since the second world war. Already back in 1871 George Meredith, the benevolent agnostic, advised Chapman and Hall against publishing the manuscript of *Erewhon*. [2] Published in spite of this advice (by another publisher!), it survived many reprintings. But it is extremely doubtful that any true utopia (which *Erewhon*, after all, was not) could find either publishers or readers today, even with the blessing of any literary authority. At the same time any counter-utopia, of whatever quality, is eagerly received. Nothing could be more symptomatic of the changing spirit of the times.

2. *Contra-Utopism in Different Keys*

Contra-utopism has journeyed a long road through history, with many twists and turnings. Many diverse ideas hide behind this general term. In order to understand the particular turn that contra-utopism has taken in our own time, it is necessary to trace its previous journey.

In Antiquity, as in the case of Plato and Theopompus, the question was basically one of a choice between good and bad utopias. The individual was himself responsible for an intelligent choice between a pure, idealistic utopia and an overwhelmingly hedonistic utopia. The latter, which is really the counter-utopia in this situation, becomes chiefly a means to the goal of pointing up the necessity for choosing the only good and true utopia. The modern anti-utopia, however, is presented as something horrible, not in relation to the true utopia as such, but to emphasize the fatal consequences ensuing from the seductive but objectionable opportunity for choice between *different* possibilities. Gradually we see the counter-utopia develop as an instrument to be used as a warning against *all* apparently desirable possibilities of any utopian nature whatsoever.

1. This book is now being translated into English under the title of *Utopia Upside-Down.* (Translator's note.)
2. Mentioned by Ross, *op. cit.*, p. 16.

A. Dis-utopia

Already in Mandeville we can see the black and white alternatives of the utopia being reversed. Now the counter-utopia is good and true, and the pure utopia is false and worthless. Mandeville stands for *realism* as opposed to *idealism*. Heaven forbid, he implies, that men should choose the ideal. It is both foolish and dangerous to the general welfare, and against man's nature. Using utopian techniques, he turns the platonic argument upside down. Hedonism is the only truth, and the summum bonum is precisely the wrong choice. Not only is a realistic attitude the only correct one, but it is the only possible one, human nature being what it is. Above all, whatever is, is best. The optimum of welfare and happiness will be reached through human nature with all its faults. Every utopian ideal would, if it could be realized (which fortunately it cannot), cause the most incredible disasters. The true utopia is then in fact dis-utopia, since virtue and goodness lead inevitably to social collapse.

Put into our terminology, it can be said that Mandeville strikes the utopia straight through the heart by replacing *essence-pessimism* plus direct *influence-optimisme* with the *essence-optimism* of "all is for the best in the best of all possible worlds". We are now back to the sources of naturalism and quietism. With Mandeville the concepts of the economic man, of the harmony between self-interest and the general welfare, laissez-faire, social darwinism and evolutionary optimism, all appear on the scene. They combine, through "scientific" rationalization after the fact, to drive out the idea of human intervention for the purpose of shaping a better social order. The result is a cynical apology for the existing order.

B. Pseudo-utopia

The suggestions thrown out rather loosely by Mandeville, that sceptical connoisseur of human nature, took hold rapidly in spite of a high initial resistance. The book at first became a scandal and was even forbidden by the authorities, but the ideas soon found official sanction in another way. They became incorporated in the social scientific thinking of the time, especially into the new economic thought. Two opposing lines of development originate from this point, according to systems which are at one only in their threat to utopism: "ôte-toi de là, que je m'y mette". Both liberalism and Marxism oppose the utopia, and function themselves as pseudo-utopias. They both maintain that utopian goals can best be realized through the laws of nature already operating in society. Utopism, in trying to alter the operations of natural law, or work against them, could only cause misfortune and chaos. Human power is already automatically discounted in the doctrine of individual self-interest, whether applied to economic progress or the class struggle, since it is in fact *self-operating* and has a mechanically regulatory effect according to the natural laws of social dynamics which it must obey. An extra-ordinary use of this human power in the form of systematic intervention contrary to these laws can only upset the natural equilibria and work harm to the general welfare. The "lawless" operations of utopism are not only impossible and superfluous, they are downright detrimental.

When it became evident that the pseudo-utopian pretentions of liberalism and Marxism could not be maintained, man did not turn back to the true utopia, but to a third type of pseudo-utopia, that of fascism nationalsocialism and communism. These do not rest their claims on a divine or natural order that excludes human assistance, but declare themselves already invested with super-natural power, whether or not divine in origin. In contrast to liberalism and Marxism, they take fate into their own hands after The Revolution, even as utopism urges, but they completely negate the primary point of departure and ultimate goal of all utopism: human dignity and worth. They promise an ideal state on earth, not in terms of an ideal relationship between man and man, but rather, in the tradition of Mandeville, Machiavelli, Fichte and Hegel, in terms of national and imperial greatness, power and wealth. This pseudo-utopia, whether or not connected with pseudo-eschatology, is nothing more than social myth.

C. Semi-utopia

The above-mentioned types of counter-utopias have left their mark on the genuine utopia. They have compelled the application to utopism of the newer techniques of natural science, and they have also aroused a rebellion against the anti-spiritual tendencies of the dis-utopia and the pseudo-utopia. Both these phenomena are seen in the work of the modern utopists like Wells and Stapledon. As a result, the utopia is very much in danger of losing its specific character. Between the influences of natural science and spiritualism, it becomes an unrecognizable object, neither fish nor fowl: a semi-utopia. Science draws it too close to every-day reality, and spiritualism pushes it too far from every kind of reality.

The classical conceptual model in the natural sciences requires, in order to be applied analogously to the social sciences, a working with exactly measurable and definable categories, with mechanical causality, empirical positivism, and above all with the strict determinism unique to the physicalist-nomothetic procedures of this type of scientific analysis. The pure scientist's ideal of a differentiation between What Is and What Ought To Be, between knowledge and value, facts and norms, condemns the social utopia to a non-scientific status as a useless pastime, when it is judged by the standards of this prevailing model of science.

As soon as utopism complies with these demands and aspires to scientific standing, it assumes the character of a social anticipation, of projection and prognosis, of an extra-polation of existing trends. It then differs very little from scientific social planning. But social planning, even if it is aimed at social reform, works with the *existing order* and moves only a step at a time. This is no radical break with the present, no turning to The Other. It is impossible that it should be anything of that nature, because historical determinism is basically irreconcilable with free self-determination of one's own destiny, the foundation-stone of all utopism.

The utopia betrays itself in quite another direction, when it fails to stay within its own province of human society on earth. This point has been discussed before. Recent utopias have not only moved back to the original point of a platonic mirroring of the divine idea in social life, but even further. They have moved right back into the infinite and immeasurable cosmos, towards metaphysics and myth, reaching to the farthest limits of eschatology and almost becoming identified with it. Thus they overshoot the age-long goal of the utopia. While Mandeville no longer recognizes the possibility of Divine intervention and the elevation of natural man, also rejecting all humanitarian idealism, Wells and Stapledon go on a search for the Divine into the farthest reaches of cosmic Space, and no longer concern themselves with the relatively insignificant troubles of mortal man on microscopic earth. To them man is only a mite among the myriad spiral nebulae of the starry infinite, for which time-space distances are reckoned in trillions of years.

Even while the genuine utopia is in its death throes, the semi-utopia is in process of giving birth to a new genre. This is science-fiction, [1] which has had its greatest impetus from American writers, especially in the last ten years. It has spread all over Europe, along with Hollywood films, jazz and bebop as a part of "the American way of life". Science-fiction is a hybrid product, frequently neither science nor fiction in the more literary sense of the word. It is related to crime stories and the comics. It has in part crowded these out, and in part swallowed them up into itself. Its career has been a stormy rise from newspaper serials to magazine fiction, [2] then to book and at last to anthology. [3] On the whole, science-fiction is a highly commercial-

1. For an excellent treatment of this subject see O. Shaftel, "The Social Content of Science Fiction", *Science and Society*, spring, 1953. Compare this with S. Spriel, "Sur la 'Science-Fiction'", *Esprit*, May, 1953, See also Basil Davenport, *Inquiry Into Science Fiction*, Longmans, Green, and Co., 1955.
2. Perhaps the best known of these magazines is Astounding Science Fiction. Other well known ones are Amazing Stories, Fantastic Adventures, Astonishing or Startling Stories, Thrilling Wonder Stories, Galaxy, etc.
3. For example, *The Best Science Fiction*, New York, 1946; *a Treasury of Science Fiction*,

ized product. In pocket-book form it has reached printings in the millions and has grown into one of the largest and most popular pulp industries. It has its fanatic fans and its book clubs. Film, radio and television have further widened its range of communication. This front of "coca-colonization" has even penetrated into France, which is already familiar with "fantascience" and has its Parisian "Club des Savanturiers".

What is this new comet in the American skies? In design and feeling science-fiction continues to remain uniquely American. It is American to the extent that it represents a facet of the American pioneer philosophy that nothing is impossible. It is also American in its mirroring of a new feeling-tone which has crept into this pioneer philosophy; it represents a retreat from unbridled optimism about the future into a rapidly engulfing pessimism about Tomorrow—a real future-neurosis. On the one hand science-fiction is a continuation of the swashbuckling romantic frontier adventures of the "Westerns". The frontier is now in space, and the new worlds to conquer are literally other worlds. The escapism is escape into the *future*, rather than into the past; there is no idealization of what has been, but an emphasis on what is to be, including a vision of endless possibilities of things to be accomplished through the invention of more and more ingenious gadgets. On the other hand there is a shift from a major to a minor key. There is a kind of space phobia, a hysterical attitude towards all that is far away and "foreign", which serves in part to conceal an even more acute time neurosis: a fear of the onrushing stream of time with the ever more drastic changes it brings; a fear that the Unknown may be Undesirable, which leads people to "keep tight hold of nurse, for fear of finding something worse".[1]

All this is highly suggestive and interesting, but relates chiefly to the special developments in the American image of the future and the parallel developments in American culture, which I hope to make a special study of at some later time. Within the frame of reference of this work we must confine ourselves to those general aspects of this development which also apply to the course of Western-European thinking about the future. This more general trend of thought which is equally characteristic of America and Europe is not fully recognized or correctly evaluated by most observers of the contemporary scene. The forms which science-fiction takes are so numerous and diverse [2] that it is not easy to reduce the shifting patterns to

New York, 1948; *The Astounding Science Fiction Anthology*, New York, 1952; *Adventures in Space and Time*, New York, 1946; *New Tales of Space and Time*, New York, 1951, and so on. There are approximately a dozen of those omnibusses published each year.

1. Hillaire Belloc, *Cautionary Tales*.
2. Shaftel begins his analysis thus: "Space cadet comics and television programs,

one basic figure. For example, it has hardly penetrated as yet into the inner sanctum of science itself, although reputable scientists and writers with scientific training also make use of this medium to try out their ideas. Perhaps its significance can best be explained by reasoning back from the tremendous attraction which this genre has for the masses. What is the nature of the attraction? For one thing, science-fiction offers an exciting set of new sensations to prick the jaded appetites of today's bored public. It succeeds, in a time when the astonishing fails to astound, in eliciting the breathless reaction, "How can such things be!", and at the same time awakens a combination of feelings of guilt, shame, fear and horror, plus an erotic-sensual interest in the abnormal. The common ingredients are: the shocker-thriller à-la-detective, technocracy, pornography, sadism, escapism in space and time, with a breath of Freud-Kierkegaard-Nietzsche-Spengler-Sartre and a sauce of Prometheus-Icarus-Columbus-Jules Verne-Wells. There is also a generous admixture of melodrama (in American terminology, space-opera), macabre machines and terrifying technology, monsters and maniacal subhumans, rockets and robots, planeteers and pin-ups, noble aspirations and tingling sex-appeal.

What are the main themes of science-fiction at the present time? In spite of the vast army of writers at work producing these books and the tremendous possibilities for imagining new and ingenious devices or combining old ones, the number of themes is definitely limited; the stories tend to be somewhat monotonous, the flights of imagination disappointing, and the human element unvarying. No matter how far they fly into space, the planeteers are disconcertingly down-to-earth. A few of the main variations will be suggested.

An important theme is war, both international and intergalactic, with fantastic weapons, projectiles and rays, and also radio-active and bacteriological materials that cause gene mutations and an accompanying degeneration of the human body. Another theme is psychic control over the individual and the masses by soul-engineers, with a similar degeneration of the human spirit. Then there are interplanetary adventures, with invasion of the earth by beings from other planets, often with an accompanying subjection and exploitation of man. Or the enslavement of man by tyrannical robots (the Frankenstein motif), or the supremacy of mechanical supermen, as the Cartesian formula, "I think, therefore I am", is applied to

five-and-dime atomic blasters, movie flights to the moon and Collier articles on space survival, flying saucers from Mars, pulp magazine covers with a thirtieth century Perseus in a space-suit snatching a wispily-clad Andromeda from the tentacles of a green denizen of Fomalhaut—these are trappings of the science-fiction fad that has grown up with the atomic bomb."

thinking machines. [1] Or the Malthusian motif of increasing over-population of the earth and the ultimate extinction of man through starvation. There are also many other themes, all in a minor key, all centering around the doom of man and civilization as a result of improbable and impossible technological achievements and a complete failure in the realm of moral, social, cultural and political achievements. Science-fiction projects the existentialist categories of sorrow, fear, want, suffering and death into the future, making it look so alarming that man can only fall back and be glad to live in the grey and comfortless here-and-now. With a sigh of relief he accepts the relative security of the known world. It is not, after all, as bad as one had thought.

This typically anti-utopian outcome of the semi-utopia is not the only paradox in science-fiction. Another paradox is that, originating in the unlimited possibilities of modern science, science-fiction ends as anti-scientific propaganda. Also, it includes in its utopias exactly those elements which eschatology is throwing out of its scheme of things, especially mythology. Finally, science-fiction loses the directed and focussed qualities of the utopia. Laden with ambivalance, it drifts hither and yon in rudderless fashion, between a positive and a negative pole.

Science-fiction makes so crystal clear what the monstrous and fatal consequences of the continued development of the physical and social sciences might be that it revives the old idea of a moratorium on further scientific research. According to Shaftel, science-fiction treats of the newest developments in "cybernetics, hydroponics, parapsychology and psycho- and socio-dynamics", along with those of "nucleonics, atomics and electronics". The scientist is frequently represented as a modern devil in human form, like Spriel's "Savant-Satan". [2] The tree of knowledge produces only forbidden fruit, as Luther and Rousseau have already shown. The greedy consumption of this fruit can only lead to man's being driven from the earth in a final dramatic enactment of the paradise-drama, which is only a prelude to worse things to come. Escapism thus ends in the suggestion that it is science which brings evil into the world. In the interests of his own self-preservation man must escape from its tyranny through a return to nature.

Most remarkable is the way in which this type of semi-utopia has assumed eschatological characteristics at the same time that eschatology is shedding its own garments only to reclothe itself in utopian dress, as will be discussed further in the next chapter. Eschatology is stripping itself of its primitive and mythical wonder-tales and super-natural images, in order to become

1. See Isaac Asimov, *I Robot*, Gnome Press, New York, 1951. This describes a new type of robot with built-in-controls according to the newly-discovered "laws of robotics".
2. See Spriel, *op. cit.*

more acceptable to modern scientific thought. Science-fiction, on the contrary, is busy picking up the leavings. No wonder is too wonderful, no natural phenomenon too super-natural, no borrowings from old myths and legends to provide themes of intervention of higher powers too outlandish. In the other worlds of science-fiction all the improbabilities of mythology and biblical literature live again as real possibilities. Prophecy, magic and apocalypse are having a second hey-day. Science-fiction is tinged with a religious belief in wonders which religion itself has rejected as unrealistic.

Most of all, science-fiction mirrors the uncertainty of the times about the future. There are still traces of the old progress-optimism and enlightened rationalism concerning the possibilities of improving the world through science, continued in an unbroken line from Bacon to Einstein. There are traces of the old influence-optimism, active and direct. Something of Promethean man lives on in the hubris, or arrogant presumptiveness of a god-like superman. In spelling out this presumption for every man to read, science-fiction contributes to the self-destruction of mankind. It leaves its readers tossing helplessly between hope and despair, power and impotence, heaven and hell.

Let us draw up the balance sheet for these positive and negative aspects of science-fiction. On the positive side goes all that the semi-utopia has preserved of the vitality of the genuine utopia, whose decadent off-spring she is. We must especially note the critique of the times, which finds an important place in science-fiction. Sometimes the critique of the times is cast in the classical form of the encounter between superior beings of another planet, living according to an exalted value system and having very few material needs, and earthlings, who are despised by the superior beings for their feverish preoccupation with the drudgery of trivial affairs. This humbling lesson strengthens a feeling of historical relativity and helps to free the ideals of even the unrivalled American Way from the corroding rust of overweening pride and self-conceit. Insofar as it does this, science-fiction keeps a path open through the wilderness of censorship, black lists, witch-hunting and mind-building, for the free expression of ideas of the free mind. It guards the road, however narrow, to the open future, and lets through the non-conformist and the man with his eyes on far horizons.

Science-fiction also carries on the tradition, in however decadent a form, of the systematic construction of another world, based on different premises and possibilities than our own. It does look ahead and think about the future. It also concerns itself with the problems of social dynamics. In trying to write the history of the future, it makes a prognosis concerning the possible further development of technology and compels the reader to speculate about the kinds of adjustments which technology will force on man and society. The influence of technology on human society is a theme of crucial importance. In a sense, then, science-fiction provides a prophetic and pre-sociological preparation for the onrushing *second industrial revolution*.

Over against these unmistakable services of science-fiction we must place the negative side, the anti-scientific and anti-cultural focus of the genre as a whole. In its culture-pessimism it points away from progress toward retrogression, and its development is on the whole anti-utopian and anti-humanistic. Man and his values are laid low by the boomerang of man's own struggle toward progress. All human power peters out in impotence and disaster. Fatalism and nihilism rule in the final outcome of all movements in the field of social forces. The far-seeing vision makes way for neurotic hallucinations, the wish-dream is replaced by a nightmare. The present is a veritable paradise compared with the inferno of the future. The semi-utopia is a transitional form leading in the direction of the negative utopia.

D. Negative Utopia

The negative utopia combines all the aspects of all the previously mentioned kinds of anti-utopias, but in a systematically intensified manner.

It is the very oldest, platonic anti-utopia in modern dress, but it stands alone without the counterpart of a genuine, positive utopia. Its creator says, this is *it*. There is *no* utopia possible anymore, other than this black and negative one.

It is the dis-utopia of Mandeville, in which cynicism is carried to a reductio ad absurdum by applying biological manipulations to the task of creating even more stupid and brutish human beings (as in the case of the epsilons in *Brave New World*).

It is the pseudo-utopia in both its aspects, that of liberal and Marxian social Darwinism, and that of inhuman and tyrannical dictatorship (for example, the work of Koestler, Orwell, Huxley, Kendal, Palmer, Jens, Gheorghiu, etc.).

It is the semi-utopia, with its eugenic experiments, its technology, its natural-science-oriented social psychology, its quasi-religion, its demonic deification of The Leader (Ford as Lord in *Brave New World*), and with its substitution of wonder-tales for the Christian religion in the spiritual diet of the masses.

The negative utopia is all this, and more. It borrows from the genuine utopia the satiric technique of axiomatic reversal. It outdoes Cyrano, Holberg, Rabelais, and all the portrayers of the world upside-down to Lytton and Butler. However, the negative utopia does not turn *this* world upside-down in its replacement of positive by negative values, but the *world of the utopia itself. The negative utopia is a caricature of utopia*. It applies the special technique of utopian thinking about the future, not to *reality*, but to the *fiction* of the utopian image of the future, with devastating results.

"Les utopies sont réalisables. La vie marche vers les utopies. Et peut-être un siècle nouveau commence-t-il, un siècle ou les intellectuels et la classe cultivée rêveront aux moyens d'éviter les utopies et de retourner à une société non utopique, moins "parfaite" et plus libre." Thus Huxley quotes Berdiaiev in *Brave New World*. The emphasis here is on the fact that utopia is realistic and possible. As in the genuine utopia, the negative utopia systematically works out the realistic possibilities of the ideas presented. The difference is, that whereas in the genuine utopia the *possible* and the *desirable* form an unbroken whole, in the negative utopia the goal is to show that the possibility under consideration is as *undesirable* as it is *unavoidable*. The negative utopia is thus deliberately and consciously destructive in intent.

In our terminology, *essence-pessimism* is related through the *élite* to a direct and active influence-optimism on one side, and on the other side it is related through the *masses* to a passive and indirect influence-optimism. The net result of these two relationships is ultimately, as demonstrated by the negative utopias, a tremendous increase in *essence-pessimism*. The general impression they communicate and propagate is that all Faustian human power, whether of good or evil intent, inevitably produces a satanic supernatural power and a far worse situation than the original status quo; further, any other, more positive course of development is impossible. Man is thus *ready* for the good (or perhaps not even that), but he is not *able to achieve* the good. Utopia inevitably becomes dis-utopia. The more fully man realizes his utopia, the more evil he unleashes in the world. Utopian striving, then, is not only meaningless but definitely disastrous.

It is not so much that utopia is *impossible*, in this view, as that man is *impotent*. The negative utopia makes a direct attack on the Achilles heel of all utopism. In the moment that man makes use of his own *power*, which is the essence of all utopian striving, his *lack of power* becomes painfully evident. In this sense every utopia as it unfolds into the future operates by necessity as an anti-utopia. Thus it is that the "brave new world" is neither brave nor new, nor is it even a world, in any humanly worthy way, but an "animal farm" or embryo factory.

It is this genre of negative utopia which dominates and characterizes the spirit of the times. It is this utopia which opens the way into a possible, nay, unavoidable other world; an evil world, but one for which man has only himself and his own strivings to thank.

3. Inconoclasm of the Images of the Future

We have just seen in what ways the de-utopianizing of the utopia has taken place. What had once been the essence of utopism, the satirical critique of the times and the systematic hypothetical reconstruction, have now become weapons to be used against the utopia itself. The positive utopian image of the future has been completely turned upside down in all its component parts: the *positive* has been *negatived*, the *future de-futured* and the *image demolished*.

A. Negativation

The negativing process, as has already been stated, has been a utopian technique from the earliest days. It was originally a contrast device, pointing up differences between the existing order and another order, or the good and the bad utopia. The device came gradually to be used with a different emphasis. Now the existing order receives the positive accent and the utopia the negative accent. In the beginning it was chiefly a matter of an occasional voice breathing a hint of a fantastic paradox. Now this paradox is the chief theme of a mighty chorus of writers, whose sound is well-amplified by all the mass-media at their disposal. The exception has become the rule, and the paradox has become the obvious.

It is clear that the utopia has contained a double charge of explosives. Not only did it cause the Middle Ages to burst into Modern Times, but it is exploding Modern Times into smithereens and itself along with it. *Every utopia is historically relative* and carries within itself the seeds of its own decay as its future is transmuted into past through the present. *The power of the utopian idea*, however, has until now seemed absolute, and has caused the utopian torch to be handed on from generation to generation. Now we are for the first time faced with the problem of whether the utopia as such is mortal, or rather liable to self-destruction; whether the utopian image of the future does not contain its own doom.

This last generation has somehow fumbled in receiving the utopian torch, and has succeeded in setting everything in flames. It seems at the least to have gotten into the wrong hands, into the hands of the anti-utopists. They are the villains of the piece who, disguised as utopists, are leading the genuine ones to be burned at the stake. Then, disregarding the amenities of a decent burial, the anti-utopists are scattering the utopian ashes to the four winds over the earth the utopists loved so dearly in life. In the negative utopia utopism has outlived itself and ordered its own execution. Anti-utopists and anti-futurists get their most clinching arguments from the negative utopia. And while we are either laughing or grieving ourselves to death over its satanic satire on the future, lustreless tomorrow lies quiet on its deathbed.

B. De-futurizing

Is this but a figure of speech? Of course, de-futurizing is primarily a spiritual process, but a deadly serious one and with unhallowed consequences for times to come. We mean by the term a retreat from constructive thinking about the future in order to dig oneself into the trenches of the Here-and-Now. It is a ruthless elimination of future-centered idealism by today-centered realism, an elimination of all thinkers about the future as poets and dreamers who are out of tune with the times. What the world really needs, we keep hearing, is realists, and above all realistic politicians; also specialists, social engineers, organizers, builders, architects, regional planners, managing directors and general staffs. We must do that which we find at hand to do, acting opportunistically, elastically, mechanically. We must only move forward one step at a time, and weigh the pros and cons of every argument most carefully. We moderns do not operate speculatively but empirically. We "think and do".[1] We are slow but sure; we move on a trial and error basis, no matter if the world's survival is threatened by our possible errors, no matter if our civilization is already on trial. The future is no longer a separate entity, but is squeezed into the day-to-day movement of the present. We have lost the ability to see any further than to the end of our collective nose.

The horizon is perhaps a bit narrower for the practical politician, a bit wider for the socialist; narrower for those who are concerned with immediate policy decisions, whether in government or business, wider for those concerned with over-all planning. But everyone takes the *existing situation* as the basic point of departure. The daily paper not only summarizes the day, but our times. Our whole civilization is becoming a one-night stand affair. Sufficient to each day is the evil thereof. The near future is more heavily obscured than it has ever been in the past, and we, in a sage act of self-limitation, choose to let it be so. The future is but a continuation of today, the prolongation of yesterday until tomorrow. We are no longer willing or able to peer around the corner of the century, or even to peer into the next decade, except when it is a question of dealing with millions of years and vast distances in space. The very size of such time dimensions renders them harmless and non-threatening to the present. Between now and infinity, however, there is a great vacuum. The same people who will animatedly discuss the next million years greet the topic of the next one hunderd years with dead silence.

C. De-imaging

Once more, is this a figure of speech? No, it refers to the third part of the process of destroying the image of the future. This iconoclasm reaches a climax in the negative utopia, which is a caricature of the future and at

1. Accustomed to European educational methods, the author has been fascinated by the title of the first-grade reading work-book widely used in the U.S.A.: *Think-and-Do Book* (The New Basic Readers, Scott, Foresman and Co.).

last delivers us into the realm of comic books, whose crooked and poorly-drawn images now replace the utopian image of the future. It is not true that modern man no longer thinks in images; only, those images now have quite a different referent. [1]

Insofar as they still refer to the future, their content is destructive, chaotic, nihilistic and absurd, revolting and full of despair. The iconoclasm is directed chiefly against the vision of another and better future. It is only a step from the caricature of these monstrous and chimerical images of the future, so filled with horror, to the rejection of *all* images of the future.

There remain then only those images which depict the world as it is or those which are based on the world as it is. There are four ways of changing the picture of the existing world; three are real, namely science, technology and politics. The fourth is an escapist technique, used by the current recreation-media, such as fiction, film, radio, television. All of these are intimately related to our own time. We no longer have time to spare for the future, spel-bound as we are by the intricate complexities of the overburdened present. This we can only escape momentarily and by highly artificial means unless, of course, we choose a permanent release through suicide. Here again we are faced with the extremes of the moment and eternity, with nothing in between. Anyway, *is* there really a future? If there is, why waste time in fruitless speculation about something which is subject to so many unforeseeable variables that we cannot possibly make any sensible predictions about it? If there is not, as we are being told more and more of late, so much the worse for us, but there is no sense in making fools of ourselves over empty visions. Negative images of the future have made us spiritually ripe for a visionless existence bounded by today.

Having described this three-fold process of negativation, de-futurising and de-imaging, we find ourselves still on the surface of the phenomenon of the iconoclasm. We have not penetrated into the heart of the de-utopianizing process. In the last analysis we must be concerned with the changed relationship between *Man* and *Time*, which is expressed in a new image of man and a new spirit of the times.

When modern man limits his time-consciousness to the *present*, we may term this a weakening of the *utopian awareness*, the source of all thinking about the future. This utopian awareness, as has been repeatedly said, operates on the basis of two inward drives: the split nature and polar tension of the spiritual life, and the urge towards self-determination of our own destiny. Out of the split personality comes the conception of The Other as possible and desirable. Out of the desire for self-determination comes the acceptance of the challenge to create an ideal society. The changes in the

1. See Chapter XVIII, section 1A.

spirit of the times and in the attitudes of mind of modern men strike at the heart of these two drives. These changes could be labelled *de-dualising* and *de-humanising*.

D. De-dualising

De-dualising is a phenomenon that is especially characteristic of the natural sciences. The pattern of thought of the modern scientist (at least according to the classical model of physics), which the natural sciences have already left far behind but which still controls most of the lagging social sciences, tends towards monism. It is a monism which considers only one aspect of a complex phenomenon and still demands for its results exclusive recognition and universal validity. This model of thought chooses an object detached from the subject, facts without values, quantity devoid of quality. It analyzes the constituent parts of a phenomenon, but does not synthesize the whole; he speaks in the indicative, not in the imperative. It places the universal language of mathematics above speculation, and frees empirical science from ethics and metaphysics. It is positivistic, mechanistically-minded, rejecting the normative and the organic. It recognizes only causal realism. Idealism is displaced into another order of reality altogether, outside science, and is considered a personal matter which is not suitable for comparison or verification. As it happens, this type of natural-science approach has been elevated to the position of ultimate standard for all scientific work, with an accompanying tendency to regard the non-"scientific" as non-existent.

This type of positivism has been greatly accentuated by the developments and applications of the technical sciences. We are now at the hey-day of scientific materialism. Everything that can be experimentally confirmed, that can be seen, touched, measured, registered and controlled, is given a high value. This has led to the specifically modern habit of matter-of-factness and to the narrowing of awareness which Whitehead has termed "the fallacy of misplaced concreteness". There are *not* "more things in heaven and earth . . . than thou hast dreamt in thy philosophy". The modern Horatio, in fact, only does *his* dreaming on the psycho-analyst's couch or at the movies. His philosophy is bounded by Existentialism and Death.

Spiritual existence is more and more forced back into the one dimension of the here-and-now, of that which envelops us (Jaspers' "das Umgreifende"), of the concrete situation which is always for every individual "that which is mine" (Heideggers "Jemeinigkeit"). Thus limited to a struggle with existence in this place and time, limited to the sorry emotions inherent in earthly existence, man must accept the fact that things can never be different. Human affairs dwindle down to an impersonal membership in an anonymous social aggregate. Life is flattened out; it lies inert, without depth, meaning, colour or value. It amounts to nothing more than an insect society equipped with aeroplanes; highly mobile, but stagnant in time. Human wits are dulled to the point where they can encompass nothing more imaginative than the threading of one day after the other on the string of time. They can no longer envision The Other, let alone believe in its realization.

Life's basic challenge, the breach between the Is and the Ought, has received the most ignominious treatment of all. It has been annulled, erased, ignored. There *is* no other reality than this rather contemptible, basically unchangeable world.

Paradoxically, the very act of eliminating the idealistic dualism represented by this breach brings about The Great Breach in our times.

E. De-humanising

The destruction of dualism leads to the destruction of humanity. Monism not only excludes the possibility of the "Umwertung aller Werte" (the revaluing of all values), but the confinement of the spirit to the tangible fact leads to the *devaluing of all values*. Realism stifles idealism, just as materialism stifles spirituality and the mass-mind chokes off the élite. Humanitarian idealism first gives way in the face of scepticism, and is finally routed by nihilism.

Let us not make the mistake of romanticising and idealising the past, of whatever historical period. There was *never* a time when man, "en masse" was overflowing with altruism, spirituality and nobility. The utopian critique of every age reveals quite the contrary. Otherwise Rousseau would have felt no need to present us with the image of the "noble savage", or Swift, with wise and noble horses. Or, to go back considerably further, we should never have needed the symbolic figure of "old Adam" (and his Eve!). Is "nihilism", then, new in name only, representing a phenomenon as old as sinful man? Does the "imbecile" in Bernanos perhaps belong to all time, and also Camus' "pest" and Sartre's "dirty hands"? Are we by nature tainted with Freudian complexes and drives? Are we all a mixture of Judas, Brutus, Macbeth, Machiavelli, Cesare Borgia, Tartuffe, Ivan Karamazoff, Raskolnikov, Attila and Hitler? Is history nothing more than the chronicle of human misdeeds leading to ultimate damnation? What (in the name of science!) is there to indicate that the great mass of humanity is any more stupid, wicked or doomed today than it ever was? Could we not rather say that the very fact that modern man refuses to believe in utopian fairy tales points to an emancipation of the human mind toward a more sober self-knowledge?

Indeed, there are no *objective criteria* for the measurement of the progress of human insight in various ages. Empirical science, with all its techniques, has not yet brought us so far. It may well be, however, that there are *specific related phenomena* in any age which indicate unmistakable trends. Nihilism is not an isolated system of ideas but is part of an organic total structure which we label the spirit of the times, the style of a culture, or cultural patterns of behaviour. In my opinion it is neither mass-mindedness nor materialism which gives such a menacing character to the times, but their intimate relationship with *technocracy*. The mechanization of life, not only in working hours but in our leisure time, extending even beyond our manual to our mental activities, extends the influence of technology far beyond its original scope and threatens to enslave mankind into the passivity of a race of automatons.

It is technical development which is responsible for our spiritual reversal. It first led to a tremendous progress-optimism and overstrained belief in the possibilities of human power, but when the course of events failed to confirm this optimism, bitter disillusionment set in. This disillusionment fell into a spiritual vacuum, for complete reliance on this same technology had already undermined the spiritual recources with which man had previously met his disappointments. The will to recovery and revival was gone. At the very zenith of human power over the physical environment man suddenly realized his impotence. Now cultural pessimism and fatalism have free play. The Balloon of the Future has burst like a bubble. Man has already driven God out of the world of human affairs; now he sees himself as abandoned by God and also personally eliminated as the guiding force in history that he had imagined himself to be. Overwhelmed by the forces of the time which he has himself unleashed, and unnerved to the point of immobility, he now lets himself be driven blindly hither and yon by these forces. He finds his comfort all too willingly in the words of those prophets of doom who maintain that things had to happen this way. In abject capitulation he renounces his rightful heritage of *human power* achieved through the age-long struggle of his forbears with their environment and prostrates himself before the whims of a seemingly inescapable destiny, steered by *supernatural power*.

The de-humanising of man is basically the loss of belief and confidence in man's own worth. Nihilism is related to feelings of worthlessness, of the nothingness of man in the vastness of the cosmos, of hopelessness that man could possibly prevail against the overpowering and unfriendly forces of the universe. As a result of the industrial revolution, man is incapable of conceiving that anything can move except through the pushing of buttons. Now he is faced with a machine too vast for him to comprehend, with buttons he has no strength to push. Once again we have the philosophy, "il mondo va da se", only with a complete change of emphasis; the world no longer runs *for* man's benefit, but *against* it.

What can man in all his smallness, small in spite of his mass-identification, do in the face of the deadly powers which he himself has helped unleash in the world? Man stands as "l'Etre" over against "le Néant". Everything goes from Nothingness to Nothingness. Nietsche and Kierkegaard, Heidegger and Sartre each interprets in his own way this same basic modern spirit, which in its western nihilism paired with inaction comes very close to the eastern Nirvana, with its rejection of the world and the flesh. But whereas Nirvana sets the future to heavenly music, this utopia sets its image of the future to a funeral march. Nirvana raises man to thin air above and beyond human existence; western "nothingness" sinks him to the lowest depth of inhumanity.

When man's utopian aspirations to raise his own humanity towards the highest values die out, then man himself dies.

CHAPTER XVII

DE-ESCHATOLOGIZING

Pontius Pilate did not succeed in putting the true Jesus to death, but in the ensuing 2000 years Christian theologians have been slowly but surely achieving just this in their efforts each to save a Jesus created in their own image. Jesus can take care of his enemies, but God has not been willing to allow him to be protected against his friends. The history of Christianity is the history of its progressive self-de-Cristianization. Truth is stronger than fiction. The dramatist's art could never construct a tragedy as grim as this true-life tragedy.

The cultural sociologist who as a non-specialist wishes to sketch the broad outlines of the historical development of Christianity, is aware that he is bound to offend from the first sentence to the last. Nevertheless the theologians unblushingly tell each other, in their professional jargon, this very tale of destruction. They do not present it as a world drama, but pass it off as an eschatological exegesis of the New Testament. [1] It is not difficult for the outsider to offer criticism, but it is difficult for him to offer constructive criticism of what is basically a demolition process. It is even more difficult, perhaps impossible, to do so in a way that will avoid misunderstanding and antagonism on the part of the theologians. The subject is a delicate one, and it is not possible for the secular sociologist to transform theological into sociological categories without committing some errors.

This hardly affects the task at hand, which is to sketch the general outlines of the de-eschatologizing process, for this process has amazing parallels to the de-utopianizing process. I fear that I risk offending some deeply held convictions, however, which I regret, but the problem is of such overwhelming importance that it goes far beyond individual feelings and detailed professional specialties. It is as much a matter of conscience as of competence to apply sociological knowledge to the diagnosis of a seriously ailing Christianity.

1. *Historical Development of Anti-Eschatological Eschatology*

The teachings of Jesus have already been discussed in Chapter VII as a messianic proclamation of a rapidly nearing Kingdom of God. We have

1. There has been a flood of theological literature on this subject in the last decades, especially in Western Europe.

avoided the issue of whether Jesus ever really lived and, if so, what he actually taught as over against the words ascribed to him by the Evangelists. Presumably no archeological excavations or textual criticism of the Bible can ever give a precise answer to these questions. It is clear, however, that the *image of the future* evoked by Jesus, as revealed in the records of the first three gospels, is on the one hand closely connected with the image of the future taught by the Jewish prophets preceding him, and on the other hand makes a historic breach in the existing situation of his day. This second aspect was the heart of the Glad Tidings. Jesus did not teach his disciples to pray, "Thy Kingdom come", in reference to a far-off, ultimate event. It had the implications of a total reversal soon to be revealed—the end of time decreed by God, which his followers would live to see. This element of revolutionary realization of another and better world here on earth, "as in heaven", also entered into our definition of pure eschatology (see p. 437).

Such a definition is not acceptable to the great majority of Christian theologians today, however. A long-drawn-out regressive movement in theology has resulted in the building up of an eschatology "sans eschaton". And as in the fairy-tale about the emperor's new clothes, which are supposed to be visible only to good people, no one dares to admit not seeing what isn't there. This undermining of eschatology is not the product of any noble or ignoble competition either to adorn or distort Christian thought. Rather it stems from a profound human need or even a bitter necessity for rationalization after the fact.

Two negative factors have set this eroding rationalization process in motion, one direct and one indirect. The most immediately obvious factor is the disappointment of the fervent expectations concerning the speedy return of Christ to this world. This expectation was quenched by the mere passage of time, and although it springs up again repeatedly, inspired by the clear words of the Bible, it is each time thereafter quenched again, often in a blood bath. The immediate promise is not fulfilled. It is thinkable that Jesus, the Son of God, could have been mistaken concerning the time of his coming and of the great reversal? Here exegesis *must* take over, and that quickly. It began already in the time of the Apostles.

Another negative factor has operated indirectly over a long period of time to undermine the expectation of any Second Coming at all, even apart from details concerning time and place. Modern man after some two thousand years represents the culmination of a new point of view concerning God, human life, the world and society which makes it possible for him, even in his role as a good Christian, to believe in a tangible re-creation of this world at a given moment, whether introduced by clarion calls, cosmic catastrophes and a battling of the angelic hosts with the hordes of Satan or not. The idea itself, the vision of a coming other and better world, has been impaired. Unnoticed, it has disintegrated under the corroding action of time. [1]

We have said that these two factors forced theology into a rationalization after the fact, in order to save what could be saved of the Glad Tidings. This is true, but it is not the whole story. Of equal and possibly even greater importance is what cultural sociology might label an attempt at rationalization before the fact by theology. It is not true that the theologian is perpetually being pulled along by the modern believer in a vain race with time. He sometimes takes the lead, and thus assumes the role of fore-runner in the true sense of the word. Again and again a theology of crisis develops which is not only an *answer* to the times, but itself a *challenge*.

It is a challenge in two ways corresponding to the above-mentioned negative factors. It de-historizes, and de-scandalizes the religious records. The de-historizing aims at purifying the sayings of Jesus and the Revelation of John of any elements of precise time computations, and at making the evangelical "soon" relative and reassigning to it the meaning "some day"; its goal is to force the biblical prophecy of fulfilment out of the concrete time-flow into an abstract eternity. This process is coupled with an attempt at dematerializing with respect to earthly prospects and focussing attention on the Beyond rather than the Here through a general spiritualizing process. Time and space undergo a similar negation, as the Kingdom of God is moved out of historical time and spatial events.

This de-historizing was, at least in the beginning, mainly a process of transposition; the de-scandalizing, however, was almost from the very start directed at elimination of the incriminated subject matter, or actually had this effect. For the latter undermined precisely that which Paul singled out as unique in the new Christian teaching, that which was therefore a stumbling block to the Jews and a foolishness to the Greeks. Here we come face to face with a fourfold paradox, perhaps the most enormous and least understood paradox in the history of Christian culture. This is what it implies:

1. There has been a continuous attempt to replace the divine wisdom taught by Jesus in his language and for his time with the human (and particularly theological) wisdom of this century, in order to purge the teachings of Jesus of what have now become stumbling blocks and foolishness even for Christians.

---

1. The strongest evidence for this is perhaps to be found in England and America, particularly the latter. The theme of "Christian Hope" in the Assembly of the World Council of Churches in Evanston, Illinois, in 1955 reflects this development. See the Appendix to Chapter VI.

2. This attempt has been characterized by a thorough-going exegesis which has had the ironical effect of negating the Jewishness and Greekness of the gospels.

3. Christianity's first theologian, the Apostle Paul, himself began this process (in spite of the wisdom expressed in I. Cor. 2 : 6-16) and opened the way for a later negating of his own doctrines and the development of a long chain of eschatological interpretations which in the end resulted in a progressive de-eschatologizing.

4. This development, which continued on from primitive Christianity through the Roman Catholic Church, has been supported both by Reformation and Counter-Reformation. Today it seems to have gone farthest in Protestantism, in which the extremes of ecclesiastical orthodoxy and a liberalism which borders on humanism appear to meet. In fact, however, the Catholic Church has also been inwardly affected by these spiritual currents.

It would be necessary to go into an extensive study of the history of theology in order to document the above contention. This, however, belongs neither to the competence of the writer or the domain of this book. We can but give glimpses of an intensive spiritual process as it has been taking place over a period of two thousand years, and risk misunderstanding at every turn.

Paul himself laid the foundations for a Christology in which the man Jesus made way for Christ, the Lord, and in which the teachings concerning the *Kingdom* made way for teaching concerning *Salvation*. Next, Paul is himself interpreted according to the Fourth Gospel of John, whose Christ-mysticism assists in the Hellenization of the Jewish-apocalyptic strain of the teachings of Jesus by covering them over with Greek logos-metaphysics. The death, resurrection and exaltation of Jesus as the Christ come to assume a central place in the sin-grace-salvation schema, while the life and heroic-ethical mission of Jesus, the prophet, and the good news concerning earthly renewal proclaimed by him, recede into the background. The Kingdom of Grace comes to dominate over the Kingdom of Glory.

At the same time there was a shift from belief in a cosmic re-creation to belief in individual salvation. Individual redemption came to be valued more highly than the collective salvation of society. This shift also encompassed a shift of orientation from *future* to *past* – and to *present*. Towards the past, in a preoccupation with the sacrificial death on the cross of Jesus, redeeming man once and for all time, and in a pre-occupation with the renewal which in that moment (or right after the resurrection and ascension) took place. Towards the present, by virtue of the factual presence of Christ for those who through the renewal of conversion and faith lived with him daily, and died in him. This was a presence both in the spirit, through the Holy Ghost, and in the body and the soul, through Holy Communion. The bodily presence extended further to the presence of the Church as the Corpus Christi. These are further shifts drawing emphasis away from the flesh and toward the spiritual body, signs of a progressive spiritualization through "transsubstantiation" of the Christian doctrine.

The Roman-Catholic sacraments of which Jesus is considered to be the priestly minister and by means of which earthly life is also sanctified by him, are visible signs of this same process. The Eucharist, which brings about communion between the resurrected Saviour and man, is the most significant sign. The priestly attendant is the mediating instrument of Jesus, lending him tongue and hands that Jesus may continue to bestow grace upon man. The believers come into fellowship with Christ through these sacraments and he affects their lives from day to day, by virtue of his past being present always and everywhere. It is mainly through the Church that this sacramental present receives more and more stress, whereas the eschatological future evaporates. In the sacrament the parousia is as it were already realized; in the Holy Mass the death on the cross is actualized over and over again, and the "donec veniat" (I. Cor. 11 : 26), literally meaning "till he comes", is more and more neglected for the past-perfect "I am come".

The regnum Christi, incorporated in the Church, has already begun, and expands with the growth of the Church—through Roman Catholicism, through evangelization, through missionary work among the heathen, through the crusades and through the inquisition against unbelievers, nonconformists and heretics. The extension of the temporal power of the Church is an extention of the kingdom of Christ. The Kingdom of God, the basileia tou theou, is as we have said in the meantime slowly fading into the background. The Church through its sacraments grants redemption from sin and rebirth in Christ during *this* life, in this earthly dispensation. Man need no longer wait for a future announcement of election to the community of believers in the new order of the Kingdom of God; he can receive his salvation now through the visible church of this congregation. By mediating the achievement of personal perfection, the empirical church exalted itself to a high magnitude of perfection.

Augustine's *Civitas Dei* unconsciously furthers this development. Attention is concentrated on the problem of defense against the temporal rule of the Anti-Christ rather than on the eventual return of Christ. The spiritual liberation of the individual from the chains of a diabolical power in a bewitched world has become more important to this generation and for this life than a time-free dream of longing for a new heaven and earth to be born in the future. Eternal life in the heavenly Hereafter can now be won through constant personal striving. This striving is reflected in the godly life filled with compassion, charity and good works, and is concretely witnessed to in the magnificent cathedrals whose towers reach upwards toward the visible heavens to the glory of an invisible God.

Even before the Reformation broke loose against the Roman Catholic Church, cosmic eschatology had largely been reworked into individual and *ecclesiastical* eschatology. The Christian Church was increasingly proclaiming *itself* as the accomplished eschatological fact of salvation, and was thus gradually assuming for itself identity with the coming Kingdom of God announced by Jesus. In this mediating role it was able to gain admittance for the faithful both to this earthly realm and to unearthly rebirth. The Church was itself a sign of the onset of the Last Times, a visible token of the fulness (plèroma) of time, an unveiling of the secret of God's plan. In short, the Church moved from the position of intermediary to that of ultimate goal: the development of the Kingdom of God.

The reformers Luther, Melanchton, Zwingli and Calvin were not protesting *this* point of view. Whatever differences they had with Roman Catholicism, and among themselves concerning Protestant versus reform orientations, and however much the Bible was re-examined as a literal proclamation of the Word become Flesh, no questions were raised concerning the teaching of Jesus about the coming Kingdom, nor concerning the Revelations of John. On the contrary, while they vied with each other in proclaiming God's mercy in Christ, and although they bitterly and fanatically fought each other in religious wars, they united in a merciless battle to put to the fire and the sword the "criminal ungodly heretics", who, chiefly in chiliast and adventist sects, held fast to Jesus' promise of the near establishment of God's glory on earth and who were ready to lay down their lives for this fervent faith. The prophetic perspective which Jesus opened on an imminent earthly fulfilment for the entire community of believers, and not only the souls of the departed, was moved farther and farther away to a shadowy, unreal end of time. The insistence of cosmic eternity thus evaporates into the bliss of beatification—a beatification for the individual elect, immediately after the end of a life lived and concluded in redeeming faith and surrender to God.

Neither the Reformation nor the Counter-Reformation destroyed the fundamental position that Christ, the only-begotten Son of God, *has already come*, and that the Holy Ghost has been present among man ever since. The idea of the predicted Second Coming became blurred and was even deliberately blotted out. The conception of a breakthrough to a long-hoped-for new time, a time of salvation and glory under God's rule, has itself been pierced and spiritually broken. It is surprising, even for the social scientist, that theological thought, while desiring to be extra-temporally exalted above the cyclical movements of the "Zeitgeist", is not only in its changing structure narrowly connected with the dynamics of the general cultural pattern, but, moreover, in the course of history works with exactly the *same models of thought*, which have successively determined scientific thought in his own field of studying man and society.

Theology of the last five centuries exhibits all the characteristics we note in the general development of science. The classical natural science, liberalism, Darwinism, rationalism, the Enlightenment, Romanticism, evolutionary optimism, philosophical idealism, cultural pessimism, existentialism, and, finally, modern natural science, by turn also made their deep imprints on theological thought. Each generation has tried to wipe out those cultural marks and matrices left by preceding generations, and has in turn introduced its own. It took several centuries to wipe out the models of thought of the Middle Ages, and then the dominating conceptions of the eighteenth and nineteenth centuries had to be successively erased. Now in the twentieth century we are preoccupied with rubbing out the last Judaic and Hellenic traces in theology. New-Testament theology is certainly a living science but its many and various approaches to eschatology have only succeeded in nearly killing it off as an idea, or at least shifted it to the realm of the inconceivable—something like the fate of modern physics.

Jacob Taubes concludes his interesting study on *Abendländische Eschatologie* of 1947 with a discussion of Hegel, Kierkegaard and Marx; this, in his opinion, seems to close the subject entirely. [1] Shortly before the first world war, Troeltsch had already issued his famous statement: "The eschatological bureau is closed these days". This was not entirely true, however. Even apart from such social-religious movements as those led by Blumhardts, father and son, and Ragaz, there was still something of the original eschatology left. There was individually oriented soteriology, a doctrine of personal salvation concerning the achievement of eternal life after death. There was also a spiritualized belief in the coming of the Kingdom of God. This was introduced by philosophical eschatology as the expected end-result of a spreading and exalted humanitarianism and the gradual evolution toward ideals of brotherhood and justice through the immanent growth of an internal kingdom of the human spirit. And in 1906 Schweitzer's monumental work translated as *The Quest of the Historical Jesus* was published, a work which represented the rediscovery of the eschatology of primitive

1. *Op. cit.*, p. 191.

Christianity in all its primary significance, in the person of the historical evangelical Jesus.

Schweitzer's work, which gradually won in influence, brought a paradoxical course of development to that climax implicit in the ambivalent tenor of his work. On the one hand his call for a revival of "consistent eschatology" was both understood and followed, but on the other hand he himself provided the impetus for a further de-eschatologizing process. This process has been carried through to its ultimate implications in a number of eschatological publications which have awakened much current interest. It can be said without exaggeration that every eschatological study which has appeared since the time of Schweitzer has systematically, if unconsciously, negated and destroyed eschatology while ostensibly supporting it.

The technique of de-eschatologizing is applied in a manner every bit as subtle and refined as in the case of de-utopianizing. The situation is very similar. We find eschatology-sans-eschaton, eschatology turned upside down, the Realm of the Future minus future, a messianic kingdom minus messiah and territory, a Kingdom of God without God. A non-Christian existentialist like Jaspers finds himself rebelling against this unchristian theology, and modern Christian theologians find themselves thinking in atheistic existentialist terms, for example derived from Heidegger and Sartre. Since Karl Barth will permit modern man to speak of angels only and no longer of demons, I dare not suggest that this paradoxical situation indicates a demonized world.

Demonic heavenly and earthly powers are a foolishness to modern thought. Theology now attempts to remove the stumbling block, the Scandal. It is not difficult to *begin* the destruction of the Scandal, but it is very difficult to *end* it. In its beginnings the process appears both innocent and reasonable. It is a question of separating out the precious and imperishable contents from the rough and perishable form, absolute values from relative wrappings. The historical Jesus, it is explained, used an image-rich language which was easily comprehensible to his own contemporaries. His words need to be translated, and his time-bound images re-interpreted so that modern man can derive meanings from them which will be equivalent to their original meanings. The first step in this process is to purify this language and eliminate the Jewish dogmatism and prophetic apocalyptics which were current at that time, as well as the messianic symbolism and eastern gnostic mythology. Then the later graftings of Greek metaphysics and Johannine logos mysticism must be carefully removed, in order to make the teaching of Jesus understandable and acceptable to the modern mind.

This secularizing process has progressed from an attack on the outer trappings of Christian teaching to a subversive penetration of its inmost core, in the attempt to make it conform to modern ideas. But what is this inmost core? For the orthodox fundamentalist it is *all* core, down to the last "a", "and" and "the" of the Bible. From the religious point of view, this position is perhaps both the simplest and the strongest. At the same time, if even one word is seriously questioned it turns out to be the weakest, for then the whole structure collapses. There has in fact been a gradual retreat on all fronts. The Catholic Church has been the one to hold on the longest to miracles, to the immaculate conception and in general to a *credo quia absurdum*. But how long will it be possible to cling to a belief which is absurd in the face of modern thought? If the existentialist conception that life in itself cannot be but essentially absurd gains ground, how can we then live by a faith which still implies the deliverance from this unavoidable absurdity?

The Church has had to give up, bit by bit, many of its irrational positions. Only an illogical intellectual tour de force can hold the last line of defense. Belief in the heavenly pre-existence of Jesus before his earthly birth is fading, along with the belief in his virgin birth, the empty grave, his re-surrection from the dead while still in human form, the recognized scars of his pierced hands, his position at the right of God's throne in the firma-ment and his corporeal presence at Holy Communion. With these the belief in the resurrection of the flesh, the immortality of the soul and life in a Hereafter, heaven, hell and purgatory as well as in a Second Coming are also fading. Modern man does not listen for the sound of the Arch-Angel Gabriel's trumpet, heralding the cosmic battle between the forces of light and the forces of darkness, nor does he get excited at the prospect of the final victory over the Anti-Christ and the glorious moment when all the faithful, both living and dead, shall be swiftly gathered up on the clouds and carried to meet their Lord in the heavens. Not only has heaven ceased to be a place, but time has lost its eschatological end-point. Christ will not come, there will be no renewal of earth. The Garden of Eden will not be re-entered and there will be no complete unfolding of human dignity in a world made divine by God as announced by Jesus.

The inconoclasm ends with the destruction of the eschaton proclaimed by Jesus. It first destroys Jesus, the historical man, then it destroys the Christ, God-sent, and finally it inevitably destroys God Himself. Here again the attack was originally directed at the biblical use of images. It concentrated itself against the image of the God of Abraham, Isaac and Jacob as a speaking, moving, intervening God, as a God of love and hate, of forgiveness and vengeance, of election and judgement. It attacked the idea that all history moved according to God's will, stumbling from time to time through incredible catastrophes but sweeping on to ultimate salvation. It rejected the idea of a God who would conclude a covenant with one particular people and choose this people of all peoples to receive His Son. Both Israel *and* this theodicy are insurmountable stumbling-blocks to modern thought.

If God indeed did send His Son to the Jews, then He must have intended for them to crucify Jesus and used them as tools for His own Purposes. He brought about the death on the cross in order that mankind might be redeemed. Jesus could only conquer human sin by being sacrificed by it. Without the cross, no judgement, no grace, no salvation. Without the Jewish misdeed, no judge, no saviour, no suffering servant and no Salvator Mundi. Without a slaying, no Resurrection—for many centuries the most convincing evidence of God's power and of man's possible rebirth to a new life. Then one must conclude that the Jews were a chosen people in this sense too, that Christianity could be born only out of their deadly sin; without their graceless wickedness, Christian grace and salvation is inconceivable. But in that case one must also conclude that this misdeed was no misdeed, but a predestined salvationary act; no cause for weeping, but for rejoicing. The early church fathers spoke, in this connection, of a *felix culpa*. The inevitable consequence is that it is not possible either to charge the Jews with sin to purge the Gospel of its Judaism without radically undermining the Gospel itself.

Modern thought goes even further in its great wisdom. It assails the theodicy as never before on the grounds of an ancient problem as old as Doubting Thomas and older, reaching right back into the Book of Job. If Holy God wills the unholy evil of this world, including the fall of Adam, the crucifixion of Jesus and the post-Christian unchristian era of now about two thousand years, then he is neither all-good nor all-beneficent. If he does not will this evil, then he is not all-mighty. This is the problem as it was put of old. The modern approach adds: If there is a personal, living God who exercises good will and wise power, why does man need to take the detour of divine grace and redemption from evil, if God did Himself admit this evil into the world? And why does God need this round-about way to reconcile a fallen world with Himself? The ancient view that this world is not the creation of God but of a demi-urge and is subject to the power of Satan, is once more gaining ground, as appears in the rejection of the Old-Testament account of the active and purposeful creation of the world and of man as a meaningful and holy act on the part of God, the *Creator*.

Here again a process of elimination sets in: God is ejected from his heavenly place (divine housing shortage!), ejected from the course of history (this world and the man cast into it, abandoned by God), and has been removed to an existence so spatially and spiritually distant that it permits of no personal communication of son to Father in prayer. God is no longer omnipresent and omnipotent, responsible for every sparrow that falls to earth. He has evaporated into the Spinozan primeval source of all being into the Platonic idea and philosophic faith (Jaspers), into the inconceivable and unreal Holy Name which expresses the unknowable and the inexpressible. He becomes the "I am that which I am not", an I-less abstraction and an impersonal metaphysical concept.

As soon as the current world image rejects the idea of this world as a *creation* of God, an image of the future which envisions the divine re-creation of this world must inevitably be discarded as a piece of outmoded symbolic furniture. Once the Beginning is subject to doubt, the End also becomes shaky. The following words concerning the fulfilment of time are still to be found at the close of the Confession of Faith of the Dutch Protestant Church: "Therefore we await that great day with a great longing, that we may rejoice fully in God's Promise, in Jesus Christ our Lord" (Article 37). But the "great day" has disappeared into the mists, and the "great longing". has become a hollow phrase for many. "God's Promise" concerning the establishment of His Kingdom conveys little or nothing to the average church member of today— certainly no more than it conveys to the ministers and theologians who handle this edifying term so authoritatively. A god of promises (even oaths) is as much of a contradiction in terms and a Christian scandal as a god descending to the sound of trumpets to rule on earth.

Modern man is turning more and more to science for an explanation of the beginning and the end of this world. No supernatural intervention is required in this picture. Increasingly, modern man is not reading any meaning into the course of events, nor does he believe that they are being moved toward a predestined end. The keynote sounded by many current authors is that of the meaninglessness of earthly existence. The time to come, tomorrow's today, has no more or different meaning than the here-and-now today. *There are no Last Things.* The other and better world that up till this age has always beckoned on the spiritual horizon, is neither existential nor real. A product of the imagination, it is no more than superstition and must be rejected as such. The biblical image of the future, according to this view, was simply a reflection of the "Weltanschauung" of a certain historical period, one which cannot stand up against the "Weltanschauung" of our own times.

The theologians are seeking diligently but vainly to square the circle. They try to retain the Bible as divine revelation while throwing out the ballast of the biblical image of the future; to retain the Christian faith minus stumbling blocks, keeping the mystical Christ and the ethical Jesus, but throwing out the prophet; to retain God as the primal Source of all things, while abandoning the Final Goal; to make Him First, and then not Last-Present, but Absent.

2. *Counter-Eschatology in Sheep's Clothing*

The striking parallels between counter-utopia and counter-eschatology will be more systematically pursued in this section. The emphasis will be on comparison, rather than on a complete analysis of counter-eschatology, and we have chosen certain characteristic categories of this phenomenon as the framework for our discussion.

A. Thorough-going Eschatology

The first half of our century (and perhaps, in retrospect, the whole of our century) has been profoundly influenced by the religious thought and work of Albert Schweitzer. His influence has been both positive and negative. He exceeds the dialectical Barth in dialectics, the paradoxical theologian Kierkegaard in paradox, and the polarized theology of Ritschl in ambivalence. He exceeds the philosophical idealists Kant and Hegel in idealism, the voluntaristic philosophers Augustinus and Schopenhauer in voluntarism, the Johannine Christian mystics in mysticism. But he also overstrains eschatology to "consistent eschatology", unleashing a de-eschatologizing process which develops in a contrary direction as *consistent de-eschatologizing*.

In dealing with Schweitzer's life of Jesus (which follows the line of thought developed by Schleiermacher, Weiss and Wrede), [1] we are more concerned with the conclusions which he and others drew from his study of Jesus, than with his actual view of Jesus. Schweitzer maintains emphatically that the New Testament, and especially the Synoptic Gospels, must be read in the way of "consistent eschatology"; that is, we must think ourselves back into Jesus' own thoughts and emotions through a process of mystical communion and historical resonance. Once we have identified ourselves with the speaking and acting Jesus, we realize that he was completely filled with one idea: that of a speedy coming of a messianic reign on earth. Jesus did not think that he was to bring about this reign himself immediately, but he expected and proclaimed it with glowing conviction. The Messiah will not be born, but will appear as the divine Son of Man and usher in the cosmic re-creation after a short period of catastrophic upheaval, that the Kingdom of Heaven may come on earth.

Jesus lived, taught, suffered and died for this alone, this summum bonum of the coming Kingdom of God. His dominating motive was not the redemption of individual man, but the salvation and rebirth of all mankind. Schweitzer feels that this inner conviction of Jesus came without a doubt

1. Macmillan, *The Quest of the Historical Jesus*. Doubleday, Doran, *Christianity and the Religions of the World*. Dodd, Mead and Co., *The Mystery of the Kingdom of God*. Holt, *Mysticism of Paul the Apostle*. Holt, *Out of my Life and Thought*.

from the late Jewish apocalypse, from the prophetic messianism, religious dogmatism and gnostic metaphysics which prevailed in his day. Presently, says Schweitzer, Jesus was doomed to the bitter discovery that he had been mistaken and misled by his dreams: the prophesied parousia failed to come about. The natural course of events disavowed his meta-historic idea. Jesus then attempted to compel God to make this dogma triumph over history by taking the role of the suffering servant and provoking his own suffering and death. The death of the Messiah was to ensure the coming of the Messiah. The sacrifice on the cross was a deliberate, well-thought-out messianic act, inspired by and in fulfilment of the Old Testament prophecy. Jesus condemned himself to death, and sought this particular manner of execution for himself alone, that his eschatological pronouncements concerning the speedy coming of the Kingdom might thereby become fact. Only if we read the Gospel as the story of a thorough-going eschatology can we understand and experience it.

The goal so far in Schweitzer's writings has been to *experience* Jesus and the Gospel anew, in our time. But just at this point comes the great and unexpected counter-eschatological turning point, inaugurated by Schweitzer himself. Having demonstrated at some length the extent to which Jesus was transported by this *idée fixe* of an immanent coming of the Kingdom, and having made the point that we can really only understand and unite with Jesus if we enter into his own thinking about this, then he goes on to say that it is impossible for modern man to go back to the image of the future which Jesus had. This image of the future is the product of a "naive" train of thought embodied in a cultural mode and in primitive materials of presentation which are time-bound and inextricably linked to the Jewish eschatological story of salvation. This imagery is secondary, and the essential eternal message, equally valid for our own time, must be separated from it. The core of his Weltanschauung must be liberated from the pinching but changeable bonds of history.

Schweitzer feels that the primary thing in the teachings of Jesus is the faithful expectation of a coming Kingdom of God which will redeem mankind from this world's evil. Equally primary is the heroic ethics of "Weltverneinung" in respect to the existing order and of "Weltvollendung" through a purposive shift toward a better world to be achieved through a dedicated striving for ethical perfection on the part of man. Should Jesus return in our own time, says Schweitzer, he would preach exactly the same expectation of the Kingdom of God and an essentially similar way of life and truth for man on the road toward this Realm of the Future. But he would do it in a modern way, leaving out ancient Jewish supernatural imagery and dogmatics.

It is up to us, Schweitzer concludes, to translate the naively imaginative depictions of Jesus into modern thought, taking a free approach to history and a liberal approach to an ossified theology. We must emancipate ourselves from the authority of the Jewish doctrines concerning God which Jesus accepted, and instead make ourselves subject to his exalted ethical will. We must experience Jesus in his "Hoffen und Wollen", focussed on the Kingdom. Modern man's communion with Jesus is a communion of will with will, of *will-mysticism*. The will determines the Weltanschauung and the Last Things, not the reverse. Inspired by Jesus, we must will the moral perfection of mankind, and actively, enthusiastically work for it. His unconquerable ethical spirit must be made to prevail through the force of the dedicated deed. Then and then only we become children of the Kingdom.

Why is this ethical-eschatological revision of the Gospel basically counter-eschatological? The point of departure seems little changed in this translation, and the recommended course of action for man is a familiar one. *But the fixed ultimate goal has fallen away.* Schweitzer no longer speaks of a *coming* (let alone a speedy coming) of the Kingdom of God, and can in fact no longer do so. We can only hope for *a* coming—the whether and the when can no longer be known with certainty. The reason is that the Kingdom will not come by an act of divine intervention in history, but through the moral will and striving of *man*. God Himself is changed. Like Hegel's rational world-spirit, Schweitzer's God is a moral world-will. This moral world-will resides in man, a Kantian conscience. God's will is not revealed, but expresses itself in human moral law and moral will, and in the ethos of loving service based on the "venaratio vitae", the reverence for life. The establishment of the Kingdom of God does not occur in supernatural fashion according to a supernatural will. It is not *transcendent*, but *immanent;* not suddenly descending out of another dimension from above, but unfolding here below.

   Instead of being the product of a cosmic revolution, Schweitzer's Kingdom of God is the result of an anthropocentric humanistic developmental process. Not in the twinkling of an eye, but step by step through toilsome ethical striving. For Schweitzer that which is fundamental is not the Kingdom of God, but the existence of man, not religion, but humanity. Jewish-Christian eschatology is reduced to humanistic culture and social ethics; Golgothe becomes Lambarene. Jesus, and his ideas, are sent back into his own time. Schweitzer maintains that true religion is independent of history. He would free it and abstract it from the burdens of the *past:* in other words, from Jewish dogma and imagery. But at the same time he thus frees it from any fixed goal in the *future*, and absolves God from responsibility for the New Covenant which Jesus preached.

The belief in a predestined end for man which can be wrought by God alone disappears. Jesus is not the Christ, not the Son of God, not the Redeemer, the Saviour or the Sanctifier. His suffering and death had nothing to do with a new heaven and a new earth. Christianity cannot offer redemption, resurrection and rebirth. Neither can it offer reconciliation with God, nor a victory over evil and death, nor a realization of a Divine Plan of Salvation for mankind. The historical Jesus has come and gone, never to return again. He has left only the memory of his illuminating human example. He did not reveal the Word of God, nor is the Church his incarnation. Instead of a sudden sacred and transcendent blaze of glory at the end of the last act of time, Schweitzer offers us a play without an ending. The play stretches out in scene after scene of endless toiling as idealistic man follows haltingly but full of hope and good will in the steps of Jesus, the great moral teacher, striving for personal perfection and fulfilment of his highest ethical potentialities. In this way and this way alone, can man live the Christian life; that is, *live in* the world as one who is *other than* the world.

In our terminology, Schweitzer continues the development from religious to philosophic chiliasm in the tradition of Reimarus, Lessing, Kant and Schleiermacher, with a shifting of the theological accent from apostolic and dogmatic Christianity to a philosophical system of ethics. But he also eliminates the eschaton of the Last Things and replaces it by a humanistic goal of self-fulfilment for man—a philosophical act with far-reaching consequences. The goal is set by man himself, under the inspiration of Jesus, or it is at least the goal that man ought to set on the basis of this inspiration. It is a goal he must set, even though in his ignorance of the future he cannot know whether it is valid or attainable. Finally, in the struggle to achieve this self-chosen goal through self-realization, he shifts the focus from superhuman to human power.

The ultimate goal postulated by Schweitzer continues to bear the same name bestowed by Jesus on *his* vision: the Kingdom of God. But it is in fact little different and scarcely more than an *ethically secularized agnostic residu*, à la Kant. Schweitzer's gospel contains no single biblical messianic idea which could give the slightest pause to modern rationalistic thought. The ethics of the will and the mysticism of the will, related to the will of the man Jesus as the ideal-type of moral willing and acting, does not flow out of faith and revelation, but out of philosophical and social-humanitarian idealism. Ultimate goal and primal source of this "consistent eschatology" are in fact *identical* with those of the *utopia*. Schweitzer's ethical voluntarism can easily be translated into the direct influence-optimism of utopian thinking about the future.

For this very reason, this de-eschatologizing takes on a heroic-tragic character. The transition from eschatology to utopia, as a necessary adaptation to modern thought, takes place just at the beginning of a period in which this same modern thought is directed toward *de-utopianizing*. This reduction, then, must inevitably have negative consequences. Schweitzer himself is in part aware of this. He points out that modern man lacks the capacity for resonance with the eschatological (read:utopian) Weltanschauung of Jesus. The nature and will of Jesus must remain alien to us, because our intellectual and emotional life contains no equivalent to his moral conviction concerning the general fulfilment of mankind. A living communion with the true Jesus is no longer possible; not because of the Jewish accoutrements of his faith, but because of his basic human convictions concerning another and better world which must inevitably come. This eschatological conception (read: utopian awareness) has been lost.

Jesus was sustained by his unshakeable Jewish faith in God's omnipotence and the constant conviction that the coming of the Kingdom had been revealed to him and through him. Schweitzer, a true modern, believes neither in God's actively intervening omnipresence nor in the revelation of the Last Things by a Son of God. He believes in Jesus the man, whose teachings contain the highest human values known to man. He calls upon mankind to realize these exalted values in this earthly existence by its own efforts, but he issues his call at just the moment when the faith in man's rational and moral capacities to renew society and guide his own destiny is on the wane. Only a vacuum remains: blind destiny darts capriciously in undetermined directions. Thorough-going eschatology makes way for thorough-going anarchy or tyranny.

Beside the liberal ethical thinker Schweitzer another figure emerges, this time from the house of reformed orthodoxy: Karl Barth, whose equally consistent eschatology has made its mark on the theological thought of our century. One would perhaps not expect a man who has returned to the work of Luther and Calvin and thus to the Holy Writ itself, to play a role in the de-eschatologizing process. It is not so surprising, however, when one considers that the great reformers were already retreating from eschatology in their fight against the chiliasts, and that Barth is primarily a disciple of Kierkegaard. Kierkegaard did not deal with mankind, but with the individual man as a person, far distanced in his despair and impotence from a personal but hidden God. He emphasizes the unbridgeable gap between the human here and now and the Other, in heaven and eternity.

In his *Commentary on the Epistles to the Romans* (1918) [1] Barth builds up a

---

1. In this work he opposes Schweitzer's synoptic Jesus with the Pauline Jesus.

thorough-going eschatology which has exercised a profound influence for decades. Just as Schweitzer's influence has been greatly magnified by his work in Africa, so has Barth's impact been intensified by his tireless battle against national socialism and German "Christianity". Barth later (1940) revoked his original eschatology and presented a new, deviating doctrine. This has won as much support as his earlier position—because Barth is Barth. His earlier view also continues to be influential through the work of kindred spirits and disciples, and is worthy of a brief description as symptomatic of our time.

Barth re-establishes the Kingdom of God as *God's* Kingdom, as the final outcome of God's will and the outpouring of divine mercy on sinful man. Man must not only live in faith and hope of this ending, but, while accepting God's judgment concerning his complete human unworthiness, he must let this firm expectation rule his whole life continuously. Barth's thorough-going eschatology maintains that man is permanently caught in the polar tensions between this sinful world and the other holy one. "Permanently" means that he feels this intensely from minute to minute unceasingly during his entire earthly existence. This unremitting tension places man every moment before the choice, before the decision of yes or no, for or against.

This tensed expectation concerning the coming of the Kingdom, which gives direction to human life, is independant of the historical stream of events. The *coming* is entirely independent of the *future*. The coming is not measurable by any human time categories of soon or late, will not be fulfilled in historical time, and is not involved in the passing of centuries. For Barth the Kingdom of God is here, the eternal Kingdom of the eternal God. Eternity is always present, from moment to moment. It is always actual and existent. Therefore the Kingdom of God is also here and now, since God's Eternity stands over time as the horizon stands over the revolving earth. Therefore the parousia is also here and now, since Christ is always present, always with us unto all eternity.

All talk of the perpetually postponed parousia is therefore meaningless, if not nonsensical. That which can never come in time, can even less stay in time. The biblical expression, "The Kingdom of Heaven is at hand" means nothing more nor less than that the eternal Kingdom of God stands before us, within our reach, deciding our life and commanding our decision. There is no question of a *future coming* on earth of that which is already come and is eternally present. There is no transition from time to eternity, and eternity in its turn leaves time to its own devices. The coming of the Kingdom is not a visible turning point in this world's time, but a revolution accomplished by God outside and beyond history—and this in spite of the fact that man must at every hour decide and act as if the boundary between time and eternity could be overstepped.

Does the banner of thorough-going eschatology camouflage a contraband cargo? He who does not shrink from a sharp answer could say that this eschatology is consistent because it completely eliminates the consistency of the old eschatology, preserving only the empty hull. This coming Kingdom of Barth's is a Kingdom of the Future *without Kingdom, without Future,* and *without coming* in the usual sense of the word.

No Kingdom. This Kingdom of God is and remains in the Beyond, not of and not for this world. It is neither visible nor tangible to human eye or hand. Transcendental, independent of man and culture, it is not concerned with a transformation of the cosmos but contents itself with a numinous being in the Godhead, remote from and inconceivable to man.

No Future. In the dialectical opposition of time and eternity the Kingdom of God is considered as an eternal category lying outside time and history, and thus eliminated from time to come and events to come. The proclamation is unprophetic and unhistorical, the content of the message static and *without perspective.* The contrast is no longer between this age and an Age-to-come, for eternity is not counted by and takes no account of centuries. For man, every period of time is *the* time, for standing in the present he is ever faced with eternity. Every day is the day of judgement.

No coming. The Kingdom is awaited as a coming event, but it can never come, as such, to man. Man comes to the Kingdom through taking his decision, through the act of choice. This view is similar to the nineteenth century "Heranbildung des Menschengeschlechts" through the gradual spiritual evolution of man, to the concept of the growth of the Kingdom in the hearts of men. The coming-which-will-not-come is spiritual and dialectical, but without sythesis. *Where* is man going? What is his ultimate goal? This remains the unknown, the impenetrable mystery. The Kingdom of God would appear to be an attribute or perhaps the very substance of a hidden God, who reveals himself only by withdrawing further into an opaque darkness. The Christian faith is here descandalized, not through rationalization, but by removing the irrational and placing it as an eternal enigma beyond the grasp of human thought, mystical and metaphysical.

The Kingdom is thus a noumenon for man, knowable to God alone. But in this case it can be *no eschaton.* The concepts of the end of time, the Day of the Lord and the Last Things were not just a space-time category, but above all a category of human thought concerning the final goal which made human existence on earth meaningful. They represented the highest imaginative projections into the future of which religious thought is capable. But the modernized expectations of *this* kind of Kingdom of God become endless, contentless and ultimately hopeless in any earthly sense. These are self-contradicting expectations: a timeless and goal-less waiting—for nothing. God's Eternity here becomes the negation of the times and the negation of all temporal expectations.

The two kinds of "thorough-going eschatology" described here, that of Schweitzer and that of Barth, different as they are, become the prototypes of further counter-eschatological developments. Almost all later ramifications and patterns are implied in the basic elements of these prototypes.

B. Endless Eschatology

Liberal modern theology had already tried in the nineteenth century to separate the historical Jesus and his time-bound proclamation from the spiritual Christ beyond time, and the eternally valid idea of which he was the incarnation: the ideal of human existence on earth. The sensational work of D. F. Strauss published in 1835, the *Leben Jesu*, made a sharp demarcation between idea and reality. Its thesis that the historical figure of Jesus was to a great extent a product of imagination and fiction gave a tremendous impetus to the destruction of the Jewishness and the historicity of the image of Jesus. It pushed aside the temporal and accidental, the human coincidence, for the sake of the divine and eternal. This is a Hellenistic metaphysical trend which fits in well with the logos-Christology of Paul and John.

Althaus continues to work along these lines in his *Die letzten Dinge* (1922),[1] revealing the influence both of Schweitzer and Barth. The two dominating motifs are: a critique of the expectation of the Kingdom of God as the end of history, and an axiological-metaphysical eschatology.

History, Althaus maintains, does not end with the fulfilment of the Kingdom of God as the city of salvation. With Ranke, he suggests that "jede Epoche ist unmittelbar zu Gott". Every time is the last time, and every moment is eternity. Fulfilment is not a future process of becoming, but the meaningful unfolding of an idea. This fulfilment of meaning does not take place *in* history, nor does it take place *at the end* of history. A historical parousia is a contradiction in terms. The future day of the Lord stands before us today and for all eternity. Every segment of time is a part of the fulfilment. Man, always placed *in* time, can only believe in this fulfilment as an event beyond and outside of time, without any observable or experienceable ultimate goal. It is so to speak a prospectless prospect, a story of salvation that somehow leaves salvation out.

Up to this point Althaus is only elaborating contradistinction between time and eternity postulated by Kierkegaard and Barth. What is new, is his relating of this concept to what Troeltsch calls "axiological eschatology".

1. *Op. cit.*, p. 76, 77.

Or perhaps it is after all not so new, since it is in the last analysis only a systematization of an idealistic-ethical nineteenth century train of thought which also found expression in Schweitzer. Althaus contrasts *the realm of ideas and highest values* with the empirical and historical world. This realm of values he identifies with the Kingdom of God. Unholy history is placed opposite holy and eternally valid values which may guide man from moment to moment in history. The nearness of the Kingdom of God consists in the continuousness of the presence of these values.

Althaus, like Barth, later revoked this endless eschatology continuing into all eternity. He recognized that it was an axiological and not a theological eschatology. The eschatology "of the moment" swallowed the eschatology of the "last day", just as the meaning of history swallowed the goal of history, and time swallowed the future. This conception was too one-sidedly vertical and not sufficiently horizontal, dominated by the "Haben" of mysticism which looks upward, without allowing for the "Herren", the biding in time, of the faith that looks forward to the distant horizon. It concentrated on the Highest rather than on the Last, on ripening rather than on the harvest. Thus, an eschatology sans eschaton—an eschatology of unfolding human dignity as depicted by utopian idealism, but without the specific eschatological re-creation of man by God.

Barth too was converted to another conception of eschatology as appears from his *Kirchliche Dogmatik* of 1940. Eternity and temporality are now brought into a new relationship with one another. The eternal God "co-exists with the temporal". Eternity accompanies historical time. God is not only prior to and beyond time, he is also post-temporal. The coming of the Kingdom of God is therefore to be considered as a post-temporal reality, at the end of this time—thus, an *expectation for the future*. Or is it? In his detailed exposition Barth seems to revert to his older position. He is left limping between the two contrasting alternatives of temporal duration and eternity. God is first and foremost "all in all" in all eternity, so that His Kingdom is inseparably united with Him before time and beyond time. It is only in its revelation that the Kingdom of God is post-temporal, in this respect still lying in the future, but it exists already with regard to the essential nature of things. The coming of the Kingdom does not mean that God at this future time *becomes* "all in all", because He was this always and already before all time; it means only that the eternal, from being hidden, will then be clearly revealed. The post-temporal now unites with the supra-temporal.

It is difficult to visualize the coming of the Kingdom on earth as a real event, as a tangible cosmic re-creation, in the *metaphysics of time*. A new trinity has been created, consisting of God, the Kingdom of God, and

Eternity, containing a new Pauline Christ-mysticism. Christ, appearing in the middle of history, indicates the turning point. He points the way toward a future already contained in the primeval past, the way toward a kingdom that *was* before him, now *is*, and always *shall be*. It did not come with him, nor will it return with him. It is what it is. It has been revealed and shall some day be seen, at the moment when time and eternity, man and God, all flow into one. It is not the Other, but the All-One. Also this end of time stretches out endlessly in the face of an open time no longer delineated from eternity. The eschaton therefore does not refer to the *last*, but to *eternal* things, which are also the *first* things. It is another definition of God's invisible essence, not of His visible acts in and for this existing world.

C. Formless Eschatology

Rudolf Bultmann [1] gives a further impetus to the counter-eschatological movement. He is influenced by Schweitzer's method of historical biblical criticism, Barth's pauline dialectical theology and Heidegger's existential philosophy. These three approaches have one thing in common: de-historizing. Bultmann develops this into a system of his own, which is best known under the label of *de-mythologizing*.

The new Testament is primarily mythical in its mode of presentation, says Bultmann. The myths which adorn the contents of the gospel message come in part from the Old Testament (which in its turn borrowed from other heathen myths), and in part from other eastern sources. The contents of the gospels are not acceptable or believable for modern man in this antiquated form. That form comes in direct conflict with his scientific knowledge (his new image of the world), with his historical experience (the perpetually postponed parousia) and with his self-awareness as man. He no longer believes himself to be the prey of supernatural powers which have chosen the world as their workshop and playground. Rather is he grasping after these powers for his own use, on the basis of the scientific knowledge in which alone he now places his faith.

How should we understand "mythical" in this connection? Bultmann considers all those ideas mythical which present the non-worldly as visually and tangibly experienceable in this world. For example: the Son of God, the virgin birth, the expiatory sacrifice on the cross, the bodily resurrection and the ascension of Jesus. Also included are conceptions of heavenly powers, resurrection in the flesh of the dead, and cosmic catastrophe. But salvation is no more tangible, nor is the content of the Christian message empirically "demonstrable". All "demonstrable" facts of salvation are

1. R. Bultmann, *Neues Testament und Mythologie*, 1948.

mythical and thus a stumbling block or a scandal to modern, non-mythical thought. In order to retain the core of the Gospel, the kerygma (message of salvation), a radical de-mythologizing must take place.

This radical de-mythologizing, directed against the imagery of the Bible, especially affects the image of Jesus, the image of man and the image of God. All these must be purified. Bultmann considers the cult of the historical and synoptic Jesus an illusion. In reality we know nothing of Jesus except that he came. This is sufficient. The human person of Jesus, his teachings, his life and sufferings, his words and his deeds, are from the Christocentric point of view irrelevant. This coming, the crucifixion and the resurrection, as interpreted by St. Paul, comprise in abstracto the eschatological story of salvation. No communion is possible with the Jesus who was indeed once a living man but who has long since been dead. Communion is only possible with the spirit of Christ. In this de-historizing, de-materializing and de-personalizing of Jesus, the only remaining concern is with the eternal ideas and the spiritual truth which he represents. This truth is eternally valid, so that it is always valid for mankind of today, in the concrete every-day life of the believers. The crucified Christ of the past lives in the present —and only in the present. There is *no other Christ to return in the future*, there is but the one and only Christ who is always present and stands timeless in time. The eschatological movement of faith, Church and the community of believers is *now*.

The purified image of man and image of God fit in with this new image of Jesus. The believer faces his decision today, in every existential moment. He is able to seize upon his potential for life through the spirit of the crucified Christ. This is what Bultmann terms "existing eschatology". The prophesied day of salvation has already dawned and is here now. Man becomes a new creature in Christ *today*, existentially. In faith he entrusts his "Eigenmachtigkeit" to God, who now acts for man. Bultmann would retain the Acting God as an admitted "mythological residue". But this God does not promise any other future. He is only present through the spirit of Christ, a silent witness to the struggles of man—man who may or may not surrender. Thus all images are *actualized*, spiritualized, and transposed in the metaphysical language of existentialism. Man, Jesus and God have only an existential encounter, in the here and now. The paths of past and future intersect in the present. The New Testament is modernized by presenting its past perfect and future tenses as one single and simple *present*.

It follows then that this de-mythologizing is *eo ipso* de-eschatologizing, and *can be nothing else*. For the eschatological image of the future is inherently *mythical*, both as *future* and as *image*, or it is *nothing*. It is mythical in the antithesis it makes between two worlds, and two aeons. It is mythical in its separation of present and future time. It is mythical in its conceptions of an end of time, of Last Days, a judgement, a dies irae, a struggle with and conquest of the Anti-Christ. The parousia, the reign of Christ on earth, the coming of the Kingdom of Heaven on earth, are all mythical conceptions because other-worldly phenomena are transformed into this-worldly phenomena with the help of Christ and God. Salvation becomes a tangible sensate experience, and therefore inacceptable to anti-mythological modern scientific thought.

In modern eschatology all that remains, according to Bultmann, is the conception of the cross and the resurrection. The preaching of these events, the Church, and finally man in the act of existential decision and surrender in faith comprise the total of this eschatology. But this mythological purification is plainly a subjective and arbitrary process, which in fact selects one myth, or the fragment of a myth, to replace another. For pauline kerygma and christology, as interpreted by Bultmann, also contain materials from Hellenic and gnostic myths concerning resurrection and salvation, and a residue of Jewish mythology lives on in the concept of the acting God. Modern existentialism replaces Greek logos-mysticism and the platonic doctrine of ideas in a similarly mythological fashion, although with much less of the religious and philosophical touch. [1] Bultmann's method of de-mythologizing, which cuts the beating heart out of the Message of Salvation in order, ostensibly, to save this message, has cut loose from all the moorings of the Christian religion and opened the way for all other interpretations including non-Christian ones. He has therefore also opened the way for a more systematic dumping out of those mythological conceptions, which he himself wants to retain in an implicit sense. It is not to be wondered at that Bultmann's disciples felt that his de-mythologizing had not been radical enough, and went on to exceed his efforts. Driven by the law of demonic logic, they had to pursue further the path which he himself pointed out, with the inevitable result that the kerygma he wished to save was not spared.

It is not necessary to pursue this process any further. At this point the de-mythologizing has already achieved the practically complete negation of eschatology. The cutting of the ties between the Beyond and the Here, together with the cutting off of times past and times to come and an exclusive concentration on the reality of the moment leaves no place for a transition from this world into a totally other world. For man there is no other life than this life, no other end than death. There is no saving message concerning the fulfilment of time. The heavenly Jerusalem will

1. As a result both religion and philosophy rebel. See the latest discussion between Jaspers and Bultmann to appear in print: Jaspers and Bultmann, *Die Frage der Ent-mythologisierung*, Munich, 1954.

never open its gates on earth. But if the stumbling block has been removed, so also has the hopeful expectation concerning the Kingdom. The suffering of Jesus is human, like unto every man's suffering. There is no portal of liberation to another better world, neither for him nor for us. The disillusionment of the God-forsaken, crucified Christ must inevitably be our disillusionment too. The iconoclastic attack on antiquated religious images has left the eschatological image of the future in fragments. Between the reality of the agonizing spiritual struggle for day-to-day existence and the rapidly evanescing sense of transcendance stands—a vacuum. Today remains forever today, a permanently present immanence *without visionary end-perspective or horizon.* For both the vision of a perspective and the idea of an end are only: illusory myths.

D. Contentless Eschatology

The counter-eschatological effects of the work of Bultmann and his followers is the indirect result of their de-mythologizing mission. This mission is aimed, or meant to be aimed, at the *form* of the biblical message. A second movement soon joins itself to the first, however, aiming directly at the de-eschatologizing of the *contents* of the message. The so-called Berner School is a part of this movement, including such writers as Martin Werner, Fritz Buri, Ulrich Neuenschwender and others. These three men all build on Schweitzer's work and all take as their point of departure the "perpetually postponed parousia". Each of them surpasses his teacher in the logical applications made of his new technique, and yet each is determined to retain the term eschatology. It is retained, however, to designate something which can be anything and everything *except* eschatology, and which can certainly not be Christian eschatology: something which contains elements of religion, philosophy, ethics, and above all, *utopism.*

The conclusions of Schweitzer's consistent eschatology of primitive Christianity form the basis of Werner's *Die Entstehung des christlichen Dogmas* (1941). He demonstrates systematically the de-eschatologizing process as it has continued uninterruptedly since St. Paul and particularly St. John. He shows how christology and ecclesiology have progressively distorted, spiritualized and destroyed the eschatological message of Jesus and robbed it of its prophetic, heroic and cosmic proportions. He describes the bourgeoisification of Christianity as the doctrine is whittled down to a concern with individual rebirth in the existing order and bliss in the Hereafter and to a sacramental logos-doctrine of the empirical Church. This has happened because the Church has made a heretical compromise with this world and has surrendered itself to this aeon—a compromise which was begun by the early fathers in the Catholic Church, and ably continued by the ensuing Reformation.

But then Werner takes the same somewhat unexpected turning which Schweitzer took before him, but even more sharply delineated. We can never return, he says, to the primitive Christian eschatology, under the "Fremdherrschaft judischer Transcendenz und griechischer Metaphysik". It is too late for that now. But neither can we accept the deviation of the Church in this respect. The position into which even primitive Christianity was coerced as a result of the unrealized return of Christ, has become increasingly uncomfortable. It has crumbled, rather than been strengthened, under the impact of an altered image of the world and "Weltanschauung" brought about by the course of time and scientific developments. Werner argues that therefore we must now move forward consciously and deliberately ... along this same road of de-eschatologizing! That is to say, we must systematically clear away all remaining fragments of eschatological transcendence and metaphysics, of Jewish dogmatism and Hellenic gnosticism. The implication is that a new Protestant dogmatics must be developed which completely abandons the time-bound eschatology of Jesus. The work must be done, unafraid, in the spirit of Jesus himself.

Buri, one of Werner's disciples, has developed this "consistent counter-eschatological" point of view in more detail. He states that the de-eschatologizing of Werner must be continued with the de-mythologizing of Bultmann. We must dare, says he, the leap from the Beyond to the Here-and-Now, from transcendence to immanence; we must take a definite stand in the only existing and only possible existential reality. Only by making the above combination can Bultmann's mythological-eschatological residue be logically and radically eliminate. [1] Then even the Kerygma, inconsistently retained by Bultmann, can be courageously removed.

Buri is indeed completely consistent. He regards the traditional story of a predetermined and divinely directed salvation as a myth born of the eternal-human longing for an other and better world. The idea of Creator, creation and creature, of the fall of creation or creature and of a coming recreation, are cosmic myths. So are expectations for the future concerning an end of time and the fulfilment of time. Real history has neither goal

---

1. The most radical elimination took place through a disciple of the Berne School, Ulrich Neuenschwander, in his *Protestantische Dogmatik der Gegenwart und das Problem der biblischen Mythologie* (Berne, 1949). He regards the gulf between the supernatural biblical world image and the modern scientific world image as unbridgeable. The dilemma of naive and uncritical acceptance of the biblical "Denkwidrichkeiten" versus total de-eschatologizing compels the modern mind toward the latter choice, which wipes out the Kerygma.

nor end. There are not two worlds or two ages, of which the second is one day to appear according to God's will. We know nothing of God's will or purpose. We know of and have to do with only this one given world, which exists here and now. This position of Buri means the terminus of all transcendental theodicy and cosmic theology, now unmasked as metaphysical cosmology and mythology.

Would Buri then have the world drama proceed undetermined and undeterminable? Not quite that, either. For Buri too retains an *eschatological residue*. Reality as given is ethically indifferent, encompassing both sense and nonsense. The Christian eschatological element which Buri retains is the will to fulfilment of life, which gives meaning to man's meaningless existence in his "Daseinsnot". In his choice between two possible worlds, one meaningless and the other meaningful, man must resolve to choose the latter; further, he must act in such a way that the meaningful world becomes the actual world, obeying the tenets of Schweitzer's doctrine of reverence for life. In other words, Buri travels the road from theocentric to anthropocentric determination of destiny, and thus from *indirect* to *direct* influence-optimism. Having demonstrated that the eschatological consciousness is waning, he issues a call to the utopian consciousness, unaware that this too has been equally undermined.

It is a remarkable thing for the cultural sociologist to observe how existentialism, which shuts itself up in a windowless present, nevertheless must form the basis for an existential eschatology. This eschatology contains, by its very nature, an insoluble antinomy. As an expectation of future fulfilment, it can never be more than a *negative* eschatology, a caricature of itself, since the eschaton has first been carefully removed. For "meaning" is something totally different from "goal", and human ascriptions of meaning totally different from divine providence and predestination. Willing is different from knowing, and rational and moral striving is different from trustful anticipation of that which has been revealed. The man who tries to restore the broken harmony between himself and this world, in respect to the *present times*, is another man than he who looks forward eagerly toward a *future* which is to be the *last times*, harmonizing with eternity.

E. Meaningless Eschatology

Buri's existential eschatology, precisely in its search for a meaningful reality, is separated only by the thinnest threads from a meaningless eschatology. Buri himself described biblical eschatology as "eine positiv zu bewertende Illusion". It is to be valued *positively* because of its inspiring ethos, pathos and heroism which Buri, with Schweitzer, would like to retain in his modernization as the will toward a meaningful fulfilment of life, and an idealistic-active attitude toward the times. But is not such an eschatology-sans-eschaton equally an illusion, particularly for the believer?

This impression is strengthened by Walter Nigg's afore-mentioned *Das Ewige Reich*, "Die Geschichte einer Sehnsucht und einer Enttäuschung", a work written under the influence of the Berne School. He points out that the chiliastic struggles for the realization of the "Reichsmythos" on earth were always condemned to failure. The disappointment over the unrealized parousia was continually and inevitably followed by new disappointments. But the "Sehnsucht" remains, and although the myth must alter, Nigg hopes that the pathos can be retained, finding new modes of eschatological expression and fulfilment.

If it is retained, however, it must be with the full knowledge that the goal can never be reached, since *the goal itself has vanished*. This is a heroic-tragic situation, and one that is rendered meaningless in advance. There is no Realm of the Future, there is only today with its cares and fears, a present under constant sentence of death. The more the rampant growth of existentialism covers over theology and eschatology, the more the danger increases that its inherent essence-pessimism, which Buri is still resisting, will choke off all influence-optimism and transmute the positive into the negative illusion.

If expectations of the future are deprived of their content, then *every expectation becomes ultimately meaningless*. It is possible to live and act in the present, but it is not possible to overturn the existing order all at once in the present moment. Anticipation is of the future or it is nothing. Therefore existential eschatology is not only without content but without meaning, as an irreconcilable self-contradiction. The existential relates only to day-to-day living, and eschatology portains to an ultimate kind of living which is the antithesis of present existence. Eschatological fulfilment is not a tidy little achievement which man can himself write into the time-table of history, but a wondrous re-creation of the cosmos by God in His own time.

This combined de-eschatologizing and de-mythologizing cannot but result in de-kerygmatizing, in a complete removal of the *primum movens*. In the end there is no holding back from the final conclusion that Christ, as Lord, Saviour and Son of God, is an eschatological myth; also that God as Creator, Administrator of the Cosmos and Heavenly Father is equally a myth. Both *Christ and God then become time-bound and transcendent in the oriental manner, and no longer suit western modes of thought*. But a Christian eschatology without a Christian Saviour and without a divine plan of salvation loses all meaning. Such an eschatology is no longer a foolishness or a stumbling block, but an intolerable contradiction. There can be no Ultima Thule without a prime cause. The gospel message then ceases to be the glad tidings of a future salvation and becomes the sorrowful acceptance of the existential Nothingness.

F. Hopeless Eschatology

Reviewing the development of eschatology up to this point, we can observe three main trends, which we will recapitulate before going into a fourth.

The pure eschatological message of Jesus was: the Kingdom of God will come soon, it is at hand.

The apostolic, ecclesiastical New Testament exegesis which followed was based not on the synoptic gospels but on St. Paul and the Gospel of St. John. It interpreted their main themes as follows: Jesus himself brought the Kingdom; it has dawned. Now we must only wait a little for the final fulfilment. This second position is a middle position of both partial and final fulfilment. It is being held in our own day by men like Otto, Cullman, [1] Reinhold Niebuhr, [2] and others.

It is seriously threatened by a third, more extreme trend, which cuts the ground from under any kind of expectation of an end as such. This trend is exemplified by Schweitzer, the Berne School and Paul Tillich. [3] It is based mainly on the delayed parousia, on the modern scientific view of the world, and, often, on existentialist philosophy. This trend we have described in its variations from "thorough-going eschatology" to „meaningless eschatology". A final fulfilment is no longer expected, but neither is there any longer a conception of partial fulfilment.

The fourth trend, which we now bring up for discussion, seems to revert to the other extreme. It is based on an interpretation of Augustine's Kingdom of God and strongly resembles the Roman Catholic conception of the Church as the Body of Christ. The partial fulfilment of the Kingdom with the first coming of Jesus is gradually extended to the view that *this*

---

1. Oscar Cullman's *Christus und die Zeit* (Zürich, 1946) has been the most influential of these various attempts to synthesize myth and history. He maintains that the mythical primal age had no beginning but did have an end: Adam. On the other hand the historical End State has a beginning (the coming of Christ) but no end. This End State courses upwards along an endless "Heilslinie" in time toward the goal of the onset of the parousia, which will take place extra-historically. The Last Days and the great final battle had actually begun with the first coming of Jesus, and we live in the Kingdom of God already through the Cristian faith in the cross and the resurrection.
2. The following works of Niebuhr are of particular interest here:
   The Nature and Destiny of Man, New York, first published in 1941;
   Moral Man and Immoral Society, New York, 1932;
   Faith and History, New York, 1951.
3. *The Shaking of the Foundations*, New York, 1948; *The Courage to Be*, New Haven, 1952; *Biblical Religion and the Search for Ultimate Reality*, Chicago, 1955.

was the *total* fulfilment. The Kingdom has come once and for all time. Any expectations for the future are therefore illusory, not because they can never be realized, but because they already *have been* completely realized.

This last position is found predominantly in English theology, and especially in the work of the Cambridge New Testament scholar, C. H. Dodd. [1] His concept of a "realized eschatology" has been developed in a number of works. With the Swiss School at Berne he maintains that eschatology is central to the gospels, as a proclamation of the Kingdom of God. But while Schweitzer and his like-minded contemporaries hold that this expectation has not been fulfilled and is in principle non-fulfillable, Dodd says that the expectation has been fulfilled and that the Kingdom of God has come, even as it was prophesied. The death and resurrection of Christ signify the inception of a new aeon, and the New Testament is the fulfilment of the promises of the Old.

Dodd bases his position on Paul and the Gospel of John, thus on the "purified" gospel. He rejects the "futuristic eschatology" of the Synoptic Gospel and of Revelations, for these are impregnated with a predominantly Jewish, pre-Christian vision. All such elements are fortunately strained and purified out of the Fourth Gospel. In this gospel the Kingdom of God is correctly represented in mystical fashion as the ultimate reality, the platonic eternal order of things in which we participate by living in Christ. What eschatology speaks of as life in a future aeon is actually the life that is here and now being realized, *today*, through the spiritual presence of Christ in his Church. The sacrament of the Eucharist is above all the means by which individual man may enter into communion with Christ and into the eternal life of the Kingdom of God. The time is fulfilled, and man stand before the Judgement today. Through Christ's fulfilment of his mission in the past, man's salvation has been accomplished by God.

We need not follow Dodd's tortuous and ingenious exegesis which replaces "futurist eschatology" with "realized eschatology". The truth is that futuristic eschatology is as such a *pleonasm*, as realized eschatology is an *antinomy*. Is there still an eschaton? Not in the sense of movement toward an endstate. At the most what remains is an inverted eschaton, a movement back to the first state. Nor is eschatology any longer concerned with the whole of creation, but only with one part: individual man, apart from mankind and the world. This shifting into lower gear now historically connects the fall

---

1. *New Testament Studies*, New York, 1954; *The Gospel Parables*, Manchester, 1932; *The Apostolic Preaching and its Developments*, London, 1936, (Appendix about eschatology); *The Gospels as History*, Manchester, 1938; *According to the Scriptures*, London, 1952 (Stone Lectures, Princeton Theol. Sem.).

of the first man, Adam, through the historical event of the redeeming death of Jesus, to the present and the rebirth in this life of each individual man, via faith and by means of man's spiritual communion with Christ. This contracted eschatology completes the historical development from individual man to individual man. *"It is finished"*—in the oft-repeated words of Jesus on the cross. Paradise *is regained*, salvation *is come*. An individualistic and egocentric redemption is welded in this life, this time and this world as an unchangeable given. The change is now in the past perfect tense, continued and preserved as a perpetual present and allowing of no distinction or separation into a possible future tense. While the Berne School eliminates God, Christ and Salvation, as propulsive forces toward a future end-goal, the Cambridge School works them back in, but only as entities rooted in the past and working on automatically and unchangingly into the present. Neither view leaves room for eschatological expectations of the future as such, or for any anticipations of a wondrous fulfilment of time. But while the Berne scholars would at least retain the ethos and the pathos of a human struggle for moral perfection, a "realized" eschatology leaves no hope for mankind at all.

The realized eschatology is a pure negation of eschatology as an image of the future. It is sheer caricature to speak of realized salvation in this age of damnation. This carrying to the extreme of ecclesiastical and sacramental concepts leans heavily on apologetics and platonism. The Cambridge School bypasses the existentialism of the Berne School, and with it bypasses the need, suffering and despair of our time. Thus the prospectless hopelessness of our times is strengthened. Berne is *empty* and Cambridge *blind* when it comes to the future. The one is disillusioned over what has not happened in history, the other petrified by what has supposedly already happened, and mankind is left between the devil and the deep blue sea. This realistic counter-eschatology without eschaton is a Christian hope without hope.

3. Iconoclasm of Images of the Future

It may seem as if we have wandered rather far afield in purely theological considerations. But resuming our position of impartial observer we find that we are now better equipped to perceive the remarkable conformity of development in the two separate phenomena of de-utopianizing and de-eschatologizing. This remarkable parallel is certainly no coincidence, but it has so far escaped the notice both of the theologians and the sociologists, each of whom are confined to their own field by their own specialist outlook. This specialization limits their insight into the basic substructure common to both developments, and therefore equally limits their understanding of the structural relationship involved. Both diagnosis and therapy are thereby hindered.

We analyzed the iconoclasm of utopian images of the future under the headings of negativation, de-futurizing and de-imaging. These same elements leap to the eye in an analysis of the attack on the eschatological image of the future.

Two further factors which we identified as crucial in contributing to the decay of the utopian images, de-dualizing and de-humanizing, are found to be crucial here also, as *de-dualizing* and *de-deification*.

A. Negativation

The clock of out theological time is continually striking the note "de". The modern view of life requires a "de-antiquating" in general, and a "de-scandalizing" of the Bible in particular. It is certainly not intended that this "de" process, however labelled, should have a purely negative issue as an over-all degeneration in the Weltanschauung. On the contrary, the intention is to save the positive and eternal values of the past from the relentless tooth of time. But subjecting these values to the trimming shears of modern civilization is like pealing the potato—it becomes more palatable, but some of the essential vitamins are destroyed. One thinks only to perform an operation on the outer rind, and ends by destroying or at least damaging the core. Beginning with de-historizing and de-mythologizing, this process inevitably results in de-eschatologizing and de-kerygmatizing, with the ultimate liquidation of Jesus Christ, both as man and as God.

In the end it makes little difference whether one takes the parousia which has not come as the point of departure, concluding that it will never take place and that the idea of a final fulfilment is an illusion, or whether one begins with the appearance of Christ almost 2000 years ago and comes to the opposite conclusion that the parousia has already taken place, is here now and will always be a reality as of the present moment, and that therefore the idea of a final fulfilment is nonsensical. The image of the future is smashed between the hammer and anvil of "never" and "already". The desks in the Eschatological Bureau are piled to the ceiling with eschatological studies . . . but the office remains closed. A time-bomb has been placed inside the door, which may blow the whole structure into the air at any moment.

All modernized eschatology is counter-eschatology, and can thus only have *negative* effects—in thorough-going as well as hopeless eschatology, in formless as well as in contentless eschatology. Dialectical theology has gone far in the direction of denial of the thesis stating a critical antithesis, but has no power to achieve a synthesis. It has only succeeded in dismantling the Bible and uprooting itself.

While the *untenability* of *fundamentalism* has been demonstrated, the *tenability* of any form of *modernism* has not been established. For theology itself has sawed off the only limb of the tree of knowledge on which modernism could find a secure foothold—the limb of the image of the future. The negativation of eschatology places theology before the same gaping void which existentialism faces us with. Modern theology and modern philosophy thus walk or stand hand in hand like the lame man and the blind man, and we are faced with the vicious cycle of one negation substituting for another.

Let us examine this progressive negativation at the point of de-futurizing.

B. De-Futurizing

The history of Christianity is the history of man's struggle to free himself from the fundamental message of Jesus: "The Kingdom of God is nigh". Its failure to come posed man with a time-problem which has not diminished with the centuries. This Kingdom was something which was *to come*, a Kingdom of the *Future*. The word "nigh" defined more precisely the limited length of time man would have to wait. The first lurking doubt was directed, not against the image of the coming Kingdom, but against the time-concept and time-computations associated with it. Could Jesus have been mistaken? Or must his time-limit be understood in a different sense? Or do the words "coming" and "to come" really mean something totally different? And how can the solution to this problem of the future be made to fit in with the time-vision of Revelations?

Jesus placed a heavy burden on the shoulders of the future—of future generations, that is. How can a good Christian free himself of this burden? Here begins a never-ending exegesis and process of interpretation, using every means of metaphysics and mysticism, in order to undermine the concept of the future. Partly this has been done by dragging it backwards into the past, and partly by pushing it out of time into eternity. One attempt at dealing with this problem leads from the Fourth Gospel and St. Paul to the attack on futuristic eschatology by Dodd, and from Augustine's *Civitas Dei* to the timeless eschatology advocated by Barth in his *Römerbrief*. The reflection of this de-futurizing process is seen in the gradual interpreting *out* of Matthew and the interpreting *in* of John in dealing with the Epistles of Paul. It is seen also in the ignoring of Revelations as non-revealing and in the centuries-long crusade against chiliasm and sectarian adventism.

There are three protagonists in this struggle against the future: the Church, theology, and time itself, which is by definition the future in process of becoming history via the present. Within this time there are three foci of attack: man, Jesus and God.

The Church, as we have already seen, would solve the time-problem by expanding first as the Kingdom of Christ, and finally as the Kingdom of God itself. This involves a shift of accent from the future Kingdom of Glory to the present Kingdom of Grace. Through the sacraments of the Church, the accent also shifts from cosmic to individual eschatology. The Church is the world (Kirche ist Welt) and relates itself to the existing order. Its members are already reborn in this life, for all eternity. All that remains is the salvation of the soul after death, effected by the mediation of the Church. The Church is the guardian of the invisible but present Kingdom of God, and he who supports the Church is a co-worker for the Kingdom and ensures its continuing work of earthly salvation. The more the power of the Church becomes entrenched in this world, the stronger its tendency to resist the coming of another world, which would make the Church superfluous. The Church solves the problem of the future by either absorbing it or stretching it out to the very edge of eternity.

Theology has always supported this development by softening Jesus' revolutionary message concerning the coming of the Kingdom as much as possible and concealing it under a haze of mysticism. It remained for Kant to arouse theology and provide it with a philosophical content for the message. Now once again this message rears its questioning head. This time it is not dealt with indirectly, by turning it over to the Church or christology, but it is attacked by direct analysis and a purposive destruction of the time-concept. This process is heralded as an eliminating of Jewish traits, but it also includes the erasing of apocalyptic prophetic elements of the Gospel, in a deliberate mission of de-futurizing.

There are three connected time-elements in the gospel message concerning the coming of the Kingdom, all of which can be ascribed to Jewish futurism. The first is the *prophecy* concerning that which is to come, a foretelling of the future. The second is a *time-computation* associated with this prophecy: it will come speedily, it is at hand, it is nigh. The third is a *philosophy of history* inherent in this prophecy, a philosophy concerning a future fulfilment of time.

All three elements are de-futurized. The first attack is on prophecy as such, a Jewish tradition that Christianity must be freed from. The Gospel is acceptable as "Wahrsagung" (truth) but not as "Weissagung" (prediction). Christianity is not a prophetic religion and en compassesno practices of divination. God reveals Himself in Jesus Christ, but He does not reveal the future. His counsel and His ways are hidden from man, and were not even known to Jesus. When Jesus spoke as a prophet he was speaking in the tongue and in the tradition of his Jewish predecessors, including John the Baptist; he did this in order to gain a response from the Jewish people. We must detach his message from the essentially non-Christian prophecy in which it is embedded. The prophecy did not come to pass, and the parousia did not materialize. We must no longer cherish the illusion that it will come to pass and that Jesus will return. We must give up all predictions and expectations for the future if we are serious about de-Judification. The Kingdom of God, however it may be conceived as a spiritual event, *is in any case not a factual event to take place in any factual future.*

The attack on the apocalyptic elements of Christianity is less far-reaching than the attack on the prophecies. The proclamation of the coming of the Kingdom of God must be retained as such, since it is an irrevocable promise made by God. Only the computations concerning its imminence are at fault. The method of computation stems from the Jewish apocalypse, which one must be careful to differentiate from eschatology. The baby must not be thrown out with the bathwater. The time-terminology which is used to peg down God's omnipotence is false and basically irreligious. We must read the Gospel as the Glad Tidings of the Coming, but we will find no answer in the Gospels to the question, "when?". "Soon" is premature, but "never" is in contradiction with God's will. The Revelations of John comprise a precious eschatological pledge, but they are worthless as a chronometer. Biblical time is not astronomical calender time. It is not quantitative, but qualitative. This time cannot be measured with secular mathematical tools, because it is completely sui generis. We may take the Coming itself as a certainty, but any suggestions as to the hour, day, year or century must be discarded as Jewish embellishments. The veil of time cannot be lifted. The Kingdom of the Future exists, and it will come in all its glory *in its time*, the time determined by God.

The most far-reaching de-futurizing takes place, not in the attack on the forms of prophecy and apocalypse, but in the attack on the *content* of the message, on the idea of the *coming* (soon or not) of the Kingdom of God. This idea, it is maintained, comes from late-Jewish dogmatics. The whole complex of concepts concerning the end of time, including the idea of *fulfilment* through cosmic catastrophe to be followed by cosmic transformation of the universe into a new heaven and a new earth, are Jewish in origin and in tradition. This Jewish cosmology rests on a theodicy concerning the ultimately beneficent workings of God in history. The Jewish conceptions of *salvation in history* is unacceptable in the modern Weltanschauung. *Christian theology must liberate itself from this Jewish theology.* We no longer believe that "Weltgeschichte ist Weltgericht". History is not a supernaturally-directed miracle play. It is an essentially human drama in which the planetary life of mankind is proceeding according to the laws of scientific necessity. The final act will be determined by gigantic natural forces of heat or cold, which will bring about extinction instead of transformation. The earth will end "not with a bang but a whimper". In this sense of a radically different and better world we can no longer believe in a coming Kingdom of God on earth. *There is no Kingdom of the Future.*

This is the end result of de-futurizing *in time.* It is further strengthened by a de-futurizing which leads out of historical time. De-Judification then combines with de-historification. True religion, according to this view, exists apart from time. Therefore we must free ourselves from the historical Jesus; not only because he thought in Jewish terms, but more generally because his message (or the message ascribed to him by the writers of the Gospels) was time-bound. Jesus taught uniquely (einmalig) in and for his own time, and that time speaks through Jesus. But this segment of historical time is now out of time, and recalls an unrecallable past. Nevertheless, Jesus partook of the eternal. The recollection of Jesus lives on today through the Holy Spirit. We must reconstruct the eternal Jesus, apart from his relationship to his own time. The crucifixion, the suffering and the resurrection of Christ are timeless, existing always, including here and now. Jesus is a contemporary of every generation, and the story of his life is an eternal, sacred story. Christ is with us in our daily existence, both in body and in spirit. We must interpret the New Testament existentially for this, *our* time. Theology thus approaches existentialism. *The Kingdom of God exists only in the present,* as the eternally actualized past. The only imperishable thing in this perishable world is the liberating work of Jesus in the heart of the struggling believer.

The de-futurizing is complete if one accepts the view that the God Who revealed Himself in Jesus Christ *is* eternity itself, incommensurable with time and history. Then there is no transition from time to eternity, and there is nothing to come which is not already here. Theology becomes philosophical speculation concerning an eternity which devours time and future. *The Realm of the Future has become an eternal category.*

The complete antipode of this timeless metaphysics produces the same end-result of de-futurizing. The anti-metaphysical, pragmatic view that Jesus has already brought salvation and that the Church is its fulfilment, so popular in Anglo-Saxon countries, breaks history into eternally repeating fractions. The school of "realized eschatology" is apparently not troubled by the warning in Proverbs, "Where there is no vision, the people perish." The simplicity of the formula, "The Kingdom is come" cancels all the force of the visionary, "The Kingdom is nigh". Time and future are erased together with their Jewish contents, for Jesus proclaims only *today.* In this sense it could be said that the Christian religion has a good future *behind* it. The Kingdom of God can no longer come, because it has already come.

All de-futurizing invalidates per se the message of Jesus, and contravenes his express warning: "No one who puts his hand to the plow and looks back is fit for the Kingdom of God".[1] Does precisely *this* one saying not have the quality of eternity?

C. De-Imaging

Paul has condemned two attitudes in respect to faith: "The Jews seek signs, and the Greek seek wisdom". He himself began the process of casting off Judaism, but adopting Greek modes of thought. Modern man does not bring the "sacrificium intellectus" to faith; rather he sacrifices "signs" on behalf of reason. Any sign which actualizes the other-worldly in this world is objectionable. De-mythologizing is basically de-imaging. This de-imaging, when followed to its rational conclusion, will also destroy the image itself in the image of the future, after de-futurizing has already destroyed the underlying expectations for the future.

All visible signs of the invisible are rejected, including the signs wrought by Jesus and witnessing to him. The resurrected Jesus appeared in the midst of his disciples and said to them, "See my hands and my feet, that it is I myself; handle me, and see; for a spirit has not flesh and bones as you see I have." De-imaging dismisses both the negative image (the empty grave) and the positive image (appearance and recognition of the resurrected Jesus). All unconsciously, man replaces the old images with new and more spiritualized ones: Jesus now appears "at the midpoint" of history, or as the midpoint of the universe. The great question is: where do the boundaries of the image lie, and once the de-imaging process has begun, can it be halted at will at any temporally fixed point?

De-imaging is not de-mythologizing alone. In the background the driving force springing from a deep urge towards de-scandalizing is always ascertainable, the unceasing struggle for adaptation to the modern . . . world-*image*. This began with a rebellion against all the biblical wonders and miracles. These images could no longer be believed, so they were treated as imagery. The progressive undermining of the possiblity of wonder in the world (Entzauberung) has occupied a considerable space of time. The wonders can either be explained away through para-psychology or science, or tossed away into the realm of the fable, as primitive efforts to understand the nature of divine power. What was once the source and strength of faith is now labelled superstition. What was once taken theologically in a literal sense, is now regarded as anthropomorphic imagery. It is replaced by a

1. Luke 9 : 62.

new-fashioned "image": Jesus as God's Sign, as The Wonder. How long shall *this* idea be able to escape the impact of the de-imaging process?

But the process of de-scandalizing is not finished by any means after thus discarding these wonder-tales out of the Bible. For the Bible is fundamentally a book of images encompassing much more than these wonders. Modern man, in his new-found "maturity and wisdom" calls it a book "by children for children". In speaking of the perfect man, Jesus refers to the image of the child: that which is hidden from the wise and understanding is revealed to babes, [1] and the Kingdom of Heaven belongs to little children. [2] De-imaging is thus more than a destruction of the Jewish elements in Christianity, it is also a destruction of its *child-like qualities*, a religious puberty rite. All of Jesus' teaching was couched in images. He created an image of men as the children of God and an image of God as Our Father. The evangelists and apostles in their turn created the image of Jesus, or rather, images of Jesus. These were recreated during many ages. Then there came a storm of iconoclastic fury. And God was not in the storm...

But the destruction of the images in the book did not happen all at once, for the storm was a fitful one—tearing this page loose, leaving that one untouched. Each act of de-imaging was an arbitrary one, continuing and abstaining at will; a question of individual taste ... and foolishness. Must we discard the image of the angel with the flaming sword, but keep paradise? What of the image of creation, and the speaking serpent? If these can be discarded, what of the concept of the fall of man? If we abandon the image of God's throne in the heavens, then what of the image of the earthly realm of the Evil One? Must we distinguish between the Devil and the demons who inhabit this world? If the deluge is regarded as an image only, do we also give up the idea of the cosmic cataclysm of the dies irae? And of course the image of the sounding trumpets at the end of time can easily be dispensed with, but this is the introduction to the crowning image, the establishment of the Kingdom of God on earth.

These questions were not all dealt with at once, but these and more must all be dealt with eventually, for all the biblical images are interrelated. The boundary of iconoclasm lies at the horizon of the last remaining image. Remove one from the total complex of images, and all the rest tremble. This includes images which are still tolerated and which at this moment few would be willing to give up: the star of Bethlehem and the manger; the word become flesh; the bread and wine of the Holy Communion;—all images referring to the essentials of the life of Christ, including his birth and death. And the Cross, the sign of the Cross, has thus far been preserved by all the

1. Matthew 11 : 25.
2. Matthew 19 : 14.

iconoclasts. But the same men who would preserve the Cross attack the Ascension and the reign of Christ, denying the image of a god who became man, or of a man who became God, in the tradition of ancient mythology and Hellenic mystery religions. Where do we draw the line between simple mutilation of an image, and desecration?

It is not surprising that the oldest of the Christian Churches, the Roman Catholic, still clings to all the biblical miracles, image-worship and the rich imagery of cathedral architecture, religious art and liturgy, nor that it kept to the Ptolemaic image of the world as long as possible, as being most consonant with the biblical image. Even today the Roman Catholic Church has retained concrete images of jubilant choirs of heavenly angels and saints, but it raises the pedestal of Mary, Mother of God, Immaculate Virgin, to an increasingly exalted place in church doctrine. The Catholic Church has evidently felt, and been confirmed in its feeling, that once the iconoclastic process has begun, there is no stopping-place short of a second and final crucifixion of Christ himself. From such a crucifixion, there would be no resurrection. Nevertheless, the Church had to accept Copernicus. Will it be able in the long run to resist the creeping secularization of the modern image of the world?

The more rapid progress of iconoclasm in modern Protestantism is not to be interpreted negatively as intentional sacrilegious vandalism. Descandalizing always seeks to find a compromise between old and new. It is not the intention simply to scrap the image-rich language of the New Testament, but to "translate" it into a form that will draw a more ready response from modern man. The images must be regarded as *symbols*—so the argument runs—symbols that still have a significance for our time if we but understand and interpret them correctly. [1] The images can be preserved by giving them a symbolic, allegorical meaning rather than a literal one. This opens up a wide field for modern exegesis.

It opens up *so* wide a field that there is danger of not being able to see any boundaries at all. Why should we not consider the Cross and the Resurrection as symbols of reconciliation and redemption, and Christ as the symbol of the God-concept? And why should we not similarly consider the presence of Christ in our time, the rebirth of man in Christ, eternal life and the immortal soul, all to be symbols? Indeed, such symbols are also present in other religions and other divine myths. According to Jung, such symbols are *the* symbols, archetypes which live in man's unconscious in all times and among all peoples, primal symbols of man's religious concepts.

1. There is an extensive literature on this subject. Of especial interest are the volumes of *Religion in Geschichte und Gegenwart*, Tübingen, 1930, and also both volumes of *Kerygma und Mythos*, Hamburg, 1951 and 1952.

The comparative history of religion, the psychology of religion, phenomenology and cultural anthropology should all support this observation in principle. Finally we must add the non-religious philosophical faith of a Karl Jaspers, who handles a similar symbolism, although somewhat more complex as fits a philosopher, in his "chiffre-schrift" (cipher-code). De-imaging, combined with a technique for the exposition of symbols, can in the end have no other consequence than to deprive the biblical book of images of its unique and specific character—whatever the conscious intentions of the expounders.

This is true, not only because one set of symbols cannot make higher pretensions than another, but because in the process of interpretation something essential is lost: the *visible* image. The living image is replaced by the symbolic image, with a corresponding shift of emphasis from outward to inward characteristics. The image *materializes* out of the Beyond into the Here-and-Now. The symbol, on the other hand, *spiritualizes* the image by leading back out of the Here-and-Now into the Beyond. A symbolic representation uses the spiritualized language of the learned ecclesiastic, not the direct and down-to-earth images of the prophet. The biblical book of images had its own unique figurative language, but the modern symbolic interpretations use the language of socratic ethics, the platonic doctrine of ideas, Hellenistic metaphysics, mysticism, gnosticism,—and the closely related language of existentialism. These interpretations use every language from the oldest to the newest mode of philosophical thought with great fluency. Only in Jesus' language, now considered to be dead, are the interpreters mute and inarticulate.

Symbolic interpretation greatly intensifies the shift from Jesus toward Christology and Christ-mysticism, and from the Old to the New Covenant [1] begun already by Paul and John. The iconoclastic spiritualization leads to a progressive de-personalization of the image of Jesus, so that Jesus, the individual, becomes abstracted into a symbol of love, perfection and holiness. This spiritualized image is a lifeless image, of shining but chilly marble. The vitality and dynamic power to inspire are gone. Faith leans more and more heavily on things unseen, including the invisible presence of Jesus Christ through kerygma and sacrament. This is a symbolic presence, as the Spirit, as the Heart of God, and as divine Redemption, which in themselves are all again symbols . . . and so on. Remarkably enough, this de-judification of the images of the Bible might seem to lead straight back to the purely Jewish "hearing" of the Word, and to the imageless God of the Jews, who is but a holy name for the Jewish "ear of the world". There is, however, a heaven's breadth of difference: this modern way of re-wording the gospel message is divested of any living *images*, including *images of the future*.

1. See II Cor. 3.

It is the basic Christian *image of the future* which forms the common focus for all de-imaging of whatever kind. De-judification, de-mythologizing, de-scandalizing, the attack on the child-like imagination, the work of symbolic interpretation and the tailoring of the primitive Weltanschauung to fit more modern views, all combine to exercise their destructive influence on this image. *All de-imaging is dissolution.* For all de-imaging is the complement of defuturizing and threatens the image contained in the gospel proclamation of the coming of the Kingdom of God. The tragedy of this de-imaging is that it cannot be confined to an elimination of the stumbling blocks formed by the details concerning the visible supporting evidence for the proclamation. It must continue its negative work until it has devalued the proclamation itself as pure imagery. No stone can be removed from this foundation without threatening the entire structure.

The synoptic gospels, not to mention Revelations, concentrate on the visible approach of the Kingdom of God: The sign of the Son of Man shall appear in heaven, the trumpet shall sound, the God-man will descend out of the clouds to establish a new age. The central figure in the cosmic recreation is Jesus. De-judification attacks the identification of the resurrected Christ with the resurrection of the Mozaic-Davidian Kingdom as the earthly restoration of a fallen Israel which is to be a beacon unto the world. But the de-imaging process goes on from there to attack all the associated imaginative concepts and successive stages in the story of salvation, including that of the return of Christ the Judge, Saviour, and Bringer of the Messianic Realm. With the destruction of the image of the visible parousia finally goes also the destruction of the concept of the salvation of mankind.

The image of the future is not only the *matrix* of faith, but also its *alma mater. Faith is basically mythical in nature, and the myth reflects in its imagery all of man's deepest convictions and longings.* The myth is divine history from the first beginnings to the final fulfilment and end. It provides the definitive image of the future in which God is all in all, and man is reunited with him in perfect harmony for all eternity. If the myth is discarded, then both myth and faith turn into metaphysics and become an abstract system of thought. Faith without an image of the future lacks the dynamic power of the believing imagination and becomes fantasy dissociated from transfiguration. *Losing itself in this world, it ends by losing the original image of God.* These two processes, closely related to de-futurizing and de-imaging, can be described as de-dualizing and de-deification.

D. De-Dualizing

The reader who has had the patience to follow the preceding analysis of the undermining of biblical imagery will now be rewarded by perceiving the key to the inexplicable drama of de-eschatologizing and the related collapse from within of the Christian faith. It is clear now that this process of self-destruction cannot be explained entirely by the delayed parousia, nor by the modern scientific Weltanschauung, although we suggested these two current conceptions as possible hypotheses. For nineteen successive centuries the delay of the Lord's return did *not* have the deeply troubling effects which we now observe in this 20th century. Also the scientific image of the world has been developing and changing ever since the 16th century, but—until the beginning of our century—*without* affecting the core of eschatological expectations. Moreover, the latest developments in physical science do not exclude the possibility of "wonders", such as a cosmic transformation. The delayed parousia, then, is surely a real factor in the process described, although it touches only the surface of our problem. Modern scientific thought and its attitude towards biblical religion is more symptom than cause in the crisis of our time.

If we seek to penetrate into the essential meaning of the course of events in our time, we must not shrink from the radical hypotheses that the eschatological consciousness has withered on the vine because the religious consciousness itself has sustained serious injury. Two foundation stones of religion in general and eschatology in particular, have crumbled. They are both predominantly mythical in nature: the dualistic view of two opposing driving forces in operation in the factual world, and the optimistic view of such dialectical movement as leading to the one highest end-goal.

The dualistic or "split" attitude of mind lies at the very core of religious thinking. It divides all existence into two orders, two worlds, two realms two dimensions, two aeons. They can be labelled the Here and the Beyond, and a distance which is something more than purely spatial is involved in that distinction. Stated in terms of power, it is the distance between human and superhuman power. Early religious-eschatological thought conceives this world to be in the grip of a struggle between human and superhuman power, and also subject to the effects of internecine warfare between various superhuman powers.

The dualistic-optimistic Weltanschauung adds that in this struggle good will ultimately win over evil. This world will finally be liberated from its domination by evil human and superhuman power. Then this earthly dispensation will make way for another, holy dispensation, with the establishment of the second or third Kingdom in all its glory. The world will thus either have returned to its divine origin or have been exalted to a divine state. The mythic-prophetic image of the future which reveals this future state forms the bridge between the two worlds, granting the means of entry to the second world for a suffering mankind living in constant expectation of their saviour.

The optimism appears chiefly in the form of *indirect influence-optimism*, the reconciliation of man with superhuman power through worship and mystery rites. We have observed dualistic futurism in this form in Iran, Hellas and Israel. The religious sense emerges out of and focuses on the contrast between the two realms of good and evil, light and darkness and God and Devil, however these entities may be variously described. Faith is permeated with the dialectical development in time from the existing to the new order, through the intervention of a previously announced saviour or messiah. We have tried to show that Jesus lived and preached in this Jewish tradition and foretold the final victory of the coming Christ over the Anti-Christ. Like the prophets before him he proclaimed the coming of the Kingdom—but now more urgently ("the Kingdom of God is nigh"), calling the alarm "watch and pray lest the day come upon you". [1]

From the very beginning, the theology and theodicy of the budding Christian religion struggled with this dualistic Weltanschauung which could never be made entirely consistent with monotheism and its associated concept of omnipotence. If an almighty God rules this world, how is it that this same world does not yet belong to His Kingdom? Why is it necessary to battle another supernatural power before this world can belong to His Kingdom? It was this question which caused the Church to declare gnostic dualism and Manichaeism as heresies. Augustine formulated a systematic monism by the introduction of the Civitas Dei into the existing order through its earthly representative, the Church.

This was the first great breach in the Weltanschauung of Antiquity. But the old dualistic views of the future lived on for centuries in the religion of the people, periodically exploding in chiliastic movements. Optimism, the other great foundation stone, remained; its ties with dualism were not so stringent. Therefore the image of another and better world could live on. It was even strengthened by the later development of evolutionary optimism and related ideas concerning natural progress. It was also supported by liberal messianism, idealistic philosophy and even by the monistic philosophy of identity, which equated the development of this-wordly reality with that of divine rationality. Dualism had indeed lost its cutting edge, but the belief in a divinely ordained beneficent end-goal remained, albeit in a secularized version. The eschatology of the fulfilment of God's Kingdom remained to cement the walls of faith, even though the cement had been thoroughly mixed with other elements. In the diluting process

1. Mark 13 : 29; 35-37.

the individualistic, evolutionary, spiritual and dogmatic elements increased at the expense of the cosmic, revolutionary, material and prophetic elements.

But inevitably the second foundation stone also had to give way, and this heralded the second breach and made a general reversal inescapable. As long as optimism dominated (whether it was pure essence-optimism or indirect or direct influence-optimism), a positive image of the future was still tenable, as such. But as soon as pessimism gains the upper hand (essence-pessimism, strengthened by influence-pessimism), and makes a solid alliance with a monism which now for the first time has the opportunity to develop into a Weltanschauung, the eschatological image of the future collapses. Only when faith in God's divine guidance of history crumbles and the goal, which was to be ultimate glory, is lost from sight, only then it becomes clear how this whole conception had already been undermined by the monistic denial of two worlds and two ages. The other realm was only meaningful if conceived as a future realm, as the fulfilment of the end of time.

Monism in its fully conscious form develops only in connection with pessimism concerning the future, and then must inevitably come in conflict with the religious-eschatological consciousness. At this point de-dualizing becomes unavoidable; man recognizes and rejects dualism as a myth, unacceptable to rational thought and unworthy of the sacrificium intellectus.

Once theology has taken the position that the other realm is a realm of imagination and illusion, it submits to the existentialist view that there is only one reality, the given, only one world, the here-and-now, and only one time, the present. Earlier absolutistic distinctions between body and soul, natural and super-natural, kairos and eternity, and world and God all disappear in this monistic world view. Now all attention is focused on the empirical world and the immanent forces active in it. No place is left for a transcendental or ontological reality, or a guided development of this world toward such a reality. All that remains is a meaningless world ruled by human power—or impotence. There stands man, in his existential "Daseinsnot", thrown into this world and abandoned by God. There he stands in suffering, fear and doubt, condemned to death.

Modernistic theology—at least the Protestant [1]—has not only taken over this monistic-pessimistic terminology, but also the underlying principles. This means that the parousia is rejected not simply because it has been so long delayed, but because the modern Christian can no longer believe in

[1]. A Catholic existentialist philosophy is also in process of development, and is becoming increasingly influential.

it at all. It cannot possibly exist, therefore it will never come. Monism compels theology back to the idea that Christ *is already come*, and away from the idea of a *return* as a separate and specific event to take place in the future. Establishing the Kingdom of Grace in this world, modern theology obscures the coming Kingdom of Glory. It retains the divine revelation *in* Christ, but denies the prophetic revelation *through* Jesus. It points up the continuing presence of Christ in this time, but shrinks itself into a non-cosmic, non-prophetic theology by doing away with the dualistic myth of cosmic transformation. The time-caesura lies in the past, not in the future. Monistic theology accepts this world as it is, as a hopeless chaos and disorganized wilderness perhaps soon to become again without form and void, as it once was. It accepts this world, for there *is* only one world, and every escape is only an illusion. The Church and faith must somehow find their difficult way in this world, the way toward a symbolic Kingdom of God, that abstract eternity which overshadows each existential moment. With this world the Church must make her compromise, if not always with this nation and this culture. The Church must accomodate itself to secularization.

Monism is now so well entrenched that it would remain dominant even without the support of pessimism. Where a stray undercurrent of influence-optimism still survives the general essence-pessimism, it is no longer an indirect influence-optimism, eschatologically directed, but a direct influence-optimism feeding into utopian attitudes. This is true of the heroic ethics of Schweitzer and of the will to moral perfection of his followers of the Berne School who still speak of a "willing" of the Kingdom of God as ethos and pathos, although they have rejected the concrete substance and actual coming of such a Kingdom. It is also true of the pragmatic-realistic churches in America which call for a "realization of the Kingdom on earth" and for social-ethical striving for a "responsible society"; it also holds for Christian socialism, for the active, reforming attitude of the "social gospel", and for the ecumenical movement. However much sympathy one may have personally for this progressive and humanitarian idealism, and however closely it approaches the social ethics of Jesus himself, the fact remains that the basic world view is completely different. The faith is in fact an *other* faith than that of primitive eschatological Christianity.

E. De-Deification

In summarizing our study of the various forces at work in the de-eschatologizing process, I suggest the paradoxical but unavoidable conclusion that the counter-eschatology of modern theology results in de-deification. In his excellent study of modern eschatology, Heering here and there very tentatively and hesitantly raises the questions of whether the arguments of his colleagues such as Schweitzer, representatives of the Berne School, Dodd, Nigg and others, can be supported by a genuine religious faith and are consistent with it. What Heering understandably raises only as a point of doubt and concern, incidentally and implicitly, we here deliberately and explicitly state as a factual and inevitable conclusion. Unconsciously and unintentionally, de-eschatologizing has contributed to an anti-Christian process of secularization which ultimately leads to atheism, or at least to agnosticism.

The *monism* which we have just discussed, which maintains that *this* world is the only possible existing reality, leads through its denial of radical transformation into *the totally other*, to be effectuated by divine intervention, along a pattern which must end in the denial of *The Totally Other*—that is, God. The dualistic view that there are two kinds of reality means that the totally other reality is considered as a pars pro toto of the divine essence. Then the *image* of a possible Kingdom of God on earth is a *mirroring* in this world of the other-worldly, and of God Himself. But the monistic reduction of the image of the world to the here-and-now dissolves the concept of the New Age into an illusion. Hauling in the boundary of vision until it touches the tip of man's nose, so that he can see no further than the immanent event, implies a cramping of awareness in regard to all transcendence and thus to The Transcendence, God. The natural order loses its counterpart of a supernatural world at the same time that human power liberates itself, in reference to the direction of this world's affairs, from a now fictitious supernatural power. However, if history does not move towards a predestined fulfilment, then there is neither Planner nor Fulfiller, neither Creator nor Recreator.

Heering cites—hardly noticing the implications—a meaty saying of Karl Heim: "Gottesglauben und Endglauben sind unzertrennlich" ("belief in God and belief in The End are inseparable"). [1] In my opinion this remark is strikingly to the point. God's omnipotence is meaningless, at least for human thought, if it is not directed toward the goal of some kind of fulfilment at the end of time, a fulfilment of that which exists now in potential in this world, a fulfilment which seeking and striving mankind can trust in.

This stated the *positive* view. We are now already in the *negative* stage, however *We must dare to think the reverse*. The iconoclasm of the image of the future has crushed to earth the belief in The End. But this also means the beginning of the end of the belief in God, at least in a God who reveals himself in time and history. Once God has been banished out of this world and out of time, the many images of the Divine Encounter—the meeting

1. *Op. cit.*, p. 205, 6. Cited from Karl Heim, *Jesus der Weltvollender*, Berlin, 1939, p. 172.

of man and God in listening obedience and prayerful supplication which forms the core of the Christian faith in God—becomes meaningless. All striving for a reconciliation of man and God, whether in this earthly life or in a Hereafter, becomes equally meaningless, reduced to a dualistic myth. Now man must choose between two evils: either he must shut himself and his faith up inside this world, thereby making God this-wordly too, or he must close off the exit to any other world and deny God's omnipotence. Thus, God may be either retained for the sake of tradition and as an ornamental figure-head in a system which functions automatically and could work just as well without Him, since it only projects indefinitely the existing purposeless order—or He may be considered as a god who will not and cannot establish a new order and thus apparently is non-existent for all human purposes, having abandoned man to his earthly lot and with no final design or function for the re-creation and fulfilment of human life.

Heering has well said: "God's redeeming love is the causa originalis and His Kingdom the causa finalis of Christian living and striving; the one pushes man, the other pulls him". [1] In abandoning this position man must accept the consequences. Without a finale, without what Ritschl calls "the ellipse with two foci", the figure of God becomes hazy; his redeeming love then acts only on individual man, and that after his death, not on mankind as such. Even the concept of a personal life after death in a Hereafter, must then lose its meaning, together with the concepts of heaven and hell, for this too is a dualistic transcendental myth. Loss of faith in the other world of *cosmic* eschatology must ultimately be followed by loss of faith in the other world of *individual* eschatology. If there is to be no transformation of this world, why should there be a transformation of man?

If both the glory of individual immortality and the future glory of this world are rejected as realistic entities, then the divine author of the effective fulfilment of these goals becomes *unemployed*. If there is no personal redemption there can be no Redeemer, if there is no collective state of salvation, there can be no Saviour. The departments have been changed around a bit, and the Original Organizer has been pensioned off. The expression, "The eschatological bureau is closed" is only a half-truth. The other half is that this bureau was under God's personal direction and that this was his main function, even within the Christian faith. The place He has vacated has been filled in a worldly manner. The Church of this world puts itself forward as the Kingdom of God. But this is a kingdom of the existing order and of an ineffective, inactive god, a kingdom which the early church fathers themselves would have called an "imperium diaboli". An eschatology sans *eschaton* is the forerunner of a theology sans *theos*.

1. *Op. cit.*, p. 208.

In the modern Weltanschauung these profound changes are registered in the altered ways of looking at the world: from dogmatic to agnostic, from futuristic to existential, from mythological to humanistic, from ontological to axiological, from mystical-cosmic to social-ethical, and so on. But however these are labelled, there are always two main components: an altered view of man, and an altered view of God, in an altered relationship to each other. Man's place on earth in relation to the universe is other than formerly, and his power and impotence in relation to superhuman power and God's omnipotence is other than formerly. In short, there is a general shift from a *theocentric* to an *anthropocentric* world view.

The modern thought of man circles around man. Man, thrown into this vale of tears (yes, it has become a vale of tears once more) against his will and trapped here permanently, has no way out. The view of this world as a way-station has disappeared. This view is neither *Christian* nor even *humanistic*. There is no God to make this world meaningful. There is only a nature naturata, no natura naturans. The only goal of life for man is death. Man can only make the best of this worst of all possible worlds, and all amelioristic images of the future are illusory and deceptive. Reality develops according to the indicative of human action, not according to the imperative of divine will. Man is subject and object of the force-field of the *praesens*, unmoved by any divine *futurum*.

Man's struggle for existence in this miserable world replaces the ecstacy of faith and the struggle with the angel. The desparate longing for "Existenz-Erhellung" supplants the aching longing for the future and leaves God in a midnight darkness. Man is called to "decision", with freedom and responsibility for his actions. If, on the other hand, he abandons his pride and surrenders his will to God, he must be well aware that God has no plan to lead this world towards an exalted goal at the end of time. *What can God expect from man, if man has nothing more to expect from God?*

However one looks at this problem, the continued *destructive* processes taking place with reference to religious eschatological expectations for the future must in my opinion end in the *de*-deification or at least in the *de*-personalization of God. Jesus, the last in the line of the great Old-Testament prophets, forcefully proclaimed these expectations of the future. If Jesus, in whom God is revealed, is denied in this respect, God Himself is denied. The first concept to give way in the process of de-mythologizing was the highly personal idea of the return of Jesus; this was replaced by the more impersonal awaiting of the Kingdom of God. This only shifted the problem to new ground, since it still involved the idea of God as Person. But the de-personalization of Jesus cannot stop at God. For how can a depersonalization of Jesus hold in a faith which maintains that Jesus, through his birth, is God become flesh, and that he was raised again to God in heaven after his death? He who defames the Son of Man defames God. Pascal's words are often cited: "Jesus sera en agonie jusqu'à la fin du monde". But two points are usually neglected in connection with this statement. In the first place, Pascal is still postulating an end of the world, and in the second place, he adds: "il ne faut pas dormir pendant ce temps-là". The contrary has happened, however. Man has indeed fallen fast asleep and would rather not be wakened from the merciful peace of his quietism by Jesus' call to the future. There is no longer an "end of the world" in the primitive Christian, cosmic sense, but only, after millions of milliards of years, in a scientific sense. In reference to *such* an end, we can safely say, "après nous le déluge".

We see that once man has begun depersonalizing Jesus, he has also unwittingly begun depersonalizing God. He is then already speaking of God in abstractions, with variations on Plato, Plotinus, Bruno or Spinoza. God becomes the ground of all being, or the highest concept of value in a hierarchical system of thought, or an eternal spirit. All the fine terminology about de-mythologizing and de-dualizing cannot obscure this naked fact. When all is said and done the "new thought" reduces to this: There is no willing, acting directing and speaking God Who will transform the world according to a Divine Plan. All ideas of such a god are but myths and daydreams which only serve to obscure reality for the worldly-wise modern man, and to block the way to a true faith. But what remains of this "true faith"?

De-Judification aimed at, and achieved, the somewhat unworthy and hasty exit of the God of the Old Testament. When he disappeared, the God of the Covenant disappeared from the world stage, with all his promises of renewal and fulfilment. The *promise* of and *faith* in this fulfilment forms an unbroken whole in the Jewish eschatology of Jesus; the broken promise takes the bottom out of faith and destroys the tight hold of God's revelation over men and their strict obedience to it. The iconoclasm does not limit itself to the destruction of Jesus' *image of the future*, but also destroys the *image of God* in all its aspects, from the Synoptic Gospels through to Revelations. Devaluing the idea of the future salvation of mankind as the foundation of Christian faith implies a desecration of the living God acting in an all-good, all-wise and omnipotent manner. In practically all counter-eschatology, the wavering faith in God hangs by the thinnest thread of an unexplained residual inconsistency in an otherwise completely rationalistic and realistic train of thought.

The progressive elimination of miraculous wonders draws ever closer to the negation of the last and greatest wonder: that of divine mercy and salvation. De-futurizing is nothing less than the recognition that a theodicy is foolish and untrue and that the bonds between the temporal events of this world and God must be cut, since God will never establish a Kingdom in this corrupt and perishable world. This destruction of the historical dynamics inherent in the Christian religion also attacks equally the dynamism of the revealed faith in God and His activity. If God is removed from the time-stream, then He is also removed from the *past* and from his supposed intervention in world history through Jesus Christ. If God is eliminated from the future, the future of God is threatened. From the human point of view, the idea of God originates, exists and declines along with His image of the future. Without a divine image of the future modern man is not so much as he thinks abandoned *by* God, as he is himself deliberately abandoning the acting and active God, as an unwanted antique. With the death of the eschatological consciousness and vision of a future glorification of mankind through the transforming action of God, God Himself dies into passivity in the minds and hearts of men.

PART V

THE BREACH IN OUR TIME

> *"Ce n'est que faute de savoir bien connaître et étudier le présent qu'on fait l'entendu pour étudier l'avenir".*
>
> BLAISE PASCAL [1]

With the above tragic concluding scene, our preliminary study of images of the future is at last completed. This historical narrative of the "grandeur et décadence" of images of the future was not intended merely as an analytical exercise, as a bit of "science pour la science". It was meant to give us a better *insight* into the *present*, that we might also possibly have a more trustworthy *foresight* into the *future*. Now we will have an opportunity to test whether indeed the preliminary study has provided us with a key to the understanding of our own time and of developmental tendencies working into the future.

It is of course my conviction that the historical material presented will throw new light on the darkness of our own time and penetrate through the black widow's veil which masks our future. In this section and the following one we shall attempt to exploit the possibilities of our material to the utmost in uncovering and making explicit the pattern of our time.

The prevailing situation in our own period, in the mid-twentieth century, may be characterized in all its uniqueness in relationship to its different past by the following paradox: The images of the future, particularly those of eschatology and utopia, each gave expression, in their own way, to the idea of a coming turning-point in time, a turning to a totally other and better time. The de-utopianizing and de-eschatologizing of these historical images of the future have brought about, all unawares to man,—a turning-point. The turning, however, is the reverse of that which had been historically envisaged.

The demolition of the images of the future does indeed lead to a change in the times, a change which has already come in our own time: *a break with the past*. This in itself makes our time de facto into a totally "other"

---

1. Lettre VIII, décembre 1656, à Mlle de Roannez, from *Pensées et Opuscules*, ed. L. Brunschvicg, p. 223.

time. Not, however—in fact least of all—into a better time. The *caesura* in time is at the same time a *crisis* in time. The breach has broken time into fragments. The change is not the upward flight of an arrow released at last from the hunter's taut bow, but the headlong fall to earth of a bird with clipped wings.

And yet contemporary man is scarcely aware of this pitiful collapse. He believes himself to be still standing with both feet firmly planted in the present. He does not know that he is standing on an earth-fault which is ready to shift and split wide open at any moment, because this hard-headed realist does not concern himself with looking into the future. But the historian of the future, looking back, will see our age as a transition to a *fourth* period to be added to the now inadequate division of history into Antiquity—Middle Ages—Modern Times.

Chapter XVIII

TIMELESS TIME

In "the good old times", time was properly divided into past, present and future. The past was mirrored in the reconstructed images of history. Foreshadowings of the future were seen in constructive images of the future. But our time knows hardly more than a continuous *present*, which manages to encompass only the short-run prospect of tomorrow and perhaps the day-after-tomorrow. Beyond that lies an endless vista, expressed in inconceivable magnitudes. Between the present and that endless vista lies ... nothing; a vacuum. Qualitatively speaking, time is not the same as formerly. The age-old interplay between images of the future and the course of time has been abruptly broken off. There remains only *time*, both as *winner* and loser.

1. *Fulfilment and Self-Defeat of the Images of the Future*

It is scarcely possible to overestimate the extent of the tremendous spiritual reversal which has so silently taken place in our day. We must fully appreciate the fact that *never* before in the history of human civilization, insofar as this is known to us, has there been a period *without* any kind of positive images of the future. Our time is the first in the memory of man which has produced no images of the future, or only negative ones. This in itself *is* already the breach in our times. From a historical point of view our time is in this respect absolutely *unique*.

Thus far we have been able to ascertain the style of life and pattern of behaviour of a period from the images of the future which it has developed. But our period is chiefly recognizable from its lusty, battle-thirsty attack on all images of the future. There are, of course, also other characteristic phenomena which make their appearance for the first time in history in this age, but none of such far-reaching significance, in my opinion, as the iconoclasm of the images of the future. This is not only true because of the unique character which this fact gives to our particular link in the chain of history, but because it heralds the dawn of an entirely new era, and may result in shunting man's future development off in an entirely new direction.

The invalidation of images of the future does not only effect our own time, but also stamps the future in its own peculiar fashion. The decades around the middle of this century may be commemorated by future generations as one of the few milestones in the dynamic development of western culture, possibly as the definitive turningpoint, *from its flowering to its decline*. Our study of time and the future will find its completion by elaborating the newly discovered, intimate relationship between the historical dynamics of culture and the *flowering and decline of images of the future*.

With this statement I have already traced the main outline of my argument, and given my conclusion in advance. But four other propositions must be established in order to give a closer delineation of my position and a more logical exposition of it. The first three will be set forth in this chapter, and the fourth in the following chapter.

In the first place, referring to the last two chapters, we will give attention to the highly significant fact that the multiple development of heterogeneous images of the future has led to a completely homogeneous result. The processes of de-utopianizing and de-eschatologizing are strikingly similar, not only in broad outlines but in details. This points unmistakably to one *structurally related underlying process*.

Secondly, we will discuss why these deeper-lying forces now pushing to the surface, are upsetting the balance and changing directions in the spiritual forcefield with the already demonstrated *result of negation and nullification of all thinking about the future*.

Thirdly, we are interested not only in the fact of this process of demolition and the reasons for it, but must ask ourselves, why does it take place *just now in our own time*? Why does precisely *our* generation have to be faced with this breakdown? And is it true that there *is* a radical breakdown? Or is this simply one of these temporary and even necessary depressions which occur in every period of history as they do in the lives of individuals? Is our modern period really exceptional in its negativism and nihilism, or does it only *seem* so because the past always tends to be idealized and romanticized?

Fourth and last, if the evidence for the uniqueness of our situation appears undeniable, and we have satisfactorily answered the question "why" with „therefore" and "when" with "now", then we must finally face the ultimate and decisive question of "where to". The vital problem is whether the dying images of the future are only symptomatic of the general situation of our culture, or whether they exercise a determining influence on the future of this culture. In the absence of a diligent application of counterforces, do these defunct images predispose western culture to inevitable breakdown and irrevocable death?

A. The Expiring Realm of the Future

In reference to the first point, we have already given an extensive analysis of the negativation-process that both utopia and eschatology have undergone. This is the first time, to my knowledge, that a connection has been made between these two different negativation processes, each of which has been separately carried out by different people in different places. The connection does not only lie in the analogous manner of elimination of the two entities, but in the fact that among all the different kinds of images of the future, *only these two* are affected. In other words, the de-futurizing and de-imaging is not totalistic, but specific in nature. Other images of the future and types of thinking about the future are left undisturbed, and are even free to continue a further development.

There is certainly no general tendency toward iconoclasm. On the contrary, eidetic representation by means of images has never been as popular as it is today. The moving pictures of film and television, the picture-books and the comics all witness to the popularity of images in the mass-media of modern communication. The graphic representation of statistics, the picture atlas, modern display art, the news-reel, the illustrated magazine, the picture magazine and the whole field of journalistic photography all give similar witness. The visual image plays a more important role than ever before. In the current mode of science-fiction such representations are combined with a new-fashioned way of thinking about the future.

Least of all is *de-futurizing* prohibitive in regard to all representations of the future. Again it is rather the opposite which is true. The novel of the future is among the best-sellers of our time, both as a caricature of utopia, as semi-utopia, and as science-fiction with its pre-occupation with long run developments of a biological and technological nature. There is furthermore so much interest in planned developments of every kind and short-run statistical prognosis that ours has been termed the "Age of Planning". And finally the secularized eschatology of Marxism and liberalism have given rise to other political forms of pseudo-eschatology and social myths which have considerable powers of attraction for large parts of the world's population in our time, particularly when they are coupled with nationalistic and imperialistic representations of the future.

There is no doubt that de-imaging and de-futurizing have specifically focussed their attack on those images of the future which are encompassed by the categories of utopia and eschatology, bien étonnés de se trouver ensemble. Thus far utopia and eschatology have been far too busy with their mutual strife over unresolvable differences to be conscious of any kinship. Men have always seen that these two modes of viewing have existed on different levels; it has also been thought, however, that these two levels were mutually exclusive and that man had to choose one or the other. There was no conception of the possibility that the two might complete each other and coexist peacefully. From our previous analysis I would draw a new and different conclusion: *If they cannot live together, they will probably have to die together.*

To what genre of images of the future do utopia and eschatology belong, and what are their basic points of correspondence? We have earlier referred to the genre in question as that of *positive images of the future;* that which they have in common is the optimistic and concrete representation, which each develops in its own way, of a totally other and better world to come in the course of time. The *basic difference* between utopia and eschatology concerns whether this other world is to be brought about by God or man, but this point is almost *irrelevant* for the *negativation process.* By crushing the elements common to both, this process dims the lustre of the underlying substance, *man or God*—and perhaps even dissolves it.

The idea of a coming, other and better world always contains the following elements, whether it is incorporated in an image of the future of a utopia or the Kingdom of God: the split between this and the other realm, optimism concerning the other as better, and even perfectly good, faith in the earthly realization of this new realm at some time in the future, and finally, a specific idea of how it will come about. Not one of these fundamental components has persisted unscathed into our time.

The dualistic conception of the world, the conception of two realms or two eons, has suffered very seriously. And it is surely this conception which is the most essential prerequisite for a split between the present and that future in which the great transformation must take place. But our age has substituted an actualistic monism for this futuristic dualism. All that exists in reality is this experienceable world in this tangible present, dragging on in the unbroken linearity of a space-time continuum, which has no counter part.

In this kind of a world all idealism is dashed to pieces against the hard stone wall of reality which presses in from all sides. The split between realism and idealism cannot survive this fencing in of the spirit. Positivism and empiricism set the tone for the age. The distinctions between Sein and Sollen, fact and value and positive and normative are carried to the extreme. All attention is concentrated on a nakedly factual existence in the here-and-now.

This concentration on existence in the present is coupled with an essence-pessimistic Weltanschauung: this world will be full of evil and human suffering for all eternity. The split between *essence-pessimism* and *influence-*

optimism (indirect, trusting in God, and direct, trusting in man) has been eliminated. The dominating existentialist world view is essence-pessimistic by definition and ex hypothesi. Existence in this world is existence to the death. "La condition humaine" is one of endless misery, despair and irredeemable inhumanity. Non-existence is to be preferred to existence. But man must nevertheless strive, like Sisyphus, to roll his heavy burden uphill toward a heaven that is not there, through days and nights that have no end.

This essence-pessimistic, monistic view of the world as a given and unchangeable reality eats into the other elements of the culture like a corrosive acid. It labels every idealistic attempt at radical improvement of the world as irrational and impossible. In other words, every faith in the future, whether utopian or eschatological, is intellectually and philosophically untenable, because any belief in goals, and particularly belief in an ultimate goal, is untenable and proven false in advance. Even if such a faith were in itself theoretically conceivable, it could never work out in practice.

Every belief in a coming realm of the future, a new human existence on earth, whether it glorifies humanity or God, is for modern thought equally *irrational* and *unreal*. Such beliefs still bear traces of the naive faith in human reason, progress and evolution which flourished in the Renaissance and the Enlightenment. They are still tinged with the ethos and pathos of primitive Christianity, chiliastic expectations or an idealistic philosophy of the unfolding of history towards a divine kingdom of peace, love and justice. But modern man knows all too well that there is only *progression*, no *progress*. There is forwards, but no upwards. The so-called highest values are not values for this world, but only the fantasies of speculative thinkers or mystics. This world is, and remains, absurd, rudderless, meaningless, purposeless. The devaluation ends in nihilism, since any meaningful direction to the course of history, regardless of whether the direction is determined by God or man, is an antinomy for modern thought. To ascribe meaning to history is either pure self-deception or deliberate falsification.

Labelling this world "meaningless" can be considered just as arbitrary a philosophical approach as the opposite, rejected approach, having no superior logical necessity and representing just as speculative an extrapolation into the future. That the validity of this position is nevertheless so generally accepted by the modern mind is due to the fact that a simultaneous attack on meaning has been launched from an entirely different quarter. By this attack the positive image of the future has received its death-blow, for this argument has demonstrated that no power on earth could ever transform our world. A paradise on earth, be it utopia or the Kingdom of God, is made inconceivable. Therefore *now* it becomes almost impossible to think that history is developing towards a meaningful end. The positive image of the future is now unmasked as only an *image*, without any significance for the *future*, since the *means* for its realization no longer exist.

There are only two possible kinds of means for such a realization: either human striving or divine intervention. There is no third alternative. But modern thought considers the first to be an *illusion* and the second a *myth*.

Sobered and disenchanted by all past illusions of the future (so the argument runs) modern man must at last recognize that there is no escape from this world. Utopian striving for the future, even when it announces itself as a "utopia of measures", inevitably involves a "utopia of men". But man cannot free himself from his own human nature with all its evil impulses, both conscious and unconscious. Just as he is, man has been thrown into the world. Just as he is, he will leave it—and it will be the same old world he leaves. It is possible that man will be able to alter his own biological nature, but whatever "brave new world" he might be able to bring about could only exceed the present one in wretchedness—as recent negative utopias have already predicted. *Man cannot achieve the good*. There is an innate *hubris* in man which leads to a perpetual vicious cycle first of over-estimation of human power with all its disastrous consequences, and then an abject conviction of the complete impotence of human power, both individual and collective.

The same attitudes destroy the naive expectations of a final victory of good over evil through a sudden intervention of a higher power. *This chaotic world has been abandoned by God.* De-mythologizing denies God's plan of salvation for this unholy world. There is no possibility of its transformation. For centuries we have wishfully interpreted our own mythical image of the future, anthropomorphically, as God's will.

The destruction of the positive image of the future finally represents the reverse side of another image of the world, with another image of man and of God. Negativism, nihilism, pessimism and fatalism with reference to the future form the counter-image of the de-humanizing and de-deification discussed in the previous chapters on de-utopianizing and de-eschatologizing. We see now how intimately these latter entities are related in their common denial of *any power*, human or superhuman, which can create anything new and better under the sun. As long as the world turns on its axis, until such time as it is extinguished by natural, scientifically explicable processes, man shall remain as he is, neither wiser nor better. God Himself will not and cannot restore the lost paradise—which is in itself only a primitive fantasy inspired by feelings of guilt and longing. Both the story of the creation and the story of the earthly establishment of the Kingdom of the Creator are equally myths.

The cosmos is subject to the rigid and immutable operations of natural law. God Himself could not change these, not even for our special little planet. There is no longer any reason for believing that God would have special intentions in regard to this microscopic speck in the universe. No Creator can create perfection out of imperfection, no Saviour can sanctify an unhallowed humanity. Man and the world, each chained to the other, can look for no salvation from any quarter. God has been banished to the Nowhere of Utopia, and utopia itself has been turned upside down to symbolize the human creation of inhuman monstrosities.

Here we find a similarly directed train of thought, permanently preserving this world as it is and atrophying that fruit of the centuries, the vital split-awareness of the future—whether seen through utopian or eschatological lenses. This can be no coincidence. There must be similar causes operating to bring about this same negative cramping of the human consciousness. Why, and why just now *in* this time, is man intent on binding himself once and for all *to* this time? With the disappearance of our image of the future, what will happen to our *future*, which now appears to be an endless prolongation of a perspectiveless *present*?

Here we have penetrated to our central problem, the solution of which should contain the key to the events of our time and our future. We will not make progress by bemoaning the sad state of decline of our civilization, for this very activity constitutes part of our problem. We must rather deepen our insight into the complex whole of interdependent causes and effects, so that we know both what to *expect* and what *to do*. If we can find a satisfactory answer to the problem of why the currents of thought about the future, which we have seen develop and move forward over a period of 3000 years of human history, have so abruptly reversed themselves, then we shall have a clue to the underlying nature of the crisis of western culture.

B. Untenable Explanations of the Breach in Time

Various branches of knowledge could be taken as a point of departure to explain this phenomenon—economics, sociology, history, psychology, and so on. But it would take us too far afield to delve into all these specialized approaches, and would not even prove fruitful. The reason for this is that the very change under discussion has also seriously affected the fundamental development of scientific thought in these specialized fields. They form a part of the total cultural pattern and they would themselves have to be analyzed for their contribution to or at least participation in the great reversal. We will content ourselves with a more limited analysis, confined to the *thinking about the future* as an entity in itself. But first I would like to eliminate certain other analyses, which are not entirely inaccurate but which are superficial and incomplete.

The first attempt to explain the atrophying of images of the future is based on the accumulated disappointment, disillusionment and frustration resulting from the *perpetual postponement of the fulfilment of historical expectations for the future*. One could draw up a striking list of such disappointed expectations. First on the list would be the "postponed parousia". Christ's return, the Kingdom of God or the Millennium failed to materialize, however fervently awaited. Other equally unrealized expectations are those of a human society operating according to the principles of Socratic humanitarianism, platonic ideas of goodness, justice, truth and beauty, and the Augustinian Civitas Dei. The Renaissance expectation of increasing human perfection and dignity has been unfulfilled, as well as the enduring end-state of perfect reason as proclaimed by Hegel, and of perfect justice, as proclaimed by Marx. Equally unfulfilled are all expectations concerning automatic development toward a general harmonious equilibrium operating for the welfare of all, as envisioned by the classical economists and social Darwinists.

Neither is there any trace of an inward development on the part of men to the point of "eternal peace, and in men goodwill", as visualized by Kant; no state of liberty, equality and fraternity as proclaimed by the French Revolution and the Rationalism which epitomized it; no irresistible progress as dreamed by the evolutionary optimists; no Russian workers' paradise, no American capitalistic paradise in which the "pursuit of happiness" could take place unhindered; no Kingdom of Heaven even in the symbolic sense, promised by those from Schleiermacher to Schweitzer who believed that human striving could at least bring the Kingdom by analogy. This completes the circle of disappointment and failure. *All* of man's highest aspirations have remained eternally . . . unfulfilled.

Has the disappointment of unfulfilled promises led to the abandonment of all expectations? Our age is indeed the "age of anxiety". Our philosophy is that of "Sein zum Tode", of the meaninglessness of human life on earth. The tense insecurity of the daily existence of the mass-man, surrounded as he is by threats of world war, atomic destruction, genocide, slavery of body and mind purges, pogroms and other forms of barbarism, despotism and sadism, means that the possibility of the complete destruction of man himself, his culture and even of all human life and the planet itself hangs every moment over his head like the sword of Damocles.

But something is not right here. Certainly, the extremes of love and hate, hope and despair do meet. Continuing disappointment of optimistic hopefulness can lead to embitterment and isolation, leading to "Weltver-neinung" ending in apathetic passivity and pessimistic hopelessness. Certainly, but these extremes do not normally meet each other in a one-way street. Rather, despair usually turns into new hope. It is typical of the divided mental structure of man that his *expectations for the future* are stimulated and stirred up by the *contrasting conditions of the present*. The psycho-genetic origins of both eschatology and utopia have been ascribed to the reverse workings of a compensation mechanism. Thus the eschatological vision of the Jews would have turned oppression and persecution into ultimate glory, and More's *Utopia* would have tranformed the existing mass-misery of the 16th century into a man-made Garden of Eden.

It is not possible, however, to reconcile the position that eschatology and utopia have their origin in the natural rebelliousness of the human spirit —and that when human misery and need is the greatest, they will provide hopeful visions of the future—with the position that the continued non-fulfilment of these visions has at last led man to give them up in our age of despair. At least, they cannot be reconciled as long as it is assumed that human nature remains the same. This is precisely the main argument for the view that the old Adam will never be able to live in a renewed world.

Again, something is not right—unless one maintains that special circum-stances have disturbed this compensation mechanism. This is improbable, since escapism has taken more numerous and alarming forms in our time than ever before. The *compensation-mechanisms are working as always, but in a different manner*, determined by fear-driven complexes. Why? This un-solved question continues to trouble the seeker. If we use Toynbee's challenge-response argument by analogy, we might say that relatively small disappointments may result in hopeful expectations for the future, but that great disappointments on the contrary nip such expectations in the bud. Then the problem shifts toward a determination of the *quantity and quality* of the disappointments involved on the one hand, and the extent and sensitivity of man's power to absorb and react to disappointment on the other.

Is the number and intensity of successive disappointments greater and more intolerable in our time than at any time in the historical past? Is man's frustration-tolerance lower and the elasticity of his reaction-potential less than that of his forefathers? Valid psychometric criteria for such measure-ments scarcely exist, nor is there sufficient historical material available to work with. We once more run aground on the barren reef of the "querelle des anciens et des modernes". Personally I would put no faith in such differ-ences in intensity as determining or explanatory phenomena. In the first place history is one long chain of the most terrible betrayals and utter collapses of human hopes. In the second place, the great reversal to an equally far-reaching and boundless pessimism has taken place approximately since the turn of the century—thus, in the course of the last fifty years. This is insufficient time for a sudden leaping mutation of the human spirit.

Above all, we risk the far-from-imaginary danger of curing only the symptoms. For these measurements, even if they could be achieved with some objective validity, would still only represent surface phenomena and would not throw light on the underlying factors which gave rise to them. The key to our time will not be found along this road. At best, it can only achieve a tautological restatement of the fact of a reversal, without throwing further light on it.

An explanation for the breach in our time could also be attempted through correlating the change in the times with the change in the image of the world. There are excellent studies of this last, including one by Becker, [1] who finds that the change begins already in the eighteenth century. Another study by Guardini [2] follows the development through to the end in our own time. There is certainly a close relationship between these two conceptions. The image of the world encompasses a view of the development of the world *in time* and thus includes a view of the *future*. It is important here, however, to avoid a tautological explanation. Are not changes in the image of the world and in the image of the future almost identical, so far as the future is concerned? The image of the future includes an idea of the future of this world and in this sense also contains an image of the world. Naturally this idea falls into place within the larger framework of the image of the world as such.

What is suggested here is a general relationship, in itself not incorrect —but not an explanatory cause-and-effect relationship. For the main question remains unanswered: why then has the general image of the world undergone a reversal with respect to the future? More sharply put, why did the radical shifts in the image of the world during the history of western civilization not work out that same way? Why did the profound changes from primitive Christianity to the Middle Ages and the successive shifts from Renaissance to Reformation, from Counter-Reformation to Revolution, Rationalism and Romanticism, and then on to Enlightenment, Liberalism, and the Industrial Revolution with all its attendant technological, political and social developments, *not* destroy the positive images of the future of former times? And why has the world image of our time destroyed *our* image of the future, in the mid-twentieth century? A satisfactory answer

1. Carl L. Becker, *The Heavenly City of the Eighteenth-Century Philosophers*, New Haven, 1932 and 1948.
2. Romano Guardini, *Das Ende der Neuzeit*, Basle, 1950.

to this question cannot be given, in my opinion, until the specific role of the image of the *future* in the various shiftings of the general image of the *world* is recognized and analyzed.

Finally one might try to crystallize the mysterious X-factor out of the dialectical movement in the history of ideas. It goes without saying that these cycles of human thought can be established over and over again. Why could not similar cycles be established with reference to specific thinking about the future? Cannot the alternations of optimism and pessimism, unshakeable faith in progress and a shattering conviction of inevitable decline simply be referred back to the general rhythm of life, or, in Toynbee's terminology, to the never-ending alternation of *yin* and *yang*? Apart from the fact that some further explanation is required of the forces that set this dialectical movement in motion, there can be no serious objection to this procedure—provided it is followed through logically. The dialectical movement necessarily continues, and cannot arbitrarily be brought to a halt. One can certainly maintain that currents of optimism and pessimism have predominated by turns in history, through demonstrable causes. But notwithstanding all currents, counter-currents and undercurrents, *positive images of the future continued to exist through thousands of years*, in many forms and variations.

Now, however, this genre of positive images of the future seems, as such, to be eliminated—destroyed beyond all reconstruction. Its fundamental point of departure seems to be permanently departed. There is no spring in sight after this autumn. The tree of life is not only losing its leaves, but is being torn up by the roots. We are beholding, not an ebb-tide, but the total draining away of the waters of civilization. The counter-currents seem to have come to a stop. We seem to have arrived at a deadlock unique in history, facing a time either without any positive image of the future, or producing only negative ones. This is the first age, since time immemorial, which is time-less, wishing no more for itself than to remain in the stagnant pool of the present.

Undulatory movements presuppose a *back* and *forth*. The undulatory movements of history have indeed represented a dialectical play of rise and fall, of drawing back and then taking a step forward, often returning on a higher level. This has implied a continuous process of replacement, renewal and enrichment, also in regard to thinking about the future; in other words, perpetual *regeneration*. But this regenerative process seems to have been discontinued. There is nothing but negativation and degeneration taking place in regard to existing images of the future, whether utopian or eschatological. The problem thus reverses itself. The breach in our time cannot be explained by the normal undulations of history; rather we must ask *why*

these undulations have ceased in our time, and why *the road back* from pessimistic
to optimistic expectations for the future *has been cut off behind us.*

C. The Riddle of Time Solved by Time Itself

Other approaches to the problem can be tried, and the author has considered many of them as he has pondered the complexities of the situation.
The reader may be spared these, since they all have in common the fact of
remaining on the surface of the problem. I have personally become increasingly convinced that the solution lies only in going straight to the core and
working from within outwards. By this I mean, *working outwards by starting
from the images of the future and their development.*

This view implies the twofold, paradoxical conclusion: (1) that the
historical images of the future have contained an autodestructive force and
that this destructive effect (also on current images of the future) was a
potential part of the historical images and can be explained by their very
nature; and (2) that this effect can therefore not (or not solely) be explained
by the fact that the historical images of the future have *not* worked (as is
assumed by the "disillusionment-theory", but on the contrary by the fact
that they *have* worked, indeed have worked effectively, inasmuch as their
ultimate decay was implied in their fulfilment. There is then after all a
dialectical process, but working at a much deeper level. It is a dialectic of
drastic self-liquidation, which explains why *this* dialectic must be self-
eliminating: it has surrendered its ultimate goal. *It is a dialectic of thesis and
antithesis, without synthesis.*

We may say that the historical images of the future contain a double
charge of explosive. In the first place they propel the present into the future
—which is their obvious function, since they are after all images of the
future. Thus they pushed the Middle Ages into Modern Times. As time
moved forward, the images of the future also leapt ahead, in consonance
with their historically relative character. This was particularly true of the
utopian images, but even eschatology was subject to continued revision and
reorientation, in spite of its shell of absolutistic dogma. These matters have
already been discussed extensively and do not need to be gone into further
here.

In the second place, and we suggest this paradoxical function as a new
working hypothesis, these now outmoded images of the future have not
only made *themselves* superfluous, but they have provided the successors
which they themselves have reared with a time-limit in the form of a
built-in time-bomb. Not only have they eliminated themselves for the sake
of later redemption through newer images of the future, but they have
already in their own operations and partial realization worked against their
successors, setting in motion a process which ends in the exclusion of *all*

images of the future. This puts an end to all renewal in time of current images of the future, an end to all thinking about the future, and writes finis to the utopian-eschatological consciousness.

With this amazing dénouement they not only explode their own present, as intended, but they end by exploding their own future, the Modern Times they foreshadowed, and the shattered fragments are even now being pieced together to form the kaleidoscopic pattern of Ultra-Modern Times. These images of the future have shaped a time which tolerates no more images of the future. Their spiritual offspring have committed parricide. Conversely, the future of times past brought forth precisely those images, which it later was going to destroy once it *had* come of age as today's present. This destruction was a compulsive action born out of an over-whelming fear of being dethroned by our now impending "new" future, which in its turn might threaten the "old" future's continuous and conservative domination of the present.

Let us consider these somewhat cryptic remarks more closely and try to make them clearer.

2. Father Chronos Devours his Children Anew

Effective and alert new images of the future, which in their turn redeem the pledges of the older images they supersede, carry out one essential task: they *propel time forward*. Images of the future are images of the totally other, and are revolutionary and radical in nature, or they are nothing at all. They are the instrument of aroused and rebellious man, as he challenges the reigning injustice, suffering and chaos of this world. They always encompass a pointed critique of the existing order, and also an incisive, far-reaching vision of reconstruction and reform for the future. In this sense their effect is a liberating and redeeming one. They rebel against ossification and dog-matism of every kind, rejecting the dead letter and bringing instead the living word. The image of the future is the great antagonist, the destroyer of the reigning image of the times, the trigger that releases change and progress with such force that they can move unhindered through the obstacles of the present.

Thus the exalted and daring image of the future of Jesus drove a deep wedge into the existing age of Eastern Jewish Antiquity. A breach was made in time. The Christian era began. Out of the ashes of the old times the phoenix of the new arose, and moved toward the future. The crucifixion of Jesus nailed down the past; the piercing of his hands and feet pierced the present, and his resurrection is the resurrection of the future. The historical Jesus is the dynamic Jesus, the great protagonist of the renewing future. *His* image of the future is the model par excellence of all positive images of the future. It represents both heresy against and catharsis for the existing order, both revolution and pioneering, as it throws open a new dimension of time.

Whenever a new image of the future itself grows old and hardens into infallible orthodoxy, the danger of hypostasy sets in and a ball and chain is fastened to the fleeing foot of time. The Christian Church of the Middle Ages threatened to dig itself in scholasticism, pharaseeism in Christian hypocrisy. The image of the future which does not move forward with its own time loses its vital force, and must seek underground methods of self-realization. But its procreative power is not thereby destroyed. Again and again it arouses for its own self-preservation those counter-forces and movements which are in rebellion against a standstill of time.

Just as Jesus revived the fading Jewish image of the future, so did sectarian chiliasm attempt to revive the weakened Christian image of the future by counter-action directed against the Church. The rebellion which developed during the Middle Ages and found expression in the Reformation was much more a reformation of the Church than a reformation of the image of the future, even though it represented a movement back to primitive Christianity. The Middle Ages themselves were burst asunder by the re-generating images of the future of Rinascimento and Risorgimento, and these images laid special emphasis on *re*birth and *re*surrection.

After this there followed a rapid succession of renewed, renewing and sometimes contradictory images of the future, influenced by and influencing new currents of thought: Rationalism and Romantism, Revolution and Evolution, Individualism and Collectivism, Christian Restoration and humanistic Secularism. These new images inaugurated new periods, or introduced new currents into existing periods. The unbroken continuation and bringing up-to-date of images of a possible and desirable other world *increasingly made another world of this world*, even though according to model and plan. In part the images of the future out of the past were not fulfilled, and therefore were supplemented or replaced, and in part they were fulfilled.

Yes, *in part* future developments conformed strikingly to the foreshadow-ings of the images of the future. This was particularly true of Bacon's visions of technological progress, and More's vision of social progress. But of even more importance is the fact that it was precisely the partial realization of historical images of the future which released further tremendous forces directed toward the course of future development. In realizing themselves, or in the successive revisions through which they strove for realization, the images of the future were coupled with fundamental structural shifts in the times. It is not possible to understand these profound structural changes without understanding the modus operandi of these revolutionary images of the future. But neither is it possible to understand the flowering and ultimate decay of images of the future without understanding the forces released by these comprehensive changes in world-structure.

The double charge which the images of the future carry, first for self-multiplication and then for self-destruction, releases itself via these fundamental structural changes, of which the images are both producer and product, cause and effect. The changes, economic, social and cultural in nature, need not be analyzed here. It is scarcely necessary to mention even the most outstanding changes, for everyone is aware how the face of the world has undergone a complete metamorphosis as a result of the revolutionary developments of the theoretical and experimental natural sciences with all their attendant technological applications and the accompanying revolutions in industrial organization, conduct of wars, political structures and the international balance of power. An almost endless succession of categories of changes could be mentioned here.

Ordinarily these changes can be summarized in the concept of "a fundamental change in Weltanschauung". This concept, while not incorrect, needs refining at two points. In the first place, historical analysis reveals that the positive image of the future forms the *primary potential factor* in this structural transformation. In the second place this observation must be further delineated by adding that this factor has influenced the Weltanschauung or image of the world in such a manner that it is currently characterized, through dialectical reversal, by a *negative image of the future*. The change in the image of the *world* conceals a more far-reaching underlying change in the image of the *times*. This change is so incisive that it has caused extensive internal ruptures, and a breach in time.

The operations of the images of the future penetrate straight through the outward hull of the world-structure to the *inward essence of the times*. And it is the times which presently strike back at the images of the future, for the images, by setting in motion the wheel of time are torn apart even as they near fulfilment; they cannot be stretched to fit the new age which they have stirred up and transmuted—and still live themselves. Through the propulsive force of the changing images of the future, man, the world and God encounter each other in the synchronous movement of time. *After this encounter, man, the world and God are changed, because time itself has changed. The key to our time lies in these sudden mutations of time.*

The images of the future influence these changes in the image of the times in a threefold manner: First, through a tremendous acceleration of tempo with an accompanying accentuation of rhythm; second, through an

unparalleled increase in the intensity of the "charge" in even the smallest
segment of time; third and last, through the releasing of the charge in a
kind of cultural nuclear fission, producing a completely "dissolute time".

A. Driven by Time

The first point, concerning tempo and rhythm, has already received a
great deal of public attention. One symbol of the general acceleration of
tempo as compared with the Middle Ages is the fact that clocks and chrono-
meters must now be able to measure fractions of seconds with great
accuracy, while astrophysics and archeology are working with millions and
trillions of years. Today, centuries count almost as days. Instruments for
the measurement of time dominate our whole life. In the Middle Ages,
man had time. Now, time has man. Time has become a scarce and precious
commodity; time = money. The present time moves so fast that we cannot
keep abreast of it. Never has the individual man had so much *free time*, and
never was the *need for time* so pressing. Time moves so fast that there is
scarcely time left for the "carpe diem". The presses of the daily newspapers
are in constant motion and man can scarcely keep up with the daily accumulation of news. Our life has become a threading-together of a series of
instantaneous exposures, each of which is in itself as dead as the individual
stills of an animated cartoon.

The images of the future have driven time with such force toward the
future that this future has now almost merged with the present. The present
has obtained such a high place in the value hierarchy and claims so much
of our precious time, that there is no time to ponder the future unburdened
by pressures from the present. As a result of this merciless onrush of tempo
and rhythm, affecting both work and play, the essence of time is contained
in the current moment and held in the vise-like grip of a *timeless present*.
Our memory reaches no further back than *yesterday*, and our expectations
reach no further forward than *tomorrow*. We live form day to day, from
moment to moment, squeezed almost to death by an unrelenting *now*.

B. The Tyranny of the Moment

Our second point is that *every moment* is charged with the highest voltage,
and reaches the most acute intensity. We have said that the centuries are
as but days. But there is also a sense in which each day is as a century.
Coupled with the tension of every moment is an almost unbearable insecurity. Every man stands at every moment before the kairos. Man's mind
is ready for sudden and drastic changes in the times, coming at ever shorter
intervals. Vistas and horizons have been radically shortened. Although the
life-span is lengthened, the thread of life may be cut at any moment and all

the world be turned topsy-turvy. A lifetime is shorter than ever before. Who can complete a life's work in the one-day lifetime of our butterfly-existence? The boisterous clock which noisily ticks away the seconds of our life, has replaced the silent hourglass and the reverberations of eternity sounded by church bells. Historical continuity has been broken, the established order of things is disappearing, man's place on earth and earth's place in the universe is rendered uncertain—everything known and familiar has been jogged loose and set into dizzy motion. Even the very near future becomes incalculable in the current complexity of interrelated motives and causes which require constantly new and constantly difficult decisions. All changes may be for the worse, so man clings desperately to the present, to the reality he knows, however cramped it may be. It is in the present that he struggles to maintain his precarious existence in the face of the ominous acceleration in the revolutions of the wheel of fortune. Thus it is the smallest segment of time which dominates time as a whole, just as the weakest link in a chain defines the strength of the whole. And it is the present moment which is the weakest link in the entire chain of historical time.

C. "Freed" Time Fettered to the Present

Our third point is that the time-chain is already broken. *Time is unchained.* Those forces whose energy has been conserved through the centuries, sealed up in time itself, have now been set free. All brakes have been removed, all restraining ropes untied. Time has become a free agent. This liberation of time is mainly the work of the emancipating images of the future. But whereas the older ones still kept time in check, the new ones successively unbound more and more of its former ties.

In our earlier historical review of images of the future we have observed the progressive freeing *of* time, *in* time — a process which has accompanied the coming of age of human thought. We have also observed that this development has never received attention as a logical, step-by-step evolution leading to certain inevitable consequences. Gradually the wrappings in which time was swaddled have been loosened by images of the future until finally they were discarded altogether—by the utopia in the first place, and then also by eschatology.

Older and mainly eschatological images of the future would have kept the wrappings tight and held a firm grip on the future by making it subject to a predestined course of events. Messianism, astral mythology, apocalypticism, prophesy and the Gospel, all these cast their net over time in order to capture it. Refining a theocracy into a theodicy, these movements all combined to confine history within a time-bound salvation story with a predetermined finale. In the course of time the imminent coming of the

Kingdom of God was first postponed to an indefinite (but inevitably coming) date in the future, and then put off to an unimaginably remote future. Finally, the idea of the Kingdom was stripped clean of all time-concepts. Life is no longer a many-act drama of salvation, portraying the fall of man, the first and second comings of Christ, and the final coming of the Kingdom of God in the last scene. The Kingdom will not come in time. Historic time no longer moves towards a definite end, nor will it ever be transformed into eternity. *The Last Time is no longer postponed, it is cancelled.*

The utopia has similarly freed itself and time from the compulsion of development along the lines of inescapable divine or natural law. It has liberated itself and the future from natural necessity, from deterministic or dialectical automatism as related to the mechanistic harmony-doctrine of liberalism, from revolutionary philosophies of history à la Leibniz, Hegel and Marx, and from "scientific" doctrines of socio-economic dynamics. The utopia places a qualitative concept of time over against a quantitative one. It treats the existing temporal order as a historically relative category, capable of radical change. The utopia is the champion of a time which is open and free in regard to the future.

All historical lines of development converge, then, on a time from which yoke and reins have been removed, a completely free time. *Free from what, and for what?*

Free, first of all, from guidance (whether for good or ill) by a supernatural power. Destiny and the devil have been banished from history. God has perhaps not been executed, but is certainly sentenced to silence. He has been ordered out of time into eternity, and events will henceforth march forward without benefit of His planning and intervention. The end of the world is no longer associated with a supernatural, but with a natural-science, time-concept.

Now the way is apparently clear for man's self-determination of his own destiny in time, for the exercise of human freedom and responsibility. We have repeatedly indicated a shift from indirect to direct influence-optimism, from pure eschatology to a manifold utopism with an active, purposeful social-ethical approach to the problem of achieving a humanly worthy society. It was always the intention to make time free for man, to put it at his service, that he might regulate the future course of developments in possible ways, toward desirable ends. Through the centuries social reform has certainly achieved something in the direction of greater social justice (raising the standard of living of the masses, redistribution of income, general suffrage, government by representation, social security, and so on). But in spite of partial fulfilment in various areas, the postulated goal of steering the newly-liberated time toward a totally new and better earthly society through the application of purely human capacities has not been achieved. It seems further off than ever.

But had not all the pre-conditions for such an effort then been fulfilled? All obstacles to the free progress out of the present into the future had been removed. Man's power over hostile nature was almost unlimited. His skill in social and economic planning had enormously increased. And yet, at the very highpoint of his outward power, his awareness of inward impotence has reached a dramatic lowpoint. Modern man finds himself forced willy-nilly into the position of the mythical Prometheus, Icarus and Phaeton who audaciously grasped too high and were struck down. Just as the way seems entirely open, man suddenly finds no way out for the future.

Obviously something unforeseen has happened; some *other counteracting force* must have come between man and his future. At the very point where this paradoxical problem raises itself, we find the long-sought key to our whole complex of problems: the pernicious and perhaps fatal miscalculations of man. In his successive images of the future he has gradually liberated time from all its bonds, both present and future. He has abolished both super-natural power and natural law of every kind. All dialectical periodicity and all deterministic theology which would eventually lead history automati-cally to a fixed end-point has been swept away. But at the very moment when man sees his efforts to liberate time crowned with success, and stands ready to redirect the redeemed potential according to his own wishes, time refuses to be ruled and turns against its old ally and liberator, and against the golden future he has already projected.

The double explosive charge of human images of the future has been *completely discharged*. Again and again, by unloading its first charge, it has shot time ahead into the future by blasting the present. Thus it has burst asunder the rigid restrictions of the existing order and of any firmly prefixed future. By its concealed second charge, however, time once set free and thus come of age now has become completely unbound and uncontrollable. Unchained, it has escaped from man's grasp. Struggling belatedly for victory over that which he sought to emancipate, man now finds himself in turn enslaved by it. Not only is he enslaved, but he has convincingly rationalized this slavery by means of a new philosophy. He has lost all power over his hard-won power. He is bound hand and foot to the here-now, and takes his orders from a highly-tensed and dynamic present.

This time-bomb, this second charge, has gone sadly amiss. At first it left a queer vacuum. There was no longer any *superhuman power* present, as far as man could see, to guide the course of events. *Human power* was not quick enough or able enough to guide the onrushing stream of the times into the right direction. The swirling waters of undammed time now filled up the vacuum in their own fashion, with malicious caprice. The new time-dictator then turned gleefully on all positive images of the future. Like every dictatorial ruler, it feared defeat by violence and eliminated all possible contenders for power in advance. "Free time" thus sits alone, autonomous, holding its own future in its hands, actually shaping itself from moment to moment. The present, as undisputed despot, bars any conception of the future as other and better. Time is not only free and open, but will allow no new reins to be laid upon it, will respond to no new pressures that would lead it to a particular future. De-futurizing and de-imaging have set in. God has resigned Himself. Man must do the same—willy-nilly, with a heart heavy with guilt, sorrow and fear. From a *God-fearing* man, he has become a *time-fearing* man. Encapsulated in the present, he is no longer able to answer the challenge of the future.

Thinking about the future is now almost equated with the original sin of eating from the tree of knowledge and provokes the stern punishment, from the *Zeitgeist*, of ignominious expulsion from the haven of the present. He who envisions the future is either a criminal speculator or a power-maniac, betraying his own times. Time is narrowed to one dimension and one order: the present. There is no backward glance to the past, and no forward look to the future. The physicist may speak of the fourth dimension, but it is precisely through this spatio-temporal continuum, in which our own future has so to speak already happened although many light years away, that the sharp distinction between the time-dimensions of present and future have fallen away.

All that remains is temporary withdrawal from the all-pervading present through various forms of escapism. Man has not lost his "split" mentality nor laid aside the old Adam, but only subjected them to the requirements of the times. The split no longer runs between present and future, but straight through the present itself. The man of today is a *moment-ridden-man*. The movies grant a temporal pass that permits man to spend his short "leave" in the approved three dimensions of the film, removed from the ever-present urgency of the world's woe. But even then there is no escape from the increased tempo of living and the high tension of each moment of time to which man has become addicted. Recreation has also provided other approved types of a "split present", in addition to the movies. There is the world of romantic fiction, including science-fiction; there is the world of the mind, which may be entered through day-dreaming and may entrap the weak in the contemporary escape of neurosis and psycho-somatic illness. There is also the world of the para-normal, which permits the participants to experiment with occultism, para-psychology, spiritualism and mysticism, so long as they refrain from trying to make any precise and factual determinations concerning the future. [1]

Whether in kindliness or in scorn, time does indeed permit man to squander his free hours in all sorts of worthless ways. Free time now plays the role of the devil creating mischief for idle hands. Ever more free time is bestowed on greedy man and for lack of time he can scarcely fulfil his task in time. For modern man's "free time" is indeed an optical illusion; this time is chained, chained firmly to the present. The royal gift has a hidden, inexorable mandate associated with it. Man is only let out of the trap of dailiness on parole, on condition that he return to it promptly—unless he prefers madness or suicide. Even this is allowed. For one cannot escape discovering, sooner or later, that existance is a meaningless Nothingness, aliving death whose only goal *is* death.

D. The Transformed Nature of Time

An increasingly irritated reader may now ask with some sharpness, what he is supposed to do with an explanatory key of this nature. What is the meaning of this personification of our time, of the "powers" of this time? Have we not, after all, set a trap and only caught ourselves? Have we not replaced one riddle with a greater one? In short, is this mystical figure of speech which refers to the present times as an autonomous and personified category, anything more than a figure of speech which would fain undo the iconoclasm of all figures, images and symbols? The reader cannot be put off with the famous philosophical answer which Augustine gave to the problem he himself propounded, "What is the time?". *He* answered, "When no one asks me, I know, but when I must explain it to someone who asks, I do not know". After which apology, Augustine proceeds to give his nevertheless famous explanation.

It is not our intention here to turn aside and climb the dizzy pinnacles or human thought regarding time-metaphysics. Without such speculations, it is certainly true that the philosophical fruits of the greatest thinkers would be unthinkable. From Antiquity to the present, philosophers have applied themselves intensively to the understanding of the mystery of time, which also encompasses the problem of history, movement and change. [2] But when we speak, in our context, of time as an autonomous entity, we intend

1. This accounts for the present suspicious view of proscopism, which might introduce a new determinism.
2. Wyndham Lewis, *Time and Western Man*, London, 1927; Louise Robinson Heath, *The Concept of Time*, Chicago, 1936; H. G. Alexander, *Time as Dimension and History*, Albuquerque, 1945; Hans Reichenbach, *Philosophie der Raum-Zeitlehre*, Berlin, 1928; Georges Poulet, *Études sur le Temps Humain*, Edinburgh, 1949 (with the continuing volume: *La Distance Intérieure*, Paris, 1952); Jean Pucelle, *Le Temps*, Paris, 1955.

it neither as a figure of speech nor as a philosophical category; rather it could serve as the foundation of a philosophical system contrasting to that of existentialism.

We mean here no more and no less than that the very *essence of time*, for the most part under the influence of preceeding images of the future, has undergone a radical conceptual change in *reality*. Previously, present-day time had no independent significance or existence of its own. The present owed its existence solely to the dimensions of past and future. Only because of its constant movement toward the future and consequent recession into the past was it indeed time and not a timeless eternity. The present was time only in its continuous striving *not* to be. By moving on to the future it added to the past or, conversely, by stretching out the past it reached out toward the future. But now, on the contrary, *the present sucks all existence in time up into itself.* The present is the only-existent, unchangeable reality. All time is present-day time, or it is nullity, non-existence, nothingness.

The personification of present-day time thus gives expression to the revolutionary reversal of the existing relationship between man and time. Time *was* relative to the human spirit, a regulative idea which served to order the observable world according to man's needs. The human spirit could move in three dimensions of time, and thus determine his own *position in time*. Utopian and eschatological consciousness formed a spiritual bond between man and his future. It could be said that time formed an *anthropological category*. But now, time is no longer relative to man; rather, man is relative to time. Man has been shrunk down to a *temporal category*. He no longer determines his own position in time; *"free time" determines his position in the present*. Modern man is seized by the kairos, overwhelmed by the existential now, and thereby cut off the time to come. Caught and paralyzed in the spider's web of the present, he can struggle neither backwards nor forwards.

The time-scale of modern man stretches between zero and infinity, two extremes which meet. At the zero-point lies the infinitesimal moment of time which rules his daily existence from second to second. At the infinity end of the scale lie the immeasurable and inconceivable distances from an incomprehensible beginning which moves on into a rapidly expanding universe with no end in sight—a vastly extended movement which totally eclipses the earth and its inhabitants. Between the microscopic reduction of the moment-bound now and the macroscopic dilation of an endless universe, lies a gaping void. *This vacuum marks the spot where the present swallowed past and future.*

Narcissus-like, the eyes of this present are glued to its own image, lost in profound self-adoration, with neither time nor energy to spare for searching out an image of the future, which could compete with it. In the meaning-less vortex of this time, which fastens all attention upon itself, positive thinking about the future becomes equally meaningless. Since any detached segment of the *present* is absurd, any detached segment of the future must also be absurd. The "free time" of the present is without course, compass or steering mechanism. All points on the time-scale are alike interesting and indifferent. Each point in time, as it is reached by the present, is de-termining for man in the same old situation, as loathsome as ever. There can be no question of a future self-determination of destiny by man, in a humanly worthy manner. Man, swept along by the almighty present, declines into quietism and fatalism.

Our time has brought a new type of man into being, and drilled him into perfect obedience. We might call him a *moment-ridden man*, for this modern incarnation of Paul Revere, the minute-man, does not ride time, but is ridden by it. If one now asks again, who hides behind the mask of the personified time of our day, it is clearly this moment-ridden man, possessed and driven by the present; it is our impotent generation with its atrophied time-awareness and shrivelled Zeitgeist. In the deepest sense our problem is that of man and the image of man, of whether his relationship to time is an active or passive one, and of whether his image of time is of a servant or an independent power. Our problem is whether he chooses, or still can choose, the dignity of a human existence powered by the human will, or whether he prefers to submit to the effortless laissez-faire of an ethically indifferent, arbitrary course of time.

It is man himself who is responsible for this double charge concentrated in his positive images of the future. Their auto-destructive activity, although certainly not intended, has nevertheless come about through man's co-ope-ration even though this consisted chiefly in what he refrained from doing. Man stands guilt-laden before the breach in time which he himself has made through his voluntary enslavement to the present. Again and again when we speak of the present-day times, today's moment-ridden man looms in the background. It is *this* development of modern man we must explain, or—more modestly—describe, according to the course of development of man's images of the future. These images themselves can be explained (or described) only in terms of an interaction of endogenous and exo-genous factors in the course of history as it moves toward a new time or rather towards a new human conception of time.

Philosophers and psychologists commonly attempt to explain the evolution of our modern culture without considering the time-element as an inde-pendent entity. All their historical erudition can but lead them astray once they have eliminated this indispensable factor in and function of the dynamic movement of human civilization. We could mention for example Erich Fromm's excellent and influential *Escape from Freedom*. His construction of a social psychology based on Freud's individual psychology is very valuable, particularly in reference to his penetrating analysis of modern tendencies toward escapism, but in respect to the time-concept his work falls seriously short.

Fromm has not recognized the split mentality as a fundamental aspect of the structure of the human mind, and therefore he does not see the purposeful thinking about the future as the driving force of socio-cultural dynamics. Nor does his own limiting empirical and anti-metaphysical attitude of mind permit him to recognize the nature and function of idealistic, constructive images of the future in history, including their destructive retrospective effect on the present ago. Fromm sees changes in the times mainly as changes in the social-economic structure, with man's adaptation to these changes and the impact of his adaptation *on* the changing social-economic structure acting and reacting upon each other in close interaction. He does not visualize any structural changes in the essence of time itself.

What Fromm calls "escape from freedom" I would call an unconditional surrender of man to the present as a totally new time, ruling in absolute dictatorship. Fromm himself, in his choice of a strictly realistic and positivistic approach to science, is the very mouthpiece of this same time. To this extent his age-dated solution can bring no liberation and his social therapy, which does not give sufficient weight to idealistic goals, misses its mark. This modern social healer is himself an unconscious carrier of the virus he would destroy.

In his excellent comparative study of various historical periods in the last 500 years, Fromm does not penetrate to the deepest level of the historical-psychological changes of structure; he does not see that escapism, ever a part of man's split mental make-up, a pre-requisite to all culture, has itself undergone a radical change of nature, to the point of being de-natured. Once it was directed mainly toward the achieving of freedom to determine one's own future destiny; now it seeks only to free a few precious minutes or hours from the iron grasp of reality; life has become a grim cat-and-mouse game in which man can expect but brief respite from the jaws of the present.

Fromm does have an inkling of the true nature of the reversal in human thought, revealed whenever he speaks of the prevailing "authoritarian" character of the modern personality—a thought which he does not pursue to its logical consequences. He labels authoritarian all human activity undertaken in submission to a concretely defined higher power, lying outside of the individual man. This power, however, is not directed toward the future, which is perpetually unborn, has no life of its own and thus no independent nor definable power. Is not this precisely the attitude of today's moment-ridden man, ruled by and chained to a futureless reality, a power of the here-and-now above and beyond himself? But then the desired change, which Fromm also seeks, does not lie in the greater development of personal freedom *within* the framework of the tangible present, but *outside* it, in a larger spatio-temporal framework which encompasses the not-yet-existent and the coming age. It is therefore a vicious cycle to seek for liberation from the present within this empirically observable present, striving for possibilities which are by definition not yet "given" and thus essentially non-empirical.

What is the power of this time? What is the role of the all-dominating present? The existing aeon of the present is the great adversary of the future, the new aeon of antithesis. *The future loses its meaning as a separate, reality-possessing entity*, in the face of a one-dimensioned timeless present, stretching motionless over an infinite time-scale as one static, unchanging moment succeeds another. Above all, it loses meaning as a possible other and better age. The dynamics of time have been transmuted into statics, and quality reduced to quantity, at the hands of man. This time and every other time is identical for him, as yesterday and tomorrow melt into an existential today, unchangeable both as to the good and the bad. Progressive thinking gives way to time-bound conservatism and philosophic chiliasm gives way to philosophical defeatism. Unsmilingly realistic, today's moment-ridden man hopes by obedience to the mandate of this towering, omnipresent today, to maintain his existence in this existing order, however shaky and insecure it may be. *But by aspiring only to win time, he loses the future.*

II

CHAPTER XIX

THE FUTURELESS FUTURE

In the previous chapter we attempted to suggest a satisfactory explanation for the great change in our own time, which is unique in the history of western civilization through the absence of positive, generally accepted images of the future. We have tried to show how this radical breach had to take place as the logical consequence of a movement in time which also revolutionized time itself, as images of the future from the past went to work and partially fulfilled themselves.

In this chapter we will try to continue this train of thought on through the present into the future. We are now no longer dealing with explanations after the fact of a change which has already taken place; rather, we are looking ahead in an attempt to foresee the weighty and probably unfavourable consequences which this change may imply for the future of mankind.

The explanatory key offered in the preceding chapter in reference to the *fulfilment and decline of images of the future*, is further developed in this chapter into an explanatory key in reference to the *fullness and decline of our culture*. This is a key which can be applied not only to the past but—and especially—to the future. Thus the history of the development of the *images* of the future goes directly on into the *future*.

The historical analysis of images of the future up to the present has had no other goal than to serve as a springboard into the future. The following pages contain the fruit—and also, we hope, the belated justification—of the lengthy preparation for this last leap. They sketch, as it were, an abstract "image of the future" in the form of a projection stemming from reasoned proposition applying to a time like our own which systematically eliminates or negates all images of the future. These propositions on the one hand form a résumé of the main lines of the argument of this study, and on the other hand they lead from the thesis to theoretical conclusions which we are now in a position to state.

1. *Restatement of Thesis on the Image of the Future*

The central thread of this voluminous work is a twofold thesis: Positive images of the future conceived in each present time are co-determining for the future of that time. Conversely the projected future is already exercising

its influence on the present through these images, and by continuous interaction it is also affecting the construction of revised images of the future.

In support of this thesis, gradually developed out of a working hypothesis,
we have turned to the vast stores of the cultural history of the west, which
overflow the bins of any purely local warehouse of history, and which
have not been adequately examined from this point of view. We have
surveyed the rich sources of positive images of the future in Hellas, Israel
and early Christianity, examined the new outpourings in Humanism, the
Renaissance and the Enlightenment, and observed the further development
in Rationalism and Revolution, in Liberalism, social Darwinism, Marxism,
philosophical idealism and evolutionary optimism. We have seen the ebb-
tide begin and tired streams at last trickle into the narrow channels of a
pessimistic philosophy of history, theological Modernism, and an Existentialism which marks them both.

In order to construct an ordered and meaningful picture of this flood of
material, we suggest the following provisional formulations; much more
work needs to be done before these can achieve any finality:

A. The prevailing positive images of the future, perpetually breaking
through the frontiers of time, have formed powerful—often the most
powerful—long-range dynamic force pushing history through time. The
pounding beat of historical dynamics, ever moving from past through
present to a future which is again becoming past, is for a large part explicable
only through the idealistic driving force, inspiring spiritual power and
rousing faith of positive and progressive images of the future. They operate
through the spirit of men, regardless of whether one might wish to define
this more closely as the magnetic force of ideal goals, as fiery enthusiasm,
radiating myth, or as a glowing, sparkling ethos and pathos. They operate,
in short, through the pulsating dynamic of ideas.

So powerful was the impact of these images that they can even hold the
non-captive observer of far later times spell-bound and lay him open to the
charges of exaggeration and overvaluing of his material. Although the
author is well aware of the danger of being led astray by a favourite idea
which has been intensely experienced so that it becomes an idée-fixe and
is magnified out of all proportion, he does not see any reason for toning
down or modifying the above proposition. Rather he would intensify and
sharpen it still further by adding: *the history of culture is the history of its
images of the future.*

B. These images of the future, in their non-fulfilment as well as in their
partial fulfilment and continuous renewal that they may yet achieve ultimate
fulfilment, have provided a more or less accurate foreshadowing of the

future, and thus have caused this same not-yet-existent future to affect current thought and aspirational action as though it were already here— especially that expectational activity which is purposefully directed towards future goals.

C. The images of the future provide a rendez-vous for time and future, where they may alternately push and pull at each other in their lovers' quarrels and embraces. This constant interaction on the force-field of historical dynamics, as thinking about the future charges the energy-potential between the poles of idea and reality, blunts the impact of the coming clash between continuity and renewal in society. The images of the future thus function as a mighty lever of progress, as they steadily push the frontiers of the spirit out into no man's land, preparing ever-new jumping-off places or suspension-bridges for the aspiring human will that seeks to set in motion a favourable course of history.

D. This movement of history in time is inescapably coupled with shifts, changes and renewals, including the unexpected, unforeseen and the un-foreseeable. For this reason every age needs and creates its own uniquely applicable images of the future. Spiritually powerful and effective images of the future are only true images of the future in the dynamic sense insofar as they develop synchronously with the times and the future; this means that in spite of having ultimately absolute goals, they must give them a historically relative setting. In this way the images of the future as a mirror of the future also typically mirror their own times, reflecting the self-image of the age. They are the spiritual progeny of their own time. But at the same time they are the progeny of the future, as their social criticism and axiomatic reconstruction tear the present apart. Formed by the present, they re-form it into the future. But the new forms which the images take on, gift of the future, find expression *in* the present, putting the seal of the future on that present even now. These images exert the pressure of an unborn but steadily developing foetal future on the present; they lighten this burden at the same time by subjecting this unknown future to the pressure of a present which is heavily laden with its known and familiar past. They plow up the present to prepare for the multitudinous demands of the future, and at the same time seek to make the future amenable that it may cultivate its soil to receive more readily the unfinished and imperfect present.

E. Just as the images of the future mirror their own times, providing an image of the times, so they also mirror the humanity of their own times, providing an image of man. Images of the future relate the encounter of man with time and the world, with history and the future. Through his images of the future we come to know man, who he is and how he wishes to be ("werde wer du bist"), what his thoughts are, what he values most highly, what he thinks is worth striving for, and whether he thinks it is attainable. The images of the future reflect his point of view concerning the direction of history, his active or passive mentality, his spiritual energy and dynamism, and the manner and means by which he would translate his ideals into reality.

The contrary is also true, however. Just as the images mirror and remake the age, so they also both mirror and *remake man*. They are not so much striving for a fundamental alteration of human nature as for a radically new manner of thinking and living, in harmony with the requirements of an other and better future. Images of the future are at once subject to and exercise a renewing influence upon the image of man and the image of the world.

While mirroring man, they also hold up another mirror which shows him how he could and should be. To the extent that they can move man to look at the changing image reflected in this other mirror, they can help him grow into this new image. Positive images of the future create an active type of man, possessed of influence-optimism, indirect or direct, with regard to the future. Their dynamic power to compel the dramatic movement of cultural events through time lies in the human intermediary, in the man moved to action by his vision of the future. *History does not unfold of itself, but evolves through man's evolving.*

F. The images of the future act and react on the nascent course of events. They are the buffer between time and the future, the crucible and test-tube of the time-laboratory, and experimental model. They are a trial balloon by means of which the adventurous may find what lies on the other side of the time-boundary; they represent pioneer path-finding, the setting of a new course. They are far-voyaging explorers, restlessly ingenious inventors, surveying and mapping a realm of the imagination and bringing it ever closer to realization in the course of time.

The foregoing also implies the very special, selective task of the positive image of the future, which is connected with its general operation as a dynamic force working through the present towards the future. For this task is not just to prepare a transition to *some* arbitrary future, but to direct man toward *that* future which is other and better, thus leading out of the present imperfection with a resolute approach to perfection. This function we have described as the giving of a timely and adequate answer to the challenge which the future has thrown out to the present. As time moves forward, the form, content and power of this challenge are constantly changing. A distorted view of the future, a wrong or belated answer to its challenge, is irrevocably revenged by the course of events, ultimately even to the point of destruction of the existing culture.

The sheer will to conserve the existing order can lead to a neglect of the challenge which the "other" future is already directing towards the present, and thus, paradoxically, to the loss of all that the present has achieved in this future. On the other hand the revolutionary breaking through and tossing aside of the existing order can equally well lead to the loss of precious cultural acquisition. It is the task of selective and positive images of the future to steer society between this Scylla and Charybdis as they act on their mandate from the future. They must find their way through the relatively narrow channel which limits the degrees of freedom of human striving for the future.

G. Looking back at the upward movement of western culture in history, it could well be said that the images of the future, in spite of a few noteworthy relapses, have played the role of pilot on board the ship of Progress on the turbulent sea of Time; an indispensible pilot, constantly meeting the challenge of the difficult reefs ahead, and throwing out guide-lines toward the future. The propulsive power of the images of the future does not lie only in their quality of inspiring the minds of men, as revealed so markedly for instance in the chiliastic movements, but also in their visionary capacity to think ahead, their revisionistic ability continually to reorient themselves with reference to the ever-changing challenge of the future to the present, as in the images of the future of the Renaissance and Enlightenment. Without these thoughtful and continuously rethought images of the future this cultural flowering could never have achieved the dimensions which it did achieve, and the course of history would have been quite different. This reversal of our above thesis is, of course, hypothetical and not verifiable, at least not on the basis of a diagnosis of the past. We may and must, however, test it prognostically, for the future. It is this converse proposition, as will be seen, which indeed forms the central proposition for the remaining sections of the book.

2. Differentiation of Images

In the previous passages we have been speaking of positive images of the future in general, without regard to their unique characteristics. These received considerable attention in the historical part of the study. We saw that widely diverging categories of images of the future can have widely diverging effects, from a historical point of view. We saw this especially for the two main types of images studied, of eschatology and utopia.

A. As time moved forward, the images of the future also moved forward (see I. D, F). The progressive development of these images of the future also encompassed changes in the structure of their patterns, as the inter-relationships beteeen the images of the future themselves changed in con-formity with changes in the image of the time and the image of man (see I. D, E).

B. The most striking feature in the development of western culture up to our own century is the gradual shift from indirect to direct influence-optimism, or the shift from faith in superhuman power to faith in human power. Divine beneficence has gradually given way to human self-determi-nation in accordance with the unfolding of human dignity.

C. The cosmic features of the eschatological image of the future gradually fade away, as "soon" stretches out into "one day", and the main accent falls on so-called *individual* eschatology. This latter has in some respects assumed utopian characteristics. At the same time utopia has taken on certain eschatological traits.

D. In a period of cultural *vigour*, when images of the future are also full of vigour, it is both understandable and from the point of view of cultural enrichment desirable that the boundaries between various kinds of images of the future should be sharply drawn. They may even be in a keenly competitive relationship, as in the case of Christian versus the Marxian and pseudo-eschatological expectations of salvation, or of Christian versus a purely utopian hope.

E. In a time of cultural *decline*, with declining images of the future, mutual strife among these images only accelerates the decline of the images as such. Differences now should be shifted to the background, and become differences of degree rather than of kind. *They must stand united or they will fall together whatever their differences.* Since we are at the moment coming into just this situation, after an iconoclastic attack which has spared no positive image of the future and particularly focused on a radical de-eschatologizing and de-utopianizing, we may conclude that the internal relationships between images of the future now require less attention than the external situation which threatens all images alike. Therefore the ensuing proposition will deal only with images of the future in general, without distinction as to kind, rank or goal.

3. The Dialectic Process in the Image of the Future

We have described how the double charge of the images of the future, after complete detonation in a dialectical process of "triumph and tragedy", has transformed the thesis into its antithesis, leading to the *breach in our time*. A time which stands out from and is sharply differentiated from all preceding time; a time which far surpasses earlier periods of essence-pessimistic world views of eternal recurrence and endless cycles; a time without meaning, direction, goal or prospect.

A. We have suggested the hypothesis that images of the future, as they forge their way through time, have brought about fundamental structural changes in human thinking and awareness. Time itself as a category of human thought has also become involved in these changes. The images of the future have first freed time from its oppressive bonds, but then time in its new unbridled independence has thrown off the last bond of all, the delicate reins of the images of the future themselves. In their continuous procreation the images of the future have produced a new image of time and a new image of man, which identify themselves with the present time. The present moment is from now on the only true time, and contemporary "moment-ridden man" is the only true type of man, in this new state of affairs. And this man of the moment is paralyzed by impotence and fear of the future.

B. The future is pushed and pulled in two directions at once, as far *forward* as possible, and as far *back* as possible. On the one hand it is pulled back to the tangible and visible present, to existential reality, to the momentary actuality of each microscopic segment of time which dominates human existence. On the other hand the future is pushed forward toward an inconceivable macrocosmic eternity, expressible only in abstract natural. science dimension of vast magnitude. The future recedes to such a great distance that it becomes meaningless to our generation, and the concepts time and future are deprived of all significant content. They can no longer be expressed in definite images.

C. The de-futurizing and de-imaging processes of our time leave only the utopia-in-caricature, the eschatology-sans-eschaton and terror-inspiring science-fiction to mirror the times. The reversal is complete. Compared with any coming time that man can visualize, this present time *is* the other and better, in spite of all its lacks, and is therefore far preferable to any future. There has been a complete change-over in the image of man from active influence-optimism of whatever form to passive essence-pessimism and negative cultural fatalism. The Realm of the Future no longer beckons on the world's horizon. Instead the world is in a slow decline from bad to worse, from terrors without end to a terrible end. Born in meaninglessness, pursuing its existence in meaninglessness, in meaninglessness the world shall come to an end. *Every effort to give meaning to it is doomed in advance.* Nothingness, chaos and absurdity, suffering and death are elevated to the position of reigning powers of the time. Their autocratic rule makes the ancient conceptions of fate from Antiquity look like child's play in comparison. The dark mysteries of Hellas become a sunny idyll in the face of this total eclipse in broad daylight.

Here the antithesis appears in its most extreme variant. Gradually, however, the extreme case multiplies and becomes the general norm; countermovements are silenced. The dialectical movement seems to have exhausted its capacity for synthesis. The present moves to the very brink of time and faces a gaping void where once great visions stood. The future has evaporated into a vacuum.

D. The mental split in man, which once drove him to seek the other and the better in the future, now also turns him toward the present. For the present provides him with innumerable refined devices for escape from the piled-up anxiety, sorrow and evil of this world, without the necessity of forsaking the here-and-now. Escapism splits these times into a two-fold present, the existent and the non-existent, replacing the image of the future by the shortlived contrived illusion of day-dream and fairy-tale. In this manner the heavy burden of free time is lifted from man's shoulders. While killing time, man can breathe easily in breath-taking ways, or in homeoepathic fashion seek a cure for his fear of life by indulging vicariously in a fear of death. Using the analogy of Gresham's Law (which states that bad money always drives out the good) one could say that lower forms of escapism tend to drive out the higher forms. The vital longing for another world can only be satisfied through a hideously distorted compensation mechanism, and the way out becomes a hysterically-sought escape-hatch. The frustrated eternal-human longing for perfection is exploited commercially by the modern mass media and on a lower level through highly temporal sensory stimulants and narcotics, as intense as they are short-lived.

E. Time contracts into the one-dimensionality of the present. The present is a timeless and futureless continuum, conserving the existing temporal order as a given, unchangeable reality. The general tempo of life is constantly increased, and at the same time each moment of time is in itself so accentuated, that we are faced with the grisly illusion that time is standing still. Standing in dead-centre of this still-standing time of an eternally enduring present, the human spirit becomes increasingly panicked at the thought of change; it cannot even face the prospect of growing old—foretoken of death and catastrophic future. Our modern moment-ridden man is equipped with blinders, which prevent him from looking in any direction but down at his own feet. This motionless present sees the future as antinomy and

contraband. Every day must be again to-day. Time must be contemporane-
ous at all times. *The reality of this world can never be any other than the reality
of today, and is not thinkable except as present, existent reality.*

Time is unbound, the future is undone. The dynamics of history fulfils
itself only in the here-and-now, from present moment to present moment.
The arrow flying through the air is every moment anew in a position of
rest. The time-scale is a collection of static points, morally and rationally
indifferent. The shifts from point to point are without meaning and without
purpose. The future has no separate, let alone higher, value as compared
to the present. The only intrinsic value of time is to be the present and
remain contemporary. Expectations for the future have no ethical value,
and the image of the future has no logical validity.

4. *Key to the Dynamics of Culture*

The exposition in the immediately preceding chapters, ending with an
analysis of the turning-point in the times, all comes under the heading of
reversal. But we seek to go further than thesis and antithesis. We hope to
have found a new key in the repeated undulations of history, ceasing at the
point of a breach in our own time, which can unlock the closed door to
the dynamics of culture and may also reveal the prospects of future developments. These prospects we wish to lay before the reader for the purposes
of testing and critical discussion.

A. It seems to me that there can no longer be any doubt concerning the
fact of an intimate correlation between the flowering of positive images of
the future and the flowering of culture, in the case of western culture up
till the twentieth century. This repeatedly observed relationship can
scarcely rest on chance. Dispute can only arise concerning which should
be labelled cause and which effect. In this regard we have explicitly taken
the position of *historical idealism.* Positive images of the future are regarded
as the primary causal factor (although not always the exclusively dominant
factor in a changing complex of causes) in cultural change. Of course they
arise out of the spirit of the times, but precisely in order to break through
these times and to guide the spirit of the times in thinking about and working
for the future. Their enkindling spiritual power radiates out over the course
of history, via the creative minority, as long as they command the faith and
confidence of a majority or a sufficiently weighty segment of society, and
as long as they have a convincing mass-appeal.

B. This argument can be sharpened and generalized as follows: *Any spiritual
or intellectual movement* (religious, social-political, social-ethical, humanitarian, humanistic or idealistic) *contains only as much historical driving power and*

élan vital as exists in potential in its ideals for the future. Further, every culture has just that future as is contained in the tensile force (both intensive and extensive) of its images of the future. The future of a culture can be perceived and measured by the power of its thinking about the future.

C. Assuming the correctness of the previous proposition, the reverse may with equal justice be stated as an a priori (see 1. G): *No culture can maintain itself into the future over an extended period of time without generally accepted, positive images of the future.* The validity of this is particularly apparent in a culture which is characterized by negative images of the future. In short, *a culture which shuts itself up in the present, has no future.*

D. In this last case the question of whether the decline of images of the future is the cause or the effect of the decline of culture, or whether the two are in mutual interaction, seems in itself of little relevance for the future. The fact remains in either case that today man's thought concerning the Realm of the Future is dying off, and that at the same time there is a somehow-related decline in cultural development. But for him who has not lost hope in a favourable new turn—and every cultural sociologist is a culture-therapist at heart—the causal connections in this situation are of the greatest importance. It must be clear that if we should have to consider the progressive decline of images of the future as the primary driving force behind this interaction, this would provide us with a highly valuable indication of the possibility of recovery and rebirth of culture through a regeneration of these images.

E. From a purely methodological standpoint, it matters little whether we deal with the relationship between images of the future and culture in terms of the classical relationship of cause and effect, or with a fixed relationship of cause and effect, or with a fixed relationship of mutual interdependence and covariance. For the purposes of analysis and prognosis the concept of mutual interaction offers sufficient insight and foothold, and the problem of unilateral or final causality (and the accompanying hen-and-egg problem inherent in it) can be bypassed. It is then sufficient to be able to say that the images of the future are a reliable indicator and barometer of cultural development as a whole. Furthermore, that they are the medium through which the movement in, out of and of time clearly expresses itself in cultural-dynamic fashion, and also announces in advance the direction it will take. This characteristic simultaneity of the images of the future, precisely paralleling cultural developments, makes it possible to use them in the place of culture as a pars pro toto, assuming their systematic, uniformly directed interaction or interrelationship with culture. For scientific purposes it can suffice, at least to a point, simply to state the fact of this relationship without pursuing further the question of cause and effect. But when culture-diagnosis must serve as the basis for therapeutic considerations, the situation is different. Then synchronous events must be more closely examined to ascertain the chronological precedence and logical priority which lead to this remarkable conjunction or concurrence.

For this reason I believe it is relevant to point out that the images of the future (whatever *their* origin) are not in my opinion a passive medium, serving only as a receiving-set for future undulations in the movement of culture, but also the spiritual transmitter, the primary agent that to a significant extent sets these undulations in motion. Our historical survey attempted to illuminate this active function of levering the present into the future (as well as the more passive one of serving as a buffer between the future and the present). There is little doubt, to my mind, that the creative images of the future of Zoroaster, Isaiah and Jesus, of Plato, Paul, Augustine and Joachim, of Bacon, More and Marx, etc., have through the centuries *made* the cultural history of the future. The Greek poets, thinkers and dramatists, as well as those who rediscovered and revived them in the times of the Renaissance, ushered in a *new time*, just as the English and French philosophers of the Enlightenment foreshadowed and helped to bring about a revolutionary epoch, the German chiliastic-idealistic philosophers an evolutionary epoch, and Nietzsche and Spengler a reactionary epoch—all through their images of the future.

The spirit of their own time spoke through these visionaries, it is true. But the goal-directed energy potential which they generated also determined to a significant extent *which* future out of a number of possibilities in a situation still open and fluid would become a part of the actual historical chain of events. They were not only prophets, but also agents who assisted in bringing about that which they predicted. Themselves under the influence of that which they envisioned, they transformed the non-existent into the existent, and shattered the reality of their own time with their imaginary images of the future. Thus the open future already operates in the present, shaping itself in advance, through these image-makers and their images—and they, conversely, focus and enclose the future in advance, for good or for ill.

F. The falling-off of positive images of the future is not in my opinion simply one of the contingent symptoms of decay of western culture, not just one among many indications of the current culture-crisis. The connection between the broken image and the broken times lies deeper, the causal relationship is more stringent. *The iconoclasm of images of the future is one of the most important, immediate and powerful causes of current uprooting and future threat to our culture.* The disintegration of images of the future carries much of the responsibility for the attendant or consequent disintegration of culture. The gradual, massive transformation of the Zeitgeist from ardent evolutionary optimism to the boundless pessimism of decline and decay is greatly furthered by negative and nihilistic images of the future. New forces of cultural disintegration are set in motion by these destructive images, which in their turn are then reinforced.

G. The monistic concentration on the existential present, with its futureless future, does not stand alone. Rather, it is the reverse side of and part and parcel of a castrated thinking about the future. *De-futurizing and de-dualizing*, whether stemming from current existentialism, modern theology, the philosophy of history or the recent anti-utopian fiction, *have undermined the image of the future and thus the future of culture itself.*

H. This view of the flowering and decline of culture as causally dependent on the flowering and decline of positive images of the future is in direct opposition to the views of cultural historians such as Toynbee and Popper. We have seen how these two men, along different lines of reasoning, have come to a similar conclusion and made *futurism* their scapegoat, the cause of evil in the world and the main source of threat to the future of our culture.

Toynbee excludes all images of the future except one: the Christian-eschatological image of the future in its old, dogmatic form. Popper also excludes all images of the future except one: the classical-liberal image, in a revised modern neo-liberal version. Toynbee is here the romantic reactionary, and Popper the realistic conservative.

At the same time that Toynbee introduces the idea of the necessity of an adequate and timely answer to the ever-new challenge of ever-new times, he maintains that only one answer can possibly be adequate—one that was already given nearly two thousand years ago. [1] As a monopolistic archaist he introduces a static and absolute element into the dynamics of history. Since *this* image of the future has little positive charge left (as discussed in the previous chapter on de-eschatologizing), it is gravely weakened as an agent for the future in this world. The elimination of wonder and mythology have resolutely pushed aside the wonder of the re-creation and glorification of this world as a possible solution to its wretchedness, and the idea of a divine story of salvation has been rejected. The exhilaration of the Glad Tidings has petered out and the modern minute-man says with Goethe: "I hear the tidings, only I do not believe them". If Toynbee then insists (which is his privilege as a private individual, but not as a historian) that

---

1. This is his position as of now, although it is always possible that future volumes of his work may introduce some alteration in this view.

only this answer will do, without revision of any kind—take it or leave it—then this actually means that *there is no answer* (see 2. E). According to his own system, this means *the beginning of the end*.

Popper, on the other hand, is the confirmed champion of a completely free time, unhindered and unlimited by any long-run image of the future. He represents and bulwarks the monistic moment-ridden man, immersed in his daily, care-laden existence. He advocates the application of social engineering, as "Realpolitik", to the concrete reality currently changing from moment to moment in the open society. His anti-futurism is the logical and chronological complement of his realistic actualism. But in my view *this actualism sounds the death knell, not only for images of the future, but for the future itself.*

It is indeed true that here we are discussing little more than two opposed points of view between which the truth cannot in the strict sense of the word at present be demonstrated. The future alone will have the last word on this. The reader must make his own free and resolute choice between the persuasive powers of these two antipodal images of the future—or reject them both, as too extreme. In any case, his choice will play its part in determining the actual future.

5. *Conclusions*

If the above explanatory key is accepted as adequate, then it must also be accepted, eo ipso, that this device not only has an explanatory, but also a predictive capacity. This key fits the locked door of the future. Are we then here faced with the discovery of a new historical law of cultural dynamics? Do we mean to imply a stringent causality, so that every culture which has positive images of the future must inevitably demonstrate a period of flowering, and every culture whose images of the future are weak and disintegrating is irrevocably doomed to decline? Is time to be forced into a new deterministic strait-jacket? Is this not just one more unallowable extrapolation from past to future, and that, after such pains have been taken to free the future from the past?

Without going into an extensive discussion of the significance of the general concept of laws of historical dynamics (a concept which is itself involved in the structural shifts of history), I believe that this terminology indeed can and must be used. But no mechanistically deterministic character should be ascribed here to the concept. This specific law certainly is not one of a divine or natural order. It has not been imposed from without but operates from within. It is a rule of, for and working through men, as a function of human power or impotence. Man sets it in motion by his own actions, and determines the direction and length of its course, and whether it will lead to flowering or decline.

Perhaps such a historical law could be reduced to a simple psychological law? *He who believes in the future, has a future. He who does not believe in the future, has no future.* In that case we should only have arrived via a long detour at a confirmation of the ancient saying, "faith moves mountains". Apart from the question of whether this feat will not also be brought about by the utilization of atomic energy—a technical revolution which accentuates the current transition from idealism to realism—this reduction is not entirely satisfactory, although it contains a grain of truth. It is not satisfactory because then the time-factor is again limited, and with it, the decisive question as to why man believes in the future in one time, and not in another. Or why the belief either in a divine predestination or the human capacity for self-determination is now present, now absent. *Thinking about the future cannot be detached either from time or from the future!*

A. Our law of history operates within the framework of the encounter in this world between man and time. In the historical drama of the challenge of the future to the present, men's images of the future play a leading role by giving answers which are crucial in regard to the future of culture itself. It is up to man, whether he wants to set off a positive or a negative charge, to put a lever into action or to explode a time-bomb. The images of the future which he puts to work contribute to determine the ultimate working of the future, for better or worse.

If man puts out of commission that unique and indispensable instrument which he has for meeting the challenge of the future—the positive image of the future—without providing an equivalent substitute, just when this challenge to our time reaches a climax, then he defaults by giving no answer at all. And, after all, this may well turn out to have been a negative answer.

B. The bridge between time and the future, formed by positive and selective images of the future, has been deliberately destroyed. This time stares blankly at itself only, and is deaf to the call of another, coming time. For while this time may be bad, it is probably not the worst possible time. The price paid for the retaining of the present is the abandonment of the future. Positive images of the future said an express "no" to the present, and "yes" to the future. Negative images of the future say "no" to the future and a hesitant "yes" to the present.

C. A time without inspiring and re-orienting images of the future, or with purely negative ones, is destroying the future from out of the present and thus, ultimately, through that future the present itself. This is the reflection of our own time and the foreshadowing of our future.

D. If a counter-movement does not set in at the right time, or rather is not set in motion by man, then our culture is irrevocably doomed to decline through forces wilfully elevated by man himself to the rank of causal laws. He would then be doomed to a futureless future by his own voluntary and unconditional submission to an automatic course of development which he himself has first made necessary.

E. In reality no time can be without any images of the future, and thus it never is entirely free and unbound. Non-existent and negative images of the future are also images of the future, with a conscious or unconscious minus sign. They too bind time and determine the future, with reversed signs.

F. Not having an image of the future also represents an attitude and expectation in time—one which excludes the future. He who does not choose for the future, or seemingly refrains from choice, chooses against it.

The above statements, deliberately expressed in the extreme form of ultimate consequences, serve as a notice of the coming day of judgement for western culture. As we have said, this is a value-judgement concerning the future, although it is founded upon a systematic interpretation of historical material which seems to demonstrate regularities of cultural flourishing and decline which in all probability will continue to hold for the future, if not cancelled by other forces.

This futureless future will not descend upon us in the twinkling of an eye. If the present is indeed unsettling the future with its weak and negative images of the future, and de-humanizing as well as de-deifying culture, then there must already be signs and symptoms of the coming decline. A *trend-line*, however vague, must be ascertainable.

For purposes of verification, insofar as possible, and as a more refined prognosis, we will in the following chapters attempt to examine more closely the present effects and probable trends in the various areas of culture, caused by the destruction of the images of the future. What are the consequences of the much-signalled turning point in our age and how do they influence the future prospects of religion, art, philosophy, science, politics, and the social-economic systems of capitalism, socialism and collectivism?

A culture is a stylistic whole, a coherently patterned structure. The future of western culture is reflected in the developments through time in all the diverse terrains of cultural life, and vice versa. Ultimately culture is an abstract, intangible concept, difficult to get hold of. Perhaps the focusing on its concrete forms of expression will contribute to a further illumination of the basic general point of view thus far presented.

PART VI

THE BROKEN FUTURE OF WESTERN CULTURE

It has been the express intention of this study to arrive at a new view of the crisis in modern culture. New especially in that the analysis seeks to step beyond the stage of discomfort and disquiet which has by now become almost conventional, and beyond interpretations of a too purely formal and abstract nature. It seeks to achieve this by using a newly constructed, specific tool of improved precision, making possible a more penetrating diagnosis and so perhaps a more concrete and exact prognosis—and even, may be, an adequate therapy. The approach is also new in that the explanatory key to be forged must not only fit the three temporal dimensions of past, present and future, but must also fit both the cultural totality, as a structural stylistic unity, and the various component parts of the cultural mosaic.

It is this last point on which we must now test, and at the same time deepen, the insight we have acquired. Culture is such a vague and disputed entity that it lends itself to almost any set of conceptualizations, and these can ultimately be neither proved nor disproved. The same difficulty presents itself, although in a lesser degree, with reference to the various subsections of culture (specifically in this case now that our western culture in itself again is a vague concept), for these seem somewhat easier to define or at least to describe. However, we are here faced with still another, very considerable problem. It is substantially easier for the cultural sociologist (at least for this one) to deal with culture as a collective concept than to refer knowledgeably to the special terrains of religion, philosophy, science, art, economics, politics, etc. Since each of these areas in turn encompasses almost inmeasurable complexities and is split into finely differentiated specialties, it would certainly be pretentious to evoke the impression of an encyclopedic mastery of these materials and to claim not only sufficient knowledge of these special fields in their present state of development, but also the right and the ability to enter into their future developments.

Here it is only possible to give a few suggestions and indications for the kind of further research that must yet take place in each of these terrains. It would be both annoying and tedious to encumber every sentence of what follows with the many restrictions and reservations and alternate possibilities that ought to be there. Neither does it make sense to weaken my own argument through an excess of self-criticism and constant harping on my own lack of knowledge. I am not going to take back with one hand the words I write with the other hand.

Therefore, in that which follows, the reader must accept in advance my lack of specialized knowledge. I do not presume to be an expert. I am quite deliberately *not* sticking to my last, in order to stimulate the professional shoemakers. My aim is to challenge the specialists, as a self-appointed interpreter of the challenge which the future makes to the treasured enclave of culture which has been entrusted to them. Perhaps they will recollect the words of Plinius, "Nullus est liber tam malus, ut non aliqua parte prosit" (no book is so bad but it may serve some purpose). Some one, after all, must clear the road to No Man's Land, regardless whether in retrospect he appears as a pioneer, though a blundering one, or whether he will only have served as a "try-your-strength" machine in an amusement park. Even that is an expression of human striving after the "higher" and thus after culture!

The material which follows is systematically organized around two combined points of departure, both of which are to some degree fictions. That is to say, the argument will be built up *as if* the writer had specialized knowledge, and *as if* the history of the future could be clearly outlined now on the basis of analysis of the foreseeable effects of forces at work today, without interference from other unforeseen or unforeseeable counteracting factors. We assume that a relatively clear, one-track line of development can be sketched into a field of simple and harmonious contours. In short, we propose to present a *view of the future* in which scientific and value judgements have been fused as consciously and responsibly as possibly—but inevitably also unconsciously and involuntarily—into an intricate pattern of "Wahrheit und Dichtung". This pattern the future alone will ultimately be able to unravel and judge as to its mixed historical contents of objectivity and subjectivity.

Writing the history of the future is not a process of historical *re*-construction, but of visionary *pre*-construction. The difficulties already inherent in the recording of history all exist in heightened measure in this genre of "future history". Both our historical criteria and our historical criticism must therefore here be regarded as "sui generis". To a certain extent *writing* the history *of* the future is already *making* history *through* the future.

I am not asking here so much for the clemency of the various experts and professional historians as for their active collaboration. I will not apologize again for the shortcomings of the ensuing partial analyses. Just because of the difficulties which this type of analysis presents, it has so far been sorely lacking, and I therefore feel all the more keenly the necessity of making the attempt. We had better begin, then, with the most difficult and complex task of all, and one that will arouse the most emotional reactions. We presume much and can offer little exactness in undertaking the examination of that subject which is generally regarded as least amenable to scientific processes: the future of Christian belief in God in the West.

CHAPTER XX

THE FUTURE OF THE CHRISTIAN BELIEF-SYSTEM

It would be a highly important undertaking to write a history of the future of religion in general, as a world problem. There is no doubt that the great religions of the East: Buddhism, Hinduism, Confucianism, Judaism, have been reached by the challenge of a future which is even now being heralded by the gigantic changes at present taking place in the structure of the world. The sweeping dynamic of these changes, however, is only in its opening stages in this particular respect. Even so, the religions of the world are already entering into a state of stormy commotion, and their respective orthodoxies may in the end become completely transformed. Such changes can scarcely be overestimated in their significance for the future face of mankind, and they are also of crucial importance for the West in the coming encounter between the Christian religion, perhaps at an ecumenical level, and the non-Christian religions.

Since our study concentrates on the future of western culture, we will confine ourselves to the future of western religion. Now "religion" is an elusive term, for it can encompass a faith or a philosophy without a god and reach from ontology and metaphysics to agnosticism and even atheism, and from individual mysticism to the spiritual aspects of social movements. It should therefore be stated that when we speak of western religion, we mean the prevailing Christian belief-system, which includes a belief in God. And whenever we refer simply to "religion", we mean the same thing unless otherwise indicated.

On the other hand, since it is our express intention to give only a broad outline, we will consider this Christian religion as much as possible as a whole, without distinguishing between Roman Catholicism and Protestantism, and even less between the various denominations within the latter, or between orthodox and liberal or literalistic and modernistic points of view. Nor will we make any distinction in the *first* instance between forces which tend towards disintegration and counter-forces directed at regeneration, although this distinction is of course of great importance in this connection. We will for now assume the existence of a general trend, which is the resultant of the various forces and counter-forces at work in the field and of the potential strength we attribute to these.

Finally a choice had to be made between two possible modes of analysis,

that of the theological scholar or that of the cultural sociologist. Our choice
here, as for all the other chapters of this part of the study, is logically for
the latter. [1] This is not only because this is our natural field of competence,
but especially for the sake of the *other* aspect, the *other* view, which this
approach permits. Through its greater distance it provides more freedom
and objectivity with regard to this subject matter, revealing more of its
general coherence of structure and perspective.

But where can the cultural sociologist find a point of departure for his
analysis? The sociology of religion has made little progress as a science [2]
since the time of Max Weber, apart from some detailed studies of such
specific subjects as capitalism, economic ethics, the social aspects of religion
or of religious socialism, and a few empirically oriented pieces of research.
Moreover, insofar as such a science has developed at all, it has confined
itself mainly to retrospective description and has made no attempts at prediction. After the penetrating and speculative work of such thinkers as
Comte, Proudhon, Feuerbach, Marx, Bauer, Stirner, Bebel, Kant, Nietzsche,
Dostoievski, Burckhardt, Multatuli, Ter Braak, Freud and Jung (a widely
diversified group, both as to thought and influence) there have been so far
as I know hardly any systematic examinations of this subject of any great
importance, which also deal with future developments. The only exceptions
would be a few indications in this direction in the work of writers such as
Bergson, Berdiaiev, Niebuhr, Maritain, Jaspers, Heidegger, Sartre, Denis
de Rougemont, Simone Weil, Toynbee, De Lubac, and a few others.
    This lack of systematic thought on the future of the western Christian
belief-system is not so strange after all. For Christians there can be no
discussion of a future in which there might be no Christianity, which to
them would be the same thing as envisageing the possibility of a future
without the only true, Christian God. Christianity rests on the belief in the
authority of God's Word, which has been revealed in Jesus Christ. In this
belief-system, Christianity is everlasting by definition. God, having revealed
Himself for once and for always, is everlasting. At the most, the future
(and that possibly a transitory future) of Christendom in the West could
be a matter for discussion, or the future of our present so-called Christian
culture, or of the Christian nations, or even the future of the Church (or of

1. The fact that Christianity is here treated only as a part of culture and a culture-
carrier does not of course imply that it is not also more and other than this.
2. W. Banning, *Theologie en Sociologie*, 1936; Charles Ellwood, *The Reconstruction of
Religion*, New York, 1922; Jean-Marie Guyau, *The Non-Religion of the Future*, (tr.),
New York, 1897; Raymond Knopf, *Religion and the American Dream*, New York, 1934;
Gustav Mensching, *Soziologie der Religion*, Bonn, 1947; J. Wach, *Einführung in die
Religionssoziologie*, 1931; And more recently, a study of the current picture in America:
Will Herberg's *Protestant-Catholic-Jew*.

one or several churches). It is possible for a Christian to recognize that the outer forms of worschip and ritual and even in some respects of dogma might conceivably change, but never the essence of Christian faith, which is eternal and has absolute validity regardless of place, time, culture or political conditions.

For non-Christians, on the other hand, Christianity is often either something already surpassed or something to be surpassed. Their affinity to the world of Christian faith and religion is often practically non-existent or unrecognized as adherence to higher values or the belief in divine guidance. In either case, there seems to have been hardly any stimulus for discussing the future of the Christian belief-system.

Nevertheless, a rational open-minded discussion of the future of this Christian belief seems only possible for those who are often labelled "unbelievers", although this term takes rather too much for granted. We would rather say that only for those who are willing to regard Christianity as a historical and cultural phenomenon on a level with other great religions, a development, which might even include the end of the Christian religion as such, is theoretically conceivable. [1] That which holds the believer in check like a taut rope, the Will of God, is in the texture of the non-believer's thought a thin thread which has been broken. And so they are free (or in honesty bound) to envisage all conceivable possibilities for the future, including also the worst.

This is the situation in principle. In practice, however, many theologians have—often still unaware of the consequences—come very near to the point of transition, as the tension has been taken out of the rope that restrained them. It now hangs slack and could easily be overstepped. However, intimations that this is so, tend to increase an attitude of rather aggressive resistance against those who take a detached view. Because of this the gulf between Christian and non-Christian thinkers, which has actually narrowed, has seemed to widen, and this is not conducive to an open discussion of a common problem.

Well aware of this painful situation and in the attempt to cause as little misunderstanding as possible, we will now broach this subject, which is in our opinion of crucial importance for the future of our culture as a whole.

The Christian belief-system centers around the biblical image of God. [2]

---

1. This development can be conceived by non-Christians *theoretically*. This is not the same thing as saying that this line of thought is also more *objective* than that of a Christian. In this respect, the Christian and the non-Christian are equally biased and neither can *prove* their point at this time. This most obvious truth is often forgotten, but it is implied in our whole discussion.

2. For the modern observer this image is a projection. We will use this expression in the following as we have used it before: as a term of psychological *description*. This

This image has always contained a representation of what God has done in the past, what He does in the present and what He has promised to do in the future. It contains a projection of man's hopeful interpretation of history and so of his expectations of future salvation. These eschatological expectations have played a preponderant role. The image of a coming fulfilment in glory is the deepest source and justification of the Christian faith and has given it its world-wide significance and influence. This sublime image of the future, through which man expresses his deep desire to rise above himself, lies at the core of the Covenant between Jahweh and Israel, and of the New Covenant in Jesus Christ.

It is a metaphysical projection which assumes a living God Who is active and discernible in historical time. As such it has been a determining and dominant factor in the development of western religion and of the social structure which crystallized around this and which we call European culture. Its strength was and is dependent on the scope of its ideal image and on the depth of the faith it inspires. The faithful stand in contact with another reality through this image of God and His future for them. It could be said that they partly already live in this other reality. Their projections do not arise out of nothing but spring from this encounter with a coming time, which though not yet born is already present in their hearts and minds.

In the beginning of this study and in the course of it, we have stated and developed the basic idea that a positive projection of a wholly other reality has its source in the split or dualistic human mind and that this split mind is also the basis for belief in such a projection, which is itself an integrating synthesis. The striving of the dualistically split spirit for wholeness, its attempt to embrace two worlds and two realms with its creative imagination, lies at the core of all true religion.

In the following we will attempt to demonstrate how in our time the split mind, which sought integration in and through these images, tends to cut its bonds with another reality and withdraw completely into the one world, the sole realm of the present and of empirical reality. Or, in other words, how *dualism* is changing into *monism*. Applied to religion this means in our opinion the end of religion, for religion is metaphysical, that is dualistic, or it is nothing.

---

therefore implies that this term contains no pronouncement on the truth or untruth of the projected image, or, in this case, on the existence of God as an entity independent of man. If God exists, a psychological mechanism to approach Him is still necessary and the terms used to describe it do not make much difference. This being said, it hardly needs adding that the personal opinion of the author in religiosis is irrelevant to our discussion.

1. *Future without God—God without Future*

The future of the Christian belief-system is a question of the development of faith and worship *in historical time*. A grasp of this development can only be achieved, in my opinion, through an understanding of the almost complete reversal brought about in the relationship between the entities God and Time. Many thinkers from diverse fields have unconsciously worked together to achieve the resolute and radical removal of God from Time: He has been shown back to His private domain, Eternity. God is no longer the animating force of temporal events, propelling the world toward its future. The image of the future as a dawning era of Salvation, the Last Day and the New Aeon—this image has yellowed with age and been gnawed through to the roots by the tooth of time. God is now no longer in man's future. For that reason above all others, God Himself will no longer exist for a future mankind.

When Nietzsche wrote his famous words, "God is dead", he said at once too much and too little. Too much, in that even now this God *lives* for countless people, albeit as a blurred and faded image. Too little, in that God has since then died many deaths in the process of banishment out of Time and the Future, as the manifold functions, related to the image of a personal god living and acting in time, are cut off. The concept of God and the faith that accompanied it have been hollowed out and voided, in every sphere where God was once thought to be active in history. He has quite literally been put out of action.

So long as God is God, He can die many human deaths without ceasing to exist as a person, however cramped His style, but one of these times could be the last time. Vulnerant omnes, ultima necat (all blows wound, the last blow kills). The extreme mortal agony might set in when theology itself no longer acknowledges God, i.e. when it denies the last days and the last hour as the work of God. If God is detached by the theologians from the *Last* Things at the End of Time, then our time will be detached from God as the First and the *Last*. Many of the stages on this journey along the road to death have been accomplished, and the end is already in sight. A few milestones on the road, proclaiming the death of various parts of God in the course of time, will here be briefly reviewed. "Milestones" is perhaps not quite accurate, since several of these points coincide both chronologically and logically. But human thought does not take all these steps at once, especially where the dissection of the divine is concerned. Rather it proceeds gradually, forging link after link in this new chain, although the finished whole is predetermined once the unity of God and Time has been breached at any one point, so that God is de-temporalized and Time unhallowed.

With respect to the future, it matters little when and where the breach took place, and just how the succession of events unfolded. What follows is therefore not an accurate chronology of the history of religious development from the mythical to the theological death of God, but I do believe that at least for our purpose the starting-point and the end-point in the progression of thought from belief to unbelief can be adequately described in the manner used here.

A. The Mythological Death of God

At first with diffidence, finally irresistibly, the conviction has grown that the Christian God owes many of his traits if not His existence to older religious-mythical ideas and images of the future from Iran, Israel, Hellas and other ancient eastern sources. These images gradually and increasingly came to be perceived as incompatible with modern western ideas. A purification of the image of God was undertaken, with de-mythologizing as the goal. Various points of view contributed to this process, and for the most part they carried German labels such as de-magicing, de-judification, de-metaphysicizing, de-apocalypticizing, etc. The intention was to revive God for modern thought, to make him live again. No one could foresee that the spirits summoned in the process would get out of control and ultimately destroy the spirit of God.

The process is characterized by a gradual forcing back of God and his heavenly satellites or enemies—insofar as these appear palpably and visibly in this earthly sphere—manifesting themselves in personal and physical anthropomorphic shapes. This therefore involves the speaking and acting God, the God Who descended to the mountain top, the Commander of His people, the Guide in the desert, the Wrestler with man, the Punisher and the Avenger. It removes that God, vested with supernatural power, Who chooses to make use of this power to direct and guide the daily life of every man, from first to last, according to His will and His purposes. But it then also includes the God Who sealed the Covenant with *one* people; it removes the God of the Oath and the God of the *Promise*.

This Promise, let it be remembered, refers to the *future* of mankind, to the ultimate conquest of darkness by light, to the victory of God and His angelic hosts over Satan and his demons who are the cause of evil in the world. This Promise represents the great, inscrutable wonder of the future, of the coming, totally other reality. For to this God nothing was impossible. To banish God as the Omnipotent Fulfiller of His own personally and irrevocably given divine Promise, threatens both His omnipotence and His personality.

God is not human, and a human being is never God. Thus de-humanization and de-deification go hand in hand. A God who no longer appears in person among men on earth certainly does not send a bodily Son, except as a mythical symbolic image. So the idea of the Messiah, the Mediator the Son of God or the Son of Man, of the Divine Saviour born of a human mother (immaculately conceived), dwelling on earth for a time in the flesh, is also tarred with the brush of the myth. Both the First and Second Coming of Christ, the man-god, must be eliminated as actual physical events according to modern ideas, and be seen for what they are: ancient images, projections of a mythical imagination. As a historical personality, Jesus was a man; an above-average man, but not God. But with this new view, a part of the personality of God Himself as an effective transformer of historical time into the new future, dies.

Gradually modern man discovers and uncovers the biblical images as mythical in nature: the resurrection, heaven, hell, the hereafter, immortality of the soul and eternal life after death—precisely all those respects in which God was thought to be active for the future salvation of man. But in the modern view, man and his reality are unalterably given by nature. The transformation into "the other" is a myth. To that extent The Other is also a myth. Not only is the Son of God a myth, but so also is God the Father, more particularly God the Creator and Fulfiller, who will re-create this world into another by His intervention in earthly history. Consequently the Holy Spirit and the Trinity are also mythical. The ideas of God and Salvation become something which have no reality except as ideas, existing only in wishful thinking and unrealistic expectations. As the expectations for the future breathe their last, all that is left is—lasting agony. The God of the future is now a thing of the past. In a strange, sad second childhood mankind has traded in all of eternity for the one soiled penny in his grasp—the present.

B. The Cosmic Death of God

The encroachment upon the old image of God is spatio-temporally extended to the Universe. God is deprived of the heavenly sphere as His personal place of habitation, and His new domicile is left in the air. This is but a symptom of a more profound spiritual and intellectual revolution which overthrows God as First Architect, Builder and Mover of the universe. This revolution not only affects His creative function, but most especially once again His task in and power over time from first Beginning to ultimate End.

The old images of chaos and cosmos, the immeasurably distant poles which it was thought God was gradually spanning through the work of His creation, are now outmoded. The image of the *aesthetic* cosmos has been destroyed. The cosmological images of Beginning and End have been displaced by natural-science studies of past and future. Cosmic catastrophes can also be explained in this manner. They are no longer revelations of God's wrath, much less the apocalyptic horrors which must precede the imminent and awaited end of this dispensation.

For this dispensation now has *no* cosmic-eschatological *end*. Thus every calculation concerning this end, including the Revelation of John, is nullified as a revelation of the future. There will be no paradise regained, no new earth and heaven, no new time and no new man. The cosmos moves toward no glorious end and there is no Realm of the Future.

God is not really the Creator, as biblical symbolism portrays Him, nor can He be pictured as the Transformer and Fulfiller. He will not one day make "all things new" according to the antiquated doctrine "de novissimis". The universe develops on the basis of *immanent*, demonstrable and definable powers, not through the arbitrary and inscrutable operations of *transcendent* powers. An unforeseeable total cosmic transformation which involves a setting aside of natural law by God's will is no longer acceptable to modern thought. The current chaos, on the contrary, can easily be conceived as concrete, real and enduring. Existing and observable nature, whose powers are increasingly being brought under man's control, has literally grown over God's head till He can hardly be seen or recognized. Or, conversely, God has been swallowed up by the concept of an autonomous, logically compelling law of nature. Super-naturally, God is no more.

C. The Historical Death of God

In the older view of a God who personally acted and directed man according to His free will, God and history were identical. God revealed Himself in history, and history witnessed to God. The stream of events in time mirrored God's face and disposition towards man, His benevolence and beneficence. The course of history was permeated with divine meaning, and moved both teleologically and theologically towards the goal and end set by God. At one point in time God had laid down His Plan of Salvation, complete with precise chronological time-table, and equally irrevocable both for man and for God Himself. The future had been written in the Book sealed with Seven Seals. The pattern of history was already fixed, and the actual weaving must inevitably follow this pattern. The end had been settled at the beginning and was known to be good. The divinely determined historical development was but the unrolling of a historical scroll which already existed in its entirety in God's hands.

According to this theocratic view, history was firmly in God's grasp and moved under His direction. And man could trustfully accept this direction, knowing that he would sooner or later be guided to the revealed final goal of this earthly pilgrimage. Then history would be fulfilled and completed. Fulfilment was equated with perfection. But in order to bring history to *completion*, it was first necessary to *break through* history. At a time determined by Himself, God was to provide for a breach in time, for a general over-turning and a transformation of historical time into the other aeon of eternally enduring time—God's own *a-historical* time which would prevail in His Kingdom to be established on earth.

In the meantime God has been removed from His position behind the steering-wheel of history. God is deposed, time disposes. The evolution of human thought regarding the future liberates historical time from an inter-vening *superhuman* power and leaves it to its *own* destiny. Time is autono-mous, and the future is no longer determined and directed by a Higher Hand. History as such is without meaning and purpose, and is certainly no longer the story of man's salvation. History never can and never will be more than history. Historical time will never be transformed into a non-historical time and time will never have an end, even though this world perishes. Eternity can never break in on our time and put it "out of commission". Along with Nature, Time has also permanently freed itself from the reins of God and driven its former master away.

The philosophy of history reflects and rationalizes this development. No longer is "the history of the world the judgement of the world" ("die Weltgeschichte das Weltgericht"). History no longer conforms to the Hegelian image of a self-unfolding divine-rational spirit. Ranke's famous "jede Epoche ist unmittelbar zu Gott" is still often quoted, but has become without meaning. God has withdrawn Himself endlessly far from *every* epoch, including the very last one. History demonstrates no progress and no upward evolution, either of a dialectical or unilinear nature. History is but a ceaseless undulatory movement. The history of earth will simply continue until, according to scientific calculations, this planet disappears or man himself destroys it. God does not fit into this picture, except for those who like Toynbee confuse historiography and theology.

While it may still be widely accepted today that God did reveal Himself at least once in history through Jesus Christ (whether or not this truly was His Son), it must nevertheless be recognized that this fait accompli recedes daily further into the *past*. Without a *coming* time of salvation, this historical fact shrinks to ever smaller dimensions. In size and strength it becomes insufficient for the leaden load of The Present. For a generation inmersed in the time-stream of the present, only those gods exist which exercise a powerful influence here-and-now. A God Whose power hides in a once-recorded, never repeated and never authenticated Word, or in a Holy Spirit of which the times show no evidence, no longer commands an audience and cannot make Himself understood or even heard. *The historical God has outlived Himself, and is dying of old age and exhaustion.*

D. The Secular Death of God

God's removal from history is intimately related to His removal from this world. Man removes God from this world and then states that this world has been abandoned by God, is Godforsaken. This world with all its good and evil, all its sense and nonsense, is now being placed out of God's reach, totally secularized. No sensible man believes any longer in a "harmonia praestabilita" for this world, or a Providential or Natural Order guided by a Hidden Hand toward a perfect equilibrium of peace, prosperity, happiness and harmony. He no longer believes in social laws ordained by a wise Providence which will automatically lead human society toward perfection. Nor does he believe in the Church as the chosen divine instrument for the realization of the City of God. *The world has become worldly.* Human society is and remains the imperfect work of man. The age-old striving for a theodicy is at long last given up. The social sciences which study human behaviour are no longer "ancilla theologiae". God is not in the social order, with its poverty, strife, suffering, injustice and misery, nor in its improved editions with greater welfare, international law and technical aid. He never was, and never will be. The death of God as a force in human society is an undeniable fact.

God has not only died a social death, but also an axiological, ethical and cultural death. In our society man struggles alone and unaided for sheer existence as he endures and inflicts evil and staggers under a heavy load of guilt and fear, without any prospect of change. He sees no far prospects. No civilization may now or ever call itself a Christian civilization, no culture ever was or ever will be chosen by God for His ends. Gone is the faith in a gradual unfolding of the highest human values, somehow wrought by God. Gone is the faith in the future of the human race through a divinely ordained process of culture and civilization, gone the conviction of moral progress and ultimate exaltation of man, gone man's trust in the final establishment of the Kingdom of God through its irresistible growth in the hearts of men. The essence-optimism and quietism of 19th century liberalist idealism are dead, and with them the God Who had chosen this world as His future dwelling place. His Kingdom is not of and not for this world. *God has become alien to this world, and man has been alienated from Him.*

E. The Philosophical Death of God

At the same time that Pascal went over from the God of the philosophers and scholars to the God of Abraham, Isaac and Jacob, Spinoza was exchanging the Jewish-Christian God for a metaphysical God as the really existent and eternal but impersonal God to Whom man is in fact bound by the "amor Dei". Then, closing off a long period of philosophical demonstrations of God, Kant a century later removed Him from philosophy on the grounds that this was a science of "pure reason", rationalizing only that which could be empirically known, and that God overstepped these bounds. He placed Him instead, as a postulate of "practical reason", in the separate field of religion. Thus epistemologically supplied with the labels "transcendent" or "noumenal", ontology has shrivelled—at least as it pertains to the absolute being of God and the philosophy of religion. Modern philosophy has in general continued this trend of *not-knowing*, emancipating itself from biblical revelation and Christology. Here agnosticism predominates, but apart from a minority of exceptions (such as the phenomenology of Scheler and Catholic existentialism), even the retention of a philosophical or metaphysical *faith* goes hand in hand with a rejection of the Christian belief in a *personal* God. This situation represents the final merging of originally contrasting lines of development, one stemming from the Christian thinker Kierkegaard and the other from the anti-Christian thinker Nietzsche. Finding expression in England through Russell, in Germany through Heidegger, in France through Sartre, in Italy through Croce, and in America through Dewey and related schools, they all coincide on this point although differing on many others. The theological point of view has in general made way for the anthropological point of view: God has made way for Man.

In all fairness and therefore apart from all the gradations in current philosophical thought which range from impersonalistic to a-religious and anti-religious systems, let us consider an example which is relatively favourable to the Christian belief-system. The choice then falls almost automatically on Karl Jaspers as a modern influential and representative thinker. Jaspers continues to concern himself intensively with Christianity, and although in his later religious writings he turns increasingly against the Christian-ecclesiastical image of God, he still bears the name of one who, while remaining outside the Church, has spiritual kinship with it. Even in this philosopher's search for truth, nothing remains of the Christian image of God but the mystical "ground of all being", a "shapeless all-shape", a "silently speaking" or a "non-revealing" transcendence; in short, a completely image-less idea expressed in a language of esoteric "ciphers" and eluding any clear-cut delineations, an idea incapable of being known and described.

And how does this hidden deity work for the *future* of mankind? Is He merely the ground of all existent being, or is He also the lode-star and goal of the not-yet-existent? Does He at least resemble the mythical Proteus, the old sphinx of the sea, who took every possible shape to escape his questioners but, when finally caught, returned to his own shape and revealed the future unerringly? No indeed, however much man may try, this God will not permit Himself to be seized or bound, precisely because He is God. He and the future remain for man a closed book. Man is wedged between existence and transcendency, his feverish search for a way out, for a bridge over the chasm, is doomed to failure as an *illusion*. Man is imprisoned for life within an inescapable finiteness, confined to the kairos of the here-and-now; in all his attempts to soar into eternity he is struck down again and again, for it is the core of the eternal-human tragedy that man is bound forever fast to *this world* and *this time*.

In our age every man is a Sisyphus, rolling his load in vain. He cannot rise above himself, above his temporality and his essential existence-to-the-death. To philosophize is to learn to die, and the only meaning to be found in life is a resigned amor fati. There is no perspective on the future, no transcendent salvation from or in another world. In his "Geisterreich der Philosophie" the thinker communes with the great spirits from the past, but there is no communication with the Divine Spirit of the Realm of the Future. Even in this deeply religious philosophy, God has no time for the man of this time, and has no other future in store for him than the endlessly repeated drama of perpetual failure in the striving to reach and grasp Him. The drama has no finale. This God is as elusive as He is incomprehensible for the ordinary mortal—and mortality is man's very essence according to this doctrine. He is a bookish God instead of the God of the Book. Requiring no obedience in surrender, dispensing no grace out of love, He intentionally remains completely obscure in this philosophical enlightenment. Except for the abstract philosopher personally, God has been buried alive.

F. The Theological Death of God

The spiritual currents of the time have all fed into modern theology, as they did in the past, in the form of rationalization after the fact. Progressive theologians have even moved on to rationalization in advance, approaching the farthest extreme of a science of godhood without God. These trends have already been discussed in the chapter on de-eschatologizing. They can be distinguished, according to their different emphases, as de-mythologizing, de-dogmatizing, de-prophetizing, de-transcending, de-scandalizing, or de-kerugmatizing. The ever-present prefix "de" denotes the consistently negative factor of debunking and denial. Their effect is always the destruction of the image of a totally other future or in other words: de-dualizing and de-futurizing. And always, in the process, irremediable damage is inflicted on the Effectuater of a divine future, and the inescapable ultimate result is: de-personalization and de-deification.

A theology purged of the eschaton collapses inexorably to the level of philosophical belief or unbelief—or even sinks beneath it. Without the possibility of a *dynamic change* in this time and this world, it peters out in the sands of existent reality, it ossifies in the dungeons of the existential present, it loses the *dynamis*, God. It is a remarkable thing that the philosopher Jaspers, who rejects Christianity, disapproves even more of this drastic theological reducing diet to which God has been subjected, so that His living biblical voice can now scarcely be heard. But other, even more progressive theologians feel that all this is not yet radical enough. Here too the long process of self-realization finally results in self-destruction. Even so, the theological God is not yet dead, nor has His death sentence been signed. Martin Buber correctly still uses the term "Gottesfinsternis" (the eclipse of God). Will God's sun once more shine forth with its former radiance? Or will he merely blaze up in one last glow of fire which the earth reflects onto the heaven? Great progress is being made in the learned preparations to light the faggots at the stake formerly erected for heretics in His name, but now intended to consume the image, any image of God Himself. This iconoclasm takes place in the mistaken belief that God, through being made imageless, can be better served or even saved. The destruction of the divine image of the future has extended to the destruction of the image of God as image. *This destroyed image of God is the negative force which will ultimately destroy God.*

2. *The Chances of Future Revival*

This brief survey, with all its shortcomings, nevertheless indicates what I believe to be an unmistakeable and threatening trend towards the gradual disappearance of the Christian faith as the traditional religion of western culture. The basis of this faith in a personal god, which one might describe as God-consciousness, [1] has been seriously injured and undermined in modern moment-ridden man. The twilight of the gods has been brought into sharpened focus as the twilight of God. The hour of darkness at noon, without tomorrow, without dawn, is upon us. Formerly man believed that God would bring about the end of the world. Now an unbelieving world is bringing about the end of God. The former belief, which implies a God, Who is active in and through time, has grown *weaker* with regard to the future. The latter belief, unbelief, is growing *stronger* with regard to the future. Translated into my general formula for a prognosis for the future: *without a widely spread and fervently believed image of the future, the Christian faith has no future.*

The above prediction will, of course, only hold insofar as no counter-

1. This does not necessarily mean (à la Feuerbach, Jung, Vestdijk) that God exists *only* as a projection of the human psyche and has no external reality. Even if God exists independently, He still has need of man and man's consciousness as receptors of the divine.

forces are put into active operation, counter-forces which can bring new life to the religious image of the future. Not to complicate the argument needlessly, these counter-forces have so far been considered as already included in the resultant of present-day developments. It is true that earnest attempts are being made from every side to modernize the old conceptions, to translate them into our own language and modes of thought, to adapt and clothe them in a manner appropriate to our time. But this is mainly true of the images of religious exemplary living; it is an attempt to infuse new life into the old models of paradigmatic experience, which had become dogmatically rigid. But the images of the *future* have not been treated in this manner. These have been hollowed out and mechanized to the point where they are nothing but a contentless and meaningless ritual; they are now the dead letter of an artificially preserving culture, without a challenging spiritual appeal, basically unconvincing. They have become without *significance* because they give no *sign* of time moving into the future—they lack the quality of the living *image* of the future. Faith which does not joyfully expect the future fulfilment of its own treasured ends of a Highest Good, which are also the revealed ends of a God Who will become all in all, *is* no faith. It is flat, without hope or goal, loveless and lifeless.

Is it possible that now, having come to this point, the images of the future might be revived? Or, we should ask first, is this necessary? Does not orthodoxy still hold integrally fast to the letter of the biblical images of the future, and would it therefore not be sufficient to counteract modernism and heterodoxy with all available resources? In a certain sense, however, orthodoxy is strongest in relation to the past, but weakest in relation to the future. The clock cannot be turned back, the fundamental structural changes cannot be unmade, we cannot free ourselves from the grip of the present, much less return to the Middle Ages or shortly thereafter. Whether we want to or not, we must *move forward with the times*, we must even anticipate the future. Even the most conservative theological trends must in the end be caught up by the tidal wave of the times. The past, even the present, is irrevocably behind us. L'histoire ne se répète pas. There is no other choice. The existing images of the future are spiritually dead. The only meaningful question is that of the possibility of an adequate and synchronous metamorphosis or rejuvenation of these images of the future into a new moving and exalting idealism and enthusiasm.

There is no earthly reason why this possibility should be completely excluded in advance; one cannot deny the possibility of miracles even in these matter-of-fact times. But on the other hand the speculative chances of such a reverse in trend seem fairly limited. Only one event is thinkable that could turn the tide completely, and that is to see the rejected original image of the future actually materialize as truth after all. I refer to the return of Christ to earth. But if this idea must indeed only be regarded as a myth, this messianic "dénouement" seems highly improbable, since from the beginning of time no myth has ever become reality. It is even more improbable that if Jesus did return he would be recognized by men, or acknowledged by the official bodies of Christianity. This theme has been given dramatic treatment in the famous "Grand Inquisitor" passage in Dostoievski's *Brothers Karamazov*.

There remains the possibility of the future appearance of a new prophetic and revolutionary figure through whom God would speak and give man a new truly religious image of the future. Many feel they are called, but few are chosen. More important, the more Christianity is mechanized and the God-consciousness of men minimized in accordance with the spirit of the times, the less chance there is of successfully giving a new content and form to eternal truth as an adequate and timely answer to the challenge of the future. A new prophet would not be crucified; he would simply be ignored or laughed at. C'est le ridicule qui tue.

Or *is* this prophet already here? Some consider the figure of Karl Barth in this light, as the originator of the dialectical crisis-theology. Barth continues the line of development begun in the Reformation, which in any case resulted in the weakening of the Christian image of the future. Whatever Barth's contributions have been from a theological-dogmatic point of view, or possibly even in terms of a fundamental eschatological awareness, he has certainly not strengthened the prophetic vision of the future. Swiss theology (with the exception of Ragaz), and English and American theology have contributed even less in this direction, the American being the most pragmatic, realistic and actualistic of all. The New World seems to hold no promise in *this* respect.

In this connection the American Frank Buchman, founder of the Oxford Group and Moral Rearmament Movement, should be mentioned. While this is undeniably a movement which has faith in its own future and therefore a movement with a future, it is primarily ethical and strongly oriented to the present; in spite of the enthusiasm it generates and the increasing response it is still receiving, it is not in my opinion predestined to become a mass movement that will rejuvenate Christianity through a positively renewed image of the future.

On the theological and ecclesiastical side, there remains to be seriously considered the Ecumenical Movement and its leaders. This movement too is moved by faith in the future of its ideal of unity, and therefore also probably has a future before it. But although this ideal is of course associated with and borne by religious motives, it is not as such a Christian image of the future. In this respect it is more a means than a goal-in-itself. Assuming that at some time the ideal of unity will be realized, *which* Christian faith will this unity then serve? As long as the road to unity is still being travelled, this question is in a sense not so disturbing (except insofar as it might disturb communication between the denominations) as it will be when the goal is once reached. What image of the future will then be offered? International unity is a necessary pre-condition, but a pre-condition of what? Where does it lead? What does it want to achieve? Unity considered in this light certainly contains a remedy against *external* crumbling, but in no way prevents internal disintegration resulting from declining power and a threadbare image of the future. [1]

The same applies, mutatis mutandis, for the many other counterforces which are at the moment working in and for the renovation and restoration of Christianity. Whatever hopes one may cherish for these movements, they are unfortunately negligible in respect to the *Christian image of the future* as a truly living magnitude, an inspiring idea, an overwhelming conviction which might once again dominate western Christianity (whether Protestant or Catholic). Therein lies the *crux* of the matter, the *cross*, on which Christianity in the end will hang itself—inviting a death without resurrection.

That another equally exalted religion on the same level and of the same type as Christianity will emerge, as some thinkers suggest, is a possibility I would rule out, at least here on earth within a foreseeable time. [2] Even as the discussion of Jesus' resurrection and exaltation continues, the resurrection and rebirth of God Himself have become highly dubious.

What kind of equivalent faith might step in to take the place of this waning one? Mystical neo-Buddhism, evolutionary or pantheistic vitalism (Alexander, Haldane), philosophical faith (Jaspers), humanism or even super-humanism (Nietzsche's "Uebermensch"), the creative art of Camus or his "pensée de midi" (both mediterranean and midday-inspirations), a religious syncretism? In how far? For how long? I do not know. But one thing

---

1. This point becomes especially clear when one thinks through the consequences of the position that only the Catholic Church is truly ecumenical, and that the terms Roman Catholicism and World Christianity are identical. See Prof. W. H. van de Pol, "Wereldchristendom en Katholicisme" in *Denken uit Geloof en Leven in de Tijd*, Utrecht, 1949. The problem of easchatology in Roman Catholic eschatology is, however, just as acute as in the Protestant Churches, as is apparent from its absence or presence in Roman Catholic literature.

2. We can certainly not exclude the possibility that other planets in the cosmos already have a long history of human or higher forms of life than those known on earth. Why, in such a case, not also higher forms of religion? Along with the chosen people, the chosen earth and the chosen man as the highest form of creation, the claim to the chosen truth of the accompanying religion also comes into question. But such a point of view leads to a hypothetical blending of utopism and eschatology, which introduces a much longer time-span than this study encompasses, in assuming a possible future contact with, and spiritual influence from, non-earthly beings or organisms.

must not be forgotten: if the present trends of thought would prove capable of destroying Christianity, not only socially, but also spiritually in and through its own adherents, then there will remain little hope for substitute currents of an ideal, religious and cultural nature.

Then nihilism would have the opportunity definitively to clear away the last remnants of culture. For not only the future of the Christian faith is threatened by the iconoclasm of the image of the future. All the structurally related and associated expressions of western culture are equally threatened; the *total* pattern of culture would then face extinction. This catastrophic development will not introduce the Kingdom of God, but rather announce the passing of a two-thousand-year-old faith. Even Anti-Christians would then have little cause to rejoice over the plight of Christianity.

Chapter XXI

OTHER CULTURAL COMPONENTS
AND THEIR FUTURE

Progress is the realization of Utopias.
OSCAR WILDE

It hardly needs saying that each of the topics dealt with so summarily in this and the two following chapters deserves a volume in itself. We are examining them in the light of one aspect only in order to bring out clearly the structural unity of the diverse dynamic elements of culture. They all seem to have been touched by the magic wand of an evil time-fairy, and are all suffering from the same epochal effect. In our analysis we are working backwards: only to the extent necessary to achieve our primary goal of demonstrating the *common fate* of their future development, are we going to give attention to the *differentiated background* of these cultural elements, and their nature and development from the past to the present.

1. *Philosophy*

When we consider philosophy, in its period of unfolding and full-bloom the queen-mother of the sciences, the purest and most comprehensive expression of upward-striving human thought, the very image of evolving homo sapiens—we see what a reversal has taken place in our day. Science now stands on its own feet, and insofar as it tolerates philosophy at all, it is in sternly scientific form—preferably highly specialized. The philosophies of science, logic and mathematics rank first, and thereafter the philosophies of religion, law, art and history; the philosophy of man himself comes last of all. Pure philosophy is in a decline, and has only itself to thank; it dug its own grave and brought forth its own matricides. Even so does it not live on, immortal, in its rebellious scientific offspring? Do they not honour their alma mater? Or does a doom rest on the thankless progeny, ensuring their destruction through the same destiny which pursued their parent?

Philosophy *had* a future, so long as it created an image of the future which could endure in time. Basically this image of the future, in all its many forms, insisted on the existence of *something other* than tangible, experience-able reality; it maintained that there was a second, equally true or perhaps even exclusively true reality. Philosophical thought was kept in constant motion by the dualistic tension between the poles of these two realities. In the course of the attempt to approach the imagined other in the midst of this visible reality, a bridge was built between present and future—the future of philosophy itself as well as of culture, for these two entities were continually fortifying each other. The other reality and the way of thinking that led there formed also the way both of philosophy and culture, by playing the role of architect and builder of their common road and movement, and by providing the basis and goal of their common development.

It matters little, in principle, how the other is labelled or defined. This other was ever the subject matter, object and objective of "speculative" philosophy, reflecting the other reality and holding out to man the mirror of a prospective future as he strove to cross the boundary of present reality. Call it, with Plato, the divine idea of the world of ideas, the Absolute, the Eternal, the Truth, Universal Peace, or God. Or call it, with Spinoza, thought or mind, as the counterpart of extension (Nature of the Cosmos); or, again with Spinoza, take mind and matter together as the attributes of a divine substance, which is infinite and eternal. Or call it the Transcendence, the Great Unknown, the All-One, the Beyond, or, with Kant, the transcendental, the noumenal, the postulates of practical reason, regulative ideas, categorical imperative, or what you will.

But whatever it is called, it should be perceived that there is more meaning hidden in the world-shaking struggle in medieval scholasticism between conceptual realism and conceptual nominalism than modern man in his conviction of superiority has been willing to admit. For nominalism was the great attack on the actual existence of this other reality, which sought to characterize it as simply a "name"; no longer as a sum total of universalia ante rem, but as universalia in re or post rem. Here the criticism which Aristotle levelled against his teacher Plato was repeated on a larger scale, anticipating the later uprising, even on into our own times, of empiricism against apriorism.

There was only one occasion, after the scholastic period, when the idea of the other reality achieved climacteric intensity in the history of philosophic thought. It came about in German idealistic philosophy "im Innern ist ein Universum auch", as Goethe so pregnantly expressed it. In Hegel both the high-point and the turning-point were reached. His portrayal of the divine-rational self-realization of the other through the medium of history, in actual and observable reality, was dynamic; but the portrayal of the end-state of this development, achieved already in his own time, was static. As in the struggle between nominalism and realism, the conservatism of the existing order annexed the idea of the other reality and thus broke off its own future by shifting it into the present. Wishing to maintain the status quo, it tried permanently to fuse the contrasting realities in the here-and-now. Man's fate was thereby sealed and a complete about-face had been achieved. The other reality and its power of propulsion toward itself—i.e. the future—are no more.

Two great figures, whose influence and significance were only perceived after their time, ran far out in advance towards this futureless future: Schopenhauer and Nietzsche. They completely levelled the edifice of idealistic philosophy and dug down to destroy its foundations. They represent the beginning of a line of development with which older and newer currents fused to make that mighty swelling flood-tide which has washed ashore in our time as existentialism. I can only give a few links in this chain of events, without any claim to comprehensiveness.

For Schopenhauer the ground of the world's being—das Ding an sich—lies in the intrinsically groundless will to live. We can experience this directly in our corporeal being, although it is in fact blind, unreasoned and unconscious, and thus condemns man to painful suffering and puts him at the mercy of agonizing desires. The world is our will, and our image of the world is conceived by this will. It is the worst of all possible worlds. It is not possible to leave this world, nor redeem it by the contemplative postulation of another, higher reality; it is only possible to annul the world by destroying its creator, the will. Schopenhauer thus constructs an anti-metaphysical metaphysics, with the help of a negative dialectic by which the creative free will again destroys itself and life. He preceded Nietzsche as the author of nihilism and the gravedigger for philosophy. It is not sufficient to abolish the will through suicide or madness, through the will-less knowledge of the genius, through the ethical-religious elimination of the will as in Buddhism, through the aesthetic conquest of the will by either bodily or spiritual flight, or through the turning toward the mystical good, true and beautiful. All these together cannot outweigh the irrational and massive impetus of the will to live of mankind, expressed in the maintenance and procreation of the species. To this end man has also harnessed human knowledge and made it a tool of the will, thus holding fast to this miserable reality which he ought to reject. Ultimately this self-repeating fatal cycle can only be broken and the definitive reversal of the power-relationship between the will and the understanding be brought about, through the extinction of the human race—not only the individual—and the cessation of procreation.

Nietzsche does not go this far, and at the same time he goes further. He goes less far, in that he would not destroy man (Menschliches-Allzumenschliches) but cause him to rise above himself; he goes further, in that he destroys God instead *(Thus Spoke Zarathustra)*, and with Him all that is related to the concept of the divine and supernatural. His *Beyond Good and Evil* has the subtitle "Prelude to a Philosophy of the Future". But by excluding the Beyond, rejecting the possibility of the real existence of a second, other world and denying the transcendent and absolute; by instead absolutizing the existing reality as that which is exclusively existent—he in effect undermines the basis of all future philosophy. The death of God encompasses the end of metaphysics as a doctrine of the eternally existent, and the end of axiology, of ethics and idealism as representations of eternal values stemming from the transcendent sphere of the eternal divine. Nietzsche's nihilism is nothing but a vacuum, a Nothingness which develops as soon as the mere biological instinctual life and its nascent will to power is advanced as the fundamental and exclusive reality, without any higher goal or nobility of meaning.

Nevertheless, after the general demolition in *Antichrist, The Twilight of the Gods* and the *Genealogy of Morals*, after the "Fröhliche Wissenschaft" (Joyous Knowledge) comes "Morgenröte" (Dawn), in which Nietzsche counters Schopenhauer's hedonistic "no" with a tragic-heroic "yes" to the world and a positive image of the future. It is an image of the "revaluation of all values" and of a "new order of precedence", of a spiritual aristocracy and a Superman (Uebermensch). This superhuman man will transform and sublimate brute force and self-assertion into a new exalted ideal of stern self-discipline and ennobled authority (master-morality versus slave-morality) and take the place of fallen gods and dead faith, rescuing culture from the profound decline that philosophy, religion, morality, science and politics have plunged it into. At the same time Nietzsche invalidates the future he himself depicts, and any other future, by virtue of his basic and fatalistic idea of eternal recurrence, which renders his own thought fruitless in advance. All things will recur in exactly the same fashion, an unlimited number of times—even Nietzsche and Zarathustra [1]—since history is without meaning and goal and predestined to unending repetition. For such a pessimistic view, even Schopenhauer's remedy offers but a temporary solution; the game that must be irrevocably lost, will begin again and again, always with the same sad result. Thus even the negativism of Schopenhauer's image of the future is ultimately surpassed. The idea of return *is* already return, and by its literal come-back [2] destroys the future in the sense of the coming of something totally other.

1. Nietzsche himself says this in *Zarathustra*: "Unsterblich ist der Augenblick, wo ich die Wiederkunft zeugte. Um dieses Augenblickes willen ertrage ich die Wiederkunft".
2. In Nietzsche's words: "In jeder Handlung, die du tust, ist alles Geschehenes Geschichte wiederholt und abgekürzt."

The influence of Schopenhauer and Nietzsche can scarcely be over-estimated. It has not only operated directly, but also through effecting and reshaping both older and later diverse and contradictory conceptions which have in common an anti-metaphysical point of departure and a concentration on factual reality, whether hyper-rationally or anti-rationally. It is felt in Comte's positivism and right on through into neo-positivism. It has affected the blending of Hume's empiricism, Marxian historical materialism, physicalism and logicism, mechanism and the behaviourism of various natural-science or mathematically-oriented thinkers, on into naturalism and neo-naturalism. It has further affected the philosophy of life, vitalism and irration-alism initiated by Dilthey, as well as his deliberate rejection of "Jenseitig-keit" for "Diesseitigkeit". It is to be found in the pragmatism of Dewey and James.

Together these trends of thought have brought about the transition from speculative to operational thinking, from the transcendent to the immanent, from the other, imagined or ideal reality to this present, concrete reality. Apart from the pattern for world-history of eternal recurrence, it represents in any case a return of philosophy to this given world, out of which thought arises and in which the thinker lives. As far as a possible other reality is concerned, the earlier metaphysics of being and of ontology gradually loses its foothold, sacrificing its object to an increasing scepticism and agnosticism and exchanging it for a more precise examination (as required by modern semantics and the science of meaning) of empirically observable and logi-cally assimilable phenomena concerning earthly existence.

These developments find outlet today in two distinct currents. The first makes short work of traditional philosophy, and in fact abolishes it. The second appears on the contrary to continue it, though in a radically re-novated form, but cuts out the ground just as drastically from under its own future. The first current, related to the striving for what is virtually direct self-extinction, does not need much discussion here. It includes, among other, the so-called Vienna Circle of Schlick, Carnap and Neurath. These men assign a part of the matter of philosophy to the various branches of science, reject a part as not amenable to scientific treatment, and retain philosophy as such only as the analytic instrument for the unity of science, as a symbolic logic and a common scientific code or sign-language that can serve all the specialized fields of science. The analytical, anti-philoso-phical Cambridge philosopher Ludwig Wittgenstein (*Tractatus Logico-Philosophicus*, 1922) [1] was also a part of this movement. The work of his

1. Note for example this expression of his position: "Die Methode der Philosophie wäre eigentlich die: Nichts zu sagen, als was sich sagen lässt, also Sätze der Natur-wissenschaft—also etwas, was mit Philosophie nichts zu tun hat. . .".

school, and that of other mathematically-oriented philosophers, served to reduce philosophy to a formal combination of linguistics and logistics.

Of even more importance than this explicit liquidation of philosophy is its implicit elimination, contained in the second main current of thought. Here again a choice must be made between a number of modern schools of thought, and only the most representative will be mentioned. Many mutually differing philosophies find a common crystallization in the anti-metaphysical orientation of modern existentialism. Hitherto separate threads in the tapestry of history come together at this point as the philosophical thought of Schopenhauer and of Nietzsche are worked through to their ultimate consequences and woven into a systematic whole. The foremost present-day representatives of this movement (influenced, as we know, by Pascal and Kierkegaard) are Heidegger, Sartre and Jaspers. We will touch only on those aspects of their basic thinking which will throw light on future developments—that is to say, on the image of the future contained in this philosophy, and, in connection with this, on the future of this philosophy itself.

Existentialist philosophy is based on the axiomatic reversal of some long-prevailing philosophical assumptions or at least of their order of precedence. Existence takes precedence over essence, human existence over the nature of things, the individual over mankind, practical action over theoretical knowledge, the particular over the general, concrete reality over abstract universality and personal problems over the impersonal system. Now it is the existential attitude which molds man's existence in a struggle with his own time, rather than the striving towards an idealistic image of future time as formerly.

There are however far-reaching mutual differences among the three representatives of existentialism named above, and also between them and other existentialists such as Marcel and Lavelle, especially with reference to the problem of the future.

Heidegger's goal is still to develop a metaphysics of true being. Since the only being which can understand and illuminate itself as a medium is man, man's personal and concrete existence is the only possible point of departure. The essence of man is his "Dasein" or existence; his existence-in-the-world. Man is thrown into this world in a specific situation. This world is immediately existent for him (Vorhandensein). The meaning of man's existence is determined by its temporality, by his consciousness of irrevocable existence unto death. The only possible anticipation of the future consists in living with one's face set towards coming death. In order to escape this picture man throws himself into this world, lapses guiltily into it and drowns his

"I" in the impersonality of the third-person indefinite, "one". Thus his existence-unto-death is filled with guilt, suffering and dread. His gaze is held by the abyss as he struggles for his daily existence, miserably aware of his nothingness and of the approaching end in an annihilating void of Nothing. This void can tolerate no metaphysics, stands apart from any transcendence and any concept of divinity. This is why Heidegger is classified as a nihilist and atheist, although he himself does not accept such a categorization. Reflective thought in his opinion can give neither a positive nor negative judgement concerning the existence of God; it must needs be agnostic. It can only say, concerning man's existence in this world, that the old gods have fled and new ones have not yet come. The most suitable attitude for man to take in the situation in which he finds himself as of this moment is a stoic-heroic acceptance of destiny, or Nietzsche's amor fati.

Sartre, on the other hand, boldly proclaims his atheism. God and the transcendental keep silence before man in our time. Since God gives no sign of life, there is in effect for us—for me—no God. Any current religious needs of man thus do not fit into this time. We must forget God. There is no other universe than that of the human subject. The existence of man is being-in-himself and his consciousness is being-for-himself. The objectivity of knowledge disappears in the face of this basic subjectivity of the individual man, as does the objective validity of values, norms and ideals. The only meaning which life has is that meaning which I choose to give it. I am free to choose, but my existential struggle is rendered meaningless and purposeless in advance. Man is alone with himself. The world stands over against him, indifferent and unconcerned, with no predetermined goals. Man is left to his own devices and must look after himself in a life of unceasing care. Since he is so completely alone, without God or any enjoined morality, he is also free; indeed he can be nothing else but free, and any and every choice is permitted him. But this is a despairing and horrible freedom. The basic undertone of this life is loathing and dread. The dread leads to an escape into diversions and pastimes, and into bad faith and hopelessness. There can be no positive acceptance of life; in the last instance there is only the negative dialectic of a consciousness which stands tortured and destructive in the face of every decision (consience néant), marking man's course towards unacceptable but inexorable death. Here again the end is that which humanly speaking cannot be called an end, but only Nothingness (L'Etre et le Néant).

Jaspers takes an intermediate position. He goes a long way with Heidegger; for him also the existential existence of man assumes a central place, characterized as present existence (Dasein) in the world and sharply brought into focus by temporality as an existence unto death. He also denies the transcendent as an "other" reality, although it nevertheless plays an important role in his thinking. For man's existence becomes truly existential only by man's resolute decision to rise above himself and this world and to relate himself to the transcendent. In order to achieve this he must first pass through this world, through the immanent, which speaks to man in the secret ciphers of the transcendent. But transcendence itself, as the other reality, can never be reached by man. His striving is an illusion. The meaning of life consists in the acceptance of the perpetual failure (Scheitern) of every attempt to transcend the here-and-now, and yet these attempts are his mandatory existential task. For the Absolute or the Beyond has no separate reality, either as a meaningful entity or as a Realm to be entered by man. It exists only as the intrinsically meaningless goal of man's perseverance, in spite of all, in the unending process of upward striving and inevitable falling back; and here again it is ultimately transformed into a resigned amor fati, although with a somewhat different nuance. But Jaspers also emphatically denies the charge of nihilism.

In attempting to understand modern existentialism and whether or not it is nihilistic, I find the oft-made comparison between existentialism and gnosis very significant. There is indeed a striking coincidence of philosophical terminology and symbolism in the two philosophies. The main difference in my opinion appears at the point where gnosis, with all its worldly pessimism, *had* an image of the future—and existentialism has *none*. [1] For gnosis retained a metaphysics and transcendence as an existing, other reality, as a kind of basic support in the background. Existentialism has cut itself off from all supports. Gnosis is dualistic in the extreme and yet ultimately achieves synthesis, while existentialism has gone from split to complete severance, is monistic in the extreme, and remains ultimately in a state of antithesis. The "nihilism" of gnosis is oriented toward a positive future, while the modern existentialist outlook is completely negative.

Anyone who desires a deeper insight into the flowering and decline both of philosophy and of western culture in mutual interaction, finds this direct contrast, in a setting of spiritual relatedness, between the gnosticism [2] of Antiquity and modern existentialism [3] fascinating and pregnant with meaning. It is well worth the trouble to examine this contrast further.

1. An excellent discussion of this point is to be found in an article by an outstanding modern authority on gnosis, Hans Jonas, "Gnosticism and Modern Nihilism", *Social Research*, December 1952. I make grateful acknowledgement here that my discussion is based on his line of thought, with some alteration to make allowance for my own point of view.
2. Gnosticism took several directions, including Christian, some more, some less radical. For purposes of comparison we make use of the ideal-type of the radical gnosticism here.
3. Heidegger is considered here as the keynoter among his contemporary philosophers;

A. Gnosticism

Dualism here achieves its most extreme expression. This miserable world cannot be the work of God, and is not to be justified by any theodicy. God is beyond and outside of this world, having nothing to do with it. For man He is the Great Unknown (theos agnostos), the Hidden One (deus absconditus), The Other. This world has been created by a demiurge and is not a part of the divine whole. It stands outside of God's cosmos and nomos. God is not revealed in it or to it, and it stands outside His power. The demiurge has brought it forth out of blind passion and ignorance. Ignorance (agnoia) is the negative mark of this world.

If the world stands in direct opposition to God, so does man in his turn stand in direct opposition to the world. It is a world both anti-divine and anti-human. Man has been thrown into this hostile and alien world, and the two entities are antagonistic and mutually incompatible. Since God's law does not reign in this world, there are no divine norms and values valid for man, sanctioned and effectuated by God's will. Man is thus at the mercy of the superhuman powers of demonocracy and destiny, threateningly depicted in the starry heavens (the constellations). The basic undertone of human life is therefore dread, despair and panic.

Knowledge (gnosis) reveals the way out of this darkness and forms a bridge to God and His divine realm of light. Knowledge is the positive tool with which the negativity of an ignorant world can be transformed. There is thus a way out from unhallowed earthly misery to unearthly blessedness. For the human spirit contains a divine spark (pneuma), held fast in the corporeal prison and chained to this world. The spirit despises the unholy world, matter and the body. This revered spiritual knowledge can lead to completely different attitudes toward the body, whether of asceticism, abstinence and discipline, or of libertinism, excess and anarchy. In any case, man's inner and spiritual self is not of this world. Through wisdom and devotion man can achieve exaltation and insight into God's mystery, and union with the divine.

God is this world's negative. But His passive existence and that other reality, though invisible to this world, are basically positive. It is true that man, with all his spiritual capacities, has been thrown into this demon-possessed world, but there is also a Thrower. World and God, and man and world are both irreconcilable opposites, but there is a spiritual bond between this-worldly man and a non-worldly God. This bond gives direction, force, meaning and purpose to man's actions in the world and in time.

also a few ideas of his pupil Sartre are included, as one who pursued existentialism to its furthest consequences, literally ad absurdum.

Gnostic philosophy thus possesses a dynamic goal of development. Man has a pilgrimage to make, and a project to accomplish. He moves from past, through the present, into the future.

The extreme negative dialectic of this line of thought is certainly nihilistic in regard to this world. But the antithesis is fulfilled by a synthesis in which the other reality plays a positive role. The temporality of this world is not absolute, but is relative and transitory in respect to eternity. Man comes from eternity, and to eternity he returns. Gnosticism combines an essence-pessimism for this world with an influence-optimism for the other world. It is, more than anything else, a philosophical doctrine of salvation, and this is why gnosticism was finally condemned by the Christian Church as a heresy.

B. Existentialism

Whereas in gnosticism dualism was strained to the utmost and yet managed to maintain an ultimate overall unity-in-duality, a radical break-through finally takes place in existentialism. Here again man is thrown into a world which is alien to him. It is not hostile, however, but what is worse, indifferent. It does not know him; he leaves it cold. Here the irreconcilable opposition between world and God, and between world and the divine spirit in man, falls away. There is *nothing else behind* this world. Man has lost all contact, however slight, with another world. He is lost and abandoned in a lost and abandoned world. The eternally silent measureless spaces of the universe are silent because they have nothing to say. The *theos agnostos* who does not visibly reveal himself is not only absent, but in the new interpretation since Nietzsche, dead. If he ever existed, he obviously does not exist any longer; or even if he does, as far as man is concerned he is now out of the picture. A god who will not legitimately manifest himself is no longer to be illegally maintained. Belief in a god has lost all meaning.

Not only has faith (pistis) in God lost meaning, but also knowledge (gnosis) of God. There is no transcendent other reality, existing elsewhere, with which the human spirit has an affinity and which it can approach through knowledge. On the contrary, any perceptive knowledge (contemplatio, theoria) of the essence of things is degraded and eternal truths are devalued. Conceptual nominalism has completely vanquished conceptual realism. There is no other reality than the immanent, existing and experienceable reality. There is no superhuman power. There are no objective ideas and ideals, no absolutely valid values and norms inherent in the nature of being. There is only the factual man-in-himself, who exists in complete subjectivity in this world. This world is naked nature, starkly present, ethically indifferent, untouched by metaphysical thought. Such a naturalism knows and recognizes only realistic existence without spiritual essence. *Thought* no longer stands in dualistic contrast to the total extension of matter, just as man no longer stands in a personal I-thou relationship to the transcendent. The thought of mind is now part of monistic matter. It has fused into immanent reality, and is one of the modalities of man's existential being in the world. Thought is, in a complete adaequatio rei et intellectus, that which is hic et nunc. It does not represent a supra-sensory idea, but is itself sensory reality. And this reality, in its modalities, is once again only accessible via the medium of man, who himself lives and thinks in this same tangible, spatio-temporal reality. This given reality, strictly material, unchangeable and exclusive, and also concretely experienceable, is one and indivisible.

With the dissolution of God and all evidence of a divine steering mechanism and any possibility of a divine incarnation in human moral law, or of another world or transcendent reality, the human soul also disappears from the scene. With it disappears the accompanying ideas of immortality and resurrection of man (or his spiritual part) and his transcending to another, eternal life. Man does not move from eternity, his beginning, to eternity, his end, but from nothingness to nothingness. He finds himself in a blind, indeterminate, unaware and soulless universe, in a chaos that knows no countering cosmos. Nothing more is expected or commanded of man than that he make pragmatic decisions and concrete choices. There is no other goal than death, and the farthest limit of being is not-being. Thus the destruction of God ends in the destruction of man.

The existential struggle of man in this world is meaningless, and all human values and dignity is eliminated. Human power is dismantled along with the superhuman. Certainly man is free to determine his own destiny responsibly, but his choices are rendered meaningless by the fact that they all lead to . . . Nothing. Man can make no decision which will lead him to anything higher, better or other. Labouring without ethics and idealism, any evolution or transformation is ruled out. His desperate striving must be prospectless. Man has cut himself off from mankind; through his temporality he has separated himself from eternity, and through his exclusive existence in this world, he has withdrawn himself from any other existence.

Existentialism keeps pace with gnosticism in fundamental pessimism regarding existence in this world. But their ways soon part and a wide abyss yawns between them as between day and night. For the so-called "Existenz-Erhellung" (existential enlightenment) leaves man in perpetual, impenetrable darkness. There is no way out of this world and this infinite existence. The elimination of metaphysics, transcendence and eschatology, so essential to gnosticism, amounts to a cutting short of all movement in time by existentialism. The existential is not only *real*, but *actual*, concentrated in the here-and-now.

There are no more polar tensions to provide propulsive power and goal for dynamic developments in time. Time has set for man the nearby limit of fast approaching death. In dread of this inevitable future man is driven back into the present, in which—at least for the time being—he lives and exists. With the future having become a vacuum, the totality of time is compressed into a one-dimensional present. Existentialism provides the rationalization for the modern moment-ridden man. His *time* is *his* time, here and now. The present is then even further narrowed down to the hour of the minute, the kairos. "Seize the day" becomes "grasp the moment". But this moment, the moment of decision, evaporates into meaninglessness even as it is grasped after, for the best and worst decision alike lead to Nothing. There are no goals, let alone one goal.

Man is not only thrown into the world, but abandoned there. Thrown but without a Thrower, abandoned, to be without memory of a cradled past or hope of a beckoning future. All that which is, is in the present, from one moment to the other, including the future which trickles steadily and hopelessly into the present time until it all ends with death. This completely negative ending, so narrowly closing off the present for every man, is the only thing which can be anticipated. Until the final cutting off, he can by way of escape submerge himself in the present. This is his falling prey (Verfallenheit) to the immediacy of existence (Vorhandenheit) in this world, his lapse into the here-and-now, his guilty game of hide-and-seek behind the back of Every-man, the piteous impersonal collectivity of his fellow-sufferers. This capitulation to the present implies paying a penalty of degeneration and decadence, and yet this is the inevitable mode of human existence. It is a backing away from a back-firing future which promises only approaching death. Death offers no perspective, no transition, no eternal life; it can only offer the "homesick" longing to rest in peace. It signifies nothing but the cruel snipping off of an isolated thread that was never part of any larger pattern, human or divine, linking man to mankind or God.

In a sense then man already finds himself in the continuous non-existence of death even during his existence in this world. The *Kairos* is perpetually *crisis*. Man's every moment is always at the same time zero-point. Man's existence in time has no duration and no relation to eternity. Movement through time is but standing still or slipping backwards, for it is pre-determined by the end, with death all ready to reverse the gears. The actual course of events enlarges every man's past from year to year and day to day, but simultaneously shrinks his future. The negative dialectic of the world and the life of man thus comes to a standstill in absolute negation and a splitt-off antithesis. The gnostic synthesis, or any type of synthesis at all, is lacking. The lack is considered and intentional. There is no place to go, no way out, for there is no future.

This essence-pessimism goes hand in hand with influence-pessimism. There is no liberation for man, in this world or from it. No power of any kind, human or superhuman, either in or outside this world, can redeem him, because there is not and cannot be such a power. The former ideational structure and tri-unity of God, man and time has been systematically broken up. This philosophical association of Time and Being (See Heidegger's main work, *Sein und Zeit*, 1927) is in the deepest sense a negation of time, especially in the concept that man's existence is temporal only and strictly limited by death; at the very least, this combination of realism and actualism is a negation of the future as such or *de-futurizing*. It is a continued process of writing all history in the present imperfect tense, a random registration of events by instantaneous photographic exposures which when chronologically arranged reveal no meaningful theme. As Büchner said, matter without force, nature without spirit. If it tells any intelligible story, it is not one of salvation, but of damnation.

Philosophically speaking this point of view seems no more or less acceptable, and no more or less demonstrable, than any other. But closer consideration reveals a great paradox in it; it raises a problem in such a manner that it *cannot* but lead to contradictory answers. In the final issue this philosophy solves nothing, but only dissolves itself. At a certain point it falls headlong, and threatens to drag culture with it into a bottomless abyss. We do not intend to give a comprehensive critique here, but only wish to indicate the potential predisposition to self-destruction on the part of modern existentialism. *The philosophy of the absurd leads to the absurdity of this philosophy.*

This self-destructive effect stems in part from the fact that the contrast with idealism, especially in the Hegelian form, is consistently carried to the extreme. Extreme realism[1] manages to smuggle in successive diverse elements of Hegelianism to the point where it threatens to remain adrift as disguised idealism just when it believes itself to be firmly anchored to the realm of the purely factual. Where Hegel made the absolute idea engulf all reality, existentialism makes absolute reality engulf all ideas. These two identifications are not as far apart as it would at first appear.

Hegel was reproached for his time-boundness, for making the self-realization of the world-reason come to fulfilment in his own time, but existentialism exceeds all preceding philosophies in time-boundness. This

1. N.B.: this realism (the recognition exclusively of experienceable reality) is the exact opposite of so-called conceptual realism, which represents the idea as the basic reality and which is therefore a purely idealistic philosophy.

philosophy, having no image of the future, is only an image of the times. It is a rationalization after the fact of our own time, however one chooses to describe it. It is a rationalization of despair, of blood ill-shed, of the breaking of faith; of illusionism and phariseeism, of flight and escape. It is a rationalization of all that is cowardly and ugly, chaotic and demonic, meaningless and purposeless. The resolute decisions and choices of the individual are worthless both for his own future and for that of mankind. Human society is conceived as the nauseating impersonal "one", or "every-man", the stupid oppressive force of the anonymous masses. To surrender to this world—and no other course than this "Verfallenheit" is open to man—means lapse and collapse, enslavement, corruption and decay. *Being does not rule time, but time rules being.*

Like the Hegelian dialectic, existentialism also fulfils itself in its own time, our day. But it comes to an end one stage earlier—not in the synthesis, but in the antithesis. This dynamic too is basically static. The end-point is simultaneously contained in the beginning. Time seizes and appropriates all man's being, from moment to moment, to the point where being itself becomes timeless. The infiniteness of human life dominates to such an extent that present reality is infinitely extended: ever changing, ever the same. The strict delimiting of human life to this reality is basically an unlimiting process, in which the Here-and-now washes over its own boundaries and floods the Beyond. Anti-metaphysical realism, just as every other philosophy, is also based on an *idea*. It is based on the *one* idea, that what *is*, is the only thing existing and being, that *this* reality is *the* reality. It is the metaphysics of monism.

Existentialism is thus itself "thrown" into the metaphysical problem represented in Schopenhauer's doctrine of the deepest ground. Being must ground itself as being; it would be incompatible with a transcendent ground for being, drawn in from the outside. The ground is in itself. Life is the ground of life. Since no outside causes for a reliable foundation can be introduced, any idea of *telos* which would point elsewhere to a beyond, must also be completely excluded. This leaves us with a strange picture of one nature, the only and all-encompassing natural being of reality: in itself quite indifferent and free of any concern, yet including as part of itself man, who is on the contrary characterized by deep concern and care and is overflowing with anxiety and unending trouble. Where, why and how did this ill-fitting constituent enter in? How is this phenomenon of an anxious part of an anxiety-free whole to be explained? Why this thoughtful self-awareness in a completely thoughtless and unaware universe?

In my view, existentialism here places itself before an insoluble dilemma. According to this philosophy man, defined as care-laden and suffering from anxiety for the nearby end, must take himself as the starting-point to establish Being; this Being, however, is intrinsically unconcerned, indifferent and unending. Next, this philosophy robs man, tortured by continuous cares and the terror of death, of all rational and ethical grounds for his own existence. For according to this view man's mortal agony and man's troubled existential life-struggle are meaningless and doomed to frustration. He just exists. His suffering is non-sensical. Its outcome differs in no way from that which is achieved by the untroubled birds of the air and beasts of the field. Since his anguished striving has neither reason nor goal, it is only so much spilled energy. His "creatio de nihilo" changes nothing in Nothingness, and makes no sense out of Non-sense. This attempt to throw light on human existence throws darkness instead, and leads to a de-humanizing of man, reducing him to the animal. In existentialism man lives until he dies, like any other animal. If man cannot even be considered to be a rational animal, how in the world can there be a philosophizing man? Is there much more wisdom in this than that of "une minute avant sa mort, il vivait encore"? It seems to be simply another elucidation of death, "la mort avec phrase".

Can this philosophy teach men to die, if it has not taught them to live? The ancient rule of giving warning before shooting is here reversed and man is told that he is dead while still living. The old wisdom concerning the primary need first to live and only then to philosophize (primum vivere, deinde philosophari), is deliberately neglected. Such a philosophy provides no guide-lines for life itself. It leaves man completely free to take any decision, without suggestions and completely without imperatives. Is a freedom that cannot lead to any good still to be considered as freedom? This philosophy detaches man not only from God, and from a transcendent metaphysics, but also, as immanent philosophy, from himself and from his future. Ecce homo: thrown into existence without a thrower, in the world without a place of habitation, in time without a future, in action without plan or vision, in movement without course or guideposts. All that he can see is the grinning open grave, that was already present beside his cradle; a retrospect, but no prospect. Rebellion is fruitless; there remains only a rebellious immersion in recreation to seek oblivion; there remains only the aimless goal of "killing time".

If existentialism is *true*, then it is *untrue*. If we can only know the individual man and his subjective choices in a personal, concrete situation, what validity could a philosophy have which is built upon abstractions and generalizations concerned with human existence as such? Should there not rather "be" as many truths and as many philosophies as there are heads to conceive them? If man can only be, without getting anywhere, then why bother with a philosophical inquiry into the whither, whence and why?

He exists, and that's that. The particular mode of his existence is obviously irrelevant. It is a meaningless occupation to analyse a meaningless existence, and also by definition impossible. If the totality of existence is meaningless it excludes the possibility of meaningful thought. *Thus existentialism, in stripping man of all except the bare fact of existence, denies even this existence to philosophy.*

But even if we follow the above reasoning and accept the conclusion that existentialism, in making a monstrous covenant with a futureless world, has eliminated its own future—we need still not accept the generalized conclusion that philosophy as such has reached a terminal point in the development of western culture, and has left all its future behind it. Philosophical *counter-movements* are always possible. Existentialism itself was such a counter-movement, and new counter-movements directed against this philosophy may still condemn it to decline as it condemned its predecessors.

Of course this is *possible*, but is it *probable?* And could such counter-movements develop sufficient force? In part they exist already, as continuations of earlier philosophical streams of thought, even in existentialism itself (Jaspers, Christian existentialism, existential theology, and so on). Where have these brought us, and where can they bring us?

One might first consider the extremely important renewal of philosophy through Husserl's phenomenology. His attempt to develop a strictly scientific philosophy which is nevertheless metaphysics in a sense continues Kant's *Prolegomena zu einer jeden künftigen Metaphysik, die als Wissenschaft wird auftreten können.* Husserl thinks that it is possible to perceive the essential nature of things intuitively. This means a "zurück zu den Sachen" (back to things), which, however, requires a preliminary work on the part of the investigator, namely "Einklammerung", or the setting in brackets, of this observed reality. Thus we would appear to arrive at a sort of intermediate entity or sphere between *this* and *another* reality. It would then become possible to demonstrate essential laws and generally valid structures of this purified reality, with the help of a purified consciousness. To my shame I must confess that this method of facilitating the examination of the perspicacious essence of reality (Wesensschau) has remained somewhat of a mystery to me, but it is an undeniable fact that practically every self-respecting thinker these days claims or at least attempts to make use of it. It is both curious and somewhat disturbing that his tendency to proclaim phenomenology as their basis is found in nearly all modern philosophical schools of thought as in itself a sufficient justification for the claim to objectivity and adequacy.

While Husserl himself was an express adherent of *idealistic* philosophy, his students and contemporaries made use of phenomenology in constructing a basically *realistic* philosophy. This was true for example of Max Scheler and Nicolai Hartmann, although they still held on to metaphysics. However, it is Heidegger who is now considered to be one of the foremost modern phenomenologists. Thus, existentialism harnessed this potential counter-movement to its own victorious chariot even before it had emerged as a full-bloom philosophy. [1]

At the beginning of this century, expectations of a spread of Bergson's dualistic philosophy might still have been cherished. Since then, however, the optimistic image of the future contained in "creative evolution" and the "élan vital" that also penetrated into the cosmic-religious area *(Les deux Sources de la Morale et de la Religion)*, has gone the way of all positive images of the future.

Any modern handbook of philosophy (Bréhier, Joad, Heinemann, Bochenski, Russell, and others) describes other developments which deviate from or run counter to the development described here. In the first place, of course, there is the never-ceasing attempt to reconstruct an ontology. Those who have embarked on this endeavour, however, differ widely among themselves, and try to push each other aside. [2] When in 1920 Peter Wust boldly published *Die Auferstehung der Metaphysik*, the wish appeared to be father to the thought. Just one year later, already in 1921, D. H. Kerler published *Die Auferstandene Metaphysik* (The Resurrected Metaphysics) in the manner of a proclamation. Ever since, a lively longing for the vanished metaphysics has continued, although one could scarcely speak of a general resurrection. No moving thought ever disappears completely out of the total stream. Whether as undercurrent or counter-current, each present in potential, always ready to be reactivated. Even the present time-consciousness is not without its ontological basis, but it is surely no bastion and even less does it provide an exit to the future.

Another counter-stream offers more hope, since it at the same time runs with other main currents of the age. We refer to Christian existentialism, which continues and modernizes the earlier influence of such thinkers as Newman and Kierkegaard. Again, as always in individualistic philosophy, ideas diverge widely. [3] The one characteristic common to all is the leap

1. This does not mean that the continuing influence of Husserl and Scheler has been exhausted. They have left other traces, as in French and German personalism. But these traces point much more to their origins than to the future.
2. It is difficult to bring such widely diverse figures as Othmar Spann and Whitehead or N. Hartmann, the neo-Platonists Blondel and Hessen and the philosophes de l'esprit such as Le Senne and Lavelle, all under one heading.

from purely subjective existentialism into the Transcendental and thus to a form of absolute Truth. Now the great question remains as to whether this development stems from the obvious attempt to infuse new life into existentialism, or from the attempt at synthesis with Christianity. The answer will depend on whether after further consideration these entities appear to be compatible, or whether existentialism ultimately does not negate all transcendence as another kind of existing reality. I gladly note that Marcel entitles his existential system a "metaphysics of hope", but pure existentialism leaves no room for hope. The earlier Christian hope is also seriously weakened. Could the combination of existentialism and Christianity under these circumstances possibly be stronger than the separate parts, or is this rather a diabolical pact of the times which contains the weeds of its own destruction? Could it not even intensify earlier Christian tendencies of earthly despair? Think of some of the somber anti-humanistic traits of Jansonism and Calvinism. We might hope the best from this union, and yet cautiously maintain certain reservations. Nevertheless this attempt deserves our sympathic attention, and it is certainly true that it contains more intensity of potential force for the future than other movements, because of its attempt at synchronization.

Catholic thinkers are the main contributors to Christian existentialism, but there is also the almost exclusively Roman Catholic philosophy of Thomism, with its various subdivisions of neo-Thomism. A noticeable revival of this line of development has taken place in the last half century, under the influence of Gilson, Maritain and Sertillanges. Within Catholicism itself this fact is not without significance, but apart from the great following which Maritain has as "humanist", this somewhat isolated philosophical phenomenon can scarcely be considered as part of the general developmental trend in western philosophy. It is so strongly interwoven with Catholic theology, that the key to its future development lies primarily there. Catholicism is its reason for existence and its goal, and the strength and weakness of Catholicism are in principle also those of this type of Christian existentialism as such and as a mode of philosophical thought.

There remains the ethical voluntarism, based on reverence for life, formulated by Albert Schweitzer. [1] No one will speak a word against it—if only someone would break the conspiracy of silence and speak about it at all! His person is respected as almost none other in our age. There is unfailing reverence for *his* life, and his work is crowned with praise. But his teachings, which unite humanitas and caritas, is as a philosophy completely outside time.

3. In addition to Wust, we find such differing thinkers as Marcel, Guardini, Lepp, Guitton, Mounier and others in this same group.
1. See *Verfall und Wiederaufbau der Kultur*, Munich, 1925, and *Kultur und Ethik*, Munich, 1925.

This is the age of irrationalism and scepticism, of rock-hard realism and plunging pessimism. At the moment no single philosophical counter-movement has a serious chance. But what of the future? Surely, things will develop according to the well-known cycles of rise and fall of cultural modes and moods and the changing outlook on the part of man? This is the critical point, in my opinion.

Human consciousness is not an accordion, simply to be pushed together and then stretched out again at pleasure. One cannot push the metaphysical consciousness back into a purely physical consciousness without suffering the consequences; it will not simply spring out again of its own accord in due time. If anything at all has emerged from our previous discussion, it is that there is an intimate relationship between the religious, particularly the *eschatological* consciousness, and the *metaphysical* consciousness. They are related through their intertwined ideas concerning another reality with its attendant higher values, to be found in another, coming time. The relationship is not a purely intellectual one, but also emotional, the fruit of the creative imagination. It developed through the religious consciousness of the last centuries in a direct line from Pascal - Rousseau - Kant - Chateaubriand right to and certainly including Nietzsche. The gradual growth of a-religious and anti-religious attitudes kept pace with the growth of the a-metaphysical and anti-metaphysical consciousness. Existentialism is not just one more philosophy which has found a chance development in this time, to be relieved in due time by another trend. On the contrary, it has written the typical and almost inevitable closing lines to a tragedy consistently developed through the history of western culture.

If the metaphysical consciousness has really been radically put out of commission and the human spirit become inaccessible, then the seeds of metaphysical philosophy can scarcely sprout in petrified soil. Or rather, such is the hardiness of the human spirit, they may sprout but will not be able to grow, lacking nourishment at the roots and willing hands to cultivate them. Then we face the prospect of supposedly unchangeable human nature changing indeed. A new sterile type of man is being carefully nurtured by our society, a man without the sixth sense for The Other. The Song of the Earth will spread over the entire western world: let us eat, drink and be merry today, for tomorrow we die. This is the only song which will arouse a responsive chord in the new moment-ridden man. This attitude may be rationalized by sonorously calling it "amor fati", but Nietzsche saw through this better than our own time can; nihilism knocks at our door.

This nihilism (and let us at last define exactly this concept of the gaping void) arises from and thrives on the systematic destruction of the image of the future and of its fundamental ideas and ideals, rooted in the deepest layer of conscious humanity from of old; it destroys the dignity of human existence through its basic attack on man's idealistic consciousness as such. This is not the ordinary case of a progressive philosophy attempting to replace ideal, which has become antiquated and dogmatic, by a new one; its revolutionary impact is purely destructive, directed to the liquidation of "*the* ideal" as such, regardless of whether it refers to the holy, the good, the true, the just—or even the wise. And as the ideal disappears, so does the idea, the possibility of imagining in one's self another and higher order, the crystalized reflection or the "eidos" of all the highest values of the existing society. Every idea and every ideal is unmasked as a false idol, an illusion; every cherished *form* of idealistic human thought is shown to be without *content*.

The essence of our entire system of basic values concerning human *being* is sacrificed to and compressed into naked existence. Existentialism makes it clear to man that this is the way he is, has to be and forever must remain, in fruitless guilt and penitence, and that he can never rise above himself or become anything better, no matter how he strives with blood, sweat and tears. Existentialism not only gives a phenomenological description of the modern moment-ridden man, but rejecting all values, it unconsciously—or deliberately—gives its nomative sanction to that which is thus devaluated, proclaiming it as valuable. It says: this is how things really are, and they are right this way, in spite of all evil. Thus a positive realism conceals a negative idealism. *Theodicy* becomes *anthropo*dicy, and brings quietism, passivism and fatalism in its train.

This new negativistic philosophy of life is profusely embroidered with terms such as choice, decision, act. These terms have themselves been rendered meaningless by the philosophy which makes use of them. A more accurate key vocabulary would read: exist = vegetate; life = existence unto death; action = non-action. Nothingness is the basic (but minus basis) point of departure of this metaphysics, and also its end-point for man. Man is the centre of being. By confronting man continuously with this exclusive Nothingness, however, it cannot but degrade him to a nihilist.

Philosophic nihilism is of course also a philosophy. But once it has penetrated into popular thought and elevated nihilistic man to a secure throne, then that man must make his own future way without the benefit of philosophy, of any kind. At this point he will find himself truly bereft, this existential, technological pragmatic man. Completely preoccupied by the "primum" of his deadly daily struggle for life, he is wilfully destitute of his former organ of consciousness for any kind of "deinde" or beyond. The chosen end-point of Nothingness is then no longer a subjectively arbitrary end-point, but *the* existential and essential end-point of philosophy itself within the framework of western culture. Nihilistic philosophy has edged to the very brink of the bottomless pit of nihilism. *This moment-bound philosophy has exposed all future philosophy to its own negative dialectic of a time-bound existence to the death.*

2. Science

At first glance the development of science appears to be diametrically opposite to the development of religion and metaphysics. What has been taken away from the latter seems to have been added to the former, in a major internal shift of attention in the world of thought. What does this mean? Is there a limit to man's intellectual capacity so that development in one area must inevitably take place at the expense of another, with the result that a decline of religious and metaphysical thought is the price that must be paid for the flowering of empirical and natural-science thought? And looking at the larger, over-all picture, what is the relationship between this flowering of science on the one hand and the unmistakable crisis of our culture on the other? Is this an incomprehensible contradiction or is there a hidden causal relationship or at least a functional correlation? Must we perhaps even characterize our modern culture as scientifically civilized barbarism?

Much has been written on this complex of questions in the last half century, in a copious mingling of sense and nonsense—both scientific and unscientific—and all of it is laden with emotion. Both optimistic and pessimistic tones are to be discerned, ranging from breathless expectation to somber premonitions. I have myself contributed to this literature, attracted repeatedly to the critical self-analysis of science in its attempt to understand its own function in our culture and its relationship to the ongoing course of events in society. I became convinced (and this point of view was not, of course, original) that scientific thought not only forms a point of departure, but holds a key position in the generation—and alas, the *de*generation—of western culture. On all sides attempts have been made to consider constantly emerging, constantly different, and constantly related, aspects of the total situation, in the hope of ordering kaleidoscopic fragments and tangled threads, if not into an aesthetically pleasing mosaic, at least into some kind of comprehensive system which might throw light on future developments.

In my own opinion these attempts, including my own, have been but preliminary skirmishes which have not succeeded in striking to the heart of the problem. They have, however, removed some obstacles which, like a modern Great Wall, had been erected in order to keep out interlopers and protect the central core of the problem. After renewed consideration, I must now conclude that here too this central core can only be reached through the use of the concept of the *image of the future* as an analytic and explanatory instrument.

Science has reached an unheard-of peak of historical development in the course of the last five centuries as a result of a powerfully generating and regenerating image of the future, in itself both fruit and seed of a basically changing image of the world. This development in western science is indissolubly coupled with the general development of western culture through the medium of the image of the future, which provides an active two-way channel of communication. The evolution of this image of the future throws light on the opaquely related rise and fall of these entities. This relationship is not only opaque and complex, but frequently paradoxical and contradictory.

One of the greatest obstacles to a better understanding of this relationship between science and culture lies in the fact that there is no general agreement on the precise meaning and content of these two entities. This is not surprising, since the one outstanding characteristic common to both is that they are each in a fragmented state. One could almost say that there are as many sciences and cultures as there are minds to think them. Both in science and in culture many forces are active, and many trends can be observed, all moving in different directions. Before attempting generalizations concerning the probable result in the force-field of science, we will examine the subject more closely. Three aspects will be considered: the historical growth of science in its various branches, the ideological presuppositions of science and its sociological role in society and in higher education. After this analysis we can see whether these different approaches present sufficient indications for a sketch of the main lines of probable future developments.

A. Development of the Sciences According to their Images of the Future

When we find a well-integrated culture-pattern, we generally expect also to find a harmonious unity of scientific and philosophical conceptions. When the classical period of Antiquity was at its peak, the totality of scientific thought was part and parcel of a synthetic whole which encompassed philosophical, religious, ethical and social-political thought. This situation remained until deep into the Middle Ages, and sharp differentiations between different areas of thought until then made little sense. But as soon as this homogeneous structure is disturbed, these splits become inevitable. To the extent that the earlier cohesion can be considered a natural one, the disruption contains an element of artificiality. This may make it difficult to build a good theoretical foundation for this breach in retrospect (in the sense of justifying the event), but the accomplished *fact* of the breach is not to be denied or disregarded. There can be no excuse from the scientific point of view, for failing to describe and delineate the factual differentiation process going on within science itself.

This is particularly true for the differentiation between the natural sciences and the non-natural sciences (variously known as the cultural or social sciences, or, in the most recent American terminology, as the behavioral sciences. [1]

The earliest, and far and away the most decisive, break with the formerly encyclopedic whole of religion, morality, philosophy and science was undertaken by the natural sciences, especially from the sixteenth century on. By means of an extraordinary fruitful combination of empirical experiment and mathematical reasoning they took their future into their own hands. Their independent and steadily increasing demonstration of power profoundly influenced the future course of development both of the non-natural sciences and of the entire culture for many centuries. Bacon's image of the future gives an amazing forecast of this development, and in the process gave a powerful impetus to the actual development itself.

This image of the future has not weakened or faded in the course of the centuries, but has grown constantly stronger. Applied natural sciences and a host of scientific applications have bestowed a halo on the basic sciences and have transformed the idea of unlimited possibilities into concrete reality. Their initial miracles became every-day fact and every man's property as a result of the staggering effect of the first industrial revolution. Their continuous flow of achievements has almost atrophied man's capacity for wonder. Every revolutionary breakthrough of natural barriers in the micro- or the macro-cosmos, whether of speed, distance, altitude or depth—and all new victories over nature in all its dimensions, including the many feats of exploitation of nature down to its last resources (almost to the point of annihilation of these resources)—all this is now in the realm of the expected and obvious. Anything and everything is now possible and nothing will surprise us. Science-fiction becomes mere anticipation. If tomorrow's newspapers were to carry the announcement that after long experimentation scientists have finally and definitively succeeded in producing life in the laboratory—the beginning of the *Brave New World*—it would be believed at once and evoke little more comment than any other currently announced scientific discovery. The original technological image of the future, so stirring in its effect, is now but an ordinary and accepted fixture in the general human consciousness: in science nothing is impossible.

1. I am aware of course of the objections—partly justified—which are raised against Rickert's classification. However, for practical purposes it is still very serviceable and easy to understand. See Franz Adler, "The Value Concept in Sociology", *Journal of Sociology*, Vo. LXII, No. 3, November 1956, which also refers to Znaniecki, *Cultural Sciences: their Origin and Development*, Urbana, 1926. Rickert's classification pertains only to the method and subject-matter of science. It is obvious that the natural sciences had and still have a greater role in the shaping of western culture than the social and cultural sciences (Geisteswissenschaften) themselves.

The revolutionary turn of affairs that set in with this independent and fabulous development of the natural sciences has been felt far beyond the realm of science itself, however broadly conceived. The struggle for autonomy and emancipation within the natural sciences was eventually taken over, after a considerable lag, by certain of the non-natural sciences. As a result these "new" sciences—scarcely two centuries old as independent disciplines—obtained a certain emancipation from the religious and philosophical authority which had held them fast, but complete independence was rarely achieved. They continued to be swept along in the train of that still dazzling comet, natural science, held there by powerful magnetic forces.

As a result of a disproportionate development, the pressure of the natural-science thought-model on *all* thought steadily increased, until the independently active image of the future of the non-natural sciences could no longer maintain its resistance. Whose name should we lend to the hopeful image of the future of these new sciences? Should it be Vico, Quesnay, Condorcet, the economists, the encyclopedists, the Saint-Simonists? Each of these has some sort of claim to the honour, but it would seem to me that only with Comte did the star of this image of the future rise to its zenith. He introduced a new hierarchical ordering of the sciences, according to a six-fold division on the basis of wealth of content. It ascended from mathematics, via astronomy, physics, chemistry, and biology to sociology, the queen of the sciences, ruling in place of a dethroned metaphysics. Where Bacon gave the natural sciences the motto, "knowledge is power", Comte provided the cultural sciences (subsumed under sociology) with the slogan "prévoir pour pouvoir". [1] This latter image of the future seems to ensure the balance of power between the natural and the social sciences.

But by the time Comte wrote this, after the turn of the eighteenth century into the nineteenth, the balance of power had already been in fact destroyed by the impact of the industrial revolution. Later writers maintained that sociology must contribute to the restoration of this equilibrium. It was a crisis-science, born of social crisis and destined to help overcome that crisis. The positive image of the future, even though it was generated by a negative situation, remained operative, and was given a tremendous new stimulus by Marx. Nevertheless, both Comte and Marx, and all their respective followers (or opponents, like Spencer), were themselves dominated by the natural sciences and its much-admired thought-methods and -models.

Comte introduced systematic *positivism*, Marx social *determinism*, and Spencer Darwinistic *evolution*, into the thinking of the cultural sciences.

1. Sometimes quoted in his words: "Science, d'où prévoyance; prévoyance, d'où action".

But this physicalism and naturalism, both in the extreme forms of Marxism and liberalism and also in the more neutral intermediate positions, at the same time provided one of the greatest obstacles to the full development of these cultural sciences according to their own lofty image of the future. This inverted effect resulted from the fact that their methods were not adequate to the subject-matter of the social and cultural sciences, formed as it always is by the free and variable work of man (including his use of scientific knowledge).

Comte placed sociology at the top of the scientific hierarchy, but so limited its freedom of movement that it could scarcely stir in any direction, let alone start on its upward course. At the same time that he assigned to it the primary task of prediction and control of the future, he also placed it securely in a positivistic framework which in effect entrapped it in the bare actuality of the *present*. For Marx and Spencer also, the future only made explicit that which was already implicit in the present situation, as they organized it in their blueprints. The subject-matter of the non-natural sciences was equated with that of the natural sciences, by having the same mechanistic laws of determinism and automatism now rule both.

The overwhelming success of the natural sciences forced scientific and philosophic thought towards a new all-embracing monism. The old ideal of a "mathesis universalis" rapidly gains ground again. The movement towards the "unity of science" has a great appeal for modern thought. In the field of economics, econometrics and mathematical statistics have achieved a prominent position in a relatively short time. Sociometry has imitated econometrics in the field of sociology, and cybernetics has just made its entrance. In philosophy, the positions of prominence have gone to logistics, symbolic logic, the theory of probability and "scientific" neo-positivism. Mathematical significs and semantics are achieving an ever greater importance in linguistics.

As so often is the case, this exclusive adulation of monism calls forth its own antithesis, which then leads to a breach. Within the non-natural sciences rebellion wells up again against the exclusive application of the techniques of natural science with the consequent distortion of the material in order to make it fit this methodological bed of Procrustes. The prophetic warning of Goethe still sounds in our ears, though faintly: "Wer will was lebendiges erkennen und beschreiben such erst den Geist herauszutreiben". It is a fact that culture itself as an object of study has been gradually removed from the cultural sciences. Cultural sociology is a dying species of sociology, in spite of the culture-crisis. An independent *science of culture* (culturology) has never emerged. Empirical sociology, social surveyism and social research, leaning heavily on the natural sciences, have on the other hand flourished mightily; but these fields have little status from the science of culture viewpoint. Thus dividedness and uncertainty reign.

The gulf between those non-natural sciences which are still resisting, and the natural sciences themselves, is steadily widening. It is a bilingual situation, with neither group "on speaking terms" with the other. Whether the two camps are described as quantitative versus qualitative, mathematical versus literary, empirical versus speculative, or simply as Science versus Art—the scholars on both sides have reached the point where they can hardly understand or even appreciate each other. Their attitudes, however, are not always the same. The natural scientists are not infrequently a-social, but do feel this themselves as a deficiency. The cultural scientists are often vague and inexact, but feel superior about it. The one is blind and knows himself lacking; the other is lame and proud of it. Neither is the reverse situation any exception, however: the mathematician, who will discuss nothing but abstract magnitudes and symbolic calculus or formulas, and the non-mathematician, who only can validate his argument by "l'art de groupper les chiffres" and delusive exactness.

It is, of course, an over-simplification to label this situation as bilingual. In actual fact it is multilingual. For autonomy, once begun, has multiplied within science, within both the natural and the cultural sciences, through ever-increasing division, differentiation and hyper-specialization, making for ever-narrower limits of each branch or subdivision. Everyone speaks an ear-shattering professional jargon in his own dialect. There is an increasing confusion of tongues. The Tower of Babel rises again in the midst of science. This time the labourers are specialized scientists, and in the deafening roar of their declamations, no man can communicate with or will listen to another, much less understand him.

Both natural and social scientists are quick to ply each other with reproaches. The natural scientist is inclined to stand on the authority of his own indisputable success and maintains that there is only one truly scientific method of work, only one possible conception of scientific truth, and only one universally valid criterion for the verification of new scientific insights. If this is not accepted, scientific work peters out in vagueness and incomprehensibility in aimless discussion and speculation, and fruitless scholasticism. The social scientist on the other hand points out that the one-sided application of these uniform methods entraps us in logicism and mathematic formulas. Man and all his uniquely human qualities are destroyed by the chill hand of mathematics which reduces a living reality to a series of functional relationships. Placing a social reaction in a test-tube produces only inaction, for social chemistry cannot survive in the vacuum required in the laboratory experiment.

Next, the blind and the lame attack each other and become locked in deadly mental combat, all the while beating nothing but air. Man's threatening self-destruction by means of his own technological weapons and the so-called mechanization of culture, is on the one hand blamed on the forces set in motion by the application of natural-science discoveries. On the other hand the social sciences are blamed for not being in the position to explain or control the tremendous social changes which are taking place, and particularly for not being able to generate a moral power to match man's power over nature. These reproaches are often mutually contradictory, such as when one side maintains that its (own) science cannot take the responsibility for the any misuse of its findings and that at the same time the (other) science is at fault for not absorbing the shock of the social shifts as they come along, and for not making the best use of discoveries already made. In another contradiction the social sciences are blamed for being too subjective and speculative, having too little concrete application or doing too little empirical research, then at the same time are taken to task for their slavish and sterile imitation of natural science methods, forcing a rigid social determinism on a subject far too complex and full of subtly shifting human interactions for such an approach.

If the non-natural sciences attempt to gain insight into the current social upheaval set in motion by the development of the natural sciences through the use of their own specific methods, they are denounced as unscientific. If they try to take a strictly natural-science approach to the problems and thus let the very core of their subject slip through their fingers, so that they lose their grip, they also lose face or scientific status. This situation has led to civil war among the social sciences, observable in frequent methodological battles. The natural sciences also have their problems. When their disciples try to stay with a strict pursuit of pure science, they are accused of being a-social, ivory-tower eggheads. When on the other hand they wish to express a sense of social responsibility, they are accused of naivity and dangerous amateurism, and the cry goes up, "Cobbler, stick to your last." This generates disunity and insecurity within the ranks of the scientist themselves, which moves by osmosis from the strictly scientific to the social-political and ideological level.

A fatal split thus develops, both between the "warring brothers" of science, and within each of the two main camps. The earlier integration has vanished, to be replaced by feelings of frustration, guilt, impotence, aggressiveness and intolerance. There is a vague awareness of a crisis in science. There is a superficial awareness of the relationship between the development of modern science and the present phenomena of social disintegration. There is a half-insight into the fact that science has made a major contribution to this disintegration, and is not now (no longer, or not yet?) able to counteract it. Finally, there is great disagreement concerning what science is, what it ought to be, what are its province, task, responsibility, its role and its function in culture.

In this confused situation, characterized by the abundant growth of highly emotional controversies concerning basic principles, the most extreme positions are procaimed the loudest, and emerge the most clearly. We hear on the one hand the view that modern science is the work of the devil, the doomed product of a fuddled Faustian man hastening toward his own downfall, ridden by the insane and godless delusion that mankind can independently provide its own salvation. On the other hand we hear that modern science is still in its childhood, with all the attendant diseases of childhood, and that through this current crisis it will come to a catharsis, reaching maturity for itself and finding a cure for the sufferings of the time.—All this, provided that new approaches are attempted in time, that new points of departure and new goals are accepted and new channels of communication opened between science and society. In short, provided that revolutionary changes take place which produce the acceptance of an awe inspiring image of the future.

The existence of these mutually contradictory tendencies indicate that the differences of opinion between the natural and the cultural sciences, which mainly concern methodology, do of course present important historical aspects and also have symptomatic significance for the present complex situation, but that they are not in themselves the main problem with reference to the future. In some respects it could rather be said they cover up much deeper and more vitally operating forces of the dynamics of science and prevent access to the right understanding of these. The dramatic process of development which bears the imprint "modern science" is not essentially touched by controversies concerning the classification of the sciences, nor through terminological and epistomological definitions, nor through the use of a kind of scientific esperanto. Only by placing it in its deeper structural relationship with the inner motivating and spiritual driving forces of the image of the future of science itself, can any clarification be obtained of what is now but a dim awareness of crisis in respect to the former foundations and certainties of science.

B. From Utopism to Counter-Utopism

Specifically scientific images of the future are the intellectual fruit of the general thinking about the future of a given time, and are rooted in it. The flowering of this general thinking about the future are mirrored in the scientific visions of the future. We have already discussed the crucial role of the utopia and utopian thought in preparing the way for a renovation of scientific thought which had been kept in a cramped and restricted state of tutelage. Utopism provides the model for all basic criticism and reversal of fundamentals, and is the primary source of all thought-experiments undertaken with Cartesian thoroughness and motivated by a purifying doubt. The utopian image of the future is the prototype of man's eternal struggle to free himself from himself and to break through the temporal ties of his own historical period and spatial ties of his own given environment. It is the classic example of that split mental capacity which enables man to rise above his animalistic initial situation on earth and which had been considered evident and invariant for centuries. It is the stimulus for making a problem or a paradox out of what seemed an obvious and natural premise. It is, in short, an indispensable instrument for the emancipation of free creative thought and for the highest development of man's mental faculties. The utopia pioneers with these highly developed scientific techniques of thought, using hypothesis, antithesis, isolation, abstraction, ideal-type, non-Euclidian geometry, non-Aristotelian logic, non-Ptolemaic astronomy, non-Newtonian physics, and so on. Utopian thinking has been especially pronounced in the most revolutionary minds through the ages, among those who have erected the milestones and monuments in the history of philosophic and scientific progress: from Plato to Kant and Bergson, from Copernicus to Einstein, from More to Darwin, Marx and Freud, from Socrates to Jesus—to mention only a few of those who have liberated and renewed the world-images for the development of western culture.

Utopism first crystallized and incorporated in scientific thought the concept of the philosophical panta rei—constant flux, continuous movement (including counter-movement). In stretches scientific elasticity to the farthest thought-boundary of the antipode, to the coincidence of opposites. Its undogmatic and unprejudiced attitude made the first approaches to the concept of alternative or complementary truths possible, and changed eternal-human absolutes into historical relativities. It penetrated into an unknown hitherto protected by a conviction of the inevitability of ignorance, and strode over barriers erected by the so-called science of its own time into for ever forbidden no-man's land. Utopism gave a universal bill of rights to science, including the right and responsibility of man to determine his own destiny; this meant also unlimited freedom of thought and expression, and the right to question all basic assumptions previously considered unassailable.

At the same time this revolutionary development towards intellectual freedom and maturity reacted to strengthen the utopian thinking which had given rise to it. It was the flowering of the liberated sciences which confirmed the new images of the future of the Renaissance and the Enlightenment and the related faith in revolutionary (or evolutionary) Progress. The basic idea of the utopia, the faith that the totally other can be made real through the creation of a completely deviant society according to one or more of a number of ancient and honourable ideals, is now intertwined with new idealistic expectations, awakened by the tremendous upward flight of the sciences. The concept of unlimited possibilities has now moved from the realm of the fantastically unreal to the cold realism of common sense if not to the downright commonplace, thanks to science.

The greatest initial contribution to this self-assured elevation of the potential of human power was made by the natural sciences. They shed their aura on the non-natural sciences as well, from which equally good things were expected in time. The ironical dialectics of history, which do not spare science, caused the natural sciences to influence the non-natural sciences in a wholly contrary and unexpected direction, from utopism toward anti-utopism.

Imitation of the classical model of natural-science thought impelled the cultural sciences to use quantification and mathematics to the farthest extent possible, leading ultimately to a capitulation to positivism and the resultant attempt to achieve value-free judgements on the part of the researcher. This implied the enforcement of a number of sharply-edged differentiations for the sake of the practice of pure science: between quantity and quality, positive and normative (Sein and Sollen), facts and value, science and conscience, real and ideal. This not only meant a preference for the observation and measurement of tangibly present phenomena, for concrete description and documentation by means of survey and statistics, or for—at most—extrapolation of existing trends on a short-run basis. It meant, above all, the reduction of scientific research to a choice between alternative means to given goals, with the goals themselves excluded from the domain of science. Goals were considered to be by definition subjective, bound to personal preferences for certain values, norms and ideals of a religious, ethical or metaphysical nature which are neither suitable for, relevant to or demonstrable by the scientific method. [1]

If this doctrine of scientific objectivity had been equally feasible for the non-natural sciences, no harm would have been done. But what actually happened was that the social scientist set himself up as an impartial observer and yet at the same time, quite unconsciously, cemented all the officially banished values into the very foundations of his work, but under a camouflage that for long a time defied detection by himself and others. The result was a supposedly neutral, but basically bourgeois and conservative social science which made unquestioning use of the values of the established order

1. See my *Kennen en Keuren in de Sociale Wetenschappen*, cited earlier.

as its point of departure. This implicit, unconscious and invisible valuation excludes all possibility of explicit modification. The axiomatic foundations of the system thus become invariant and absolute. They are not amenable to criticism or disagreement, let alone reversal.

With the elimination of ideal goals as unscientific and utopian, the utopian procedure of axiomatic criticism and regeneration is also eliminated. In the natural sciences the valuation of the material was indeed irrelevant for practical purposes; earthquakes, eclipses and volcanic eruptions took place without regard to human judgement. But in the social sciences hidden (and frequently ossified) value-judgements on the part of researchers gave scientific sanction to certain types of events, or tended to lead events in a certain direction. Marx quite correctly revealed (or unmasked, according to one's valuation) much of this kind of science as untrue or even as *class*-science. But then he used for his own anti-bourgeois valuation *exactly* the same untenable procedure of implicitly incorporating his different (but of course equally variable and historically relative) premises into a rigid system of so-called invariable categories and immutable natural laws of his own making. By this seemingly strict scientific reconstruction, completely in line with the then prevailing rules and standards, he intentionally and emphatically strengthened the trend in social science toward anti-utopism and counter-idealism. Liberalism and Marxism, however opposed in other respects, were united in that they assumed that society was regulated by a scientific law, theoretically definable and predictable in its exact workings. Or, in other words, society—like nature—was an automatic, causally determined mechanism, based on a single, exclusively valid set of axioms and operating independently of human valuations and wishes for its own good.

The consequences were hardly less than fatal. On the one hand the practitioner of the social sciences had to refrain from pronouncements concerning desirable future developments on pain of banishment from his professional brotherhood. On the other hand science itself was drawn into the struggle between the Marxian and liberal schools of thought, the image of science itself was obscured by political considerations, and scientific research was sucked up into various ideological currents; none of these could break through explicitly to the surface of the conscious mind, because of the tabu on values and ideals. Progressive thinkers could only be classified as non-bourgeois and therefore Marxian thinkers. The time-honoured utopian method of continuing axiomatic critique and reconstruction, so indispensible to the general vitality of science, was narrowed down to a one-sided forced choice between the biased extremes of ultra-liberal science and ultra-Marxist science. Both doctrines were duly canonized and each has its standard version, authoritative and absolute. Each also has its revised version, of course; neo-liberalism is somewhat becalmed through loss of spiritual momentum, and neo-Marxism has become even more grossly immoderate through massive accretions of power.

Once again, this time along a different road, we come upon an essential aspect of the crisis in science. Here it is the split in the human being between the pure scientist and the private individual. Previously these were two sides of a personality, united and undivided in one mind. It was precisely such minds which were to be found among those considered to be the leaders of culture, the creative and therefore also the responsible elite. This status was destroyed by the contrived separation between the mental functions of perception and valuation, intellect and emotion, and scientific and philosophic insight—in short, by the separation between searching realism and seeking idealism. "Chassez le naturel, il revient au galop". These repressed complexes must find expression in some way, in unnatural and distorted ways if not in natural and fully conscious ways. According to the usual cycles in scientific thought, [1] a rebellion against this rigidly static attitude was inevitable. And once again some revolutionary minds are attempting a major overthrow. Related to anti-utopian but dialectical Marxism, a new current of thought is indeed emerging which might once more be labelled utopian. It represents a modern version of that evolutionary optimism of the previous century [2] which the forces of disillusion had converted into its opposite. It is most frequently referred to as "scientific humanism".

This so-called scientific humanism is not so much an offshoot from transatlantic evolutionary optimism developing from the "American Creed" to the "Atlantic Charter", but forms part of a very different stream of thought emanating chiefly from Great Britain (with Bernal, Huxley, Hogben, Mannheim, Haldane, Russell and others). It can be recognized from the "bold new look" of a systematically planned and projected, positive, *image of the future*. The assumption is that another and better society can be achieved with the help of purposefully directed scientific developments and the disciplined use of human power on the basis of these developments. Has not science already to its credit an almost incredible progress in the battle against sickness and death, hunger, poverty, unemployment and sub-human living and working conditions? Why should it not as well be able to master the problems of war and over-population, of education,

---

1. See my *Wentelgang der Wetenschap* and Mannheim's *Ideology and Utopia*, both previously cited.
2. Automatism and determinism, an integral part of both classical-liberal laissez-faire and of orthodox Marxism are here exchanged for *their* opposite, free, responsible and planned self-determination of destiny.

democracy and world government? Why should man abandon the struggle toward increasing civilization now, when the harbour of scientific victory over evil, fear and suffering is almost in sight, now, when for the first time in history we seem to have built up a reservoir of almost unlimited scientific potential and only steady steering is needed?

The fact that the representatives of this school have ties either with Marxist communism or with atheistic humanism or both presents an obstacle to unbiased analysis of the valuable elements which may be contained in these ideas. Instead, both religious (eschatological) and socialist (realistic-political) forces in established western society, with all their attachments to "neutral" science, tend to regard these modern utopian ideas as unfair competition and have mostly reacted with an upsurge of counter-utopism and anti-futurism. It happens not infrequently that truly progressive thinkers are also personally attacked as disloyal, dangerous to the welfare of the country, heretic, defeatist—in this atmosphere of aggressive and in part irrational defensiveness. And so in this respect these thinkers still must pay the same personal price—although methods and labels have changed—which their early utopian forerunners usually have had to pay. But if the result is that regenerating images of the future from progressive scientific minds can no longer come up for honest scientific discussion, then this means the systematic cutting off of these vital sources of nourishment, so essential to spiritual survival. And this can only result in death by starvation both of the cultural sciences and of culture itself.

C. The Age of Science, or Science of this Age?

The lines we have traced in the two preceding paragraphs meet at a point where a dim but uncomfortable awareness dawns that science has run into a blind alley, that there is a crisis of science. On the one hand the common development of the sciences now appears to have resulted in irreconcilable differences and even in mutual obstruction. On the other hand, the moving spirit and mainstay of the sciences, namely the original images of the future, have become seriously undermined, and this pertains to both the specifically scientific images and the general utopian images. However, one important link is still lacking for a considered judgement concerning the future of science: the link between the situation in science and the prevailing culture-crisis. The developments in science are both cause and effect of the general crisis, as science and culture interact. The relationship between the ups and downs of western science and western culture are as complex as they are paradoxical. They are a special case within our general problem of finding the key to the flourishing and decline of cultures in general. Here we can only discuss a few aspects of this large, but still somewhat neglected area of the history of culture.

If we look back several hundred years and compare the situation then with our own time, the most striking change that has taken place is the gigantic growth of the influence of science on society. [1] An influence as intensive as extensive, it operates on society as a whole as well as on the individual, and is reflected in tremendous changes in the structure of society and culture patterns as well as in the minute events and actions of daily life. Our culture is pre-eminently a "scienticized" culture, our society a "scientific society". Our time proudly bears the historic label, "age of science".

The age of science. Now the crucial question for the future is, where is the direction and leadership for continued progress coming from, the *age* or the *science?* If we anticipate ourselves and simply answer that the primaire agens is the age—that is, *our own time*—then we have touched the core of the inconspicuous and yet revolutionary development of the last centuries, whose effects have led to the already discussed breach in our time.

In order to understand this radical change in, but also of time we must go back to our earlier explanation concerning the double charge in the images of the future. The first charge carried the image to new heights, and the second exploded the heart out of it. The images of the future liberated time, and then time destroyed the images in order to retain its freedom. This tragedy of death by success is repeated here in the field of science.

The scientific images of the future were fighting in the front lines during that war of emancipation. Having first liberated themselves from an anti-quated past, they were strategically situated for helping to free an age still mouldering in irons. It is also thanks to this scientific struggle for a new world-image, in which many intrepid and far-sighted scientists paid a high toll, that our time finally gained its freedom from chaining conventions and from a conservative ideology of vested interests. Time itself has now become free and independent, but also undisciplined and unrestrained. Set loose from old moorings, absolved from following a mandatory course, our age now remains adrift with no goal other than to continue to stay afloat through each day and to make the most of the "present".

But this free age, we can now add, does have its own unique style of life. It holds captive that very science which worked so hard to free it. This is the core of the reversal. For science had scarcely freed itself from the encyclopedic grip of dogma and scholasticism and won its battle of "la science pour la science" when it almost immediately lost this hard-won freedom. A show-piece among other present-day idols, it is carried along on the gigantic chariot of that modern Juggernaut, our Triumphant Time. The bitter pill is sugar-coated, however, at least in the western world.

1. See Bertrand Russell, *The Impact of Science on Society*, London, 1952.

Science does not languish in visible chains, but moves in apparent freedom. The truth is, however, that Time—our time—has hired Science. Its position is not that of grand vizier, but of feudal vassal.

This modern phenomenon of a spiritually enslaved science has many implications, some of them very profound indeed, and reacting back on science itself. They resolve themselves into two groups, one centering on society, the other on the university.

1. SCIENCE AND SOCIETY

If our time makes use of modern science, this relationship affects both master and servant, and in a predominantly unfavourable manner. The misuse of power corrupts both subject and object. Indeed, our time now takes care to be always covered and justified by science, its hireling mouthpiece. Science applauds at the right time like any paid claque, and delivers the required "oratio pro tempore" on demand. It functions to rationalize, legitimate, sanction and confirm the course of events. Science is, all according to circumstances, an apologist or an advocatus diaboli, building both foundation and façade for our time. Our time is free and always goes scot-free. Looking at it the other way round, as long as science strictly limits itself to the mandate given it by the times and never tries to stir outside the narrow channel of current events, it will remain positivistic and empirical and completely comme il faut according to the currently prevailing scientific code. To the extent that its descriptions cover reality, science will be covered and shielded by our time.

But what do we mean by this unscientific imagery? Two things. In the first place, the moment-ridden man of our time-shaping generation *is hiding behind the scientific approach*. His endeavours are no longer tinged with the charisma of magician or medicine man, but bear the seal of silence. He reduces all reality, including religion, philosophy and art, to scientific activity; he entertains himself with scientifically produced artifacts, he works, lives and dies in a scientific manner, with the blessings of science. And science works, lives and dies for him—for his happiness and progress, for his comfort and recreation, or (according to what the times decree) for his misfortune and ruin. In the second place, modern science is completely subservient to actual reality, and is more time-bound than in any previous age. Precisely because science has become so indispensable to our time, her independence is threatened to the extent that her value increases.

Of course the scientist has always been the child of his own time; science (together with philosophy) has always captured the essence of an era in its conceptualizations, and one can know an era from its science. Of course science has often served kings, nations or special interest groups as well —becoming, in Marxian terminology, class-science. But in our time the highest bidder can purchase scientific power in any desired quantity or quality for any purpose out of stocks on hand. Government, industrial and commercial enterprise, labour unions and employers' organizations, the army, the press, the entertainment industry, organized crime, advertising and even occasionally the universities (although in most countries these are far from being the highest bidders).

He who pays the piper calls the tune. Scientists dance to this tune that they may have bread—and in thus acting remain scientific and therefore honourable men. This is more true today than in any previous era. Modern science is of and for this time. Never before in the history of human civilization has any age commanded such an army of scientists, and never before has science *as science* so completely submitted to becoming a jack-of-all-trades, taking on any job which the time requires. Science is the mercenary prostitute of our time; it is the modern Babylon, the biblical "mother of whores".

The mantle of science adorns the age and all the manifestations of the daily stream of events. All the prestige of scientific knowledge serves only for the further glory of our time. Science has proved itself to be useful, trustworthy, modest and ingenious. Again and again it arouses universal approbation and acclaim by supplying logical reasons for our behaviour, whatever that behaviour may have been, and by explaining all the currents and movements of the time. It is impossible to recount it all here. Is it a question of the behaviour of an individual man? Psycho-analysis has descended to the deepest sub-cellar of his soul and lovingly nurtures all the excrescences which grow there. The work which is assigned to him and his chances for promotion are all under scientific supervision. His recreation and education are in the hands of scientifically manned mass media. Scientific staffs supply the weapons for economic conflicts of interest. A suitable scientific theory stands ready for every political action, whether in the field of economics or biogenetics, whether in central planning or geophysics. Warfare too not only finds its scientific techniques but also its ideological justification clothed in scientific garb.

Even culture has found a scientific-philosophic basis which lends itself to the transformation of the abnormal into the normal (existentialism), or to the anaesthetizing of the current crisis by labelling it a transition stage from a lower to a higher level of social existence (Sorokin). Whatever our generation does or fails to do—things which may fill future historians with horror or strike them dumb—we do it all in the best scientific manner, and thus with a good conscience. The indulgences of faith are now replaced by the general pass of science. Our time is inviolable, for science is at once its shield and standard-bearer.

Or perhaps its Achilles heel? As we examine the events of our time more closely we come across inexplicable contradictions and remarkable phenomena which warn us that something is wrong here. On the one hand, we find that science, using as foundation the Baconian postulate that knowledge is power, has climbed to the very zenith of influence in an incredibly short time. It has achieved a position of complete ascendancy, bringing all human behaviour, twenty-four hours a day, within its compass. There has been no muting against this forcefully imposed yoke. We not only live in the age of science, we actually live scientifically in every respect, according to the will of science. Science is today the driving and determining force in our existence. It is the source of all basic changes in the social structure, and stands in the wings at the scene of every revolution in our habits of life. It is responsible for the great transformation of human society and the creation of one world economy. Omnipresent, it has even penetrated into the home of the average man, ruling his destiny both as an individual and as a member of masses.

On the other hand, we are faced with the paradoxical situation that in spite of this incredible extension of the sphere of influence of science, its position on the social ladder has gone sharply down. The modern scientist has, generally speaking, a diminished prestige, status, independence and authority. The work of a science, which has become subservient to society, is carried out by an equally subservient intelligensia.

Even apart from the derogatory epithet "subservient", the entire concept of the intelligentsia has become devalued. It carries vague connotations of a caste to whose members an odium clings, of an undefinable something which is not sound, which is strange, maladjusted and eccentric to the point of being embarassing or hardly decent. The attempt has been made to establish nuances by differentiating between the concepts intellectual and intelligent; the former has gradually become something which is not "bon ton", scarcely better than being an artist. This social devaluation of the intelligentsia is certainly related to the transformation from former independence to present subservience. Formerly men of science and knowledge belonged to the aristocracy of the spirit, a select and distinguished minority which fulfilled a leading role in culture. The platonic philosopher-kings were at the top of this aristocratic hierarchy. Now trained intellect can be hired by the hour, week or month. This new proletarian class is forced into compliance with the demands of the ruling powers, which can afford the luxury of a private army of picked scientists.

An increasing proportion of the intelligentsia now has employee status and is made use of both by business and government. Brain-work is now for sale like any other commodity. A subservient intellect is by definition unfree, servile and passive, prepared to carry out well-defined tasks without any display of initiative. Frequently the scientist-servant is forbidden to publish his work independently or to express himself freely. Conscience must bow to prescribed regulation. Il y a des accomodements même avec la science. The subservient intellect is both extension and instrument of the "scientific society" with its centralized mass organizations, and it is fuel and lubricant of the modern social machinery. Subservient intellect = serviceable intellect, one that is without principles, pliant, docile, efficient and indifferent to the nature of its tasks. It has declined from *being* a discipline, in the best scientific sense of the word, to being *subject to* discipline.

Hired science may lead to the possible distortion of knowledge and truth according to the dictates and opportunistic considerations of political ideology or tactical propaganda. These may originate in various organized pressure groups in society, or in unscientific and even perverted interpretations of the general interest. Scientific results are often determined in advance by the requirements and goals of those who are paying for the research. The subservient in science far outnumber those who are still working in the so-called liberal professions, but even where formal freedom and independence exist there is a progressive deterioration as the times produce more and more conformists, and dissenters are mercilessly persecuted.

Science provides an arsenal of arguments for the rationalization, both before and after the fact, of anything that man wants to do, will do anyhow, or has already done. References to scientific research have come to replace references to the Holy Writ as the source of authority for those who would wield temporal power. Just as in earlier times both parties to a conflict were certain that God was on their side, so now every group has scientific truth on its side—scientifically fabricated according to prescription and delivered with alacrity. Subservient science serves every purpose admitted as legitimate by the age, to the best of its ability: capitalism and socialism, tax collector and tax payer, the munitions industry and pacifism, private enterprise and the cooperative, employer and employee, exploitation and recreation, advertising and boycott, art and barter. Just as the rain falls on the just and the unjust, so does the subservient intellect serve both good and evil. Its main orientation is towards today's values of productivity, efficiency, utility and rationalization. Science is put under steadily increasing pressure to become an applied discipline, useful to its age. Each demand for the services of the intellect encounters a liberal supply; the times see to this. Happily "conscientious objectors" still resist, but they are scarce, priceless and unpaid.

We do not mean to suggest the misleadingly romantic notion that science was formerly as white as the lily and is now as black as night. Science still has its independent advance outposts, of impeccable integrity. Their relative influence, however, is declining. The accelerated development toward a subservient science has not been without retroaction on science as a property of culture, and on the brotherhood of its practitioners. Once reckoned among the leading élite, the scientist gradually has been forced down into the position of middleman. Unorganized in a highly organized society, he now faces the threat of being pushed even further down the ladder. In times of depression, the unemployed brain-worker belongs to the most drastically disinherited, and is lumped in one group with the white-collar worker. It was in the thirties that the term "intellectual proletariat" became common in Europe. In times of prosperity the economic value placed upon the intelligentsia lags increasingly behind the rising standard of living, so that it is frequently in many respects worse off than skilled labour. Is this simply a question of demand and supply? Is it really true, as more prosperous groups maintain, that the scientist must make sacrifices for his chosen calling? Is this the price which must be paid for a fundamental democratization, which no longer permits scientific education to be the privilege of a closed priesthood, of a chosen few?

In my opinion the decline in the social value placed on the scientist weighs more heavily here than the purely economic explanation. The loss in status, prestige, integrity, and moral and spiritual authority is the crucial element in the situation. It is as if science had cheapened itself by success, in a battle for recognition too easily won. This popularization is closely associated with the incorporation of science into commercial exploitation and production for wholesale consumption by the mass media, including science-fiction and pseudo-scientific advertising. For the public, the magic authority of the practitioner of science, working in the seclusion of his study or university, has been transformed into the sinister intention of the man in the white jacket, the perverse sorcery of the laboratory and the evil genius of the wonders of technology: a demonic blend of Svengali, Fu Manchu, Caligari, Frankenstein and Dr. Knock. Amateur psycho-analysis, astrology, spiritualism, chiromancy, radio-aesthesia, magnetism and quackery in every form wear the trappings of science, as to a great extent do hypocricy, exploitation and deception. Through its omnipresence, through the scienticizing of man, society and culture, and through the coupling of science with any random event as a matter of course, it has quite literally become "common" property. From the economic point of view it is at the same time indispensable and without value, since it is as available as the air we unthinkingly breathe. No longer does science receive an honorarium—a recognition of merit—but is simply paid wages on the basis of production and current market prices for mass consumption.

Science has tumbled from its pedestal as a dedicated servant of pure truth and gives itself alike to tycoon and errand boy for ready cash, as a woman of the streets will offer herself to the first comer with money in his pocket. No longer a possessed Faust or even a thoughtful Kant, it has rather taken on the role of the practical factotum and busybody, Wagner and old Zampe. Speaking through every mouth, swaying in every wind, it is every man's friend and speaks for every actor in every scene of every act of the current world drama—but it speaks from the lowly prompter's box, and it speaks from a manuscript provided by the stage manager: the Times. Of Schiller's description of science in his era of transition, "Einem ist Sie die hohe, die himmlische Göttin, dem Andern eine töchtige Kuh, die ihn mit Butter versorgt" (For one it is a high heavenly goddess, for another a good cow which keeps him in butter), all that remains is the butter. And this, only for so long as it is not required to make way for cannons, and other assorted weapons produced by science.

Differences in status or standing, although still in evidence within the world of scientists and university graduates, are more and more levelled off in public life. There little distinction is made between the university-trained individual, carrying out some assigned job in industry, business or government, and the scientist (in the narrower sense of the word) who makes a profession of scholarship and research on the highest level. The demand of the times that science and knowledge be serviceable and practical, useful and realistic, has achieved an equalization and standardization of scientists together with a loss of science's essential norms and standards: freedom, integrity, critical independence and foresight. The various layers of the intelligentsia are becoming increasingly uniform in structure. Gradations and nuances disappear under the common stamp of subservience, coupled with an incalculated mentality of actualism and realism, which kneads and molds even the most timeless and universal materials such as metaphysics and theology according to the concrete requirements of the times.

How does the intelligentsia react? If it is forced into this subservience on behalf of all kinds of interests concerned only with their own ends, and if it allows itself to be degraded to a technical consulting service carrying out orders indiscriminately, then it must eventually decline either into apathy and atrophy, or into moral dislocation and disequilibrium. Both symptoms are already present. The first goes almost unnoticed, but is therefore all the more treacherous, the second reaction is most spectacular and distorts its cause even further. Both reactions are mortally dangerous, for the intelligentsia and science itself as well as for the culture of which they are—and have always been—the vital spiritual element and unifying force.

The second reaction, that of dislocation and upheaval, is at least a reaction, in the sense of conscious counter-action, still giving evidence of vitality and a critical application of intellectual gifts. Nevertheless, something is wrong. The term "unattached" intelligentsia has begun to achieve currency, an increasingly negative connotation. This unattached roving intelligentsia forms a group apart, capable of going off in every and any direction. In part withdrawn into voluntary isolation, in part forcibly banished by society, they are nevertheless not yet quite a pariah caste. Politically shelterless, socially adrift, they are everywhere guests and nowhere at home—spiritually "displaced persons". Science, as it has unfolded from its point of departure, finds a provisional and uncertain ending here in a loss of mental foothold. No longer earth-shaking, but earth-shaken! Outside the narrow borders of their own specialties, treading the terra incognita of human relationships in society, the scientists fall prey to the general crisis of science, and cannot but lapse into this roving state.

This unattached intelligentsia consists largely of frustrated intellectuals. In the course of the fulfilment of their professional duties they have been led into conflicts of conscience, tensions and repressions which have exploded in rebellion against the existing order and the extremisms of the ultra-revolutionary of the ultra-reactionary. In Europe particularly, fascism and national-socialism has had a magnetic attraction for a number of these unattached intellectuals. It is then not to be wondered at that many of the most intelligent and most idealistic intellectuals have in turn succumbed to the irresistible fascinations of Eastern-European ideology, even though they may be well aware that behind the iron curtain the old intelligentsia is being ruthlessly crushed. If further proof is needed that science is in a crisis, then what could be more convincing than the sight of these intellectuals of the West using the freedom of speech and publication which they value so highly to aid and abet a world power which denies this very freedom and teaches explicitly the complete subservience of the intellect to totalitarian ends?

And yet, what is it that drives this unattached intelligentsia along this path of death, but a deeply felt, passionate sense of social and cultural responsibility? Their protest against our bourgeois, complacent science grows out of an attitude of self-criticism which should in itself be acknowledged with respect. The tragedy is that they have been misled by an inadequate diagnosis into the application of a theory which will produce the opposite of the desired results, and the use of a means which dangerously intensify existing evils. Remarkably enough, the most intelligent and far-sighted of these intellectuals are well aware of this too. They know that the present political communism for which they are working will leave them only the choice between complete submission and death. Moved by a fatalistic self-contempt, they are apparently ready for both. They have lost faith in themselves and in the future of the intelligentsia as the vital organ of the social structure and the motive-power for social progress. Their image of the future is negatived. They despair of their own spiritual influence, of its worth and its power to move men. This intelligentsia is the greatest enemy of the intellectual, undermining the very basis of its existence, stripping it of all meaning as an entity in itself and as the leaven of culture. In deep horror of American influences in Europe, which they term "Americanism" and consider anti-cultural, over-optimistic and hyper-mechanistic, they do an about-face and give their allegiance to another, equally anti-cultural, over-pessimistic extreme—and one which may well destroy all the values which have been built up by European civilization through the centuries since Antiquity.

Coupled even with the sharpest perspicacity—and how much more pronounced when this is absent—is a shocking blindness and incredibly naive self-deception. The self-educated man, trying to achieve intellectual mastery over all fields of knowledge as a homo universalis, makes way for the dilettant, who in respect to anything outside his own ever-narrowing intellectual enclave, lets himself be swept along by propaganda and ideas produced for mass consumption. Culture is terra incognita, a spiritual vacuum for most of these men, even—and often particularly—for the best of them. For the most part they believe the essence of cultural dynamics can be caught in the aprioristic and unscientifically rigid categories of an often misunderstood Marxian materialism, and of causal determinism. In this deterministic course of history they see themselves as playing their "determined" role, midwives of Marx assisting the historical process towards its predestined conclusion. They make a vociferous intellectual virtue out of the dire distress expressed in "man glaubt zu schieben und wird geschoben".

They do not sufficiently discern the general relationship between the specific crisis in science and the over-all crisis in culture. The very lack of a science of culture in the real sense of the word is avenging itself in our scienticized culture. Our most learned specialists are often cultural illiterates, whereas critical-idealist philosophy with its accompanying conceptions of an encyclopedic and synthetic nature have been destroyed in our modern scientific culture. Simply tacking over to one special form of non-bourgeois science, moreover set in a framework which denies the values which are the foundation stones of western science and culture, can do little to help them save the twenty-five centuries-old treasure they both guard. Only when sufficient spiritual courage will have been mustered to shift the discussion from the means to the goals does the objectionableness of *this* proposed reform, and the necessity of some *other*, equally far-reaching reform, become evident. Only then is non-bourgeois science liberated from the bonds of Marxian dogmatism (as oppressive as any conservative bourgeois ideology), and only then will it be accessible for other alternatives of axiomatic reconstruction.

But unfortunately we are moving around in circles. We call for reconstruction and reform. But reforms always mature far in advance and are slowly prepared by the ideas of a small number of creative intellectuals, the élite of a nation or a science. Now, however, the idea of an intellectual élite is practically a contradiction in terms. The emotional reactions now elicited by the mere use of the latter term are proof enough of this and neatly demonstrate one of the main characteristics of the crisis in science. Intellectuals no longer constitute an élite and do not want to be a minority; on the contrary, they too become swallowed up by the masses. Science and its representatives in society are now moving in the opposite direction, i.e. away from a preparation of future reforms. At the same time, there is a small top-layer busily preparing the self-elimination of true science (and of scientists), so that any possibilities of a future rehabilitation and for new developments become literally unthinkable. The intelligentsia of today are equally representative of and represented by modern mass culture, steeped in the present.

The intelligentsia now swarms with civilized barbarians, cultural and learned ignoramuses or nonentities, to throw in all the terms that are used to describe this situation. For the masses they cloth nihilism and neutralism with scientific dignity. Within science itself they introduce the mass characteristics of the industrial machine-man: uniformity and passivity and a resistless drifting along with a reality which changes from moment to moment, as the forces of various vested interests of the established order pull the strings. The intellectual deteriorates from individualist to marionette, from apathy to atrophy. Is this picture too somber, too one-sided, too much of a caricature, too simple a generalization? Will there not be some healthy reactions which will serve to restore the general equilibrium when the pendulum swings too far?

The faith expressed in the "une minute avant sa mort il vivait encore" should always find support, but the cheap optimism of the vis medicatric naturae (the healing power of nature) when transferred to the social field can do more harm to the possibility of regeneration than any form of tragic but active pessimism. In the present case this is all the more true so long as the training of the intelligentsia continues to strengthen this unfortunate development. Science and the intelligentsia are not simply imaginary entities; they are made into what they are in any given time by real people who in accordance with their ability and the training they themselves choose to undergo are systematically cultivated into men of science. Modern scientific training herds these men like so much live-stock within an enclosure, strings the fences with barbed wire, and puts up a sign: caveat intelligentsiam! This stock-farm, feeding trough and county fair for scientific products, is united under the symbolic roof of one institution, called the university. This institution can be recognized by the pedigree it issues in the form of a diploma, the trademark of the doctoral examination, and the miserable collection of types known as its faculty.

2. SCIENCE AND THE UNIVERSITY

If we add the university to science and society in our analytical scheme for determining the changes which have already entered into our culture, we find that the contradictions within modern science are only an indication of deeper underlying problems which the development of science as a whole has forced to the surface, there to dominate modern society. The independent development of the university as an agent of science accentuates the paradoxical dislocations in our present situation. For example, here are two facts which it is difficult to reconcile with each other. In the first place, there is a swelling chorus dedicated to singing the swan song of our culture. The theme is that culture is heading into a decline—perhaps an irrevocable one. The point here is not whether the opinion is correct, nor that it is held by authoritative observers of the social scene. The important fact is that this feeling of impending doom, regardless of source, is gradually mastering the minds of men in our time. And the leitmotiv of their current swan song has become that the source of this pernicious decline is the poisonous mushrooming of science.

Let us leave aside the question of whether culture is indeed doomed, and consider only two contradictory attitudes. On the one hand there is an increasing acceptance of the possibility of such a doom, and of the conviction that science will actively contribute to it. On the other hand—and here is our above-mentioned second fact—there is the rather self-assured attitude adopted by those who share the responsibility for the present situation, the "producers" of science. We refer to those who both engage in scientific work of their own and who are responsible for the intellectual procreation of scientists. In other words, we refer to the university. How does this modern focal point of scientific development and training, this source and seed of culture, react in the face of the threat to culture? What is it doing, what is it thinking, how is it mobilizing its not inconsiderable forces in the face of impending crisis?

Of course, "the" university is an abstraction. Each university is a separate entity with a life and style of its own. In speaking of the modern university we will try to delineate the dominating type and its actual course of development by pointing out a few ideal-typical characteristics, drawing a deliberately exaggerated picture. The university in general appears to be an isle of tranquillity in the midst of turbulance. Or rather, it has withdrawn from the turbulence. It sits in gracious calm on top of a fire-spitting volcano. Heroism? Quixotism? Or just the well-founded conviction that this volcano really is nothing but an innocent windmill, and that the culture-pessimists are nothing but swollen windbags? Imminent downfall of culture? Come come, the university says benignly and gives us an encouraging pat on the shoulder or a wink; we mustn't let ourselves be carried away by exaggerated reports emanating from bilious melancholics or ulcerous neurotics, and neglect the daily work that presses upon us. Let every man do his duty, as the day requires. No, a culture-crisis is most certainly not admitted within the reinforced concrete walls of the university. And so, in sharpest contrast to the keenly-listening Middle Ages, which thought constantly to hear the approaching hoof-beats of the apocalyptic riders, the modern sage pays no attention to the pounding at the gates, and averts his head from the handwriting on the wall.

Has the cry of "wolf, wolf" perhaps gone up once too often in false alarm, so that now when danger really threatens there is no one to listen? On the contrary, there has scarcely been any articulate cry of alarm to be heard, especially concerning the state of the university. [1] Those who attempt to speak are like a voice crying in the wilderness. This failure to react hints of an intellectual inertia and spiritual poverty one would not expect from the university. The institutions of learning remain silent in every language, where the crisis of culture, of science, of the intelligentsia and of *itself* is concerned. [2]

Is not the term "crisis" perhaps tossed about a little bit too casually in some of these cases? Is it not rather the problem of that imperfection which dogs every human institution? Can we not confine ourselves to the constructive social criticism which every age requires? In my opinion today's dislocations have completely shattered the normal frame of reference in respect to human efforts which inevitably, owing to our human imperfection, are lagging far behind our human ideals. This time something more and something different is at issue. It is no longer a simple question of the same, but of much harder work, in order to catch up with the times or to keep abreast of them. The very raison d'être of the university is threatened, its basic idea is at stake. The extent of this crisis of the university

1. The following two books ought to be required reading for all university scholars: *The Crisis in the University* by W. Moberly, London, 1949, and Ortega Y Gasset's *Mission of the University*, London, 1946/52.
2. Although the crisis of the university takes different forms in different countries, the crisis itself is an international phenomenon.

can be measured in the three dimensions of the chasm that yawns between that which the university now is or is in process of becoming, and that which it needs to be or should most earnestly be trying to become.

What *is* the typical modern university today?[1] The plain and unadorned truth is that it is a more or less haphazard assortment, an amorphous mass of unattached areas of specialization, unattached colleges, unattached teachers and unattached students.

a. *Unattached areas of specialization*

The university is a factory, operating a conveyor belt according to the best techniques of mass production and producing in anticipation of miscellaneous orders from society. It applies itself to the manufacture of spare parts for the replacement of worn-out sections of the social machinery or the building of new units for this gigantic mechanism of the "scientific society". The product must of necessity be standardized, to be used for mass consumption. It is somewhat doubtful whether there is any treatment or even trading of living human material in this setting. In America particularly, where state universities have attained such a tremendous size, it has become almost a cliché to refer to them as diploma factories. But almost everywhere institutions of higher learning are being turned into centers of distribution of official passports entitling the bearer to one of a number of impersonal jobs where skilled brainwork is needed and must be carried out by the subservient intellect.

The university puts its marketable products on display as in a department store or supermarket. Some have a greater assortment than others. In America the specialties may include the undertaker's profession, novel writing, the beautician's art, landscape architecture and interior decorating. But the basic principle is everywhere the same. How do I make an atom bomb, how do I handle personnel problems in my staff, how do I undertake a cost-accounting, what kind of cotton can I grow in Egypt, how can I most effectively preach the Gospel, how do I become conscious of the unconscious . . . all this can be bought across the university counter, provided that it is listed in the catalogue. In principle, one can buy anything and everything one pleases, but only odd parts, bits and pieces out of the total inventory of science and knowledge. The buyer has free choice, but no one can obtain more than a tiny self-sufficient scrap of the totality of knowledge, a scrap which has itself been assembled from various isolated sub-specialties. The university itself has become a large-scale industrial enterprise in which the individual student has a very small place indeed and

1. By "typical modern" we mean the large urban universities. For smaller, regional or denominational universities and colleges, these phenomena are as yet less pronounced.

has no way of comprehending the whole. His opportunities for such comprehension are steadily decreasing as the university pursues an ever increasing specialization in preparing its apprentices to be useful in the megalo-concerns of modern society. This cramping of the field of consciousness is an accurate reflection of the progressive hyper-division of labour and narrowing of individual fields in an industrial civilization.

b. Unattached departments

Our remaining points flow from the above. Each splintered faculty of a university grows increasingly independent, even more so than the corresponding departments in the above-mentioned department store. Moberly speaks in this connection of the "chaotic university". Even this gives it too much honour! I would rather call the modern university a *non-university*. The university has sacrificed its *universitas*, and made a mockery of itself as the great symbol of the indivisible totality of knowledge. As a rule it is nothing more than a collection of independent colleges under one name and one roof—and often not even that. The faculties have eclipsed the university. That which separates is more significant than that which unites. The university is no alma mater, but at best an unloved step-mother that one must occasionally visit for decency's sake, preferably when she is not at home. The university is the officially sanctioned system of watertight compartments, a proud modern incarnation of the Babylonian confusion of tongues. Each faculty claims its own original contribution by erecting its own heavenward-aspiring tower. It incidentally contributes also to the transformation of university education into a "spectacle coupé", a collection of excerpts.

c. Unattached teachers

The current trend toward super-specialization has made a euphemism of the so-called intellectual bi-lingualism in the sciences. The teachers have been appointed as specialists assigned to the training of specialists. No one knows any subject but his own overblown speciality, and each man isolates himself behind the barrier of his own esoteric terminology. There are no accredited translators; any attempt at translation is discredited, and he who steps into it risks being brought down under a barrage of insult and abuse. The only thing which the members of various faculties have in common —as a rule—is the town of residence, the institution which hires them, social position and academic title. Occasionally, as chance wills, several of them may deal with the same student. But this is not a significant aspect of university life, for the modern university is much less a "Gemeinschaft" (folk society) than a "Gesellschaft" (urban society). The broken contact cannot be re-established by "meetings" alone—these are in themselves one of the time-consuming evils of our time. Nor can it be remedied by the personal goodwill of the individuals concerned and personal "interdisciplinary" friendships. A heterogeneous collection of men of goodwill cannot weave academic splinters into an integrated whole worthy of the name of university.

The currently officiating representatives of the academic profession are themselves captives to the spirit of the times. They have strengthened routine, continuity and stability behind the bulwarks of tradition, conservatism and immobility. They suffer from the very disease they should be remedying. Instead of actively working against a further progression of the disease, they are frequently the mouthpieces of the prevailing forces of our time, the exponents of a mouldering culture. They perpetrate "le trahison des clercs", and shape a learned barbarism.

d. *Unattached students*

The students also—however much they establish themselves in a net of clubs and societies—fall prey to the unattached state; the pieces are assembled only in the office files. The majority of students are known to their professors mainly through the class registration lists and the examination papers they turn in. Fellow-students are more often competitors than confreres, in a keen competition which is but a trial run for the later, "real-life" struggle for existence, with every man for himself. The university is chiefly considered to be a continuation of the secondary school, the approved last step on the educational ladder. How often does it happen that a student is really "reached" by his studies, and leaves the university another (if not a better) man, capable of intelligent reflective thought and critical judgement, alert with constructive interests and sympathies? For most students it is rather a necessary evil, a hurdle which must be cleared, a quarantine station which holds the monopolistic power of granting the entry visa to a job in one's chosen specialty. And only specialists, who themselves acquire a monopoly of more and more knowledge about a small and smaller field, have a chance at placement, promotion and success "on the outside".

The super-man of our time is not the encyclopedist, the generalist, the one who seeks universal knowledge, but rather the super-specialist. It is the man who knows more and more about less and less, until at last he knows everything about nothing. The student life was once considered to be a rather irresponsible one, and yet in their gay and carefree ways many students managed to pick up a little something from everywhere. The carefree aspect of student life has almost disappeared, to be replaced by the hardships of the student who must "work his way through". And yet these restrictions on their freedom from care are not nearly as bad as the lack of an intellectual frame of reference of a universal character. The university imparts scattered fragments of science and knowledge and thus makes out of its students "scatter-brained" specialists. They are "scatter-brained" because we have made them that way; we require them to be so.

Of course the truly superior work that the university continues to accomplish cannot be ignored, but its worthy attempts to restore the civitas academica are unfortunately much too feeble. And so I see the crisis in the modern university plainly indicated by a symptomatically splintering situation of differentiation progressing toward disintegration. I previously cited a few lines from Goethe's *Faust*. The lines which follow are: "Dann hat er die Teile in seiner Hand. Fehlt leider! nur das geistige Band". [1] This is precisely the situation of the average student in the average modern university (which without that spiritual bond *is* no university). Clutching his fragments of knowledge in his hand, he is delivered to society by the university as a worthy product and producer of science. Thus cultural barbarism spreads like a weed through our society.

As we have already said, the existence and extent of this crisis can best be comprehended by contrasting with the negative aspects of the current situation the positive aspect of how it should have been. We have so far only indicated the extent of the university's shortcomings, shortcomings towards the students and also toward science, society and culture. But are not these deficiences comparatively simple to remedy? Unfortunately, not so simple, for these shortcomings are characterized by a simultaneous over-doing. There is "too little" because there is "too much". Increasing specialization has led to an overloading of the student's mind with details. The long years of study are growing too short for cramming in everything which the super-super-specialist must know about his ever reducing field. Post-doctoral and post-graduate work is becoming more and more necessary, and the towers of higher education rise ever higher until they are indeed skyscrapers, surpassing all previous altitude records. But they gain only in height, not in depth or breadth! This vertical building is incompatible with expansion in other dimensions, and a spiritual deficiency of the inner structure cannot be compensated for by piling more loose bricks on top.

That which the university should be, is not something more, but something totally other. With Ortega y Gasset I am personally convinced that only that university which endeavours in well-considered ways to achieve

1. Goethe was referring to the new techniques of analytic and increasingly differentiated research in chemistry (the so-called encheiresis naturae), and added: "Spottet ihrer selbst und weiss nicht wie". Whether this is a fair criticism of chemistry I do not know, but as a general criticism of scientific development, particularly in the university setting, this prognosis strikes home. And yet Goethe had in all probability no inkling of coming developments in micro-physics and the splitting of the atom!

the cultural moulding of its students—of *all* its students, without exception—
is truly fulfilling its essential task. Such a cultural education would certainly
include a systematic carry-over of the precious heritage of great thinkers out
of the past into the future, and the furnishing of insight into the origin and
development of the highest cultural values. It would include an orientation
concerning the fundamental structural changes which have entered into
our western culture with corresponding changes in the image of the world
and of society. Equally, it would include introducing all students to the
burning questions of our day and to the divergent forms of "Weltanschauung" as man struggles for his present and future existence. In short,
the camera lens of the university would be focussed on *that which moves
the world*.

Inseparably linked with this cultural transfer is the cultural preparation
of students for the task of their own generation. This is a matter of training
outstanding citizens, future leaders and managers in the key positions of
society, people who are something more than pure specialists. Of producing
individuals who are able to contribute actively to society through their
capacity for critical and creative thought. Individuals whose academic
training is precisely what has given them a sense of social and cultural responsibility that will guide all their actions, wherever they are placed in
society. Individuals who transform the subservient intellect into the serving
intellect, not being confined body and soul by contractual stipulations regarding work, but retaining the inalienable right to serve in the broadest
sense, free to contribute to the progress of culture.

Academic training in the best sense of the word sharpens the judgement
and teaches how to discern where a "yes" is called for in answer to society's
needs and where a decisive "no" is demanded. This training should serve
to develop students into critical, individual thinkers who can if need be
even stand isolation and solitude with the strength to swim against the
current of the times. Individuals who can resist the flood-tide of public
opinion, and who even have the courage to launch a lifeboat and save what
can be saved from the impending shipwreck of culture. This training should
prepare the student to fulfil the indispensable function of an intelligentsia
worthy of the name: openly and purposefully to be the world's bad conscience about its cultural decline. In a word, what needs to be done is to
undertake the selective transformation of as many students as possible into
a new creative minority, wrested from the flood of total massification. The
university is now confronted with the crucial experiment which it must
undertake to fulfil its cardinal function: it must contribute to the formation
of this creative minority without which no culture can long survive, for
without this creative minority (to use Toynbee's valuable terminology) no
adequate answers will be forthcoming to the challenge of time and the future.

Only when we contrast the existing university with this ideal statement of the goal of the university, can we reach full awareness of the extent of the current crisis in the university, and of the inadequacy of most of the current attempts at reforms, removing unevenesses here, giving a new coat of varnish there, and at best treating only symptoms. To fulfil or even approach the goal just outlined, requires nothing less than a full-scale rebellion of the creative minority of our generation, particularly its university contingent. This is the only counterbalancing answer to the so-called rebellion of the masses, and is the necessary condition for the revival of genuine creative leadership in science. A spiritual revolution is called for to complement the industrial revolution. Unfortunately, nothing seems more remote from the average, tradition-bound university, the very prototype of conservative thinking in our time, than the possibility of rebellious brainwaves. The endeavour to achieve continuity and retain established ways is valid only insofar as this serves to preserve and pass on the highest achievements of the past. But in the modern university—and we are of course overstating the case to make our point—what we find is *discontinuity* with reference to the most valuable elements in our historical heritage, and *continuity* with reference to those elements which have the least value for our own future development as a culture. The outstanding innovation in the history of thought since the Middle Ages is precisely this specialism of science and knowledge which now threatens to destroy the university. And it is in the attempt to specialize, just here, where the university has wanted to adapt itself to the needs of our time and set its sails into the wind, that it has degenerated into such a dramatic picture of this sorry time, reflecting the disintegration of culture. In spite of all conservatism and even anachronism, the modern university is in this respect typically the university of the modern moment-ridden man. Its crisis stems from the decline of positive goals for itself and the culture of which it forms one of the critical foci.

A positive image of the future of and for the university can only stem from the premise that the university itself has one of the most crucial functions of all to perform for the future. By its very nature it is a kind of transformer-station processing the ideas of yesterday into the ideas of tomorrow. Because of its function of scientific mediation between preceding and following generations, it must ultimately produce thoughts which have not been thought before, or not in this particular way. A petrified university works both against itself and against science. The university cannot, may not, have any orientation to the future but a dynamic one. If it is not an intellectual and spiritual vanguard, it is nothing. I am far from asserting that the university has always answered to this ideal image in the past, but now the problem is of more significance than ever before. After the profound changes of the last 150 years, and in the face of the coming changes of the next 50 years (which promise to be far more radical), there is only one way open to the university, the institution which must give direction to future scientific developments if we are not to deteriorate further as a society: it must cut entirely new paths into the future, and do it while there is still time.

D. The Future of Science

The matters which we have discussed in the preceding sections are not generally evident, not to those directly concerned nor to outsiders. But this much has gradually penetrated, that the whole-hearted faith which has prevailed for so long, that science can bring us within reach of our goals and also has unlimited power to achieve its own goals, is now making way for a pronounced ambivalence of attitude. [1] This sometimes leads to a splitting off into opposing images of the future, one positive and one negative. But even where two sets of values are still encompassed in one system, there is at least a strong shift from the positive to the negative value elements. Idolatry is mingled with criticism, satisfaction corroded by anxiety, and faith undermined by frustration and disillusion. Scarcely anyone doubts that science is capable of continuing to make enormously rapid progress, but the paradoxical question is also being pondered of whether this progress may not destroy both us and itself through a no-longer-controllable tempo and excess of demonic successes. We are becoming aware that Promethean man cannot storm the Olympian gates unpunished, and that the sin-ridden descendants of Adam and Eve cannot unaided free themselves from their creaturely impotence. The self-awareness and confident pride originally awakened in man by science begins to waver before new feelings of inferiority.

Clouds are beginning to gather about the still-shining head of science, and disquieting storm-portents are appearing, although as yet they keep their distance. Does every ascendancy already foreshadow its own decline? Do scientific developments only accelerate a predetermined and inescapable cycle of rise and fall? Can the sorcerer's apprentice not control the spirits

---

1. This ambivalence is not entirely new. Ever since the Middle Ages there have been undercurrents of mistrust, running through Catholicism as well as through Luther, continued in such diverse figures as the romanticist Rousseau and the mystic Goethe. There is the feeling that scientific pursuits will have negative effects on culture and religion, deriving either from a Mephistophelean inspiration (the Faust-legend) or from man's rebellion against the supernatural (myths of Prometheus and Icarus, of Albertus Magnus, doctor universalis, and Roger Baco, doctor mirabilis). But after the industrial revolution, in the eighteenth and nineteenth centuries, the development of science became overwhelmingly identified with social progress. This too is a continuation of earlier currents of thought, represented by Francis Bacon, Godwin, Adam Smith, Bentham, Spencer, Condorcet and Comte.

he has evoked at the crucial moment? Will unchained nature at last revenge itself on man? Will the undisputed master of nature become the slave of technology? A vague and indeterminate disquiet, evoked by historical, philosophical and biological parallels, is on the increase as the fact of the antithesis between *scientific civilization* and a *humanly worthy culture* leaps more and more clearly to the eye. By way of illustration, here are a few arbitrarily chosen items.

1. The progress of military technology to the point where the potential exists for the total destruction of the planet earth, and the species man.

2. The dissipation and exhaustion of the earth's sources of energy and its interior mineral capital.

3. Industrial automation with the threat of mass-unemployment and the further mechanized, spiritually deadening use of ever-increasing leisure time.

4. Soil exhaustion as a result of the pressures of increasing world population, with the ultimate alternatives of hunger or world war, or both.

5. The moral dislocation of "underdeveloped areas" as a result of enforced transplantation of western industrial civilization.

6. The barbarian expansion of totalitarian dictatorships based on scientifically refined techniques, with the threat of the development of new bestial human types.

7. The depersonalization of man and the technocratic mass-culture, also in western democratic lands. The ascendancy of the mass un-man and the decline of the homo humanus.

8. The inadequacy of man's power over himself and over his newly-won, incalculable power over the micro-cosmos and the macro-cosmos.

As far as the future of science is concerned, these future dangers inherent in the applications of its findings, and the presumable excesses of its blinding successes, do not alter the basic fact of unlimited possibilities for science as such. At many points the climactic developments are still far in the future, and record will outstrip record in one scientific field after another. The capital investment in scientific research, both on the part of private industry and government, is continually on the increase. In spite of complaints that we already have too much of a good thing, the century of science has just begun.

But this century of science is becoming a two-edged sword. The present, which now dominates everything, compels science in its subservience to become moment-ridden. Bound fast to its master, science must march with the times, and thus also cooperate in the campaign against the future. Scientific control or determination of the future would also mean a restriction of the present and of its complete freedom. In that case modern free time would again be captured, harnessed and shaken out of its self-adoration and preoccupation with present actuality, and given reality. Away then with all earlier concepts of finality and causality, away with outmoded determinism and historicism. Let us replace causality with probability (in the short run) and relations of indeterminacy. Prophecy gives way to foresight, and this in turn gives the field to prognosis, which is then altered into trend-extrapolations (from today until tomorrow), only to be rejected in its turn on the ground of the basic unpredictability of human behaviour. And then too, there is always the danger that these attempts to study the future will become unempirical and speculative, because wishful thinking, religious teaching and romantic utopism can hardly be kept out. All this goes to show that the future is neither measurable nor knowable and must therefore be eliminated from the subject-matter of science. Thus the exalted scientific image of the future, envisioning the progressive pushing back of the boundaries of the unknown, evaporates. As the age wills, anti-futurism reigns in the house of science too.

In this respect there is still some difference between the natural and the non-natural sciences. The natural sciences are permitted the innocent pastime of concerning themselves with immeasurably distant time-spans whose astronomical remoteness leaves the present untouched. When a fiery explosion or slow death by freezing is predicted for the earth, millions of millions of years hence, it is easy for us to shrug our shoulders and say, "Après nous le déluge". The social sciences are, with good reason, much more time-bound and in a dependent-variable relationship to our age. They should precisely concern themselves with current doings and misdoings, and evaluate present developments in the light of future outcomes. They should, if necessary, criticize or condemn. But this age does not wish to hear itself judged, nor run the risk of condemnation. For this reason society has pulled the reins of positivism and empiricism very taut on the social sciences, giving this fountainhead of dangerous thoughts, this cradle of critical idealism and laboratory for utopian reconstructive experiments, little opportunity for free movement. King Today keeps Crown Prince Tomorrow at the greatest distance possible, with the help of an enslaved science. The age has so intimidated the social sciences that while the latter see the very object of their studies visibly crumbling before their eyes, they still rigidly maintain their impeccable approach of empiricism—even though it is doomed in advance to impotence. There is nothing which they can say or do for the future of a culture whose destiny is so intimately tied to their own.

This is not just an isolated and contrived paradox, without further consequences. The defection of the social sciences and the decline of culture are inextricably linked, and this connection is already visible. As soon as the social sciences turn their back on the future, the future will turn against science and culture and hand them over to the free play of forces beyond their control. It is common today to speak of a "cultural lag", meaning the incapacity of man to "live up to" the developments of human power over nature. Now this cultural lag is no more than a typical time-lag. And the very use of the term "cultural lag" in this sense demonstrates again how the social sciences confine themselves to an interpretation of some given situation in reality as it has developed to date. The term "culture" in this context does not mean anything more than "social heritage" of the past. No association whatsoever with the future and with the vital forces in the dynamics of culture. And thus the social sciences play the repetitious role of a guide on a conducted tour through a museum and no longer function as pioneers and pathfinders exploring the promised land of the future.

Afraid of losing the security of knowledge in the status quo, afraid of new discoveries which might turn all its neat systems upside down, it would rather have time stand still. It wants to preserve and cling to a kind of closed order which the industrial revolution itself made impossible. A neurotic fear of the totally other drives it to a compulsive preoccupation with the myriad tangible facts of the here-and-now, where it can weigh, measure, count and calculate to its heart's content. The social sciences step haltingly from one moment to the next whilst events are madly rushing on. We are told that at the Council of Nicea no votes could be counted because the faces of the bishops kept changing, one into the other. In the same way the face of reality is always changing as it is being studied. Anything is possible. At any moment any irrefutable fact may be completely overthrown. But if we are never finished with the sheer *gathering* of facts, performance will always lag behind pretension and meanwhile the world changes—seldom for the good. Time-bound science is fact-bound science, and nothing more. Its immobilization before the facts of day to day is a going backward in the face of the wild onrushing of history. In its almost stationary and inelastic inertia it reflects the lack of daring foresight and youthful capacity for adaptation which is causing or accelerating the decline of our culture.

Science and culture meet in yet another paradox. He who would at any price save his life, shall lose it; he who would at any price hold on to this age, shall lose it. The more man tries to dig himself into the present, the more completely he is buried by it. The science which developed at the hands of a creative minority with leisure time who knew how to free themselves from the bondage of their own time and move toward the future, has now bestowed leisure time on the masses. The rebound of this action has robbed science of much of its own free time, which is its very life's blood. The Greek word for free time (σχολη) is not only the linguistic root of *school* and *schooling*, but the psychological root of a free and fruitful pursuit of science. Modern science struggles under the heavy pressures and tensions of our time, and scientists themselves are overburdened and over-strained.

Society holds a whip in one hand and a chronometer in the other, and the scientist fumbling at his forced labor must inevitably sacrifice quality to the Moloch of speed. There is no longer any time for writing (or reading) carefully wrought masterpieces which embody a lifetime of thought and study. A lifetime is now much *longer* than ever before, and yet much *shorter*. The essay replaces the major work, and the encyclopedia article, the journal article, the summary and the excerpt of excerpts supersedes the many-volumed book wellfilled with footnotes, appendices, annotations and bibliographies, product of the great system builders.

Scientific work that in earlier times would have been written out with great care, and discussed and re-discussed on the printed page, now remains unwritten, or at best receives a cursory scribbled note. How did the out-standing men of science of another era find the time for their tremendous correspondence with their colleagues, all written by hand, when today's scientist is always desperate for time simply to finish his own assigned work? How was an encyclopedic type of knowledge possible to earlier generations of scientists when we can scarcely keep up with the knowledge in our own narrow specialty? Science was once the Elysium of the free spirit, where new worlds could be created at will, out of space and time. Now it is a ball and chain confining man to the present. This present is so extensive and complex that it requires the total and undivided attention of science, allowing no spare moments for non-contemporary considerations.

There is no eight-hour day, or "English weekend", or undisturbed vacation for the subservient intellect in the scientific society. His exploitation exceeds that of the proletariat in the nineteenth century. Though he often comes in contact, in his work, with the problems of leisure time and culture, he has neither leisure nor culture himself. Subject to permanent pressure, he is driven straight into the arms of the mass media and has his own opinions molded along with those of his less well-trained contemporaries, as the times require. Here too he submits to the yoke. And once he steps outside his own specialty he loses whatever claim he has to distinction and authority and merges into the anonymous majority, falling pray to the mass de-personalization of our society.

This absorption of the creative minority into the masses is not simply a personal problem for time-pressed intellectuals. [1] These sacrifices on the altar of the times will determine the future for all of us. A sufficient measure of freedom and leisure time is a sine qua non for the existence both of creative minority and of a culture as such. We have already indicated over and over again what a crucial role the creative minority plays in time's great game of challenge and response. Its members can produce new ideas, both analytical and constructive, both critical and speculative, contained in powerful images of the future. The combined effect of the factors we have been discussing, subservience, hyper-specialization and over-work, these three modern occupational diseases of the intellect, must inevitably lead to the breakdown of the intellectual nobility and their extradition to the masses. And this massification—that is the crux of the matter—leaves society without the possibility of the development of a new minority able to do creative thinking for the future. A democratization which prunes down and nips in the bud every offshoot of spiritual aristocracy can in the end but destroy itself.

The effect of these same factors on the future of science and knowledge with which this chapter deals, is in principle the same. Current empirical science is on the whole no longer working under the stimulus of an idealistic *image of the future*. It is rather a faithful reflection of the *image of the times*. The two are becoming increasingly identified, so that the pattern of our age is a pattern woven by science. A cross-section of science gives us a cross-section of the times, and moment-ridden man finds his replica in moment-ridden science. This science is mute in all languages concerning the impending future, and has insulated itself against all challenges by the future. It will deign to explain the future only when it has become present, or preferably, past. After all, science has its hands full with today's problems. Why anticipate those of tomorrow? Mañana.

As soon as the watchword of science says "today", then its negative dialectic of degeneration will move implacably towards its appointed end. Science has breached the fortress walls that guarded time "temporarily" within each of the successive ages of the past, and the force of the ensuing flood has prevented damming operations or any restoration of general equilibrium. The tools of science have boomeranged, undermining their own master and former liberator.

Science, in its headlong pursuit of progress, has all unwittingly created an age and generation no longer capable of reaching out beyond itself. If

1. For this reason we do not here mention the "managerial illnesses" such as stomach ulcers, high blood pressure and heart attacks, which have a more private nature of their own.

this were but the movement of a pendulum which could be counted on soon to swing in the other direction, we need not be so concerned. But, as this process accelerates, the pendulum will be wrenched loose from the clock. Unless it can be repaired we face the prospect of society's crumbling into a rubble of broken parts of a highly complicated clock-work, a rubble for which science will be made accountable. Now the future no longer appears as a separate entity, but as a monotonously steady lengthening of the present. And because of this illusion, the present time stands helpless before the noiseless approach of the actual future; before an unexpected End of the Times such as has overtaken other defenceless and undefendable cultures in other ages. We know these other cultures from their ruins, and from the spiritual testament of their once inspiring images of the future, which we in our turn should have passed on to the future.

If science had not sold its soul to the present in order to prosper as it never had before, it could be purposefully taking thought for the future. Such a science might have less thanks, but more utility. Instead, science is indifferent to the future and is nurturing a decadent culture which may well destroy it.

According to science, history teaches us that man has never learned from history. Is it not then high time that science at least attempts to learn its lesson for the future? Or can one in all seriousness raise such a question? Can science free itself from the trap it has fallen into, and burst the chain of rationalizations which keeps it there? Again we are faced with the question of the probability of counter-currents and counter-movements which can lead to brighter prospects than those we now envision. The possibility of a more favorable turn of events can certainly not be ignored, and it would be meaningless to write a book like this if resignation to the inevitable were the only possible attitude to take. If there is any hope—and there is—it is that science itself—because it is science—will come to its senses and assist in bringing about a revolution in the spirit of the times. I say *assist*, because this is something that science alone cannot do. But, on the other hand, if we are to remain realistic, we must not assume too high a probability for such a turning of the tide.

At the moment two counter-currents stand out, among a host of other isolated phenomena. Both of them, however, as yet tend to strengthen the course of development of the negative dialectic, rather than work against it. One, originating outside of science, works against the scienticizing of our time. The other, originating within science, directs itself against a scientifically irresponsible conduct of the affairs of our time.

The first reaction might be called the reversal of *isms*. There is a revolt against the domination of natural-science thought, against mechanism, materialism, logicism and rationalism. The rebellion has spread, sucking up strength from many old roots, until it represents a protest against all theoretical science, and against all operations of the purely rational intellect. Other sources of acquiring a higher or deeper knowledge are put forward: art (Schopenhauer and Nietzsche), history (Dilthey), biology (Darwin, Goethe, Bergson, Spengler, Freud). More emphasis is placed on emotion as opposed to the rational faculties (Romanticism), on will (Schopenhauer, Nietzsche), intuition (Bergson, Husserl), utility (James), and on living and becoming. They are all characterized by a certain type of philosophy of life, and the central figure in this web of life-threads is Nietzsche. This kind of philosophy presents itself by various names, such as vitalism, intuitionism, pragmatism and irrationalism. These various threads have been caught up at present in two main knots. One may be labelled existentialist, opposing both metaphysical philosophy and theoretical science, and in its agnosticism and scepticism delivering man up to the blind forces of the age; the other is downright anti-intellectual.

The growing influence of existentialism on the practice of science implies a further retreat of science into the security of empirical positivism. The converse of this is a retreat from all transcendence, from values, norms, goals and ideals, and thus a retreat from images of the future. The anti-intellectualist current is represented by such thinkers as Ludwig Klages (Der Geist als Widersacher der Seele) and Theodor Lessing (Der Untergang der Erde am Geist). The views concerning the over-intellectualization of western culture held by the philosopher of culture, F. S. Northrop, are not unrelated. These, however, will be discussed in the following chapter. Once again it is clear that extremes are meeting and the result is the threatened destruction of human reason.

These scientifically trained scholars expect nothing but evil from academic science. It is a parasite on true life, a by-product and a cause of the degeneration of a spiritually dying culture. This is the case, not because science has inadequately fulfilled its task (for example, in regard to the future, as I personally suggest), but simply because of the very existence and unlimited development of science as such. This is but a prelude to a more general reaction and a more far-reaching reversal which may take place if the crisis of culture intensifies with the increase of a specialized and rationalistic scientism.

The second counter-current, however positive in its attitude towards science, also threatens to take a negative course. It originated in the circles of idealistic natural scientists animated by a lively sense of social responsibility.

Their eyes have been opened to the tremendous time-lag between the forces their own work has released and the power of the social sciences to overcome the present obvious incapacity for making a constructive use of these forces for the good of mankind. They are trying in a more or less organized fashion to come to an understanding with the social scientists, both requesting an accounting for the current state of social disorganization and demanding systematic planning that will work toward a solution of these problems. From among the scientific humanists have already come several far-reaching suggestions for such a solution.

At the same time the social sciences have been as far as possible disguising themselves as natural sciences, in submission to the "Zeitgeist", and therefore confining themselves to empirical phenomena capable of quantitative treatment—achieving even then but a doubtful recognition from their older sister sciences. Now from these same natural sciences comes the sudden demand that the social sciences become non-natural and set to work in the speculative sphere.

Having achieved freedom from values at the expense of so great an effort, having rejected social ethics, the philosophy of culture, politics and idealism, having narrowed down the scientific consciousness to the very pin-point of empiricism and violently silenced the personality of the researcher, should social science now sacrifice this hard-won scientific maturity to naive and unreal wishful dreaming for the future? Perish the thought! The response of the social sciences to this appeal has been pitifully meagre. Some are inclined to reproach those natural scientists who have achieved preeminence in their own highly specialized fields for presuming to enter the equally highly specialized fields of the social sciences as amateurs. Others say (or think): it is not reasonable for you to expect us to repair the damage which your own work has assisted in bringing about. We can describe and explain this damage, but we cannot remove the causes or counteract the consequences. *We* are guiltless, and we wash our scientific hands of the whole affair. They consider these demands, coming from unscientific qualified observers, to be irresponsible and unscientific, and as further proof that this shunning of responsibility and this escapism from the future into the present is in accord with the only valid standards of pure science. Moreover, they say, do not these natural scientists who grow so emotional when they look at society and culture, strictly apply these rules in their own field? Especially in times like the present the social sciences should abstain from any subjective hopes and utopian images of the future. This is imperative, a scientific must.

Thus we see that while the one counter-current would call a moratorium on all science except that which supported its own point or view, the other only serves to conform the empiricist prejudice of the times. The one demands desperate measures, an impossible setting back of the clock. The other would square the circle it personally helped to inscribe, and its prescriptions fall on deaf ears. Thus the hope of a better future, with the help of science, wavers between the hammer and anvil of these contradictory positions, which seem incompatible and equally aggressive. The future itself will show whether science is able to find an adequate alternative solution to this dilemma and we will then know whether we were justified in retaining great expectations that science would help save our culture.

3. *Humanism*

Before making a closer examination of humanism, a concept which has represented many varied and yet related meanings in the course of the centuries, it is perhaps necessary to explain why this particular cultural component is here given a separate place with precedence over other ethical and spiritual movements and currents.

This does not stem from any preference for humanism as an ethical doctrine. The position has been taken that ethics and value systems have been sufficiently covered in the discussion of the development of religion, philosophy and metaphysics; social ethics will be included in the later treatment of socialism and capitalism.

Furthermore, an ethical representation of the image of man is always implicit (for the most part unconsciously) in the manner in which the social sciences are practised and in the way in which their scientific ethics are developed.

Neither do I mean to express any personal preference for humanism as a spiritual movement of our time, above other current idealistic and spiritual movements. This is certainly not the reason why humanism was chosen above, say, anthroposophy, theosophy, Sufi, Christian Science, spiritualism and all the various movements based on psychic phenomena, and sects stemming from Chinese and Indian approaches to truth.

Nor are we primarily interested here in humanism as a recently independent development. Before the Middle Ages it was an integral part of Christianity itself, but with the disintegration of Christianity it has gradually come to be a typically profane faith without a personal God and without supernatural revelation and absolute redeeming truth, instead basing itself on natural, human and this-worldly capacities. There are other philosophies not based on belief in a personal God which might well deserve equal attention.

As I see it, *all* these diverse religious and philosophical developments with their respective images of the future are ultimately grounded in a metaphysical eschatological consciousness and represent a higher order of escapism into an other, supra-mundane reality which we have already extensively discussed. A special examination of these developments within this frame of reference must therefore be omitted, however interesting and instructive for the sake of comparison a description of these styles of human imaging concerning man himself and the cosmos might be. As far as their future within our modern western culture is concerned, they are all more or less branded with the mark of the "Zeitgeist", that weakened and undermined eschatological consciousness, that crippled ability to envision the future which characterizes our generation. They attempt to survive through conformity, through becoming precisely that which they would not and should not be: realistic, empirical, positivistic and non-mystical. Such an adaptation can scarcely lead to any other fate than that which is befalling a similarly-adapting Christianity.

Humanism is then selected for separate analysis as an almost ideal-typical counterpart of the numerous spiritual movements based on eschatological consciousness in all its gradations, and because it is the direct fruit of the utopian consciousness. Thus humanism as we mean to use it almost defines itself; or rather, the basic unity of the temporally changing contents and forms of this humanism, including its metamorphosis into neo-humanism is indicated. [1]

Humanism as it is used here refers to the idea of human existence as a dynamic becoming-process for man, as a vision of the gradual unfolding of man, through and for mankind, towards a higher type of manhood, an ideal image, which can only be approximated in reality. This idea of the self-elevation of man through self-awareness and self-education, includes both the individual man (and his "Vollending der Persönlichkeit") and his attitude toward his fellow-man in society. It is thus an I-We relationship, as compared with the I-Thou relationship of a personalistic religious faith. This is the dual ideal of man as a member of humanity, and, to put it the other way round, of humanity in man. It is the ideal of the *humanly* unique personality and worthy man. The idea that man can transcend himself and elevate himself to a higher level of human existence and co-existence, by

1. There are endless definitions and innumerable interpretations of humanism, since the term encompasses many differentiated ideas. Arthur Liebert, in *Der Universale Humanismus*, Zürich, 1946, offers in place of the three unfree, traditional-dogmatic forms of humanism (theological, natural-science or historically determined) four differing free forms: scientific, religious, artistic and ethical humanism. Then there are the diverging views of thinkers such as Maritain (*Humanisme Integral*, Paris, 1936, *Vers un nouvel Humanisme*, Inst. de Coop. Intell., 1937, and *Pour un nouvel Humanisme*, Renc. Intern. de Genève, 1949), humanistic personalism as in Denis de Rougement, or the humanity concept as in Thomas Mann (*Der Adel des Geistes*, Sechzehn Versuche zum Problem der Humanität, Stockholm, 1943).

conquering the self and rising beyond it, implies the idea of human dignity, of the acceptance of the challenge to strive, individually and collectively, toward a free and responsible self-determination. This humanistic image of the future supplements (or counters) the invocation of superhuman power (indirect influence-optimism) with the invocation of human power (direct influence-optimism) as the main highway to the goal of human existence. This highway has *not* been completely barricaded by the guilt and impotence deriving from "original sin", but only temporarily blocked by obscurantism and primitive techniques.

This core-idea, developed with many different nuances and accents, has ridden all the ups and downs of the history of western culture. It is present in the Socratic-Platonic-Stoic ideas of "know thyself", of eros, agape and paideia. After having passed through Hellenic and oriental philosophic systems, it turns up again in the duality-in-unity of romanitas and humanitas. Next it takes on the form of the Christian humanitarian ideal of charity and mercy. In the Middle Ages it lies behind the ideals of knighthood and womanhood. In the twelfth century it suddenly mutates in the new gospel of Joachim van Fiore. It is found in Cusanus, the transition figure between the Middle Ages and Modern Times, in his image of man as a microcosmos and a microtheos. It is found in Florentine humanism and in the Renaissance, as Pico's image of the uomo universale and dignitas hominis. It is found in Erasmus as biblical humanism. In the eighteenth century it is philosophically and ethically based in the idea of humanity as developed by idealistic thinkers ranging from Kant to Herder, Lessing and Wilhelm von Humboldt.

Again and again we find as a constant element in this core-idea the concept of a rediscovery of man, resulting in his spiritual elevation through renewal. The note of a *new man* in a new world, of the realization of another and better reality in earthly life itself, sounds constantly. This is what now binds humanism and Christianity together and then again drives them apart (if there is disillusionment about the humanity of Christendom). This latter process began as soon as the humanistic scholar, the lover of the classics and the arts, separated himself off from the theologian and the clerical. It was the element of renewal, related to that of rebirth, through which humanism could fulfil its role of champion of critical and social idealism. When the Renaissance break-through into Modern Times took place, it was this same upwards-striving humanism which came in direct conflict with conservative realism of the earlier age.

This humanistic concept of a revolutionary renewal of existing reality towards a more humanly worthy society, to be accomplished by man himself, is the very essence of the utopism which came into its own at this time.

We have traced this development from the Catholic humanist More to the Anglican dignitary Swift, that philosophic misanthrope who almost over-stretched the utopia into the anti-utopia. We have seen humanism reach its highpoint in the ethical idealism of Kant, in his ideas on the "Würde des Menschen", attainable in the human *becoming* through moral effort. At the same time that this ideal of humanity continued to dominate the eighteenth and nineteenth centuries, even exercising a strong influence on theology, and that its general acceptance as an image of the future was spreading out-wardly, its inner force began to diminish. For its character of a *task*, demand-ing human effort, faded away as the idea gained ground that history of itself moves toward higher levels. Liberalism, social Darwinism, Marxism, evo-lutionary optimism and historical determinism all contributed to the undermining of human power, fostering instead passivity and quietism.

This prepared the way, even before the disillusionment of two—or two and a half—world wars in the twentieth century, for a basic change in attitudes. The ideal that had once been considered almost too easily attain-able had now become utterly unattainable, and thus unreal. Nevertheless, the idealistic human striving, even while it was being increasingly under-mined, remained for some time the basis of the concept of western *culture*. This was considered to encompass every means by which man could raise himself spiritually and ethically to a higher sphere, including religion and ethics, art, belles lettres, philosophy and pure science. In contrast, *civilization* represented all lower-order striving for its own sake, including all meeting of material needs, technology, applied science, and so on. As ever against the dominant human ideal, Stirner's extreme reaction *(Der Einzige und sein Eigentum)* and his plea for the purely egocentric man appeared as little more than an isolated eccentricity. Nietzsche, however, brought about a definitive breach in the humanistic tie between the image of man and concept of culture. With the destruction of the prevailing Christian-humanist values and the gradual transformation of the somewhat bourgeois ideal man into the aristocratic Super-man (Uebermensch), the iconoclasm against the image of the future of man and humanity broke loose.

We find off-shoots of the Super-man in Spengler's heroic-Faustian man, and later on in the ennobled-Germanic man of blood and soil; in a certain sense we find them in the instinctive-vitalistic Freudian man, and finally, we find these offs-hoots in the anti-idealistic and anti-humanistic anthropo-logy of modern existentialism. The penetrating influence of Nietzsche has reached in to the very heart of humanism in all its twentieth-century forms. This is particularly true of that philosophy which bears the name of human-ism, a system built up chiefly by the Anglo-American Schiller and by Dewey. This humanism is not only antagonistic to all theistic and super-natural ideas, but opposes all philosophic dualism and idealism. It recognizes, in naturalistic and positivistic fashion, only this one, given, existing and experienceable reality. It has a pronounced natural-science tone, its methods are empirical and its concept of truth is pragmatic and utilitarian. It is permeated with common sense, cash value and the pursuit of happiness in concrete and practical ways. Its social ethics (closely related to the Social Gospel movement) inclines predominantly toward eudaemonism. In short, as monistic realism it becomes sheer *hominism,* and by an ironic twist of concepts such as the whimsy of history frequently permits, forms the precise anti-pole of classical *humanism.*

Is not present-day humanism, by comparison, a new *counter-movement?* Humanism has reconstituted itself on a national and an international level, and inscribed universal human values on its banner. Once more the dignity and worth of the human personality takes a central place along with individual and social self-realization, the freedom of thought and belief both inside and outside the Christian framework, and the communication with all the great thinkers of the past. In short, this is again the ideal norm of humanity or the dignity of man which should be constantly pursued and towards which end society should be transformed. The *old* image of the future seems to be restored in all its glory; but what of its inward, spiritually renewing power? To what extent is this rehabilitation also a regeneration?

This modern humanism is inspired by the great minds of the past. That is as it should be. But in order to live as a creative force for the future it must bring forth its own fruitfully idealistic and foreward-thinking minds. It must do more than stand up against the prevailing existentialism and philosophic nihilism; it must be able to rise above today's philosophic levels and convincingly stem the flood-tide of de-dualizing and de-futurizing. The tragedy of the present situation as I see it is that the more the humanist movement grows in numerical strength, the more danger there is of a decline in spiritual strength.

For numbers require organization and a "party-machine". Importance in numbers also implies a continuous struggle for official recognition of the movements "existence" as a "denomination". And all this forces it irresistibly to the place of actuality, social work, government subsidies, etc. In short, in trying to obtain a standing equivalent to that of the official churches, it is running the risk of a devaluation similar to that which the churches have suffered, namely of becoming institutionalized, conformist, materialistic and opportunistic. It is inclined towards, or feels itself compelled to seek the spiritual support of atheistic existentialism, and also seeks to relate itself politically to progressive socialism. These tendencies narrow its basis and so limit its field and scope in advance.

Historically, humanism in its noblest expressions knew scarcely any organizational ties other than those of the Florentine Academy or the international contacts between outstanding humanist scholars and artists. It spread over Europe and from there to the rest of the world, growing into an invisible community of believers through the power of its spirit, establishing a spiritual aristocracy. Here the old problem of the élite versus the masses with reference to culture-dynamics presses forward again. Must not this humanistic-idealistic organization submit to the "Zeitgeist" in spite of itself, and take on the form and face of the times? Are not "movement" and "direction" subordinated to administrative mechanism? Is there not danger that its national and international organization will cause it to degenerate into a self-contradictory *moment-ridden humanism?* It is self-contradictory, for the author is convinced that *true* humanism will have to be future-*oriented* and future-*determining*, if it is to be at all.

The more success such a programmatic organization gains, the more it risks losing, for like a victorious invading tribe it is in danger of being assimilated by the vanquished. A humanism which has immersed itself in problems of practical policy easily falls victim to a bourgeois Weltanschauung and may end up as an unrecognizably distorted monster with its jaw clamped firmly on its own tail. It is subject to the same disintegrating effects of time which have caused Christianity to crumble into secularism. In the end, does it make any difference whether our Christian-humanistic culture finally collapses under a Christian or a humanistic label? Modern humanism is running around and around in a self-sufficient, anti-utopian and seemingly everlasting present. The dying-off of the utopian consciousness means the destruction of the spiritual foundation upon which any true humanism, as an image of the future for man and humanity, must be built. Does humanism defend itself with all its might against a pessimistic view of man, or does this modern pessimism penetrate its present representatives? What is the position of the humanist movement with reference to the revival of rejected and abandoned expectations of approximating an ideal human society on earth? What *is* the humanistic image of the future, how does it operate, and what is the road to it? Does it combine with other specialized movements, such as international socialisms or world federalism? Is it in process of building its own international organization, according to the temper of the times? Or does it choose a more spiritual path, and put its faith in the power of the idea?

If modern humanism *has* such an image of the future, which means it consciously opposes the spirit of the times, then it *has* and *will bring* a future. At the moment it arouses such visions on a very modest scale indeed, and to an inadequate extent. Instead, several of its leaders explicitly reject the historical form of humanism in respect to its optimism and proclaim the need for a realistic humanism. They feel that this changes nothing essential in humanism. In my opinion, however, the very heart is taken out of humanism, inasmuch as its ideal goal comes to be considered as a mere matter of historical form. The emergence of a new forward-looking spirit, rising high above the dead level of our own time and placing its stamp on the new era which has already dawned, is something which can only be hoped for; we cannot, alas, now foresee it.

Pregnant with coming evil as our time is, it can no longer be characterized as a time of optimistic expectations for the future, and least of all with reference to man and the use of human power. Man's awareness and confident image of himself has been threatened to the very core. The classical humanist was a prophet of salvation. Will the modern humanist, whether Christian or non-Christian, be able to follow in these footsteps? We can only quote the words of Thomas More: optarim verius quam sperarim; this is something to be wished for rather than expected.

Possibly also Thomas More would have expressed himself even more cautiously if he had lived and written in our time. For it is in this period from 1500 to almost 2000 that those basic cultural changes have taken place which have made the difficult task of humanism so infinitely more difficult. Five centuries ago humanistic thought was still embedded in a spiritual current that flowed from a symbiosis of medieval and Hellenistic thought. This was before the time of the astounding meteoric rise of the natural sciences and the fantastic accumulation of technological discoveries, before the industrial revolution, the rise of the proletariat and the gradual cutting in half of the length of the average working day. It was also before the periods of Revolution and Rationalism and of Enlightenment and Progress. Humanistic thought was at that time still rooted in or intimately related, in its principles, to Christian thought, forming the base for a duality-in-unity of a Christian-humanistic culture. This was, in short, before the literal mechanization of the world-image, and before the partly figurative mechanization of culture and of the image of man and society.

While the sixteenth-century and twentieth-century humanistic ideal may still be in essence the same, the carrier and agent of this ideal, man, is no longer the same; he has been revolutionized into—or has evolved toward—a new type, one which according to pessimistic observers represents a dehumanized, anti-humanistic type of man. It is not necessary to review here the argument upon which this view rests. We have already said a great deal about the changes which have taken place in these last five centuries in human thought and behaviour and, not least, in man's attitude towards the future.

It is true that a spiritual process of destruction is going on alongside of the development of military techniques of physical destruction on a scale previously unknown to man? Or is it true that with the construction of machines which are taking over more and more human tasks (not only muscular tasks, but increasingly complex mental work) and thus becoming man-machines, that man in his turn is increasingly conforming to mechanical modes of living and becoming a machine-man? Is technocracy, which now dominates leisure time as well as working hours, one of the chief factors in the current spiritual debacle which characterizes the crisis of modern culture? In our view this approach has some truth in it but does not penetrate to the heart of the matter, to what the Ancients called the *nervus rerum*. This can only be reached by analyzing the underlying connection with the reversal which has overtaken the formerly accepted humanitarian images of the future of our generation, and has painfully constricted the very idea of humanity as such; both of these phenomena stem from the same subterranean source.

The deterioration of the Christian-eschatological image of the future, based on faith in a superhuman power, is a process which has actually been taking place for two thousand years. But in the second half of the last five hundred years the process has increased in tempo and intensity. The results were not felt immediately, because there were all kinds of positive images of the future, based on faith in human power, to replace them and pervade the Zeitgeist. Humanism ranked with these new images, as a declaration of independence from Christianity and a proclamation that man could determine his own destiny and undertake his own moral elevation. There were many others, some mutually complementary, some irreconcilably antagonistic toward each other; there was the faith in man's capacity to control natural forces and improve his natural environment, faith in enlightened government and education, in rationalism, liberalism, Marxism, social Darwinism, planned socialism, and in the optimistic doctrine of predestined and inevitable progress, evolved in the "American Creed". All these images of the future contained expectations of the achievement of some kind of optimal social order by and for man, and some kind of optimal development of the worth and dignity of the individual. There was a social-utopian element in all of them.

At this point a pincer movement begins, as we have indicated earlier. Next to the de-eschatologizing process, which has been a long-drawn-out movement, the de-utopianizing process is now set into stormy motion, so that both processes will meet toward the end and close the circle, cutting off the culture's life-space. Only then does it become evident that man has lost all images of the future and almost literally put his head in the noose. The philosophic theme shifts from optimistic faith in man to suicide. Courage and spiritual readiness are seen in retrospect as a foolhardy trigger-happiness. The urges to do looks overdone. The tremendous upsurge of

Faustian energy is now seen as a pact with diabolic powers, and the mastery of nature is unmasked as slavery. The rational approach to life turns into irrationalism, and an overreaching progress-optimism subsides into a somber pessimism of decline.

The religious faith in an ultimate state of glory for man, to be brought about by a higher power, had been progressively replaced by the faith in humanly wrought progress. When the last fragments of this new faith were shattered against the stone wall of present reality, the tyrant Present took the reins into his own hands and cut man adrift from the grip of his historic past as well as from the call of his beckoning future; suddenly man found himself alone and abandoned, standing before the gaping void of a lost faith, supported neither by divine or human power . . . supported by nothing. He tore down his "rock of ages" himself, stone by stone. He not only failed in his attempt to build another and better world with his own hands, but lived to see his world turn into a diabolic opposite of what he intended. Then he was indeed naked and defenceless before the raging elements which he himself had evoked and could no longer master. As long as there was an unshakeable faith in an eschatological end of time, all temporal suffering could be endured and other positive images of the future could be dispensed with. As long as the utopian idea of a better society here on earth was a living and glowing hope, the transition from Christian to humanistic images of the future could take place almost unnoticed. Only when both kinds of positive images began to deteriorate was there any awareness of crisis. With the loss of faith in his own capacities, man also realized that there was no longer any faith in God to fall back upon as a last resort. Man is caught in a trap of his own making.

Man's undeniable failure to control his own destiny provoked a greater feeling of impotence and depression than helpless submission to a superior power had ever done. For the distress which man brings on himself is much harder to bear than the blows of an impersonal fate of those wrought by God's will. The idea of remote supernatural force acting upon man in arbitrary and incalculable ways can make an essentially intolerable situation more tolerable, simply because it cannot be altered. Human impotence is under such circumstances regrettable, but must be accepted as heroically as possible. But once man has taken power into his own hands, his spiritual situation is profoundly altered by the transfer. If he is then forced to admit his impotence anew, then there is nothing for it but to recognize that he has himself called forth the evil power of the time, which now frustrate all his good intentions. He alone is responsible for replacing the formerly remote alien powers from a higher sphere with other, earthly—but equally cata-strophic and adamant—powers. The devil from without suddenly becomes the devil within. We ourselves are our fate.

Thus a new feeling of guilt is added to the increasing feeling of impotence, and further undermines man's self-confidence. The murderer of humanity has been unmasked, and to everyone's horror it proves to be man himself; man, who had previously been conceived as a being filled with divine love and compassion for human-kind. Now modern man knows that he has no one to blame but himself for the catastrophe he faces, and that his impotence stems from his own immoderate lust for power. In his dehumanized mass form, man is the product of his own technology. The age of anxiety is his own creation. His own arrogant pride tripped him into his present fall, and he is a helpless spectator at the scene of his own débacle.

It is this frustrated, disillusioned, guilt-ridden, self-doubting and fearful man that present-day humanism must deal with. And not only that! It must not only counteract the forces of the times that work toward the increasing deterioration of the human spirit. It must also take stock of the other forces and counter-forces which seek deliverance for society in one direction or another but nearly all lead into a vicious cycle or a dead-end. Fear, ever a bad counsellor, is driving man along the wrong path. It is part of the tragedy of our time that solutions are sought which only serve to aggravate the crisis of culture; one of the causes for these errors is a lack of clear insight or a wrong diagnosis of our ills. This is particularly true of those solutions, however divergent, which seem so appealing because they again relieve man of his long-awaited and hard-won power to determine his own destiny, and absolve him of a responsibility he has found too heavy to bear.

It makes little difference in this respect whether the solutions point back to the security of the closed society of the Middle Ages, a theocracy whose earthly embodiment is an ecclesiastical hierarchy in which every individual has his assigned and unchangeable place with no freedom or individual thought or action, or whether they resort to an autocratically-led mass movement in which individual freedom is delivered up to a despotic, machine-implemented rule of terror. Neither the reactionary nor the revolutionary solution can be reconciled with the fullest development of humanistic values.

The neo-liberal version of "laissez-faire", in which the self-interest of every individual becomes the tool for the implementation of the general welfare, cannot be relied upon in the present situation either. If history has taught nothing else, it has taught us that freedom for some exists only at the price of lack of freedom for others, and that the automatic harmonizing of individual self-interest and the general welfare is a pathetic illusion. This approach too represents an attempt by man to escape from the responsibility of purposefully working out his own destiny. The same applies to the various movements of eastern fatalism and passive mysticism, which all tend toward determinism and occult-astrological determinations of the future and exclude in principle the possibility of free will and goal-directed human activity. Western philosophies in the vein of Nietzsche and Spengler, in which fatalism and mysticism result in boundless influence-pessimism and nihilism, tend in the same direction. The culmination of all these pseudo-solutions to the crisis of our time is found in existentialism, which reflects and also sanctions prevailing scepticism, realism and actualism as the only justifiable attitudes for man to take toward this time and the future.

It is on this battlefield of arrayed forces that humanism finds itself. It is caught between two driving forces: the progressive social changes which are working towards the shaping of a new type of man, for whom everything now human seems strange, and the powerful strategies that reject the human dignity of a responsible determination of personal destiny and strip the individual of his last shred of independent initiative. Humanism was the long-time defender of the conscious application of human power and therefore sometimes collided with those who put their trust in supernatural power only. But now it finds itself caught in a trap unwittingly forged by human power, and held there by forces, which may destroy both the essential values and expectations for the future of humanity which it championed and cherished. So powerful is the attack of these forces that even humanism itself cannot quite avoid unconsciously absorbing and assimilating this new spirit of the times. Of course modern humanism cannot stand apart from the times, and it is essential that it have a firm grasp of reality insofar as current world events are concerned; but it must also be able to stand above this reality; it must be able to outlast it. Connections between humanism and communism, or between humanism and existentialism, however mutually contradictory these systems of thought may be, are no longer anything out of the ordinary. But this kind of undermining of the image of the future through an undermining of the image of man is unquestionably fatal for humanism.

Nevertheless, if there is still a chance for the regeneration of our culture —a possibility in which I still believe—then humanism, with its neo-classical image of man as an image of the future, will certainly play an important role. This critical review of its present plight—brought on by its own organizational revival—must be considered in the light of the intentions of the writer (as must similar reviews of other areas of culture). Our goal is to achieve an impartial analysis of current developments unhindered by self-deception, and to make a constructive contribution to the history of the future.

CHAPTER XXII

A MODERN DEPTH-PSYCHOLOGY:
LEVER OR BARRIER TO RELIGION AND
CULTURAL REBIRTH?

One field of our modern science of culture can no longer be ignored in the broader context of this book. I mean the branch of psychology and more specifically the psycho-analytical trend, which has developed since Freud. The latter claims the ability to revive religion and culture on the basis of its new insights. The assumption is that its new scientific knowledge of diagnosis and therapy, which extends beyond the individual to the collective processes of mental and spiritual illness in our time, has released an almost magical potential for the application of antidote and cure for religious and cultural decline. It would provide the means for overcoming the crisis initiated by the uprooting and subsequent decay of western culture.

These trends offer a new perspective and point to a technique for regeneration; therefore they are attracting increasing attention, albeit within a limited circle of the intelligentsia. They are moreover attractive in that they are grounded in a fusion of western values with eastern elements. I refer here to a development first represented in the groundwork laid by C. G. Jung and his Swiss circle, and then carried further through the publications of one of his influential but independent students, Erich Neumann, now in Israel.

Both Jung and Neumann attempt a renewing synthesis between all religion, including even the oldest religion, and science in its most modern form. Through specific psychological developments science could construct universally valid categories which will cover all religious experience from the time of the cave man until the present. By means of this capacity to penetrate through to the most fundamentally human drives, the archetypal forces of the soul, it can remove the obstacles of deterioration and petrifaction which are blocking man's way at present. It can re-open the road for progress, it can once more tap the sources of human civilization, releasing the flow of their healing and life-giving waters.

If this far-reaching claim has hardly been mentioned so far, it is because, in the author's opinion, the claim must be denied, or can at any rate not be accepted as long as its rationale and application and argumentation rest on a basic philosophy which keeps it from reaching its avowed goal, or even leads it astray. For this underlying philosophy contains a destructive potential.

Having thus already anticipated my final conclusion on a matter which will shortly be examined more closely, I will also state my main objection. It would seem to me that *this* kind of depth-psychology completely fails to lead out of our time; on the contrary it is deeply immersed in our time and heightens to a considerable degree its precariousness. In the view presented here it increases the pressure at the breaking point of our culture and widens the breach that already exists, thus hastening an explosive breakthrough of the latent crisis. In other words, my quarrel with this psychology is essentially that it claims to have discovered scientific laws and relationships of an absolute nature, objective criteria which will apply to all religious phenomena at all times, and consequently valid principles for cultural therapy. These pretensions can and should be uncovered as a typical fabric of our time, woven to the pattern of the present, and therefore of relative historical value only. Possibly even of negative value, in terms of its genetic origins and basic premises, or in terms of its own systematic construction and inner consistency. This analytical psychology must itself be analysed, its own unconscious nature and drives exposed and the paradoxical fact demonstrated that it suffers from the very disease it would cure. More, that far from bringing a cure for our time, it could well aggravate the present serious condition with its high-brow patent medicine. This psychology is full of undeniable good intentions but also full of self-delusion. The main source of its delusion is that concepts which apply to the limited life of individuals are transferred to the nearly unlimited field of collectivities and their unfolding sequences. [1] Psycho-analytic methods which are valuable for individual therapy are stretched and strained to apply to a wide range of metaphysical and sociological material. All cultures and their different styles are interpreted in the same terms and these terms are typical of the modern mind. Uniform trends are discovered everywhere and uncritically extrapolated. Every and any culture is thus made to develop or alternate mechanically or according to identical causal principles and fixed laws. In consequence of this approach, psychological diagnosis of a retrospective character is confused with cultural prognosis and guidance. Only one direction for the future development of mankind is considered possible— and *therefore* desirable.

We cannot, of course, give an exhaustive treatment of these cultural-therapeutic conceptions of Jung and Neumann here. Our considerations will be confined to those aspects which bear on our central problem of the

---

1. For an excellent discussion of this, see **Louis** Schneider's *The Freudian Psychology and Veblen's Social Theory*, N.Y., 1948.

future, and we will examine the thought-model they propose for deciphering this future. All other aspects, however important and interesting from the point of view of depth-psychology itself, will be disregarded.

1. Notes on the Religious Ideas of Jung

Jung's renewing ideas have been incorporated in an extensive body of important works covering a wide yet well-integrated field. [1] He has evolved his own special terminology for the expression of these ideas. A summary of this almost unparalleled wealth is a perilous but indispensable undertaking. [2]

A. Extract

1. Over against the orthodox view that God really exists "in and for Himself" as an independent entity, Jung offers a heterodox view that might be formulated as follows: in the course of time the divine was evoked in different forms and shapes by man's inner being; it is a function of the human soul, more specifically of the unconscious which encompasses the individual and the collective (racial or inherited) unconscious. God's existence is not absolute and transcendent, completely apart from the human being and psyche. He does not exist beyond man's existence in space and time, independent of the historical unfolding of humanity. He is not an extra-human and super-human metaphysical Being, but man's psychical emanation and epiphany.

2. The divine receives its shape and becomes manifest through human psychic projection of mythical, symbolic and ritual images and figures which do not in themselves have reality but which flow from real experiences, aspirations and ideas. The divine factor is creatively at work deep in the unconscious (of the individual and the collectivity), appearing in successive historic-heroic renewals and transformations of its ever-changing image-projections. But is is rooted in an unchanging foundation of archetypal

1. Works by Jung of special importance in this connection are: *Answer to Job*, London, 1954; *Essays on a Science of Mythology* (with Kerenyi), New York, 1949; *The Integration of the Personality*, New York, 1939; *Modern Man in Search of a Soul*, New York, 1934; *Psychology and Religion*, New Haven, 1938; *Psychological Types*, New York, 1923; *Psychology of the Unconscious*, New York, 1949; *The Secret of the Golden Flower*, 1932. Pantheon Books, New York, has put out an edition of his collected works in English.
2. Such a task has been successfully achieved in the very relevant area of the psychological-religious concepts of Jung, by an authoritative thinker of our times in this field—Martin Buber. I have also made grateful use of this summary. Although Jung himself sharply disputes Buber's interpretation, I find myself in full agreement with its main points. See Buber's *Gottesfinsternis*, op. cit. p. 94-115, and 157-162 (Anhang: Replik auf eine Entgegnung G. C. Jungs).

patterns and trends which surge up out of the unconscious, molding and changing the conscious mind which, in its turn, again modifies the unconscious.

3. It is out of this continuous mental process of interaction and self-realization that modern consciousness grows. Nurtured by the unconscious, it is yet a process of liberation from the unconscious and its darkly threatening powers over the weaker "I". For modern consciousness, God or the idea of the divine is only thinkable as something pre-eminently human, as a factor or function at work in the human soul; it becomes, in short, a purely psychic and therefore merely immanent quantity, or quality. Man, in seeking the divine and finding it, encounters himself; as an "I" he contacts and finally becomes merged or identified with his own higher and deeper self. It is at this point that a would-be empirical science expands into metaphysics and mysticism, even in its terminology.

4. However, Jung has chosen a brand of mysticism all his own, and it is preponderantly an anthology of eastern gnosis, ancient Indic variants of mysticism and medieval alchemy. According to Jung's personal psychological image-projections, for which he claims universal validity on scientific grounds, this human Self is the spiritual replica, the natural twin of the image of God. The human and the divine are indentical. The Self of the human soul is the locus of the divine. Separately and together they form an all-encompassing totality. It follows that depth-psychology too has an all-inclusive, scientific and philosophical validity. All-inclusive in this all-encompassing Weltanschauung, is intended to mean: reconciliation on a higher level of bipolar constellations and diametrical opposites into a harmonious union. This does not only mean the unity of God and man, but in this unity each part again contains its thesis and its antithesis in perfect synthesis. Each (both God and man) encompasses its positive and negative, good and evil, light and darkness, salvation and damnation, its masculine and feminine (animus and anima), its superior and inferior, and so on.

5. In this view, then, God, or the divine, always and intrinsically contains this counterpart. Therefore God is not only good but evil too. The old projection which man has clung to for centuries of an almighty, all-wise and beneficent godhead, holy and perfect, is withdrawn as the human psyche develops toward a higher and deeper consciousness of the Self. It is withdrawn from a supra-mundane outer world and is transplanted to the earthly, inner world of the human Self. It has been provided with the fundamental attributes of divine ambivalence or dichotomy. Henceforth good and evil must also co-exist in the human spirit on equal terms. For according to Jung they are but the two sides of one and the same thing, together representing in man the contrasting aspects of what may be called the divine.

They are joined in "hieros gamos", in holy wedlock, in a sacramentally indissoluble, alchemistical blend of the human-divine antipodes of positive and negative into a "Ganzheit" of which the human psyche is the retort.

6. This inexorably implies the exit of the traditional religious belief in a supernatural Being who represents an image of immeasurable perfection and holiness. As Jung says, "The modern consciousness abhors faith and therefore all religions based on faith". This outmoded faith in God's perfect holiness and holy perfection, bound to an unconscious projection, is now giving way before the process of man's increasing Self-consciousness. The illumination which depth-psychology provides not only fosters this process, but confirms the outcome and rediscovers the truth of ancient gnostic wisdom. In his Self man now finds again the undivided dualistic union of a divine power which is also satanic, and which joins the holy to the unholy. Conscience (the voice of the divine good) is in this profounder view replaced by the soul (the operational center of good-evil). The trinity finds completion in a quaternity, in which the devil is included as an independent force; and "der Geist der stets verneint" is recognized as that basic divine-human element which necessarily negates every positive.

7. In a more recent work, *Aion*, Jung pursues the logical consequences of this line of thought with reference to evangelical Christianity. Christ himself has no other meaning than as a symbol of the Self. The Gospels can then by no means be grounded in a transcendent revelation of the work of God, nor can Jesus be considered as the Son of God. Jesus Christ as a projection of the unconscious also possesses, according to Jung, the divine-human double nature of a totality "welche sogar die animalische Seite des Menschen in sich begreift".[1] This Christ no longer stands in mythical contrast to man, high above his I and his Self, but is realistically imprisoned in this factually experienced, closed world. He has been forced back into the psyche of the human individual, and has become one with that "qualvolle Suspension des Ichs zwischen unvereinbaren Gegensätzen"[2] which reigns deep within it. This psychological approach necessitates the dismantling of all symbols and thus a complete de-mythologizing of the New Testament. Here modern psychology and modern theology meet. But the former in its total consciousness cannot leave the gospel-message of salvation intact. The Christian kerugma is one more projection which must be withdrawn, along with all other images of salvation and fulfilment.

8. This modern withdrawal of antiquated, one-sided idealistic projections must be considered, according to Jung, as a meaningful spiritual enrichment, and as spiritual progress. It is the end-product of a laborious maturation of

1. *Op. cit.* p. 69.
2. *Ibidem*, p. 74.

consciousness and self-liberation of mankind achieved at the expense of the unconscious and thus also at the cost of the oppressive forces which had a stranglehold on the human psyche in its more primitive stages. Having achieved this literal self-consciousness, man recognizes these forces as the incarnate struggle in his own Self of the divine totality, which encompasses the Christ and the Anti-Christ, the light and dark. This implies the modern image of God or the divine, for these coincide in that they both *preclude* an ideal image, either of man or of God. At the same time both reflect a god-man, and a man-god, who meet in the Self. The eternal conflict between the Janus-headed pairs of opposites and the unending struggle between the human and the divine have thus been fathomed, illuminated and definitely settled.

9. This progressive self-redeeming expansion of consciousness is realized through the modern thinking individual, and can be termed his existential "individuation". The gnostic double-being which crystallizes out of this process is in Jung's view the herald of the god-man or man-god to come. This being will be deliberately half-hearted and half-blooded, a hermaphrodite, a fully conscious unity of angel and devil, intellectual man and instinctive beast, doer of good and doer of evil, saint and sinner in one. In this way the great reconciliation between man and God, man and cosmos, and man and world is achieved in this exclusively given, actual reality. Suffering and evil will always remain in this world, but man, who consciously absorbs this inescapable situation into his Self and achieves a meaningful assimilation, will no longer regard it as the manifestation of an oppressive and tormenting higher power. He will be able to free himself from his torturing fears of dark, inscrutable, evil forces, which cruelly and fatally overpower him. His discovery has enabled him to bring these forces within the compass of his higher consciousness and thus to master them. He now accepts them freely as the divine-human, inalienable essence of earthly existence.

B. Critique

There is no doubt that a new conceptual apparatus of great value has been developed. This is most clearly evident in the new method of analysis of the psychology of religion and of the history of religion. I will not venture to estimate how successful it may be in the clearing away of rigid ritualism, sterile symbolism and meaningless religious compulsions. Let us for the sake of the argument accept the possibility of the dethronement of reigning archetypes of the unconscious through their conscious unmasking, and the possibility of a purification and liberation of the spirit through the progressive removal of unconscious restraints and resistances as man grows in self-awareness. Let us further recognize that from the point of view of individual psychology, these diagnostic insights may form the basis for a successful therapy.

We are primarily concerned here, however, with the more far-reaching claim to powers of cultural therapy, especially with reference to religious reconstruction and renaissance. I agree with Buber, although partly on other grounds, that such expectations are unjustified. The technique developed by this psychology contains a destructive rather than constructive spiritual tendency. Since Neumann carries both the arguments and the claims still further more clearly demonstrating their untenability, I will confine myself to a few remarks at this point.

1. The gnostic-mystical incorporation of blasphemy and humanly degrading evil, of fatal negation and the dark demonic into the image of God and man has far-reaching and almost incalculable consequences. To the end that man may be liberated from unconscious projections of excessive, anxiety-arousing constellations which are caused by ignorance and a lack of self-knowledge, the forces of evil are wrested loose from the ungraspable firmament and fixed forever in the center of the human Self. Paradoxically, at this point a striking kinship with another spiritual current of our time appears. We refer to existentialism. This, however, takes the reverse approach of making anxiety and dread the lasting essence of human existence (See Chapter XXI, 1 A and B).

Gnosticism, in the modern dress which Jung gives it, contains as little perspective on a totally other and better world as existentialism. This possibility is denied in principle. The wholly Other, and anything wholly other, are anchored fast in the divine-human ambivalence of the Self, along with unconquerable evil and inescapable disaster. This God who contains in himself, and in his human reflection, an inherent hellishness, is incompatible with an eschatological projection of a glorious fulfilment for this world. And this man who contains within himself both divine and satanic potential, and in whom good and evil are amorally reconciled, stands in implacable opposition and unresolvable contrast to the utopian images of an ideal human society on earth, and to any idea of attempting to approach the good society.

2. On the individual level, a mere elucidation of the concrete situation and of the conflicting workings in the force-field of the personal unconscious may have a therapeutic effect, transforming crisis into catharsis. But does this almost automatic healing mechanism also function on the social and cultural-psychological level? Is not such a transplanting in direct contradiction with the expressly stated principle (correct, in my view) of individuation, which means that the modern consciousness can only be attained through a long and laborious struggle for self-liberation on the part of the individual mind? Is there any realistic possibility that this modern conscious-

ness could spread to any extent from creative individuals to the reigning masses? The coming into full awareness which Jung describes demands hyper-intellectual gifts, united with a special mystical predisposition. How is it possible to anticipate a generalized conscious acceptance of the tragic and demonic in man and in God, or to transform this doctrine into a strong public opinion, if this understanding can only be reached along a road which climbs to the highest peaks of human thought and descends to the deepest layers of the psyche? Finally, how can this new understanding be arrived at with absolute certainty? For how is it possible for an *empirical* method of psychological analysis to make definite pronouncements concerning the exclusive *validity* of this particular mystical projection of a gnostic type, or, which amounts to the same thing, concerning the non-validity or part-validity of all *other* metaphysical projections and images? When and how can a genetic psychological interpretation ever prove that certain images are real and others not? This would mean that it has come nearer to the transcendental "Ding an sich" than Kant, finally succeeding in distinguishing indisputably between the real and the unreal.

3. Not only is the prescribed process of attaining consciousness only accessible to a small creative minority or élite. But there is more to make one doubtful of its advantages, which even for this group are not guaranteed. The very attempt to popularize this process can easily lead to completely adverse results through a misunderstanding of the concepts involved. For the new-old, double-natured God, who embodies evil and disaster to the very highest degree, this God-Satan, as a "deus absconditus" indeed, now has his abode in the bosom of every man. And so every man is always at the same time good and evil, is both positively and negatively charged. What does this mean for the average mortal whose eyes are opened to this evil necessity and unalterable condition? Does not this leave him to gaze dizzily into a bottomless pit of utter chaos and mad confusion, where crime is unavoidable, animal instincts are sanctified, and where the void of all-devouring death is the only certainty? The Old-Testament image of original sin seems to be confirmed and strengthened in this new teaching, but now without the purifying faith in and the striving counterbalance of divine redemption, without the divine voice of a monitory conscience. But also without faith in human dignity and the attainability of a meaningful existence by responsible human effort. This kind of consciousness has a pronounced nihilistic potential. It presents a void which cannot be filled, it offers darkness at noon as the essence of human existence.

Is it true that complete consciousness of self is eo ipso identical with human elevation and progress, even when this consciousness is characterized by the discovery that such elevation and progress do not exist and never can exist, because God and the devil are indissolubly chained together? Even when it perceives that there is no self-liberation which can lead to a deliverance from the divine-satanic evil of this world? Or does this insight perhaps rather lead to a buttressing of the foremost components of the current culture-crisis, such as pessimistic-fatalistic passivism, existential-realistic existence-to-the-death, general apathy of the masses, indifference and resignation? Is this really a self-emancipating type of forward thinking, or is it a translation in its own way of the prevailing spirit of the times, with all its decomposition and decline?

4. What goal does this development of consciousness, this insight into man's own human-divine power, contained in the Self, serve—when compared with the former belief in super-human power? In terms of purposeful self-determination of human destiny, this theory does not leave any conceivable goal! Or, rather, the possibility of such a goal is explicitly denied. Earlier aesthetic and ethical values, norms and ideals with their corresponding images have been deliberately destroyed in an iconoclasm which leaves standing only the one image of ultimate ambivalence, of both God and man. A philosophy which strips a higher world of all transcendence, and denies all ideality to higher values (which Freud still ascribed to the moral consciousness of a super Ego), can tolerate nothing but deliberate disillusionment in regard to an unchangeable good-bad world. Nothing but unconditional permanent surrender to the hard and cold reality of the actual moment with its inevitable negative strands and demonic perversions.

This view of God and man leads to a world-view which compels acceptance of the unalterably given fact that man cannot rise above himself, that he cannot escape the stranglehold of his divine-satanic Self, that he will never live to see the crowning victory of the positive over the negative, or man's elevation to an ultimate summum bonum. His newly acquired power serves only to recognize and accept his everlasting impotence to change the monstrous alliance sealed in the human psyche and in the patterns of human behaviour. It is possible then that the human consciousness in freeing itself from the bondage of ancient mythical images may fall prey to a new type of mythical regression. Man may thus succumb to his own self-conscious, superior power as to a "force majeure", to the spirits evoked within himself, and retreat into atavism and barbarism. *This* manner of "becoming conscious", seized by unqualified hands or immature minds and turned out ready-to-wear, may function as a tragic boomerang for the development of religion and culture. Is this doctrine, so obsessed by a diabolical unconscious, itself possessed? Its further development in this respect certainly gives food for such a thought.

2. *Notes on the Religious-Cultural System of Neumann*

Erich Neumann builds further on the ground-work laid down by Jung, and expresses himself in the same somewhat difficult specialized jargon. The claims of depth-psychology are more pronounced in this work for two reasons. On the one hand, Neumann has pieced together the many incomplete fragments of thought scattered throughout Jung's work, and has carried them through to their logical consequences. On the other hand, there is one point of difference between them; Neumann regards himself as a left-wing-protestant—even though he is of Jewish origin, a convinced Zionist and deeply versed in Chassidism. Thus the claim for a possible synthesis between science and religion narrows down here to a compromise between modern depth-psychology and the Christian faith .[1] This point of view has been given explicit formulation in two recent books by Neumann, dealing respectively with the renewal of ethics and of culture through religion. [2]

A. Extract

Although Neumann is a man of great penetration and has written passages which reveal a fine and sensitive perception, his style is not always clear enough to meet the requirements of his analytic task. Sometimes he appears to contradict himself, and his terminology is not precise nor stringent enough to support his argument. Nevertheless, I trust that the following brief summary of those of his ideas which are relevant to our discussion, is fairly accurate. [3]

1. Depth-psychology is able to penetrate through to the religious foundations and primal sources of the human (individual and collective) unconscious. These are accessible in the collective images or archetypes of the human unconscious and can be found in all forms of ritual, mythology, mysticism, dreams, and other forms of symbolism.

2. The central factor at work in this human unconscious is the numinous or the divine. The divine reveals itself solely as a force, a spark, which moves

1. This is also the case with other students of Jung, such as Hans Schär of Berne, who seeks a synthesis of theology and psychology.

2. *Tiefenpsychologie und neue Ethik, Kulturentwicklung und Religion.* See also two publications in English: *The Great Mother*: an analysis of the archetype, New York, 1955; *The Origins and History of Consciousness*, New York, 1954.

3. This concise summary could not make use of literal quotations, since Neumann often prefers extensive and somewhat vague descriptions to precise formulations. It must be remembered that this paring-down has been undertaken for my own purposes, although I believe I have been fair to Neumann in the rewording, for which I am responsible. The value of this method is that it points up ideal-typically the points of agreement and disagreement between our views, and makes explicit the implications which follow from this.

and acts in the deep of the human soul. The divine is pre-eminently human. Theology is anthropology.

3. Divine power, once thought to be above and beyond man, resides rather in the inner world of man and is *his* power. It is contained in the primal life of the soul, which was originally for the most part unconscious. It can thus be demonstrated as a transpersonal content within the uniquely personal Self of every individual. In the human Self this non-I stands opposite the I as its hidden center of power; not metaphysical or "jenseitig", it lies in the farthest reaches of the realm of human experience, at the antipode of the conscious mind. It is in the empirical inner world of the individual Self that the human and the divine mysteriously meet.

4. The findings of depth-psychology concerning religious archetypes leads to the view that the divine can only be fathomed and understood as the purest idea of polarity. [1] God is ambivalent and antipodal, precisely in that He is God. Bipolarity and antithesis represent the divine principle. The divine is by definition metaphysical *and* empirical, essential *and* existential: a unity of absolute opposites. God is not only light, he is not only pure and masculine, but he is also dark, impure and feminine. God is holy and God is hell; He unites love and hate, purity and plague, the sublime and the ultimate degradation, the over-world and the under-world. The divine is also of the devil, and the satanic partakes of the divine. God reconciles all contrasts of being and not-being, of good and evil, of solid and fluid, celestial and infernal, of white and black, truth and untruth, righteousness and unrighteousness, beauty and ugliness, since He Himself encompasses and generates all these contrasts in His double-nature. God is not the Great Unknown, once one has grasped this point of view; He is rather the Great Generator, working simultaneously to create and destroy in the vast force-field between positive and negative poles. God Himself is the center and the universe of all the angels and demons, heavenly spheres, infernal regions and purgatories, sanctifications and desecrations, the focal point of all the extreme and antithetic conceptions which have ever emerged in mythical images and configurations.

5. This divine coincidence of opposites resides, as has been stated, in the depths of the human psyche, in man's Self. Only thus can individual man truly conform to the image of God. Every man is as it were God's twin, or rather, identical with the divine, which is eternally and actively present at the core of human existence. This divine is the secret center of the human soul, and its manifestations can be perceived by enlightened spirits in their own Self. Thus the human Self, be it consciously or unconsciously, *is* itself this growing expanding totality permeated with the divine, and embraces

1. *Ethik*, p. 157 ff.; *Religion*, passim.

a polarity which is an exact replica of the structure of the divine. This paralleling polarity of God and man is followed through to its logical end in the earthly world, where intermingled God-man and man-God live out their common life. Consequently this world was, is and ever shall be an extreme contrast world of light and darkness, both civilized and barbarized, evolving and degenerating, humanistic an demonic, beautiful and bestial.

6. The attainment of consciousness by man implies the spiritual appropriation of this axiomatic duality of values which is invariably inherent in all being, whether divine, human, worldly, or spatio-temporal. It is a self-liberation from hitherto unconscious and therefore incomprehensible forces which seemed to dominate human life in cruel and arbitrary fashion. Now they are grasped and handled, both figuratively and literally, as forces belonging to the human Self. Man's earlier, instinctive ostrich-like reaction can now be replaced by deliberate, intelligent effort toward a harmonious integration of the somber shadow which the immutable law of nature or of fate has immured forever in the divine center of the soul. This awareness can come about within individuals who have reached a higher level of spiritual development by means of a gradual psychic process of individuation and centroversion. It is a process of revelation of the divine-human Self. As a result of this revelation, man no longer faces overwhelming superhuman configurations of an inimical fate, or the destructive determinants from an inaccessibly distant cosmic field of forces. He now recognizes these for what they are: the divine-satanic, good-evil powers which are generated deep within himself, and which he may absorb by learning and assimilate by suffering.

7. This understanding of man's double nature and of his true and permanent position in this world, an insight for which Neumann claims exclusive validity, must result in a revolution in our current system of ethics and morals, based on obsolete images from the unconscious. The present system has fulfilled its mission in a historical stage of transition; its disappearance now is now not only inevitable, it is a necessary condition of progress to a higher spiritual level. In the first place the fall of a superhuman God must be automatically accompanied by the dethronement of a superhuman, heteronomous moral law. The new ethic can only be autonomous, arising from within, in the divine-human Self. The withdrawal of the divine from a supra-mundane realm to the inner realm of the human soul involves also the transplanting of moral aspiration to psychic soil and sources. But in the second place, these moral aspirations of man are now characterized by an essential duality of values, they are in the literal sense and per definition ambivalent. Morality now logically includes good and evil, the sacred and the satanic. For according to this gnostic view God also loves evil and also hates good. Evil thus has a right to its own place under the sun. The most highly evolved, truly moral man is he who recognizes the evil in his own

bosom and acknowledges its equal rights with the good, lovingly and reverently taking it up into his total humanity. If this state of full consciousness has been attained, it is no longer possible to believe in a one-sided idealistic value-system. Such a system is then recognized for what it is: delusive and unrealistic, representing only one part of the human personality [1] and therefore forcing man to attempt the impossible. For it is impossible, inhuman and contrary to the divine principle to demand a single-minded course towards the good, the true, the beautiful and the just. This means misguided neglect of the ever-present, equally primordial counter-current of negation and malignancy. Now at last the command "resist not evil" can be grasped in its true meaning and taken seriously. If man behaves and misbehaves in full awareness of what he is doing, he will be able to serve society better and more responsible than before.

8. At the same time this new insight, consistently and consciously thought through, implies a systematic revolutionizing of all religion and religious aspiration. Reduced to the briefest possible formulation, worship of God becomes worship of man himself. The encounter between man and God takes place in the Self. It occurs by way of dialogue between the I and the not-I, through a becoming aware of the divine content of and the center of bifoly power in the unconscious. This dialogue is a dialectical art which can onld be mastered by mystical man. Religion is mysticism, mysticism is anthropology, and anthropology is rooted in depth-psychology. [2]

Outmoded, unconscious religion rests on an outmoded, unconscious mysticism. This mysticism is disqualified as nihilistic and uroboric. Uroboros is the snake that bites its own tail. It is the symbol of a primordial longing for the restoration of the lost paradise, of the objectionable, one-sided aspiration toward holiness and perfection, or for mystical union with a deity of sublime holiness and consummate perfection. Such ideal images of a coming pleromatic state of salvation contain a renunciation of this world and its evil, and the mystical awaiting of a better world, which will never come. They are caused by the fixation of unconscious incest with the Great Mother, that is our planet Earth, or by the unconscious fear of castration by this Terrible Mother. They have their origins in the twilight life of earliest man, in his desperate attempt to escape from the suffocating shrouds of mythical night, and they cannot but lead to equally desperate and dangerous fear reactions, which make a hell out of this world. [3]

1. Or rather, prescribing as a model for the masses what could only hold for a select élite, according to an overstrained moral code which by the very impossibility of adherence leads to double morality, hypocrisy, repression, and all the accompanying complexes which represent distortions of behaviour.
2. See especially the third essay on "The Mystical Man" in *Religion*.
3. *Religion*, p. 92, 121 ff; 187, 201 ff. *Ethik*, p. 95 ff.

The new, conscious religion is based on a renewed, conscious mysticism, realistic and heroic in nature. This mysticism may be poorer in escapist dream-images and unfulfillable illusions, but it is much richer in understanding and a sense of reality. It accepts this world as it is and necessarily must be, because it has recognized the polar structure of the divine and the human, and the inevitable inclusion of evil and corruption in both. The modern, self-conscious mystical-religious man has adapted himself to this situation and is strengthened by the open encounter with and reconciliation of the primeval conflict between God and the Devil which rages so painfully within his Self. Re-emerging from this open struggle in his soul, he then is better able to assist the world in its heavy task of bearing a split destiny. The symbol of this mystical maturity and achieved integration is the "mandala", the closed circle, in which there is perfect harmony and balance between the radiations from periphery to center, and from center to periphery.

9. The regeneration of ethics and religion in this sense is only possible after earlier ideal and mythical projections of the unconscious concerning the existence of a separate realm of the divine with its values have been "drawn back". [1] The unmasking and demythologizing of these ideas, which belong to a primitive stage of spiritual immaturity and faulty self-knowledge, are the conditio sine qua non for mankind to become aware and reach psychic maturity. Thereafter, the completed break-through of the conscious and the rediscovery of the true god-man, revealed in the Self, opens up a tremendous prospect of regeneration and progress. Once the inscrutable forces of fate have been rendered impotent and the redeeming solution to the riddle of the Sphinx has been discovered, there will no longer be any need for the repression of dark instincts and demonic drives. There will then be an end to obsessive feelings of guilt and fear, to the helpless suffering and complex mental ills which these cause in an endless vicious circle or an unavoidable chain of cumulative destructive action and reaction. The current rigorous system of ethics and religion forbids the resigned acceptance of evil and has led to a deeply imprinted bad conscience and a constant compulsive preoccupation with sin. But evil, thus repulsed, only returns by a detour via the unconscious to cause far greater harm to the individual and society. It seeks negative compensation in aggressive and destructive impulses, in atavistic and barbaric reactions, in moral insanity, social instability and epidemic wars. We have had bloody demonstrations to the effect that these forms of compensation are "one of the primary causes of the crisis of mankind", and therefore the "outstanding problem of our time". [2]

Conscious insight into the basic psychic structure of the demiurgic god-

1. *Religion*, p. 164/5.
2. *Ethik*, p. 78.

devil and the sacral beast-man means spiritual self-liberation, activating freedom and joyful living, and the inrush into stagnant ethico-religious pools of the fresh pure waters of cultural creativity. For it means acceptance of the actual world and of its concrete transitional situation, which is spatio-temporally at once a beginning and an end: a consciously assimilated and self-reconciled divine world, under the eternal simultaneous rule of God and of the Anti-Christ in man, bearing its inalienable essential burden of suffering and evil, chained fast to a holy-unholy matrimonial coupling of mutually counter-balancing opposites.

10. This development toward a liberating self-consciousness could also go astray and have a contrary effect if the emphasis is misplaced, as Neumann recognizes. Its purpose is always the conscious renunciation of a one-sided distorted striving toward ultimate perfection, and the recognition of ine-radicable imperfection as a basic element of God and his human counter-part. But this consciousness, meant to bring about the realization of this duality of values, could swing man too far and drive him toward the oppo-site extreme of monism. Not this time a monism of the over-optimistic All-Good, but that of a starkly pessimistic All-Evil. Man and his world then become *solely*-evil rather than *also*-evil. The original divine aspect and center of the Self is then denied. The mystical encounter of the human spirit with a hitherto unrecognized divine element in itself then becomes meaningless. Man will become one with his shadow, evil incarnate, and his work will be satan's work. Without counter forces the world is irre-trievably doomed to religious, ethical and cultural uprooting. But, Neumann says, the recognition of this dangerous possibility is tantamount to its spiritual disarmament and so brings it automatically under control.

11. The enlightenment concerning the true dualism of human existence which depth-psychology brings, is on the contrary meant gradually to foster the realization that there is in every human creature the same divine energy, actively working in diametrically opposed directions. It creates out of nothingness and also reduces to nothingness. All men are bound together by this unchangeable spiritual duality of the fertile and the destructive. Mankind is thus in eternal togetherness in the face of death, demonic infinity and the shared acceptance of powerlessness before a universe filled with inescapable evil which it must itself ceaselessly unleash. The growing reali-zation of this will finally drive men to voluntary association, to forming a solid front for the purpose of deliberate restraint of and defence against their own individual and collective evil excesses of power. Once every man knows himself to be no better than his neighbour, then this blood brother-hood and solidarity of evil will bring about a general brotherhood of man much more effectively than has hitherto been the case. [1]

1. *Ethik*, p. 110, 159.

12. The experience of unity of opposites which arises from man's scrutiny and contemplation of his inner Self is comparable in Neumann's view with that which religion terms the "gift of grace" and art calls "being gifted". These are regenerative powers of the unconscious, constantly and through an inner urge working towards this state of awareness. They are striving and able to heal this sick world. The rapprochement between the I and the Self is both the life-task of the individual in his search for inner integration, and also automatically provides a restoration of the social equilibrium whereby the current culture-crisis will be overcome. [1]

B. Critique

This critical evaluation stands completely apart from my respect for Neumann as a person and for his good will and lofty aims. I wish here to confine this evaluation as much as possible to the implications of the basic concepts for our areas of concern namely religion, ethics, the image of man, the image of the world, culture, the spatio-temporal situation and the future of mankind. I will arrange my critical remarks in this order.

1. RELIGION

The return, for the sake of a regeneration of religion, to an eastern gnosis-type of dualism as the only and absolute truth, implies—and also intends—a revolutionary upheaval and a heretical break with the currently dominating, mainly monistic ideas of western religion. This doctrine dese-crates the sacred God of western tradition, for it reveals that the divine is possessed by the devil. There is an "imago dei" placed within man, but it serves at the same time as "advocatus diaboli". The existence of God becomes an anthropological function of the human psyche, a two-fold function which also fulfils the role of satan, to the end of time. Older ideal images of God are withdrawn because they are invalid projections of the human psyche in an imaginary mythical world of the beyond. The real God is entirely unmythical, He is a psychic principle; He is present *in* the human soul and nowhere else. Personal experience of this God is possible through the conscious encounter with the Self. [2] The divine becomes a consciously humanized central factor in the psychic force-field. It is a bi-polar agent, moving and moved by the alternating current of energy between positive and negative, good and evil. God has his classical model in Pan, the archetype of the Christian devil. [3] God-satan requires of man that he shall be evil too. [4]

---

1. These last ideas come from a series of lectures delivered by Neumann in 1954 at the International School of Philosophy at Amersfoort, The Netherlands.
2. *Religion*, p. 175/6.
3. *Ethik*, p. 135.
4. *Ethik*, p. 121.

Apart from all other consequences, the main implication of this last idea is that the divine arch-principle does not operate in one, but—intentionally and with equal strength—in two diametrically opposed directions. The resultant gravitates necessarily and perpetually around the existing equilibrium of forces. An ultimate victory of the good can never be achieved. The contest with the devil remains undecided through all eternity. [1] God, no less than man, is impotent under any circumstances to divest Himself of His satanic character, no more than man can He ever be saved for once and all by suffering. The God of Love is obliged, for such is His nature, to love sin, demonic evil and stinking impurity, or even to have a predilection for them. [2] All possibility of a glorious fulfilment of history is absolutely excluded. It is in this sense unthinkable that a Kingdom of God should miraculously break in upon or succeed history. And equally unthinkable is a redeeming return of Christ. For Christ is bound to share his rule with the Anti-Christ, precisely because he is part of the divine in man. Rebirth opens no prospect of perfection, for evil too is eternally reborn. [3] Because of the God within him, there is for man no other time and no other future than the contemporary here-and-now. God, who is present in man and *only* in man, is of the ever-present only, an actualized and moment-ridden God. Any purely divine, perfected future, God's future, is deliberately sacrificed to the religious requirements of the present. The eschatological perspective of an ultimately perfected re-creation is utterly destroyed. [4] The question is whether precisely this perspective was not the indispensable foundation, the very cornerstone, of at least the Christian religion. For it was the express desire of Neumann's psychological renewal to assist and remain in close contact with this religion.

2. Ethics

The regeneration of ethics requires a similar preliminary rejection and deliberate removal of all earlier, primitive and infantile projections from the unconscious. What is involved here is again nothing less than a "revaluing of all values", as well as a "beyond good and evil". The traditional distinction between good and evil, the contrast between holy and sinful, the distance between the exalting and the degrading, are obliterated after more conscious analysis. A state of being simply good or simply evil no longer exists, [5] since one man's good may be another man's evil. [6] And so a superior farewell is

1. *Ethik*, p. 39.
2. *Ethik*, p. 148/9, 157.
3. *Ethik*, p. 39.
4. *Ethik*, p. 95/6
5. *Ethik*, p. 147.
6. *Ethik*, 123.

bidden to all the long-cherished values of western culture, for the very reason that their value is so high—too high. The good, the beautiful, the true, the just—all these are one-sided overgrowths and naive illusions, left-overs from the *kindergarten* phase of unconscious culture. For a progressive and realistic consciousness, only the basic duality of all being and thus also of all values is tenable. Earlier half-true ideals and lop-sided value-hierachies must, because of their monochromatic and monolithic construction, be expelled from modern thought. This must now learn to express itself in the new bi-lingual double-talk, in the language of dissonance and cacophony. There is only one model of values: the deistic-demonic conflict of the soul, the human drama of the choice between integration or disintegration of the split deity struggling ceaselessly in man's innermost being.

As far as its value-content goes, the new ethic can only be bound to the autonomous human Self. Along with the old values all commands and prohibitions of a heteronomous morality are permanently overthrown, from the Mosaic laws and the precepts of the Sermon on the Mount to Kant's categorical imperative. A higher authority projected by the unconscious no longer exists. There is no "Sollen", no "ought", no conscience, no rigorous code of righteous behaviour, no canon of deadly sins, no virtue or noble striving for the good life in the undivided, pure and simple sense of good-ness. [1] Nor can any guilt or moral responsibility adhere to evil. The murder-ed one is equally guilty with the murderer. [2] The concepts of punishment or retaliation for committed evil must therefore also disappear. [3]

To recognize one's own evil and to commit it consciously is ethically "good". [4] Every man ought to seek a gentleman's agreement between the warring divine-diabolical forces in his Self. [5] The pact between Faust and Mephistopheles provides an appropriate model for an "irreproachable" ethic. [6] To wish to be one-sidedly good or virtuous is "evil". [7] It is absolutely necessary for every normal man to commit a certain amount of evil. [8] This, provided that it is done consciously, does not defile the world. [9] One must have the "moral courage" not to wish to be better than one is. [10] For the sake of purity, one must be impure and sacrifice innocence. [11] The "mys-

1. *Ethik*, p. 102, 124, 132 ff.
2. *Ethik*, p. 10.
3. *Ethik*, p. 129.
4. *Ethik*, p. 132.
5. *Ethik*, p. 86.
6. *Ethik*, p. 135.
7. *Ethik*, p. 132.
8. *Ethik*, p. 119.
9. *Ethik*, p. 118.
10. *Ethik*, p. 127.
11. *Ethik*, p. 126.

terium iniquitatis" is not a dark mystery, but a consciously soluble problem.
It can be stated as follows: evil is a normal psychological fact of human-
divine nature and it has to be integrated harmoniously into every individual's
life. Such inevitably subjective and arbitrary harmonization forms the sole
criterion of the new "total" ethic—"total" because it encompasses good and
evil. This ethic will decontaminate man and make him pure. It is better to
be in good health, than to be good. [1]

This is the tenor of the entire work about the new ethic: a necessary
dethronement of the old ethical values and their replacement by the one
value of conscious assimilation of evil, which needs sufficient "Lebensraum"
and independence within the balanced totality of the soul. A straight, ethically undifferentiated code of conduct, valid for all people at all times, can thus
no longer be prescribed. The only course offered is that towards an autonomous synthesis of each man's situational and personal evil. [2] This integration is an individual task and its ethics will differ according to each
individual's constitution or condition. But whenever a successful personally
"right" symbiosis is achieved, there will also be an automatic delimitation
in respect to such outgrowths as libertinism, nihilism, animalistic vitalism,
or materialism. For these too are again one-sided, literally "no good",
because they lead to the other extreme, namely that of the conscious sever-
ing of all ties to the divine-spiritual aspect of cultural evolution. Success
resides in a balance of equal powers. If the good is given its rightful place,
but no more, then evil will automatically keep in its place. But then evil
must be given the room it needs, and no less.

It is clear that Neumann himself wishes to call a halt at some point to the
demons of destruction which he has summoned from the unconscious and
sanctioned existentially and definitively. However, once the Self is un-
fettered, why should it have to listen to *his* all-too-human voice of warning,
however commanding or entreating? How can this depth-psychology
explain, let alone guard against, the development of a modern attitude of
mind which would also invoke the conscious attainment of "awareness",
but only to deny the existence of any divine center of power in the human
soul? An attitude that can and does go even further and would deny the
existence of any higher humanistic or spiritual arch-instinct in man or of a
value-creating, spiritually exalting agent or energy of any kind? The valuable and the non-valuable, which were originally distinguished according
to the tree of knowledge, have now been deliberately merged. This ultra-
realistic ethics deny and devaluate a separate ideal realm of values. After this
dethronement of all hierarchical and criteriological value-systems—what

1. *Ethik*, p. 116.
2. *Ethik*, p. 123 ff.

ethical checks and restraints can there be on the sliding scale of dual values
to prevent a degradation to inferior values or an elimination of the scale
itself, so that finally nothing is of value?[1]

3. IMAGE OF MAN

Man remains the image of God, even according to this point of view.
But, like God, he is profaned, perverted and debased, so that in the very
depths of his soul he is as demonized as he is deified. Just as a supernal,
overpowering God is reduced and split into a half-god, so man, through
illusory self-conceit, overblown as God's chosen creature, is reduced to
half-man, after the archetype of Cheiron, the centaur.[2] The dangerous and
poisonous process of religious-humanistic inflation can only be neutralized
by a genuine and healthy deflation which can bring the two poles of human
existence into their true relationship with each other. If the earlier deification
of man was the product of an optimistic perspective which would be realized
after the separating out of the last judgement, now a reification takes place
which immortalizes sin, suffering, evil and death without the prospect of
any coming reality other than the existing demonstrable order of things
from the beginnings of history. Neither God nor man can ever cast off the
old Adam and change the inherent ambivalence of human nature.

By a single deadly blow the substance of human dignity is removed from
the new image of man. The conscious self-liberation of man has only brought
insight into the divine will to evil and the diabolical lust for destruction
which are irredeemably sealed in his breast. From this, there is in the last
analysis no liberation. In this sense mankind is permanently denied all
possibility of self-elevation, since the essential duality of all values entirely
excludes any third higher value-alternative. Man now knows himself to be
the slave of his own spiritual offspring, which he can neither reject nor
separate himself from: the evil which God has made operative in him. And
there is no way of getting rid of this evil: no God who can overcome it,
no devil to be overcome, no man who by struggling for perfection can
emerge victorious in the end. This evil is all-destroying but indestructible.
All that man has achieved by his consciousness is a definitive recognition
of his own enduring impotence. The classical image of man is bereft of
idealism and power, without any substitutes. The new image does nothing
but mirror man as he always was, and now is more typically than ever:
a cruel mixture of monster and machine, the mass un-man, beast of prey,
murderer of his own kind, devil incarnate. At the same time the tiny bit

---

1. This criticism of course does not imply that a serious effort to renew and replace
worn-out values and norms is not necessary. It only means to point out that following
this path may produce opposite results from those intended.
2. *Religion*, p. 115.

of humanity still accorded man gives him the illusion that he has been provided with a divine spark, or that he is called by an inner voice to another and better way of life.

Neumann presents this new image as a heroic one, but in effect it is tragic rather than heroic. What is the individual to do, who has accepted and identified himself with this new image of man? Is he to choose suicide, asceticism, deliberate childlessness, vacant contemplation, neurotic aliena-tion, misanthropic solitude, spiritual impotence in the face of a meaningless existence, or rather the escapism of sensual surrender to wild desires and delirious debauches, to spiritually deadening or stupefying and time-killing diversions? The results of this attainment of consciousness would seem to be highly ambivalent too. For in the long run, what other alternatives can there be than either a radical break with a situation which is unbearable and hopeless or a complete compromise with reality as it is? The first course means the end of life, through suicide or insanity. The second means re-conciliation and collaboration with the powers that be, even when these are anti-human and evil. Man can either open his eyes wider and wider, or he can squeeze them tightly shut again, to protect himself from the blinding darkness.

4. IMAGE OF THE WORLD

The new image of God and man forms the central theme which conditions all further variations. If man cannot wrest himself loose from the mutually antagonistic forces at work in his Self, then there is no other world for man to live and die in than this split-polar world. For then neither his religious nor his ethical striving can ever bring about another world; on the contrary, they will only serve to buttress this existing world. Even mysticism, if it is to be conscious and modern, must be based on acceptance of this world. For this world of men—pregnant with God-Satan—is necessarily and natu-rally as it is. It cannot and therefore should not be different.

Utopian projections and idealistic images of a coming other and better world are unreal and only serve to inhibit a healthy development. They stem from infantile wishful dreaming and from uroboric incest complexes, which the modern consciousness must uncompromisingly reject, knowing them to be incapable of fulfilment. The omnipresent and always actively working negative forces nip in the bud any positive images of the future of whatever kind. The Realm of the Future is left dangling in the air and cannot be consciously provided with a solid foundation. There is no ground for hope of a paradise to be regained, of a blessed hereafter, or of a cosmic renewal in perfection of heaven and earth, nor is there even any hope of approaching a more humanly worthy society.[1] Here again the

1. *Religion*, p. 169, 187, 201, 217, 221; *Ethik*, p. 95/6.

achievement of consciousness implies an iconoclasm of all idealistic images of this kind. The human longing from which they spring can never be satisfied. Therefore the conscious renunciation of such unattainable happiness is man's only hope to struggle free from this Tantalus-torture without ultimate Self-sacrifice. [1]

After this reconciliation with the existing, invariant structure, there remains but the one eternally harmonious image of the mandala, [2] the closed circle and enduring cycle, of an inwardly divided world-being which, by virtue of the Self, is ever revolving yet ever the same. The most intelligent thing that the aware man can do is to accept this world heroically, since there is no other. In the language of every-day existence, this turning toward the world of real things, this "in-der-Welt-sein", means a whole-hearted acknowledgement of the *present*. The present draws into its circle all past and all future as belonging to its unchangeable order. Since the present is thus lengthened ad aeternum, man must (if it is not to bring him ad nauseam) experience only his own life-time as Time; in spite of all, he must accept the spatio-temporal reality which presents itself to him as the only secular possibility. He must unreservedly put himself at the disposal of the concrete situation, [3] and make the best of it within the permanent limits of its good-evil. He must attempt a tolerable synthesis of these irrevocably joined antithetical elements.

If this conscious, "engagé" attitude is to stand firm against the onslaught of the unconscious, which keeps conjuring up the most tempting illusions about the future, then a strong mental defence must be erected against these irrational dreams. Any futuristic illusionism, though positive, is primitive and escapist and must be exposed as deceptive and dangerously misleading, even as chaotic and negative, for it would deny and abandon this world for another which can never exist; in short, for nihilism. [4] The world is *not* a waiting-room. The streetcar named desire does not have heaven as its destination. To await that which cannot come is a waste of time and energy which is sorely needed for the present.

The modern consciousness must therefore deliberately free itself of all still persisting time-honoured but false conceptions of Jewish-Christian messianism or prophetism regarding the coming new age. It must purge itself of all apocalyptic eschatological images of mythical origin concerning an end of time and a meaningful development and fulfilment of history according to a predetermined divine plan for the salvation of mankind. All such images of the future, projected by the unconscious into a time-which-

1. *Ethik*, p. 105.
2. *Ethik*, p. 151; *Religion*, p. 148/9, 165, 177.
3. *Religion*, p. 128, 156, 199, 204-7, 211, 219, 220/1; *Ethik*, p. 88, 147, 158/9.
4. *Religion*, p. 169/70, 187, 199-204.

is-not-yet, must be ferreted out as completely untrue. The part-truth in them can only become effective by consciously drawing them back out of this distant spatio-temporal prospect into the reality immediately present to man here-and-now. The man who achieves this understanding will recognize that he is *himself* the messiah, at every moment and at every place where he happens to be. Every man is a messiah if he has freed himself, through becoming conscious, from those unconscious and incomprehensible constellations which seemed to exist beyond man's reach and power, as soon as he has liberated himself from misconceptions about fate or the will of a higher providence which actually threatened his future and his capacity to determine his own destiny. Man can work his own redemption by localizing this power complex within his own being, thus saving his energy for concentration on the complicated problems of daily life.

This world view is as tenable and valuable for the possessor as any other, and deserves the same respect as any other profoundly held conviction. Therefore I do not feel that it is justified to attack its values directly. I will reserve my criticism until a point is reached where the wide theoretical divergence of viewpoints will be less apt to be confused with one of personal feelings. It will become more concrete in its implications and thus more accessible to analysis if it is brought to the field of cultural dynamics and the future of culture.

5. CULTURE

The antithetical God-man image of Neumann's depth-psychology stands in almost diametrical opposition to my own line of thought concerning a synthetic cultural sociology. All the more so as my conceptions also take for point of departure the split mental structure of man—albeit very differently conceived. At the same time it might be said that this contrasting conception is an unintentional mirror of the times which gives a literal demonstration of my thesis! However that may be, it will be of interest to consider and test these opposed systems with reference to their common subject matter: culture and its dynamics.

a. We come directly to the heart of the matter through the definitions which Neumann uses for the concepts "culture" and "cultural development".[1] Culture is: "The emergence of man through . . . confrontation with the mythical world". As to cultural development: „. . . the development of human culture, like that of the human mind, is a process of demythologizing". According to Neumann the unreal mythical world built by the unconscious is one of catastrophic, invincible powers, of deadly loneliness and dark despair.[2] The conscious removal of this other,

1. *Religion*, p. 218.
2. *Religion*, p. 109.

illusory arch-world of myth would therefore automatically imply a reversal in the direction of hope and progress.

I take the contrary position, namely that certain de-mythologizing processes must be regarded as intimately related to the *demolition* of modern western culture, with de-eschatologizing and de-utopianizing as decisive factors in the process. But, as we have seen, Neumann expressly (and logically in his system) bans eschatology and utopia, and all other idealistic images (except of course his own particular image of progress). A whole arsenal of invective will scarcely suffice him in his scourging of these psychic derailments; they are pathological, uroboric, inflationary, psychotic, unstable, introverted, somnambulistic, fragmentary, anti-cosmic and negativistic, as well as low, dangerous, poisonous, dissolute, unmanly, untrustworthy, antediluvian and sneaky. He regards them as primitive, infantile, embryonic, as pre-historic, pre-logical or pre-natal, and therefore irreconcilable with these modern ideas of depth-psychology. This enlightened view must publicly condemn these images as symptoms of regression. Their retention in modern consciousness could only be considered as ultra-reactionary romanticism, nihilistic world-hating mysticism, fruitless escapism and the convulsive fixation of an incestuous oedipal complex on Mother Earth. In short, all this would have to be rejected as re-mythologizing.

It is not necessary to recapitulate my own position here, but let us examine this contrasting one more closely. What is the basis of its claims to benefit culture? The achievement of a culturally progressive and consistent de-mythologizing according to the system developed by Jung and Neumann is highly unlikely! For their doctrines contain a generous and colorful mixture of eclectically gathered mythical images from many vanished and widely disparate historical culture-periods up to and including the present. The concepts "regression" and "re-mythologizing" are certainly not inappropriate here, although of course this turning of the tables, reversing the point of their argument against themselves, indicates nothing concerning the validity of *these* specific projections (any more than the Jung-Neumann argument indicates anything concerning the validity of the projections they have chosen to reject).

This doctrine of the "modern consciousness" is based on old images which have been patched up and polished—images which are chiefly drawn from spiritual currents originating in ancient oriental gnosis and gnostic movements (chiefly of manichaeism) which were violently persecuted and finally eradicated by a victorious Christian doctrine. But a host of other images has been added to these and the result is an ingenious mixture of ideal and mythical projections stemming from and identified as to Iranian,

1. *Religion*, p. 90-2, 95, 121.

Indic, Cabbalistic and Chassidist, Egyptian, Hellenistic, Germanic, medieval-mystical and even modern existentialist sources.

The entire gallery of mythological types is displayed in lavish fashion, and used as needed to demonstrate any point. The Old-Testament myths centering around Jahweh are there, the Greek myths of the eternally accursed Tantalides and Danaides, those of the tragic titans and heroes from Prometheus to Sisyphus, and other figures of destiny from Perseus to Oedipus, from Chronos to Gaia and Pan; there is the symbolism of Amor and Psyche, of Krishna, of Horus, Isis and Osiris, and also of the battle with the Great Dragon, of Hagen against Siegfried, or Faust against Mephistopheles, or again of the Nietzschean Zarathustra against gods and men. How is it possible that this depth-psychology should remain unconscious of its through and through mythical character and is unable to disabuse itself? As far as archetypical regression goes, does it really make any difference whether one expresses a strong personal preference for the ancient circle-symbolism of the spiritually purified geometric mandala above the similar cyclical image of the purely animalistic uroboros?

b. It would appear to me that Jung and Neumann (just as in another way Karl Mannheim) are too much captivated by, and unconsciously captives of, their discovery of mythical archetypes. They are misled into overextending their significance by presenting them as the primal forces of cultural dynamics which in dialectical fashion eliminate themselves as man comes into awareness. This progressive elimination is regarded as the main stimulant for the development of culture. They apparently fail to notice the fact just mentioned, that they introduce other (whether older or newer) leitmotivs in the place of those they eliminate. In consequence they overlook the two following aspects. In the first place, they do not recognize that progress need not necessarily and exclusively depend on the negative process of elimination of old concepts, but may equally or even to a greater extent depend on the simultaneous positive introduction of more adequate, consciously synchronized and reoriented ideas. In the second place they fail to perceive the central role of powerfully working images of the future with respect to cultural dynamics. Such images are contained in a number of older archetypical projections and in those newer ideas which represent substitutions for and adaptations of these former projections. These images of the future often have been able to influence the growth of culture with sometimes overwhelming force, precisely because of their deep archetypical roots.

Since these images of the future which form the unique historical matrix, truly the Great Mother, of all cultural energy and progress are neglected or denied any importance by Jung and Neumann, the conscious self-liberation from all archetypical projections without distinction as to kind (except their own kind) is automatically considered to represent cultural process. The elimination of the most far-seeing and fore-shadowing projections is included in this general iconoclasm of archetypes and in this burning of all bridges behind them to the future as a, or even *the* exclusive road to victory over the present culture crisis. As a result Jung and Neumann remain blind to the possibility that this indiscriminate destruction might not after all represent progress, but might as well be a sign of dangerous disintegration.

c. If such a complete liquidation of all archetypes and images of the future (except those implicit in their own system) were really to take place, what would then remain? Where would this progress lead to? What goal could such a perfect (?) state of consciousness serve? According to the Jung-Neumann image, the "I" in its meeting with the "not-I" would then finally succeed in penetrating through to the creative nothingness or zero-point of the Self.[1] It would achieve direct contact with the creating-destroying center of energy, the throne of the divine, which also manifests itself as the demonic evil of destruction, chaos and the void.

With the best will in the world, I am unable to see how this self-liberating situation of intimate mystical communication with an eternally ambivalent Self can provide an impetus to the revitalization and renaissance of a declining culture. Where does this magical new culture-dynamic energy come from, and where does it go? Is it to arise from the realization of this zero-point and negation? What could be its ultimate goal, now that every positive ultimate goal for a coming time has been decisively removed?

Is this energy then to feed into the ambivalent present, into the concrete situation of the moment? But how in heaven's name (the word be forgiven!) can one expect a deliberately disillusioned people, purged of all idealism, to be roused out of its cultural apathy and pessimistic frame of mind, for the sake of an evil and insane world, overflowing with misery which is the very cause, and an unchangeable cause at that, of this general feeling of frustration? How is mankind to be inspired by a new and mightily swelling pathos (which is also demonized!) and a vigorous ethos (which preaches both good and evil!), how can it be moved by an ecstatically bursting enthusiasm (which must be negative too!), to sally forth united and save our threatened culture and cultural values (not undividedly acknowledged!) from the Great Dragon, the Devouring Mother and the horrors of destruction? Just how will a glowing spark from this modern consciousness of an enlightened few succeed in lighting a "feu sacré" in the masses?

Is it not precisely the generally growing awareness of the untenability of naive progress-optimism, arising out of the actual situation in this mid-twentieth century, which lies at the source of the all-pervading scepticism?

---

1. *Religion*, p. 166, 173, 176/7, 185, 195, 208/9.

How then should a homoeopathic cure of still more awareness concerning the ineradicable evil and endless demonic doom to which the world is subjected lead to an automatic turn for the better? What the concept of original sin plus the hope of Christian salvation can obviously no longer achieve—can this now all at once be achieved by elevating original-sin-sans-salvation to a permanent pedestal? Can mystical acceptance of the mystery of life as thus revealed, ever lead, even at its best, to anything more than a stoical "amor fati", resignation and contemplative surrender to new mythical concepts of eternal recurrence or a nirvana?

It is perhaps no cause for rejoicing that there are those who take a different view from the author's. For this may well mean the loss of a battle-ready legion armed with a vital quantity of spiritual power, which might have enlisted in a more worthy cause than the passing present: our on-hurrying future.

6. Image of Time

This depth-psychology enunciates plainly what it intends and can do: to nurse culture through its present crisis of illness and lead it toward a healthy, fully conscious course of development in the future. No one can doubt the readiness of the intention, but I for one doubt strongly the ability to carry it out. In my view this new doctrine may well result in a continuation and perhaps an aggravation of the current crisis. It seems profoundly and characteristically affected by the highly contagious epidemic of spiritual consumption, the stalking white death of our age.

The spiritual hallmark of our time is deeply imprinted on just this line of thought, which intends to leap beyond our time. In spite of its claims to absolute and universal validity, its mode of operation is overwhelmingly time-bound, both in design and result. It is an ideal interpreter and chronicler of its time. The modern Zeitgeist breathes from its every pore. No other time could have brought forth this psychology and no other time than our own can come forth from it. It is a capacious funnel, catching all the current isms, placing its own peculiar imprint on them, then forcing them back through its narrow neck upon the age from which they came. Here are all those isms—and not one is missing—which we have pointed out and discussed as symptomatic of the pattern of our culture, as signs of the times.

We rediscover here the pronounced anti-futurism and anti-idealism, with their retinue of iconoclastic de-eschatologizing and de-utopianizing. Following in their train are actualism and realism, mixed with relativism, opportunism and most notably with an evil-and-doom-accepting quietism. And then, of course, pessimism and disillusionment concerning man. Further there are many ideas which are closely related to modern existentialism, to a perennial cyclical fatalism, to a recently reviving vitalism, to irrationalism ("innere Dämonie"), neo-mysticism, neo-liberalism (the "laissez-faire" of self-interest for the sake of harmonization of the psychic force-field), to nihilism (with respect to current values and the accepted value-hierarchy), and so on.

This depth-psychology is thus an ideal type and prototype of our *moment-ridden culture*. The indicated therapy toward a realistic actualization of human existence in timely conformity with the given order of things is very typical of the thinking of our time. Through this advice it becomes a part of and participates in the shaping of the crisis of our culture. Its "modern consciousness" is at once product of and program for the intellectual and spiritual life of this generation; *its* actuality is none other than *the* actuality which it mirrors from and recommends to our time. In this respect it is at one, structurally speaking, with all the strikingly parallel developments of moment-ridden culture discussed in this work; moment-ridden science, philosophy, religion, art, humanism and socialism. Moment-ridden, not because any product of culture could ever be brought forth at any other moment than its author's own present, but because they remain entirely within the narrow enclosure, the closed circle, call it the mandala, of the here-and-now.

Indeed, this depth-psychology assumes the quasi-scientific form of general validity and empiricism in conformity with the style of our scienticized times, but just as typically the historical-relative breach in our time and culture emanates from all its work. It does not operate against the current, but drifts with it, albeit it as a subversive "fellow-traveller". In its extreme psychologism it portrays only the present interim stage of decline and decay, of voluntary submission to and reconciliation with a hopelessly depraved, chaotic world.

Neumann rightly says that the evolution of the West through the last 150 years has been characterized by increasing penetration into consciousness of the "dark side". In his view this fact, which every area of art and culture reveals more and more clearly, should be recognized, and given free reign. [1] In this darkness lies danger, as long as it remains in the unconscious. But—so runs the argument—once it has been made conscious and its rightful part in the course of events has been recognized, then in this same darkness lies "the opportunity for every future development in the West. . .". [2] This is indeed true if one equates conscious tolerance of and broad concessions to evil with cultural progress. It is not true if one considers the current culture-crisis as in part responsible for the growth and spread of such a cult of the devil. And in the latter case this depth-psychology, while remaining

1. *Ethik*, p. 88 ff.
2. *Ethik*, p. 91.

tragically unconscious of its self-mystification, actually becomes the active fulfiller of the doomed destiny it would exorcize. The portal to a hopeful future still stands slightly ajar; but this depth-psychology, in dropping its fallen divinity onto the world stage like a "deus ex machina", threatens to slam the door shut for good and all. It may then represent the last link in the crumbling chain of our time. It may be the last expiring tendril of an old vine, rather than a fresh shoot of a new ethic, religion and culture; no tender harbinger of a new spring, but only the conscientious postman, whose duty compels him in spite of himself to deliver the death announcement to the addressee.

3. *Summary: The Image of the Future of Depth-psychology*

As befits the ideal-typical method, I will formulate my conclusions concerning depth-psychology as pointedly as possible, in a manner commensurate with its immoderate over-estimation of its own leading role in today's culture of bringing salvation to future mankind. [1]

A. Its claim to a salutory self-liberation of modern man has a tendency towards future self-disintegration. This tendency is introduced by indissolubly uniting the forces of negation, destruction, pollution and death with God, man and the world, as their essential constituents. It also activates this process by its attempted annihilation of all transmitted cultural values (be they religious, idealistic, humanistic, ethical or aesthetic) as being untrue and invalid in their existing forms. It furthers this by tossing the concepts of good and evil, exalted and degraded, constructive and destructive, into one diabolical stew. It rejects all objective rules and criteria of conduct and of life, and replaces them with subjective caprice and the arbitrary standards of personal temperament and private circumstances, as the solution to all problems, including those conflicts arising out of man's social relations with his fellow-man.

B. The problem of the theodicy is reduced to a problem of anthropology. It is not Christ, who will return and reign in His Realm, but man himself who shall become king of this world, ruling it through the power of his Self. [2] In this Self, and nowhere else, is God's habitation, and this God is no more and certainly no better than his human counterpart. Most certainly not, since this God is also Satan himself, dwelling in man's soul. This God loves evil as part of Himself, and so equally does man in his Self. [3] God is

---

1. Neumann at any rate should not hold this sharpness against me, since it merely confirms his own view that all renewers of ethics and religion will inevitably be regarded as malefactors in their own time. See *Ethik*, p. 29.
2. *Religion*, p. 217.
3. *Ethik*, p. 148/9, 157.

played out as Saviour, as Salvator Mundi, and so, of course, is man. The world lies torn asunder, at the mercy of his capricious grace and destruction, his love and hate. God offers no way out, and man can even less offer himself a way out from his own divine-satanic Self. Nothing new will ever appear under the sun. The circle is closed in the harmony of an enduring, unshakable disharmony.

The unsolved problem of why and for how long an omnipotent god will tolerate this meaningless disharmony and a world that denies him has ceased to be a problem at all. For this god is a god who denies himself, and who wills the evil and the impotence. These negative destructive aspects are an integral part of his bipolar nature. This new definition of God is so deviating and His new image is pictured with such contradictory and diabolical traits, that for the layman at least it is difficult to imagine how this could lead to a renewal of the Christian-humanistic religious faith. A foretaste of this development is to be found in the sardonic description of the orgiastic Belial worship, with its veneration of evil as sacred, in Aldous Huxley's counter-utopia, *Ape and Essence*.

C. A paradoxical relativity is spread like a net over the entire world. Orwell's prophetic description in *Nineteen Eighty-Four* of the "double-think", a systematic approach to falsehood, has actually come true here. Evil = good, God = Satan, harmony = disharmony, vacant circle = supreme fulfilment; these are only a few examples of this new mode of thinking. To add a few more: now = timeless, the all-in-all = the void, destructive = creative, synthesis = antithesis, holy = hell, [1] love of neighbour = love of self; [2] and, of course, all these equations are reversible.

D. With the aid of this ambiguous set of concepts, the problem of ethics is reduced to one of psychology. The method of treatment of the individual neurotic patient is simply transferred to the entire soul-sick, unstable and disintegrating mass of mankind. Thus the prescription for culture is simple: reconciliation and peace at any price with that great enemy of real progress, i.e. the rigorous ethical frame of mind thrust upon man by the collective unconscious. Therefore, unconditional surrender to an irresistible and ineradicable evil. In terms of current foreign policy: not "containment", but "co-existence". The process of becoming conscious effects a drastic shift from the transcendent to the immanent. The superior force of evil which was once conceived as coming from above, is now assigned a permanent place within. The evil power remains the same, a "force majeure", but now instead of being produced unconsciously, it is self-created in full consciousness; that is, it is created by the Self. However, man's responsi-

1. *Ethik*, p. 134.
2. *Ethik*, p. 107.

bility is thereby diminished, not increased. For with this transplanting of a supernatural mythical world to the observable psychical world, all objective, absolute standards of conduct fall away and are replaced by standards as subjective as they are relative. The goal has shifted from a moral perfection which man must strive for to a spiritual health which must at all costs be preserved and protected; this objective may require the commission of evil and the giving in to bad instincts or impulses, with the deliberate denial of human values and dignity.

Confirm the evil in this world, and the world's evil will be overcome! This rule bestows a new sanction upon the "Blond Beast" (the blacks are black enough as they are), and this time it is not philosophical but strictly "scientific". Consciously committed evil is to be far preferred over the pernicious feedback of unconsciously committed evil. It is the lesser evil of the two and there is no third alternative.

But was Christian man really as unconscious as all that, reared as he was for centuries with the idea of original sin? Why should the impending collapse of western culture be ascribed to the repression of evil impulses at this particular moment? Human nature being what it is, it would seem probable that his psychological process of repression and conversion of evil drives has been going on for the last two thousand years or more. Why should it all of a sudden have become any different or any stronger now, at the very moment when ethics are much less rigorous than they ever were (particularly thanks to psycho-analysis and depth-psychology etc.)? And, on the other hand, does not this very phenomenon of moral slackening fit in very well with the experience of the decline and disintegration of formerly flourishing cultures? It would seem to come nearer the truth to say that this new ethic simply tends to corroborate the most recent phase of moral uprooting and confusion. For it rationalizes whatever it finds, it becomes a scientific accessory after the fact, and so aids and abets the unfavourable development of our culture instead of arresting it. How this could lead to a recovery, in direct contradiction to all that history teaches us about the fundamental changes of cultural structure, remains unexplained—nor *can* it be explained, in my view. Moreover, any awareness of the possibility that this ethic might lead to quite another and fatal kind of repression seems totally absent. For now it is the moral and spiritual striving for the good and for a better future which could undergo repression.

E. There is no doubt that depth-psychology, in its own special field, contains material which is exceptionally valuable and useful. But its claims in the area of cultural sociology must be emphatically disputed. In this field it is neither modern (based as it is on ancient mythology) nor scientific (with its so-called empirical pronouncements on material which is largely metempirical, such as religion and ethics, and with its generalization from individual to collective psychology and psychopathology, applying psycho-analytic tools to the analysis of the complex processes of cultural evolution). In this respect it not only lacks in depth, remaining as it does on the marginal surface of the current situation, but it can scarcely be accepted as psychology, having rather the flavour of cultural mysticism. The result is not regeneration, but rather a further degeneration of an already declining ethics and religion. Its ethic is a modern paean in praise of evil, its religion but self-worship. The human Self is the new graven idol of the future, elevated above God.

F. Its future achievements for culture? Its good intentions cannot be doubted, but these would seem to conform to its own doctrine of the equivalence of good and evil, and may therefore be expected to have un-avoidable evil counter-effects. This crusade against all unconscious arche-typical image-projections heaps "scientific" fuel[1] on the flames of the iconoclastic holocaust already raging against all positive, idealistic images of the future of every kind. This active support to the typical representatives of our moment-ridden culture puts a heavy burden of shared responsibility on depth-psychology for the possibly injurious and even disastrous effects of destroyed and negated images of the future on the ultimate future of the already wavering culture of the West. This psychology which establishes negation as an elementary constituent of the divine-human totality, has itself no "awareness" whatsoever of the psychology of negative thinking about the future.

The waxing of this depth-psychology and the waning of our culture are but two aspects of the same phenomenon, and each explains the other. They ride on opposite ends of a seesaw which is firmly anchored in the here-and-now. Depth-psychology is child and also herald of the times. It could only spread in a time that has no future. While it is sucking our culture dry, the sands of our time are running out. For this self-appointed champion strikes down all spiritual defences against the evil of current reality, and nips in the bud all spiritual striving towards a humanly worthy, other and better future.

---

1. This really represents an extension of Freud's work, particularly of his *The Future of an Illusion*.

CHAPTER XXIII

ART AND CULTURE

*Die Künste scheinen heute wie durch das
Dasein gepeitscht; es ist kein Altar, an
dem sie Ruhe finden, zu sich zu kommen,
wo ihr Gehalt sie erfühlt.*

Karl Jaspers[1]

Once again we stand at the threshold of a vast territory. This time we are
faced with art and all its branches: the plastic arts, architecture, belles lettres
and poetry, music, design and applied art, dance, theatre and the films.
Once again I remind the reader that I have no specialized knowledge in these
areas. But in any case professional competence is of only limited advantage
here, because in matters of art taste is the final arbiter, and taste is a highly
subjective phenomenon. Value judgements are unavoidable in any discussion about art. Therefore, no great harm can be done if an unqualified
observer joins in the discussion with his personal bias. Moreover, the cultural sociologist cannot and may not ignore art, so long as he remains aware
of his own limitations.[2] The cultural sociological approach to art seeks to
discover the specific social and stylistic relationships, on the one hand
between art and culture in general or between the forms of art and culture
in specific historical periods, and on the other hand between art or its
various forms and other specific areas of culture, such as religion, philosophy,
science, ethics, social behaviour patterns, etc..[3]

1. *Die Geistige Situation der Zeit*, Sammlung Göschen, Bd 1000, Berlin 1949, p. 140.
2. The sociology of art as a specialized field within cultural sociology has received
little systematic attention. Winckelmann, who concerned himself with the art of Antiquity and was sharply attacked by Nietzsche, and Taine, author of *Philosophie de l'Art*,
might be considered as forerunners. Today, Sorokin is probably best acquainted with
the field, or at least is its most assiduous student. He claims to have made a quantitative
and qualitative study of more than 100.000 paintings and pieces of sculpture, and the
outstanding musical, literary, dramatic and architectural works, of the period from the
beginning of the Middle Ages through to about 1930 in eight leading European countries. He has also studied paleolithic, neolithic, primitive, Chinese, Hindu and Egyptian
forms of art. See P. Sorokin, *Social and Cultural Dynamics*, 4 Vols., New York, 1937-41;
it includes an extensive bibliography.
3. Among the best-known of these studies are: M. Dvorak, *Kunstgeschichte als Geistes-
geschichte*, Munich, 1923, W. Passarge, *Die Philosophie der Kunstgeschichte in der Gegenwart*, Berlin, 1930, and Herbert Read, *Icon and Idea*, Cambridge, Mass., 1955.

It is not our intention to offer a comprehensive study of this entire field, but only to examine certain parallel developments of art and culture in the course of history, in their undulations of flowering and decline. We will also focus particularly on the function of the image of the future in this dynamic process, with especial reference to the present and its prospects.

There is a good deal of material on the first-mentioned relationship, that between the rise and fall of art and that of culture, although not as yet very systematically organized. The second aspect, however, the correlation between art, image of the future and culture, is, I believe, being introduced for the first time as a relevant category of sociological research. [1] Since the latter special relationship depends on the former general one, we will first briefly refer to the various attempts to trace causal and functional relationships between the dynamics of art and of culture on the basis of available research in art history and archaeology.

In the first place an attempt was made to demonstrate that the development of art and of the different forms of art is subject to inherent historical laws and regularities. [2] Periods of flowering and decline in art were supposed to occur in the same sequence and follow a pattern which is universally valid in any culture in any historical period. Moreover, this sequence of alternatively dominant phases in art was assumed to coincide with specific similarly recurring phases of development, which every culture passes through.

Next, it was tried to prove that art, now considered as a whole, is subject to specific phases of development and that these phases run parallel to the phases of culture, also considered as a whole. This concept dates back to Hegel's *Aesthetik*, which lays down a three-pronged line of development: symbolic-classic-romantic. [3]

1. Chapter II of Sorokin's *Social Philosophies of an Age of Crisis*, Boston, 1951, contains an excellent review of a number of outstanding theories and studies on this subject. It is one of the best and most reliable productions in the very comprehensive work of this author who is as erudite as he is subjective, and who blends European and American approaches to scholarship. The following selection of hypotheses concerning the dynamics of and relationships between art and culture is taken almost entirely from Sorokin's résumé.

2. In *The Revolutions of Civilization* Flinders Petrie, the Egyptologist, maintains with considerable emphasis that all art forms do not develop simultaneously. On the basis of his considerable historical source-material, he suggests the following sequence: architecture, sculpture, painting, letters and music. Paul Ligeti in his *Der Weg aus dem Chaos* suggests another, equally uniform succession: architecture, plastic, graphic. Other writers, some of them specialists in one or another art form, suggest other sequences, but the idea of "lags" between the development of the differentiated art forms is common to them all. Usually architecture is considered to precede the graphic arts, and music mostly rounds off the list.

3. The archaeologist W. Deonna proposes the thesis of a general dynamics of art

Other researchers, using as a point of departure prehistorical, classical, medieval, renaissance and modern or ultra-modern art, go yet a step further in this direction. They conceive of a cycle of development which not only links art and culture in a pattern which must be repeated with every *new* culture, but also links them in a kind of "eternal recurrence", so that the same pattern repeats itself endlessly *within* every existing culture. Thus every culture would repeat the trio pre-classical, classical and post-classical in its music, and the triptych lyric-epic-dramatic in its literature, in an eternally fixed art-program, moving perpetually from identical endings to identical beginnings in a rigidly automatic "da capo" operating to the n-th power. [1]

If one strips all these theories of their deterministic wrappings, removing the causally determined necessity of automatic recurrence, if one also eliminates any aesthetic interpretations of the history of culture, which would consider art to be the primary determining agent of culture—then there still remains, on the grounds of the available material, a sufficient core of agreement on the connection between the dynamics of art and of culture.

The varying ways in which art is practised and the changes in the forms of art which predominate are intimately related to structural changes in the dynamics of culture. Aesthetic consciousness and cultural consciousness find a "commune mesure" in the development of human values and norms. Show me your art, and I will show you your culture. But it also works the other way around. Give me a picture of your culture, and I will tell you what kind of art goes with it. A culture shines through the prism of its art and the soul of art is reflected in the face of its culture. The score of the symphony of art-forms also keynotes the synchronous course of development of the culture. Cultural developments at every point in time find their counter-image and resonance in the artistic endeavours of the time. Art forms the *counter-point* of every *point* in time of every culture, both in its upward and its downward movements.

according to an invariable succession of archaic-classical-decadent, applicable to every type of culture. He brilliantly marshals support for his position from his extensive research in paleolithic, neolithic, Greco-Roman and Christian art.

1. There are many variations on this theme, and the succession is sometimes two-fold rather than three-fold, as with Dvorak and his contrast between idealistic and naturalistic. Other alternatives to be found in the literature are: haptic and optic, plastic and graphic, classical and romantic, Greek and Gothic, organic and mechanical, "einfühlend" and abstract, etc. Sorokin himself correctly rejects all these theories as too uniform, unilinear, evolutionistic and mechanistic, but then comes up with an equally mechanical fourfold classification, corresponding with his fourfold classification of culture: sensate, ideational, idealistic and eclectic. In his study entitled *The Commonwealth of Art*, New York, 1946, Curt Sachs suggests a new fundamental antithesis between art styles as they ceaselessly undulate through history: that of ethos and pathos.

It can also be said, and it has been said, that art is the highly sensitive indicator on a barometer of culture or of the cultural type of man and society. But the simile of the barometer can be carried even further than in its reference to the existing situation; the barometer also gives prognostic indications of things to come. Now I do not believe at all that art-forms must always necessarily develop in the same sequence, and even less that the same tableau will unroll again and again within each culture in an unending chronological succession of primitive-classical-decadent periods or something like that, with the implication that the culture as a whole must follow this same course of development. [1] But I am convinced that in any given period art can act as a barometer by giving *indications*, both of its *own* further development and of coming developments of the *culture* as a whole, insofar as no counter forces come into play. At this point it emerges that the image of the future presented by art holds a key position, or rather that art holds a key position in that it *is* an image of the future.

It is not possible, however, to present this thesis of art as a special mani-festation of the positive image of the future without already having implied a hypothesis concerning the *nature and essence* of art as such. *Sociology* of art cannot do without a *philosophy* of art!

1. *Art and its Images*

For my point of departure I will first return to the earlier-discussed *dualistic structure* of the human mind. The split and torn man, and no other, is able to conceive of another reality than the present, sensately experienceable one. He differentiates between being and not-being, reality and appearance, existence and essence, fact and value, the actual here-and-now and the idea, which is the "hic et nunc" of the-other-and-higher. Naturally, these dis-tinctions were not at first made deliberately and systematically, or by means of any of the terms we are using. Rather it was an instinctive and intuitive process, emotional and subconscious. Precisely these capacities therefore came into play which are the specific property of artistic natures. The possi-bility of and capability for such a *splitting of space and time* into every-day reality and the other, unknown, form the "conditio sine qua non" for all artistic experience and for the development of all artistic expression.

Along this path, and sometimes along this path alone, something which is *culture* gradually becomes differentiated from *nature*. [2]

1. In this regard Sorokin's arguments concerning the untenability of these generali-zations, based on innumerable examples from the history of art, are in my opinion convincing.
2. I am not prepared to say that art is always the first causal factor in the development of culture and that "split" artistic thought is also the matrix of all later religious, ethical,

Where the beginnings of culture are observable, one also finds the earliest beginnings of art. Therefore I propose to take issue with the long-accepted philosophical view of Plato and Aristotle that art is basically an imitation of nature (natura artis magistra). This view confuses the nature of art with the content of its representations. As I conceive it, even a meticulous copy of nature, if it achieves the stature of a work of art, is essentially a work of recreation and transformation of the real into the other and a beginning of all that is typically "cultural". This "other" is the medium through which art places its world of semblance opposite the world of actual existence. *Art is arti-ficial*. Through its spiritual power and ideational awareness, it distances itself from the existent and approaches the other with its sixth sense. It creates a second realm with its own hands.

Thus, according to this view, the *split mentality* forms the basis for all artistic activity. But not for artistic activity alone. It is also the common foundation for all constructive cultural efforts. What is unique for art is the *way in which* it sets its own stamp on the representation of another reality, the *specific manner* in which it connects this with the existing world. *How* does *art* perceive the other, *where* does this other lead it, and *in what form* do these impulses of the soul find expression? I will concentrate on answering these three questions, which fall particularly within the scope of this work. A few of the essential elements of all art [1] will be crystallized in the process of applying our cultural-sociological category of the positive image of the future—a category which I believe also to be adequate from the point of view of the sociology of art. Indeed, especially adequate. For whereas positive images of the future can also be expressed and communicated in non-aesthetic forms, our main thesis here is that true art is unthinkable without containing and transmitting as its essence a positive image of the future.

If in the following the three components, the *positive*, the *image* and the *future*, will be treated separately, it should be emphasized at the outset that only taken together as an integrated whole do they become meaningful.

A. The Positive

How does the artist see the Other? The non-artist can only attempt a second-hand verbal reconstruction of the process. It is a beholding with the inward eye, trained and sharpened by outward observation. The second realm is seen with a *second sight*. This inwardly directed seeing also includes

philosophical and scientific thought, but the capacity for aesthetic conception and representation is at any rate one of the oldest and most fruitful sources of culture. See Herbert Read, *op. cit.*

1. Art consists of other elements than those discussed here, but I am by-passing those which are not relevant to our purposes.

a silent listening, an interception from other spheres, a sensitivity to and communication with the unseen. This intuitive perception generally precedes conscious reflection, the image precedes the ratio. Living in the imaginary world of beauty is the artistic mode of perception of the "normally" invisible and inaudible, of the ordinary mortal's "unknown" and "unknowable".

The world of the totally other is a wonder-world of the super-human. How shall the nameless be named? For some, it is the world of the divine and eternal, of the All-One or of the Primal Source. For others, it is the world of the absolute or the idea, of the essence of things, of the "it" or the "self", of the world soul or spirit. For still others, it is a world of bliss, of immortal life, of cosmic perfection, the realm of light, of perfect humanity, a Garden of Eden, or a Nirvana.

The perception of this other world is a visionary one, but for the inspired artist it takes on as visual a form as our own world. The seer sees *reality*. It is an *other* reality which appears as pure fantasy of optical illusion to those who are not thus gifted, but it is a living experience for the artist and therefore to him genuinely existing, real and *positive*. For him the non-existent *is* the existent. The artist's gaze includes the not-yet in the dimensions of time and space, in his own Kantian modes of perception, with which he creatively calls the other world into being and gives meaning to being in this world, experiencing both worlds as one.

B. The Image

These inspired aspirations of art, its yearning contemplation and realization of the Other Realm—here conceived as the essence of all art—find pregnant expression in the concrete *image*, which is the aesthetic design for an organic fusion of content and form, chosen and modelled by art for its appearance in this world. [1] The self-realization of the artist's personality takes on a living form in the image, stimulating him to the realization of the Other. The image is a visible and audible sign of the invisible and inaudible. The creation of an artistic *image* is art's *art* of incorporating the incorporal and of realizing the unreal. Art breathes the breath of life into its pure ardours and so art is a vision of the Other and also of the image, art sets the blood of life flowing through its veins, art purifies in method, a way to reach it. The image of art is a *symbol* in the literal sense of a "coincidence" of this and the other world. As a symbol it is hidden revelation, veiled vision, restrained expressiveness. [2] Its symbolic language

1. The distinction still often made between aesthetics of form and of content is in my opinion contrary to a correct iconographic understanding of the artistic image, which can only be regarded as an undivisible whole.
2. If it can be said that the artistic image "disguises" itself as a symbol or a parable,

is not the language of this reality, but a secret language. The image is an art-istic, and thus highly character-istic transcription of the great unknown. It needs to be re-transposed, interpreted and explained.

But the artistic image, from whatever branch of art, is more than a bridge between two worlds. It is more than a *projection* into the unknown: it is above all *prophecy* of things to come. It is more in that it not only reflects what the mind's eye of the artist has beheld, but also what the artist has in mind, his object or his intention. The image, or rather the finished work of art, has covered the distance between the beginning and the end and has reached final perfection in human imperfection. The image is the outer form in which art encloses, metamorphoses and discloses itself, in which its naked soul is garbed but still recognizable to the initiate. It is both an original prototype and an ultimate ideal type. It encompasses the first and the last Adam, the total meaning of existence. Just as much as religion and ethics, art sets a goal and a norm for mankind.

The image, as an artistic creation, speaks, sometimes even shrieks—or whispers—of a finality, of some kind of last goal and boundary in time. It may be paradise, a new heaven and a new earth, cosmic unity, serenity, a complete absence of desire, a condition of peace and joy, or an ultimate synthesis or totality. Whatever its external form and whatever its particular idea, the artistic image is always an expression of an approach to perfection, of a transformation through beauty into the good and the true, the "summum bonum", and of a liberation and salvation, whether through divine grace or through the good works of man. Art opens the azure portal to the *other, golden realm :* the kingdom of the heavens, the harmony of the spheres, the cosmic meaning of existence, the great mystery, the holy grail, the All, the nameless, in short, the concept, however labelled, of the numinous and luminous.

The ways of art are at least in part inscrutable. It sometimes prefers to work through extreme contrasts, and as long as art is true to itself, evil serves the good, and the ugly enhances the beautiful. In this case the grotesque, the monstrous and the horrifying only buttress the ideal, the perfect, the sublime; the negative and inhuman are relevant to the super-human and positive. The Inferno is part of the Divine Comedy. The wild witch's sabbath is followed by the serene chimes of the angelus, the dies irae by a hallelujah. After an all-destroying Walpurgis-night, the new dawn ushers in a total rebirth. The unchained elements of nature are gathered up in the

then its symbolism must be of a kind with all similarly oriented symbolism, with the archetypes of symbolic transformation and interpretation. And art does indeed always demonstrate a network of ties to the symbolism of the unconscious, to that of dreams, fairy-tales, myths, mysticism, of cosmic speculations and metaphysical ideas about the divine and about human life, death and destiny.

pastoral, as man's fall is gathered up in the Plan of Salvation and the dialectical antithesis in the final synthesis or apotheosis. Hieronymus Bosch and Hell Breugel, Grünewald and Goya, point in apocalyptic-allegorical fashion towards a heavenly exaltation. Even Lucifer, the fallen demon-angel, remains a bearer of light, diabolus est deus inversus. The blind and groping mephistophelian *Faust I* is completed by the radiant and ecstatic *Faust II*. [1]

In its image art always presents, whether directly or indirectly, straight or controversially, the image of the highest value, either an image of God or the divine, or a replica—an image of man of the most exalted, god-like dignity.

C. The Future

The contemplation of and union with the Other inspires the artist to his art. The Other is the *primal source*, and also the *ultimate goal*. Art is the shuttle which moves constantly back and forth between the two poles which in the deepest sense are one, weaving its trends into the cultural pattern. Art is intrinsically a process of moving and being moved, or it is not art. The finished work of art is a finished movement in itself, but at the same time it is a movement in the development of art as a whole, and finally it causes its public to be moved and so moves its culture. Art has its source in emotion, in being moved, and it causes emotion. It moves the spirit of man, so that he is shaken and moved to change his direction. Art flings man into the other world, it brings him beside himself and raises him above himself. True art splits the earth-bound human atom and releases its energies for another order. It appeals to man and rouses him, it stirs and agitates and drives him forward by its mysterious power.

The artist is the ideal-type of the citizen-of-two-worlds. He flees into the, his, other world, seeks and finds his inspiration in that other sphere, and has intercourse there with his Muse. There he plunges into the stream of oblivion, drinks from the eternal fountain, partakes of the nectar and ambrosia of the gods, plucks the golden apples from the tree of beauty, accompanies Orpheus on his pilgrimage to the underworld, associates successively with Apollo and Dionysus, cavorts with nymphs and fauns, encounters graces and spirits, makes the acquaintance of heroes and demigods, and discovers angels and demons and other living creatures, shadowy forms or radiant apparitions. His other world lives, moves and is inhabited, has its own nature and cosmos, its own illogical laws and irrational phenom-

1. As we know, Goethe left Faust II as a sealed testament. He felt that his own confused time would not be able to appreciate this work properly. Only after the year 2.000, he thought, would men be able to understand it. A tragic miscalculation of a great and forward-looking spirit, who is now both more revered and more remote than ever before.

ena, its own rhythms and motives. It is a dynamic, mobile world which in its restless movement offers a place of rest to the soul of the artist, the fixed point for the artistic transformation and transfiguration of the existent.

Before the artist can function as a *transmitter* of images, he must be able to *receive* them. Only the possessed can take possession of the spirits of initiated souls. Expressive creation follows upon introspective imagination. When the possessed are "receiving", this includes both a turning in upon themselves and a stepping out of themselves; a fulfilment of their own humanity, and an overstepping of the boundaries which limit the ordinary man. The reception of images out of nothingness, or at least out of another dimension, occurs by means of a sixth sense. It touches the paranormal in a kind of telepathic transmission of higher and deeper psychic powers. The artist is driven into a state of spiritual transport and rapture, into the trance of the seer and into the split awareness of and sensitivity to the *other*, the beyond.

He flees into the other world, this artist, but so long as his split mind does not become irrevocably alienated, he returns. He climbs higher and higher, mounting the gradus ad Parnassum, yet ever again turns back in his tracks to rejoin earthly reality. The artist is Prometheus and Epimetheus in one. Having successfully sought and received *in*spiration on his pilgrimage into the unknown, he now turns to *ex*pression. Flight and return, beholding and tangible molding, revelation and manifestation form an indissoluble and hardly distinguishable whole for the artist. In this back and forth, this dynamic alternating displacement lies the seed of an irresistible impulse and even revolutionary and explosive drive toward the onwards and upwards. The *dynamics* of and towards the other can be like *dynamite* for the existent. The tensely charged energies of art can function as a link between the two worlds and along this road, or quite directly, it may become a lever for regeneration and renewel.

Art is a bridge between the Here and the Beyond. It knows or is the art of synthesis between the immanent and the transcendent, for which so many philosophical systems right up to our own day have striven in vain. It lives and gives new life to the existent out of the dialectic tension between reality and idea. In art the encounter between time and eternity takes place, between the here-and-now, and the somewhere-and-sometime. In short, one essential of all art is—in my view—a forward-striving, for in its seeking and groping it reaches out toward the other world, it fathoms and scales a land of promise, it paves the way and points to the future new eon. Art is not only "moving" and not just a movement, but it moves in a certain direction—toward the future.

Art as a "directed movement toward the future" is more than one description out of many other possibilities. What we offer here is a thesis with vast implications on which our further argument will be built up. To begin with, this thesis rejects the currently accepted view that art is essentially the purest means for expressing its time-period. Art may be this too, but secondarily, rather than deliberately or basically. On the contrary, true art of all times breaks through its own time. Artistic creativity might even best be characterized as an escape from the clutches of the actual present. Art is the gang-way in the air, leading from time to eternity and vice versa. A temporal time-bound art is in itself un-artistic. If art denies the supra-temporal, or at any rate the coming time, it denies itself.

For this reason, a true understanding of the language of art not only illuminates a specific historical period, but forms the instrument par excellence for the sounding and prognosis of the unfolding future of which that period is the seed-bearer. Art always contains in faintly dotted outline a tendency or a trend, a prevision and a program of that which is not yet. Just as the interpretation of dream-material is necessary for the psychiatrist, so the cultural philosopher cannot do without the interpretation of art-material if he wants to arrive at a profounder diagnosis of a sick time and a prognosis concerning the probable future course of development. Art reflects what lies deep in the soul of the times. At the same time it emanates a highly sensitive split foreknowledge of cultural development; it reveals, it prophecies. It is more than a sign of the times. It pre-senses through its image-reception, and pre-dicts through its image-transmission. In its supernatural state of being possessed, it reveals the signs and foretokens of the new time. Art, always eccentrically located on the farthest periphery of the times, contains the heartbeat of the future. [1]

Art works in the shadows of tomorrow, bringing to realization its presentiments of that which is coming and already lies visibly to it on the

---

1. This view of art as containing future-oriented elements is not a brand-new discovery. However, I believe the systematic sociological application of this concept to be new. After completion of the manuscript I discovered a very pertinent book by Hans Sedlmayr, *Verlust der Mitte*, Die bildende Kunst des 19. und 20. Jahrhunderts als Symptom und Symbol der Zeit, Salzburg, 1948. He makes use of this same insight, although primarily for the purpose of analyzing modern art and understanding the present age. In the appendix to the fourth edition (1951, p. 253 ff.) he gives somewhat more attention to this point on the basis of a quotation from G. Revesz, *Einführung in die Musikpsychologie*, Berne, 1946; "Bevor noch der Mensch im stande ist, die in ihm wirkenden kollektiven Kräfte und Zielsetzungen der folgenden Zeitperiode sich bewusst zu machen und begrifflich zu formulieren, tritt in der Kunst, vor allem wie mir scheint in der Musik, oft mit einer überraschenden Lebendigkeit und Wahrhaftigkeit alles das hervor, was dem Verstand noch verborgen als treibende Kraft im Menschen, individuell und kollektiv, bereits lebt und wirkt. — Die Kunst kann Vorbote der Morgenröte, aber auch Ankündigung der Finsternis und eines drohenden Gewitters sein".

horizon. It lives already now in the far prospect, and draws its creative material out of that. It witnesses to these perspectives and would convince men of them. It communicates its deeper and wider views. It is the medium which reveals what is as yet hidden from the masses and sweeps them forward towards the great unknown, lifting a tip of the future's veil. Inspired and inspiring, art personifies the striving toward the other as the higher and better, which is both exalted and exalting. Impelled by the other world, and insistently propelling toward it, all art is progressive. In its hope for the restoration of a paradise lost, regressive-romantic art is progressive too, for its regression is stimulated by the longing for a better time in the future. Even this regress is moved by progress in time. Art moves from *trans*-cendence to *as*cendence.

D. The Positive Image of the Future

The image with which art works is a *positive image of the future*. The image of the future which art evokes is always an image of the *ideal* and of the highest *idea*, of evolution and elevation, of a bringing to perfection and a glorification.

The artistic image clothes and conceals itself in a symbol, as a sealed expression of and a key to the other. Through a visible or audible representation it conveys the meaning of something else and other. But ever and above expressing itself in symbols, art also expounds a deeper *meaning*, it offers a point of view through its symbols. The symbolism of the image and its ultimate intent or meaning are intimately related. In the last instance, all forms of art are "representational", art always expresses itself in images, all artistic images are symbolic and every symbol "graphically" indicates the meaning or guiding idea of the work of art.

1. Meaning

The unequalled wealth of *images* which characterizes art in its greatest periods is also a wealth of *meaning*. In and through its symbolic images art is *intent* on something. Art is a sublime "Sturm und Drang", a captured "perpetuum mobile", actively at work in space and time.

By virtue of its guiding idea the beauty of the artistic image contains a tremendous power. The image is the crystallized idea, which turns like a flower to the sun of its ideal; it is a mysterious and magnetic effluence of frozen fluidity, it is a fire of ice, an earth-bound stormer of the heavens. Through its active idea of the other, symbolically formulated, the artistic image possesses and expresses a norm of self-unfolding activity, and a meaning and goal for that activity. There is a tenor in its motionless extension, it has a tendency. It contains, intentionally or not, a purposeful answer to the ultimate question: whither?

The true image remains symbolic. Its energy and dynamism reside in its compelling and convincing "impetus" to achieve the spiritual translation of the symbol, which then has the effect of revelation. As a result of this strain and exertion the fundamental idea is grasped, the normative ideal which moved and inspired the artist.

Penetrating through the outward form into the inward meaning, we come into communication with the symbolically revealed spiritual life of the artist, and thereby with the other. We obtain a view or a vision of the other. The horizon to the other is opened, a new *perspective* moves us towards it.

2. PERSPECTIVE

All art holds out such a perspective to the imagination of its spectators and listeners, unfolding for these who fathom the meaning of its images.

I would suggest that the introduction of perspective into the art of painting as a technical means of image presentation is closely related to the perspective which all works of art contain as prospect of a coming time. [1]

The complete realization of the perspective painting was a revolutionary accomplishment of far-reaching and literally far-seeing implications. It meant that it was possible to add a third and even a fourth dimension to an image projected on a flat surface. The canvas recedes into the background, the surface is hollowed out so that it has depth and transparency. One can now see through the painting as through a window, into the far distance and to the very horizon. The representation itself is no longer a portrayal of a higher world in which man has no part, but the spectator is now, through the medium of the eye, literally moved toward and brought into direct contact with it. [2]

1. This is possibly a reformulation in my own words of an insight which has already been expressed elsewhere.
2. The presence or absence of perspective in art is certainly not a criterion for the evaluation of art. It is rather a criterion for symbolic and stylistic meanings. The elementary linear perspective was already known in Antiquity, both theoretically and intuitively. It is no coincidence, however, that it was not fully developed until—and through—the Renaissance. The way was prepared during the transition from late-Gothic to early-Renaissance in the fourteenth century, especially through the fresco's of Giotto and Duccio. Developed further in the fifteenth century through such men as Brunelleschi, Masaccio, Piero della Francesca and the Van Eyck brothers, it was perfected by Alberti and Leonardo da Vinci, both in respect to mathematical-geometric foundations and the use of colour perspective. The ensuing general spread of the use of dynamic-stereoscopic techniques of perspective in painting is closely related to the development of the new world-image and the new image of the future in this period of revival and rebirth, as contrasted with the world-image of Antiquity and the Middle Ages, both in respect to space and time. The palingenesis develops before our very eyes in the forward-moving perspective.

The alternations in dimensions and distances which perspective introduces result in an optical illusion. The new image is an ingenious blend of semblance and reality. The pictured objects not only develop plasticity, but mimic movement. Moreover, the total picture becomes visually mobile, according to the position of the spectator. Without perspective, it is extremely difficult to give the impression of any kind of movement.

More than the quality of mobility is involved, however. Perspective gives sharper relief to the tenor of the image, the meaning of its movement is more clearly defined as to its direction and goal. It is no longer so much the representation itself which is a miracle, as in more primitive paintings, but its moving subjects and objects make a wonder from higher spheres enter into this world. The images become visionary. The miracle visibly takes place in the psyche of the figures on the canvas. The *infinite* has been transplanted to *finite* reality, and the *other* world merges perspectively with the *existing* world. The dynamic of a divinely inspired world spirit is imparted to the figures of the painting. The wonder takes place within the spectators who steep themselves in the artistic creation. It is a moving event. The spectator not only looks through the transparent picture, but is spiritually transported to the transcendent. [1]

No better example of all this than Rembrandt in the whole of whose work a mobile and supernatural light illuminates this gloomy world and disperses the shadows of space and time through its symbolic lustre and warm glow. This leaps to the eye in the unique gradations of light and shadow by means of which he, the seer, makes the invisible visible, and the other—the supernatural and the divine—conscious and perceptible. His pictures irradiate the misery of this earth with their passionate assurance; the certitude that a higher order of divine bliss will ultimately triumph is conveyed *in* his perspective and so held out *as* a perspective. In this graphic perspective a faith is proclaimed and asserted, faith in a coming new eon.

In the perspective of pictorial art a technique and a vision have curiously emerged. But even the apparently frozen movement of temple, cathedral or sculptured piece, whose materials contain a radiation of tremendous pent-up energy, through the technique of perspective, come to move in their very immobility. In their impassivity history is made to pass. The perspective

---

1. The great flowering and influence of the art of painting is unthinkable without the technique of perspective. It is the prerequisite of Raphael's Sistine Madonna and the murals in the Vatican, of Michelangelo's paintings on the ceiling of the Sistine Chapel, of Dürer's Apocalypse and of Grünewald's Isenheimer Altar. Only in this form could they perfectly express religious, apocalyptic and chiliastic (Grünewald) *expectations of the future.* The same is true for the grandiose phantasmagorias of the baroque masters of the brush.

of painting and architecture can be compared with the depth which counter-point provides in music, both as a foundation of polyphonic and polymelodic composition and of its total harmony. [1] Bach's Art of the Fugue brings this technique to its highest development in music. The transcending function and the futuristic aspect are practically the same. Specialists will be able to point out parallels for other art-forms. For all true art intrinsically aims to transform the here-and-now into the other and the coming.

3. ART SHAPES THE FUTURE

In analyzing the perspective meaning of the art-image, we once again discover the basic meaning of all artistic activity and endeavour: *the idea of the positive image of the future*. Was not this idea already implicit in the Greek term "kalokagathos", the ideal union of the beautiful and the good, which is also as it were the relating of the now and the then, the here and the there? All art is basically a "view", an idealistic "Weltanschauung", even so-called realistic art, for it is still a purposeful re-creation. It incorporates these traits stylistically-aesthetically in its elementary components of dynamic rhythm, contrast and tonality, of proportion, symmetry and harmony. *All* art is perspective in its forms of expression, providing a model and an example. *All* art is representational, and *all representational art is*, in a certain sense, *a representation of the future*.

Having arrived at this point, we can now make note of the fact that we have made significant progress. At the beginning of this chapter we took as our point of departure the traditional view—in itself entirely correct—of the intimate relationship between the dynamics of art and the dynamics of culture. This relationship now appears to be located in their image of the future and this discovery enables of a clearer and deeper analysis. We have laid sufficient groundwork to be able to outline this relationship. Shifts in the kinds and styles of art, perceivable in the development of the perspective meaning of their image, are structurally related (both as causes and as effects) to shifts in the cultural image of the time and the future, especially in the ideas and expectations, the predictions, the values, norms and ideals

---

1. Dr. R. Mengelberg, in *Muziek, Spiegel des Tijds* (Rotterdam, 1948), states that new dimensions have been added to music in western culture, especially through the chord, the harmonic triad, and the new rhythms utilized in instrumental music. In the field of sociology of music, Max Weber was once again the pioneer, with his essay on "Die rationalen und soziologischen Grundlagen der Musik", published in *Wirtschaft und Gesellschaft*, Tübingen, 1925. Also of importance are the essay by Kurt Blaukopf on "Musiksoziologie" in *Soziologie und Leben*, edited by Carl Brinkmann, Tübingen, 1952, and a separate work entitled *Musiksoziologie, Eine Einführung in die Grundbe-griffe mit besonderer Berücksichtigung der Soziologie der Tonsysteme*, St. Gallen, 1950, and the study by Andreas Liess, *Die Musik im Weltbild der Gegenwart*, Lindau, 1949.

concerning the coming times. The specifically *artistic* image is flesh of the flesh of the general *cultural image of the future*, and thus finds itself in continuous interaction with it. The alternations of cultural optimism and cultural pessimism are reflected in the subtle shifts in art's inferences about the future. Similarly, the flowering and decline of artistic images and their perspective meaning has its effect on the future developments of cultural history.

It is clear, then, that the above rather lengthy exposition of the essential meaning of art and its images was indispensable in order to be able to resolve the connected problems concerning the future of art and the future of culture. Now we can take for our point of departure the two-fold position that (1) the current decline of culture, or of its components, particularly through a systematic mutilation of images of the future, will in all probability be ascertainable in a general derangement of art, and (2) an eventual decline (or even loss) of the artistic image of the future, as representing the loss of that essential element which fuses the perception, the symbol and the meaning of the image into a work of art, could and perhaps *must* have fatal consequences both for the future of art itself and, because of its great influence, for the future of culture.

2. *Art's Image of the Future*

Art does not stand alone, but is always embedded in the whole of culture. Its relationship to the other areas of culture changes with the course of time. This change is in itself significant, both for art and for any given period, as well as for their common, interrelated development.

Traditionally, aesthetics was one of the foremost branches of metaphysics. [1] But here too, we find that a clearly marked transition has taken place in modern times, a transition away from an all-inclusive metaphysics and towards specialized fields of science and philosophy: history of art, the science of art-techniques, philosophy of art, psychology of art (Lippe, Volkelt) and sociology of art (Guyau). Metaphysical aesthetics has become outmoded and largely superseded by the modern methods of science. [2]

1. This branching-off began with Plato and Aristoteles and continued with Plotinus and the neo-Platonists, and on through to the idealistic philosophy of Kant, Hegel, and Croce, of Baumgarten (who established the term "aesthetica") and the Hegelian F. Th. Vischer.
2. This situation is related to the fact that idealistic metaphysics itself, as we have said, has gradually made way for an anti-metaphysical philosophy—whether in the form of positivism and naturalism, or vitalism and irrationalism, or of realism and existentialism. It is interesting to note how these new philosophical conceptions of our own time are heavily influencing both theoretical views concerning aesthetics and the actual practice of the arts, as well as its basic philosophy or its general "Weltanschauung". Here the simple statement of these relationships must suffice.

In summary it may be said that the gradual elimination of aesthetics from metaphysics is accompanied by an explicit rejection of metaphysics by aesthetics. Thus rendered free and independent, aesthetics concentrates more and more on factual empirical reality and the actualities experienced in daily life.

Similarly, it could be shown how the "scienticizing"—which is typical of our century—and especially the marked accent of natural science and technology, are also reflected in the modern views on and practice of art. [1]

In the same spirit, it would be possible to trace the parallel development of religion and art. [2] It is obvious that the iconoclasm of orthodox-Protestantism and the continuing disintegration of eschatological representations cannot remain without profound effects on religious art and on all art which has religious experience as its source of inspiration. A declining church-membership, atheism and agnosticism, or an abstract philosophical-impersonalist faith, all work toward the detachment of art from religion and the Church; these patterns of thought and behaviour turn it away from the supernatural and from an idealistically conceived higher reality, and incline it toward the realistic but chaotic here-and-now. Religious emotion and aesthetic emotion should certainly not be equated—in certain respects they are even antithetical—but the weakening of both can have its origin in the same fundamental uprooting and can be caused by parallel life-sapping forces of cultural dynamics. The analogy lies in the *progressive hollowing-out* of the metaphysical-religious and of the aesthetic *image of the future*. The latter is the point to which I will confine myself in this context.

In its own time, almost all great art was "modern" art, a renewing and regenerating art which stepped outside its period, misunderstood and shocking to the conservative resisted and despised and opposed with might and main. But this does not mean that all "modern art" is for that reason always a sign of artistic health; it may also be holding its own death's-head in its hands, it may be tolling the knell for all art. One may strike new paths into the future, overstepping formerly conceived boundaries and pushing

1. Certain forms and kinds of art develop more in the direction of skills and professional competence, of applied and utilitarian art, or engineering competence. Technical, geometric and abstract, or concretely practical considerations may dominate the artistic impulse of the work of art, and the demands of an occupation bound to material production quotas may frustrate the urge of vocation. The mechanization of art can undermine its organic character, and render impotent its spiritual dynamic force. When art gains in scientific content, it not infrequently loses in artistic form. The age which has bound science to itself now threatens by this devious route also to enchain art.
2. Much attention has been given to the relationship between religion and art, but too little within the total frame of reference of cultural dynamics.

up to new spiritual heights. One may also, however, strike paths which come to a dead end or lead downwards into an abyss. It is difficult to avoid on the one hand the trap of reaction, perennially set for all modern art as such, by the philistine, the petty bourgeois, the traditional lauder of bygone times, the conventional Victorian and the timorous provincialist—and on the other hand the trap of revolution set by a radically and fundamentally different modern art, out to catch and destroy all preceding and following art. The labour pains which accompany the birth of a new era and the last convulsions of the present period may produce a similar outward effect, either way confusing to the observer.

It is suggested here that the modern art of *our* day (wrongly but unavoidably considered as a whole) is basically different from the greater part of the modern art of previous ages. The defenders of today's modern art can indeed point to a centuries-long history in which the theme of the despised, misunderstood and embattled artist, who was in retrospect recognized as one of the greatest, is repeated again and again. They can point to suspicion and prejudice and resistance which stemmed from the misplaced application of old norms or current values to new art forms for the appraisal of which no new and suitable criteria had been established as yet, so that critics were drawing upon an outmoded image-terminology even while a new and deviating vocabulary of images had already developed. All this is indisputably true. We must always be aware of this danger and be honestly willing to learn to understand the newly emerging language of art with its different expressions. We must make the necessary effort for this and genuinely attempt to enter into this new artistic experience, keeping our minds ever open and not judging, let alone condemning, lightly. But even so the said phenomena constitute no proof in themselves.

The fact cannot be altered that a renewal of art may overshoot its goal and that not *all* resistance may be disqualified *in advance* on historical grounds. This seems to me to be particularly true with reference to our modern so-called non-representational art. When we have a situation where not only one image-vocabulary is replaced by another, but where the image-representation in its stylistic unity is radically rejected as such, then the question at once arises: to what extent does this art still contain a meaning, in how far can it have artistic qualities and values for lovers of art?

In my view the "modernity" of today's art is marked by a specific character. It has an element, or rather a lack, which is in basic conflict with the essence of art as such. The situation in which we find ourselves is not only that art's wealth of images has been converted into a poverty of images, but the artistic image is increasingly losing its primary intent and meaning, its positive and perspective *image of the future*. Is seems to me that this statement can be demonstrated to apply to nearly all that presents itself as modern art in our time. But we will have to content ourselves with a few illustrations mainly from the plastic arts, specifically in the field of painting. [1] And once more our ideal-typical method requires that we do not discuss the few exceptions which even today prove the rule in decreasing numbers. Our goal is to demonstrate, from the *cultural-sociological* point of view (and thus apart from the problem of judging the artistic merits of individual works of art), how both *the image and the future* have been pinched and broken in modern art.

A. Modern Art

Our discussion will begin by referring to one of the major modern developments in *painting* which took place in the last decades of the preceding century: *impressionism*. [2] As the name indicates, this trend involves the reproduction of flashing impressions. This art concentrates on quasi-photographic instantaneous exposures, on the capture of the fugitive moment. All *art of the moment* is in basic contrast to an *art of the future*, just as the transitory and the eternal are always in conflict, or pass each other by. The development of this style is one from the imaginary to the purely sensual and sensory, from the visionary to the merely visual. Impressions are not derived from the other and higher, but exclusively from direct physical experience, therefore from actual reality. In consequence, this development is also one from *idealism* to *realism*.

Realism deliberately opposes the idea of the transcendent, its symbolic representation and any metaphysical or metempirical purport of the image. It is against all mysticism and symbolism. In this respect it makes little difference in principle whether realism develops further into neo-realism, sur-realism or magical realism (strange contradiction in terms). As a rule it remains primarily oriented toward immanent reality. Volatility and lack of depth characterise it; it remains on the surface; the retina functions passively as a light-receptor, as the spectral host to a spectacular gamut of flashy colours arranged in blobs, stripes or dots. But for the most part these rays do not touch the soul in any deeper, ideal sense of meaning. Impressionism corresponds to modern materialism (or matter-realism) and to the intensity and acceleration of the modern hurried tempo of life. In its over-drawing

1. In this connection see Sedlmayr's most interesting book, already cited. Out of a wealth of literature, particular attention might also be called to B. Champigneulle, *L'Inquiétude dans l'art d'aujourd'hui*, Paris, 1939. Any illustrated work on modern art will provide ample material for further illustration.
2. This trend in the art of painting, and other trends to be mentioned later, are also found in other branches of art, and often under the very same labels. In this respect painting can serve as pars pro toto for art talis qualis.

of outward events this art tends to become movement without inner emotion.

This led, in the first quarter of this century, to a new reversal to the other extreme, which ultimately meets the first: *expressionism*. [1] Expressionism appears originally as the direct antipode of impressionism. It sharply attacks materialism and mechanicism, realism and naturalism and the purely sensory rendition of momentary and purely external impressions on the eye. In short, it appears to aim at the rehabilitation of the super-sensual, the other and higher, the inner depth of emotion, the ideal image of the future. It appears to usher in a new era of spiritualization and inspiration.

Indeed, all this was expressly declared in this radical and revolutionary movement for regeneration. The tragedy was that time was striding on and would not permit a simple setting back of the clock. Therefore an entirely modern setting must necessarily be found for the old ideals. At the same time, the reactions against the purely visual, subjective and sensory style of the preceding school of painting was so extreme, and such very modern views were held about complete freedom in regard to the categories of space and time or the difference between appearance and reality, that a violent shift took place in favour of the ideal *content* at the expense of the plastic *forum*. The latter was disdained and disregarded, so that finally the image itself was sacrificed to the basic idea. Generalizing about these two movements, it can be said that impressionism eliminates or curtails the *future*, and that expressionism eliminates or curtails the *image*; thus the image of the future was crushed between the hammer and anvil of movement in time.

Expressionism is more than a specific pictorial art-style, since it assigns a radically changed place to the artistic image. Therefore it is of interest to review briefly the ideas of various schools of expressionism. A number of trends developed under different labels: cubism and dadaism, divisionism and constructivism, futurism, archaism and surrealism, abstract and absolute art, and, especially in architecture, the "Neue Sachlichkeit".

1. CUBISM AND DADAISM

Cubism seeks to express the suprasensual and a higher truth in the logical-mathematical essence of simplified forms (cubes, segments, prisms). [2] The

---

1. Expressionism also does not remain confined to painting, extending rather far beyond to almost every realm of art. At the same time it is not a sharply defined movement and disintegrates into a number of isms, each following hard upon the heels of the other and all mutually overlapping. These developments to some extent appear to lead impressionism on to neo-impressionism and to turn its realism into super-realism. In this confusing diversity many differences of classification have arisen, not only—and understandably—with respect to individual artists (who will be named as little as possible here), but also with respect to specific groups.

2. To this end it detaches itself from the "natural" external forms, as they are visually

resulting image is an imitation, not of nature, but of analytical, experimental natural science.

Dadaism attempts a similar simplification, particularly through studied naiveté and primitivity. The image resembles that of pictures by small children and is to remain, quite literally, artless.

2. DIVISIONISM AND CONSTRUCTIVISM

Divisionism is mainly based on the scientific analysis of complementary colours (including light and shadow). The images show an abundance of dots (pointillism) or mosaic-like arrangements of elementary colours. [1]

Constructivism is equally methodical and technical in its design. Here too, everything is calculated as exactly as possible on a scientific basis. These constructions are mechanized and as a rule the image actually contains machines or parts of machines. To the layman, at least, these works of art seem made-to-order productions without individual life or emotion.

3. FUTURISM AND ARCHAISM

The movement toward renewal in art next moved in two currents, apparently running in opposite directions but both connected with the main stream.

Futurism appeared at first to hold real promise for the image of the future, both in name and starting-point. It was born of fervent enthusiasm, dynamism and youthful vitality. [2] But it overstrained its original idea, its optimism became puerile, it turned into hysterical excess and immoderation. Finally, futurism became diverted into fascism and fizzled out in politics. This movement made too hectic an attempt to actualize the future and its image became completely disproportioned.

Archaism, on the other hand, presented a new form of systematic primitivism. It wanted to go to an extreme of simplification and schematization.

experienced in their three dimensions. The different surfaces of objects are subjected to a geometrical analysis from which emotions, values or qualities are eliminated. These surfaces are spread out, ex-plained as it were. Their colours too are distributed separately over clearly delineated spaces. This distended or dissected rendition of surfaces and colours is carried out systematically, in cool deliberation on a scientific basis.

1. The maximum effect produced at different distances by the vibrations of light is meticulously calculated by means of physical and mathematical theory. The component colour particles are carefully distributed in order to become recomposed in the observer's eye.

2. Its founder, Marinetti, wrote that a rushing automobile was more beautiful than the Venus of Milo. The works of futurism showed the feverish darts of contemporary forces, the tempestuous dynamics and hurried tempo of modern life, in the surging and lurching of its lines and figures. Combined with cubist trends, it literally pushed all aspects of the world around, shoved together or took apart, turned inside out, top to bottom, back to front, etc.

This was realized by an innovation which went as far back as possible, not to the romantic idyll or the ethereal or mystical idealism of the last five or six hundred years, but much farther back, namely to the so-called primitive cultures and arts.

In the image this is expressed in the first place by a return to a two-dimensional rendition. In other words, perspective, the introduction of which had meant a revolution in art, is now banished deliberately. This, of course, implies the explicit rejection of perspective in its double meaning for the image as we have described it, both as technique and as message, as a conscious expression of the image of the future. Where futurism inflated the image of the future to the point of explosion, archaism undermined it. Works of art became child-like and wooden, its forms and figures were flat and nearly static. If futurism was too dynamic, archaism lacked dynamism. These images were like wax-works: "Alles schon da-da gewesen".

But this orientation toward the so-called primitive implied yet another possible mode of presentation. In a complete misinterpretation of the nature of these antiquarian, partly prehistoric forms of art, this pseudo-imitation served as a license for depicting the barbaric and bestial. Archaism here developed into a kind of neo-naturalism, which painted nature as it "actually was", without the varnish of civilization. And it was taken to be "primitive", i.e. uncultured, vital and brutal.

In this form archaism merged with surrealism. The surrealist artist does not paint what is observed consciously and with the senses, but projects onto the canvas that which is hidden in the subconscious and deepest unconscious reaches of the soul. The image renders freudian primeval drives and instincts, suppressed desires, dreams of lust and frustration and violence. It thus becomes an expression of existentialist conceptions, of the absurd and the demonic, of cruelty, nausea, despair, chaos, death and Nothingness.

The striking resemblance of these works of art to pictures made by mental patients has frequently been pointed out. However that may be, and even if these surrealist works are essentially no more (and no less) than what they intend to be, unvarnished replicas of our present deplorable cultural situation, it must be recognized that they are as a rule quite devoid of idealism or perspectivism and that these trends "culminate" in negativism or even complete nihilism.

4. ABSTRACT AND ABSOLUTE ART

Here the various side-currents again reach the main stream. All ties with a visible, palpable reality in space and time are severed, all emotions are barred. Instead of irrational, these works become hyper-rational, severely systematic compositions of abstractions and formulas. Logically, their end lies in a void, in a colourless and shapeless plane (all-white or all-black) or in one single line or point. This is the summmum of simplification, the expression of the dehumanized and dedeified All-One.

5. "Neue Sachlichkeit"

This relatively recent current had its beginning in modern architecture (Le Corbusier et.al.). Here too sensory perception makes way for abstract essences and pure reasonableness. The new image, making use of modern materials, is simple and sober, its lines naked without superfluous ornamentation. It is hard, cold and efficient. The concrete is combined with the abstract. The finished work must be functional. Utility is more important than beauty, serviceability must prevail over art.

Rational matter-of-factness is exclusively intent on the here-and-now. Only the actual present is considered to have validity and to be of any consequence. The future is swallowed up in the order of the day.

B. Sociological Interpretation.

At this point we can try to take stock of our findings so far. But how shall we reasonably appraise the assets and liabilities? Authoritative scholars in this field cover the entire gamut of possible judgements, with the accent on the two extremes: jubilant acclaim and cold repugnance. This is true both of the narrower point of view based on painting and the plastic arts alone, as isolated material, and of the broader cultural-sociological point of view. In the first case the favorable or unfavorable judgement depends primarily on a personal preference for either modern or classical art. The worshippers of classical art complain of the lack or even the complete absence of style, the lack of a logical unity or meaningful structure, the sacrifice of the idea of the microcosmos in modern composition, and of other ideal or technical deficiencies, in comparison with periods of flourishing artistic achievement in earlier times. On the other hand, those who plead the cause of modern art view with enthusiasm what they consider to be the notable gains of modern art as over against the art of the past: its rediscovery of vital and cosmic essences through the abstraction from practical activities; its transformation of the world and of life in this era of scientific transformation; its return to the sovereign biological basis of aesthetic principles of to the true, universal archetypes which lie beneath the visual distractions of reality; its truthfulness in revealing the eternal human condition of crisis and despair and its fundamental courage-to-be in showing the meaningless chaos of this world. [1] On this level, a firmly principled "no" meets an equally decisive "yes". And neither side lacks for good reasons and upright inner convictions.

1. Herbert Read, Werner Luft, Paul Tillich, a.o.

Where learned specialists are completely unable to reach agreement, can the cultural sociologist presume to gird his loins and enter the battle? The task is the more precarious, in that on this terrain meanings diverge widely according to whether a cultural optimist or a cultural pessimist is speaking! From the theoretical point of view, it makes little difference that since the time of Nietzsche and Spengler most cultural-sociological judgements concerning the course of development of art show a predominant and increasingly pronounced trend of grave condemnation. The distinct transition from optimistic to pessimistic valuation, however significant in itself as a basic attitude of mind, offers little foothold from a strictly scientific point of view.

Nevertheless, these as-yet incomplete cultural-sociological analyses contain valuable indications. Their increasingly pessimistic point of view has obviously been subject to the converging influences of writers as diverse as Karl Jaspers, Ernst Jünger, Berdiaiev, Ortega y Gasset, Holthausen, Sorokin and others. A rough classification will indicate the main features which in general reveal themselves in these depreciating characterizations. The outstanding features mentioned in current cultural appraisements of a pessimistic nature can be summarized as follows:

1. THE NONSENSICAL

The representation of the meaningless and the irrational as the normal and invariable face of human society. The exploration of the portals of insanity, the breaking of barriers to psychopathy and schizophrenia. Analogies with neurosis, narcosis and nightmares. The hideous systematization of the absurd and the unbalanced. The portrayal of the fundamental disintegration and incoherence of human life.

2. THE EXISTENTIAL

The ultra-realistic answer to the challenge of current trends of thought. Identification with science and technology. Utilitarian, calculating attitudes. Materialism and disillusion. The portrayal of man as completely alone, hopelessly struggling against an alien world, foresaken by God and his better self.

3. THE PERVERSE

The preference for the morbid, the immoral, the obscene and the ugly. The salacious portrayal of excess and abnormality. The descent into the cesspools of sin, lust and crime.

4. THE DEMONIC

The evocation of a grim ghost-world, of a defiling hell on earth; the release of all the forces of darkness and evil. The regression of humanity to bestiality and a brute state of nature; the permanent victory of the devil and the Anti-Christ: Satan conduit le bal.

5. THE NEGATIVE

Development of the theme of chaos and waste land and ultimate all-pervading death. The portrayal of a petrified, frozen world of planetary destruction and decay. Eternal recurrence in meaningless cycles. The denial of human values and dignity. Images of damnation and moral impotence. It would seem possible to reduce this five-fold classification of valuations in current sociology of art further, to only two main ideal-typical points of view. For the first, modern art is chiefly characterized by its loss of faith in God, in divine guidance and supernatural reality, i.e. by the loss of an *ideal image of God*. [1] The second sees modern art chiefly (generally in combination with the first) in terms of its loss of faith in man, in man's task and active ability to achieve something [2] for himself and for society, therefore in the loss of an *ideal image of man*.

Modern art, thus assessed, robs the world of divine radiance and enlightenment. God is dead and the world is waste and empty as it was in the beginning. Once more man is debased to a lowly creature, inferior by nature and incapable of any good. The art of this age makes itself the interpreter of this radical tarnishing of the world, this animal degradation of man. The world thus portrayed is raw and gray, false and ugly, infernal and meaningless, an earthly vale of tears, a place of punishment and torture. Man thus portrayed is at best a robot, an automaton, a depersonalized being, a mechanized mass-man or marionette; more often he is a monster, blood-thirsty and bestial, an under-man and an un-man, satanic and amoral; a hideous mask even more hideous in the unmasking, in the public exposure of his spiritual nakedness; shockingly mismade, crazily disproportioned, a wicked, biting caricature of himself; in the end man becomes but a manikin made up of lines, surfaces, angles and spheres, without life and without soul.

C. Cultural Analysis

The sociological analyses of art which we have just reviewed in brief, may certainly contain a core of truth. But the great difficulty that presents itself, when one attempts to appraise the diametrically opposed views in this field, is that they have too much the character of emotional and qualitative valuation and subjective tastes, over which there is no disputing. I believe, however, that we have collected and sifted enough material to offer a

1. See A. Müller-Armack, *Das Jahrhundert ohne Gott*, Münster, 1948, and also his *Diagnose unserer Gegenwart*, Gütersloh, 1949.
2. See H. Sedlmayr, *op. cit.*

conclusion along the lines of a more objective and exact argument. Obvious-ly no strict natural-science verification and mathematical measurement is possible here (although Sorokin attempted, by dint of prodigious labour, to achieve just this—and was doomed in advance to failure), but I do believe that a generally acceptable and reliable criterion is available. After having already theoretically reduced the different typical aspects, which experts have pointed out, to two underlying categories, namely an ideal image of God and an ideal image of man, I suggest we subsume them under the single category of the *positive image of the future.*

I think it would be possible to ascertain and verify that in modern art —at least of the western variety—the formerly underlying ideal image of the future has been thoroughly eradicated and destroyed. This has in part taken place consciously and rationally, and in part unconsciously, simply in conformity with the prevailing fashion. The current attitude of mind is more and other than merely anti-Christian and anti-humanist, it is overtly *anti-idealistic* and *anti-futuristic.* It follows, and powerfully re-enforces, the process of dissolution of cultural ideals and the pessimistic convictions with reference to the development of culture, the unbelief concerning the coming Kingdom of God on earth, and the scepticism concerning any kind of progress optimism or utopianism, as realistically impossible and therefore as merely pious wishes or delusions. Idealistic optimism concerning the future has been replaced by suspicion and despair, negativism and nihilism, a "carpe diem" and "après nous le déluge", a going around in absurd circles of meaninglessness and estrangement—in short, by a miserable, purposeless, struggling "Sein zum Tode". Life is a living death in the dungeons of the eternal present, a slow strangulation in the inescapable every-day straitjacket which is called the world of men. Every positive image of the future, whether it is represented as paradise regained or heaven, as the good society where freedom and justice reign, or even as no more than education in art and the raising of culture through art—all these have lost their appeal for art and have lost their inspired medium in art.

Now, to what extent can this translation into the terminology of the positive image of the future be actually applied empirically and demonstrated to grasp the development of modern art in adequate categories? We will test our line of thought with a few examples—examples which, if amplified and added to, could certainly give a more complete demonstration of our point.

1. FLATLAND: NO PERSPECTIVE

The deliberate mistreatment and literal flattening out to the point of extinction, of the pictorial perspective—the once precious fruit of a centuries-long process of artistic development and refining of style—cannot be other than a mirroring of the symbolism of modern society. There can be no question here of a chance invention or would-be "modernism". This shift is structurally and culturally in close relationship to the shift in the prevailing cultural attitudes. Perspectiveless painting and drawing delineate in their specific field a perspectiveless "Zeitgeist". Modern ready-to-wear ideas of the masses, which follow a fashion launched by a spiritual élite, is predominantly characterized by existentialist ideas of a basically prospectless course of events. Man is sinful and insignificant, the helpless plaything of evil forces he has himself evoked and which now rule in this somber death-shrouded world of measureless misery. Is this the worst of all possible worlds? No, worse than that—it is the only possible world. Hell is nothing other than a reflection of this world. The events of history can never be more than "memoirs from the House of the Dead". Man here-and-now, and everywhere at every time, is helpless, hopeless and senseless. Man's visionary perspective on another and better world is utterly destroyed. The reduction and liquidation of perspective in the practice of art is the counterpart of the general spiritual shift and indicates a lack of resistance against this overwhelming flood of spiritual sickness. Art has abolished perspective as untrue and misleading, as an optical delusion, on the grounds that it does not exist, just as God and other false projections of primitive superstition and naive self-deception do not exist. Perspectiveless painting leads the way in what it supposes is honesty and a critical sense of reality, of which the world stands in dire need. In so doing, it believes itself to be doing a service to the culture of its day, but it does not point the way to a culture of the future.

2. CHAOS: NO STRUCTURE

From an existential philosophical point of view, there is but one reality, no matter how one twists and turns it about. The world may be turned upside down, or observed from this angle or that, but it ever remains the same evil, unredeemable world in the endless indifferent universe of space and time. This aspect of the negating of the earthly image of the future is also reflected, consciously or unconsciously, in the forms which art has adapted for its use.

Too little attention has been given, in my opinion, to the basic significance of an artistic conversion which corresponds to the existential image of the world and of the future.[1] I refer to the remarkable blurring of the difference between "above" and "below" in modern plastic art, so that they become interchangeable without any noticeable effect. The possibility

1. Sedlmayr, *op. cit.*, mentions this phenomenon, and also Paul Tillich in *The Courage to Be*, Yale University Press, 1952, but their interpretation is not sufficiently penetrating.

of turning a painting in any direction and holding it upside down if desired, without altering its message to the observer, is well known and a popular subject for jokes, scorn, or (what is usually the same thing) incomprehension and misunderstanding. The deeper meaning is anything but funny, and it were better to understand this message.

The deft obscuring of the distinction between above and below corresponds to that of existentialism with reference to the past and the future, which constantly meet in the *now*, and with reference to the Here and the Beyond, which are absorbed into the secular space of the only, immediately present and observable reality.

All former distinctions and positions have been overturned in the consciousness of our time.[1] Life is approaching death. The supernatural is completely explicable in natural terms. The subconscious rules the conscious daily human round. The supramundane as the idea of the good is a fiction, and the incarnation of evil is purely mundane. The underworld and the subhuman are the driving forces of this world. The past, primeval man and primeval times, are ineradicably omnipresent. Time and space can be spun around, the past and the future tense interchanged, the here and the yonder shoved into different positions, taken to pieces, reassembled in various ways, twisted or straightened out—it is all quite indifferent and irrelevant. Whether one looks through the glasses of Genesis or studies the horizon through a telescope, from the Flood to the New Earth of Revelations, from one end of the world and its history to the other, it is all the same; every distinction between beginning and end, depth or height, closed history or wide-open prospects, disappears. From the creation to the destruction of this planet, man shall never experience any other destiny than the one he has experienced thus far. He is a puppet in an insane danse macabre, swept along head over heels toward the bottomless abyss of death as the inescapable end of all. He goes from nothingness to nothingness. He stands ever before the yawning void of life in which all coined standards finally dissolve and disappear.

This is the condition of man and the world; another, better and more perfectly ordered future is unthinkable, impossible and unfulfillable.

3. UNDERWORLD: THE ERUPTION OF SURREALISM

The human figure in modern art witnesses to a deep self-disdain, self-

1. This curious and prophetic pronouncement by Nietzsche came to my attention in Sedlmayr's book, *op. cit.*, p. 137, after the above was written: "Stürzen wir nicht fortwährend? Nach rückwärts, seitwärts, vorwärts, nach allen Seiten? *Gibt es noch ein Oben und Unten?* Irren wir nicht durch das unendliche Nichts? Haucht uns nicht der leere Raum an? Ist es nicht kälter geworden?" Cited from the fragment, *Der tolle Mensch*, 1881. (Italics ours.)

hatred and self-incrimination. This is not in itself entirely new. The utopia was also strongly self-critical in its portrayal. It also turned things upside-down and delineated entirely different human types. But the goal there was always constructive. Even the embittered misanthropy of a Swift could pass for an educational children's story. An important place was also given by the Christian religion to the fall of man, but at the same time the prospect of reconciliation and redemption was raised. The mask and caricature always played a role in art, but even the most monstrous portrayals were counter-balanced by mild irony or liberating humour. [1] Surrealistic man, hurled to the canvas, is no longer a self-ordained lord of creation in an anthropocentrically conceived cosmos, but has on the contrary reduced his rank to that of a slave of chaos. Surrealism is basically not super-realistic, but infra-realistic. Its people are beings from the underworld and the unconscious—subhuman and non-human beings.

In its images of man, surrealism carries out the task set forth by Nietzsche for the coming times which he envisioned in his time: "Der Mensch ist etwas, was überwunden werden muss" (Man is something to be surpassed). But this task cannot be accomplished as long as an idealistic image of human perfection is born by man on his course through time, through its alleys and over its chasms. The artists themselves are now signaling the iconoclasm of the future, the destruction of the centuries-long creative work on the image of man by their own predecessors, and thereby the self-destruction of man. They recognize as a given fact only man's in-dignity. Nurtured by and nurturing modern attitudes, they portray the machine-man, the Neanderthaler, the criminal, the neurotic, the beast of prey, the prisoner caught in the process, the member of the lost generation on a lost frontier, the atomic-age man, the glacial being.

The decisive and truly depressing fact does not lie in the unprecedented low-point to which this existentialist creation has been hurled, but in the sumultaneous cutting off of every possibility for regeneration and recovery. Man is spiritually flayed, rendered lifeless, stripped of every shred of dignity —not only as a reality, but especially and above all as an ideal. This time, we have portrayed for us a Daniel who is torn to pieces in the lion's den, a Jonas who is devoured by the whale, a Jesus who moulders in his grave. From here there is no way out, no deliverance, no resurrection and no rebirth. Man is here shown for the first time as he really is, was and ever shall be to the end of time, a treacherous creature who in his own death-

---

1. Sedlmayr, *op. cit.* p. 199 ff., points out that the grotesque and ridiculing caricatures of Daumier nevertheless had a relatively good-humoured and innocent character. He considers Grandville *(Le Monde à l'Envers)* as a transition-figure, because of the appearance of features which he describes as demonic, gruesome, icy, inhuman, cynical and destructive.

throes murders his fellow-man—an abortive by-product of nature. Pure surrealism portrays this ape-man of every age in all his revolting guises with a pitiless eye, now using bold black strokes, now shrill colours. There is no Darwinistic evolution here, certainly not on a spiritual and moral plane. Rather there is a firmly established state of disorder: the fall is once and for all, whether of angel, beast or man; hell on earth is his only abode, a rotting corpse his sole destination.

4. ICONOCLASM: GRAPHIC DEVALUATION

The discarding of the image of man as a christophoros or a lightbearer, as a chosen tool or a self-appointed tiller of progress, also implies his end as a participant in one of the most sublime activities of the human spirit: as a bearer of art. The pitiless destruction of active faith in the future inevitably leads to self-destruction on the part of man and the vehicle of his hope: art.

Modern art is consistent and true to itself in launching a direct attack on *this* art with its tradition of future-oriented norms and values. It attacks the artistic values of the beautiful, the "kalos kagathos", the humanly and divinely beautiful (Hellas to Renaissance to Holland's Golden Age etc.); it attacks the roots and rules of humanistic-religious aesthetics. Baudelaire's "fleurs du Mal" have quickly reproduced themselves and bear abundant fruit. The "revaluing of all values" of Nietzsche, a lover and creator of art and beauty, is tragically pursued to the art-deadening extreme of the anti-Nietzsche. The artists revolt, against the entire world and humanity, including the pursuit of art itself. They revert to the diametrical antipode of what had been recognized as the essence of art; in stern antithesis to superior artistic values they proclaim the ugly, the false, the nonsensical, the contradictory, the unruly and the chaotic. For these are the eternally and universally valid reality-values. The highest values of western man and culture are devalued as utterly unreal and illusory. The Idea and the Ideal are put to the stake; classical art shares in the devaluation; art as such is artificial, dishonest, stupid, unnatural. Surrealism especially will portray the real, the unvarnished truth, untroubled by thoughts of art and beauty. The representation of a coherent composition does not give a true picture of reality, it is a lie. Reality presents a caricature of such a concept; only a shattered image of disharmony and disintegration gives the true picture, which will finally develop into an image of the only and final truth: Nothingness.

3. *Decadent Art: Measure and Matrix of Cultural Decline*

If it were possible to isolate art and let it be "l'art pour l'art", if it could be maintained that art is an independent field of human activity which need not consider non-artistic problems of culture and human society—then all that is written in the above might have some significance as a description of interpretation, but it would have no further consequences. It could be considered "science pour la science"! However, this view would in my opinion be based on a misunderstanding of the cultural role of art and of the artist in society.

The author is of course well aware that the cry of "decadent art" has been raised many times in the course of time, and especially in recent centuries, accompanied by many malicious words of censure and scorn. He is also aware that many works of art thus condemned have later been reckoned among the neo-classical masterpieces which are now held up as praiseworthy models for today's modern art.

But history does not repeat itself . . . always. And it would be a grave mistake to speculate that the same happy fate is automatically in store for the art, which is at present decried as decadent. I do not believe in this view which implies that there can be no such thing as decadent art, but that this label only reflects the passing mood of one generation which is still steeped in its old traditions; or in other words, that so-called decadent art is actually a progressive, experimental avant-garde, a healthy attempt at renewal which at some time in the future will itself again become outmoded and will then raise objections against "modern" art, etc., etc.

Let us admit that it is extremely difficult for a contemporary observer to distinguish between seeming and genuine decadence, between vitalizing renewal and deadly disintegration, between artistic enrichment and corruption. But this can be no reason for refraining from any attempt to make such a distinction or even for denying its existence. Certainly it is possible that serious errors are made with regard to specific *individual* works of art, but I do feel that the cultural-sociological approach offered here can be of some real assistance for a just evaluation of the *general trends* of contemporary art.

Art in all its forms is, as we have said, not just a mirror of its period, but also a pre-reflection of the future. And even more: art has great influence on the shape of things to come. Its images not only picture a possible future or a probable development. Works of art are of historical import because they influence future history. In addition to its acknowledged diagnostic and prognostic function, art also has a constitutive and regulative function.

Formerly art was to a great extent merged with the general optimistic, active style of life and thought reigning at the time. It was natural that it contributed to a clear expression of the Zeitgeist's expectations for the future. This is why art's specific role in creating the future has so far seldom been noticed or analyzed and why its specific spiritual and psychological influence on the dynamics of culture have hardly been pointed out. However, now that art is submerged in the present, now that it no longer depicts and points out a new age of perfection, it still exerts its influence through its transmission of images. This time, however, in a negative and nihilistic way, opposed to the future. This kind of decadent and frustrated art is a heavy burden for the future development of culture. In its present violent reaction, modern art is a serious threat to its own future and to that of the culture it produces and which had produced it. Modern art is more than a mirror of temporary woes and more than a prophet of woe. It has a great responsibility for the woes which may possibly come.

A. Message without Vision

We have defined art as essentially a *movement*, moved by and towards a positive image of the future. From this definition it follows automatically that if art has no such image of the future as its leitmotiv, it must be regarded as decadent or pseudo-art. Modern art is declining art insofar it no longer believes in anything, not in God or man, or in any meaning, value, norm or ideal on earth or in heaven, at this time or at any other time. If it has no positive faith of any kind to inspire it, it has no artistic ethos or pathos.

Modern art of that kind has no message and no promise. It blindly gropes for nothing. It expresses itself inarticulately, incoherently, brokenly. In arbitrary, confused images it speaks of an incomprehensible imponderable doom which must take its inexorable course. It has nothing of any value to impart about anybody or anything.

This art has lost its inner eye, its vision. As an instrument of image-reception, the artist traditionally used his specific visionary sensitivity to conceive the future and contributed to the recreation of this miserable world of the present. Now, he merely registers the Zeitgeist with special predilection for the prevailing mood of doom. He writes the sign of his own times on the wall and no longer erects imperishable monuments and milestones along the road mounting to the radiant perspective of a better future. Art has become the limping art of a lost horizon. It no longer brings about a synthesis between this planet and the universe, between the Now and the Eternal, between this world and the other, between man's inner world of conscience and the vault of the heavens on high. The balanced unity of its dualistic-perspective imaginative capacity has split apart into disharmony and disintegration. Thus rendered an ineffectual shadow of its former self, art can no longer project the future, let alone give voice to promising prophecy. Profanation is all that is left it.

Cut off from the un-real, chained fast to the real, art can now raise neither nor its public. No longer can it build a bridge to the Realm of the Future. But he who does not believe in a future of any kind, is unwilling and unable to evoke an image of the future; he may be willing to produce true art, but is unable to do so. In former eras modern art was both symbolic and exemplary. It was creative in a transitory present and therefore it was itself unperishable, for by force of its creative idea it belonged to another age. Its images were radiant anticipations of future glory, of a new world. Now "modern" means the representation and perpetuation of this age and time. Modern art is totally blind—to the future. It is no longer the avant-garde, but the rearguard which covers a cultural retreat to the last lines of a beaten generation.

B. Submission and Conformity

Modern art has sold its soul, it has exchanged its essence for an existence, in the midst of actual and factual reality. It has had to do so—let there be no doubt about this—if it would not starve in a period where Time dominates all and will recognize no art but its own art. Modern art has had to relinquish its own independent position and point of view. The artist no longer inhabits the lonely look-out, which afforded him a view of the far distance, undisturbed by the madding crowd, and which enabled him to carry out his work of styleful reconstruction and recreation of the world. He has become both enslaved by and addicted to his age. He literally repeats what the times dictate. He produces meticulous copies and replicas after one and the same model. He takes a pride in not being different, in being realistic and in depicting just what normal mortals see and hear, the world as it is. He is and wants to be just one particle of the Zeitgeist, no more than a loud-speaker for the collective conscious and unconscious. In short, modern art deliberately wants to mirror this crazy world and no other. Heaven on earth is out of the picture, but earth is portrayed as hell and thus perpetuated.

So art leaves us but the choice between escapism and conformism. Temporary escape into pipe-dreams or permanent submission to the sickness of the times. There is no escaping the omnipresent reality of today which encircles humanity, including art.

Therefore art has also had to conform and adapt itself to the tempo of our modern times. It has to overstrain its dynamic to remain up to date. It has to go along with the rapid changes in fashion and present its new models at ever shorter intervals. And these models must constantly be changed to supply the general demand for ever new sensations which must be more eccentric, exotic and extravagant day by day.

So the age produces a moment-ridden art which becomes standardized, commercialized, technical and subservient to technology and the mass-media of the amusement-industry. The times distort art till its forms are sufficiently useful, efficient, "sachlich" and elastic. Modern art has become polite art. It signs its images of the times "truly yours".

It is true, of course, that the Zeitgeist is present in all works of art. But at the same time, true art rises above it as a timeless mediator with the eternal. In its period and through it, art of all times was a foreshadowing and an interpretation of another time, in the existence and the coming of which the artist must believe, if he wants to express himself in an inspired artistic way. If art does not lead out of its own day and age, it will succumb to it and compulsively portray it, in helpless protest and shattering disillusion, till it collapses.

The more timeless art is, the stronger in the long run its timely effects and the longer its life. For the future recognizes rebellious visionaries. The more art gets attached to its own time, the shorter-lived it will be. For the future rejects those who are slaves of its past. The future demands that art, art above all, respond to its challenge. Art which ignores the future, will be ignored by the future and therefore contains the germ of its own negation.

C. Dialectical Auto-Destruction

The development of modern art demonstrates a demonic dialectical trend of insidious self-destruction. It is demonic, in that art itself, following the false promptings of the times, regards its own death agonies as the growing pains of a youthful life-force. Unconsciously, it is making a boisterous show of its own dance of death. Complacently enthusiastic, modern art follows new direction after new direction in rapid succession, proclaiming each to be a counter-movement against decline and decay, hailing them as tangible proofs of potential revival and rebirth, whereas they are as a rule so many milestones on the road to ruin.

Naturally there are those among the pioneering renewers of modern art whose genius shines through any style and whose art cannot be disguised by even the strongest time-bound trappings. These artists still manage to give shape to the shapeless, to make the crudest material immaterial, to create a mystery in the midst of the ear- and eye-splitting manifestations of the times. Even in apparently unconditional surrender to the art-deadening present, this art still retains an indefinable something of timelessness which it can carry over to the future—a glowing spark of inspiration which the most rampantly gone-to-seed modes of expression cannot smother. But we are referring here to the more impersonal, symptomatic currents and trends which characterize modern art as a whole. And these seem to me to be caught in a vicious circle which spirals downward.

Each swing of the pendulum bears its own label in the various branches of art. But they are all basically related and run the same general course. The three main turning-points may be described respectively as (1) the transition from idealism in art to all kinds of manifestations of realism, (2) the introduction of various iconoclastic procedures, and (3) the development of expressionism as a counter-movement to impressionism. All three counter-courses indicate, each in its own way, a paradoxical dialectic which, at least to the outside observer, appears self-destructive.

1. FROM IDEALISM TO THE NEW REALISM

The transformation of idealism into realism (of whatever style) reduces original art to copy-art, and dilutes its inner symbolism to a photographic snapshot. [1] Art can only flourish as a moving dynamic if it is moved by the unbroken tension between the poles of idea and reality. Art can only appeal to reality from the vantage point of the un-real idea, thus moving it by the force of the contrast with its ideal symbolic meaning. Art can only survive by the graceful transformation of actual matter and through its supernatural transfiguration of the natural experiences of the common man. Thus we are faced with the—in itself entirely justified—counter-movement of *surrealism*. It seeks, thoughtfully and responsibly, for the idea behind, under or above observable reality. It is thus a protest-movement against mechanization and materialism, and against the misrepresentations of the truth as it is experienced by the conscious mind.

Nevertheless surrealism is, perhaps more than any other movement, a sham-manoeuvre which bears the imprint of our mad, infatuated times, a typical illustration of all modern intentions of regeneration. Where does surrealism look for the hidden idea which underlies the reality of the rational-empirical consciousness? In the *un*-conscious and *sub*-conscious of an unreal and irrational dreamworld, in repressed and censored complexes—unmasked psycho-analytically by Freud and ideologically by Marx—in the primal human instincts, death-fears, sexual-sadistic desires and uncontrolled urges, in a Nietzschean and nihilistic will to power, or in existential moods of doom. What a fateful self-deception!

This apparent insight into the concealed and genuine truth is taken over lock, stock and barrel from the modern image of the world and the modern view of man, society and life with reference to the concrete situation. This view sees reality, and nothing but *naked reality*, through the trebly realistic spectacles of a Marxian doctrine of dynamics, depth psychology and existential philosophy. Time once more renders to art its bill of actuality, now disguised as a time-dominated science and philosophy. It is the synchronous and up-to-date reality of our time, *im*pressed upon the subconscious, which is *ex*pressed by modern art. It is this reality which is accepted as eternally valid. Surrealism in the last analysis *remains within* the framework of the here-now and does not overstep its bounds. Its idea was an alluring illusion. The same insane world which was first consciously observed, returns at a gallop via the subconscious. It is the same reality, only still cruder—bestial,

---

1. Even photographic art is only thinkable as the representation of a meaningful idea.

demonic, amorphous, quite simply hideous and horribly ugly. Apparently the soul's cellar does not house the soul's ultimate idea, but rather the soul-less and meaningless chaos of the raw world of the senses. Conscious and unconscious are identical in content, differing only in the outward form of presentation. Surrealism is thus no regenerated idealism, but cramped realism.

2. FROM IMAGES TO NEW FUNCTIONS

A second line of development, if carried to its logical extreme, results in a loss or a voiding of the intrinsic meaning of the image of art, specifically where its form of expression is concerned. This is true of all art now being increasingly subjected to a process of image destruction. All the expressive imagery by means of which the Other can be symbolically revealed, is radically ejected: harmony, melody, symmetry, perspective, colour and tonality are stowed away in the art museum, along with the traditional aesthetics of measure, rules and regularity. The new artistic image is atonal, abstract, absolute or functional. And all this too is done in the name of an idea; not an idea of transcendential or ideal beauty, however; it is mostly described as "reasonable Sachlichkeit", a rational idea. Shorn of all romantic and sentimental trimmings, this art-form seeks to relate itself to modern machine technology, modern materials, modern hygiene and comfort, and to the modern stream-lined simplicity of standardized mass-production. Here again, via this detour of neo-rationalism and neo-realism, the sights and sounds of our time are approximated. These currents adapt art to a realistic, industrial culture. This reorientation too bears the times-tatoo. Its basic idea is anti-idealistic. Its image is an exact technically perfect cast of existing reality, and the image's tenor denies any other meaning or message to art than that of efficiency and economy.

This style may hold its own in industrial architectural constructions of concrete, steel and glass, or in industrial designing and streamlining of utilitarian articles, but when it comes to art for art's sake, where there is no question of utility, the logical outcome of this approach is a series of horizontal and vertical lines and black-and-white planes, of colourless shadings and toneless sounds—in fact imageless images, without inspiration and without communication. And at this point this form of art, which is so pre-eminently this-worldly, turns into its opposite: it becomes estranged from the world, it loses contact and completely misses any meaningful mark. Art which divests itself of images will finally find itself devoid of artistic impulses and exhausted must bleed to death.

3. FROM IMPRESSIONISM TO THE NEW PRIMITIVISM

Seemingly the most hopeful movement to appear on the scene after the shift to materialistic, sensory impressionism, was the revolutionary counter-shift towards idealistic, non-sensual expressionism. Here the explicit desire was at work to go *back* to older values by leaping *forward*. In futurism a new image of the future developed only to become embroiled in political developments and go under ingloriously in its hyper-dynamic exaggeration. This dismal outcome set in motion *futurism's counterpart*, archaism, which turned back to the infantile stage (da-da), to a pre-historic or at least primitive world-image.

Again we find an anachronistic self-deception! For this primitive image of the world was seen through the sharply focussed lens of the modern world-image. The wilful abandonment of perspective and the quasi-naive representation on a two-dimensional plane, without the enriching matrix of living inspiration which the fine art of so-called primitive people always had, can only produce a pseudo-primitive, contentless art, a mere aping. The same is true of modern imitations of primitive folk music, or of poetry without words, rhyme or meter, in simple imitation of primeval sounds or rhythms. This archaic expressionism remains entirely on the surface. It is false and contrived, in that the basic presupposition of the artistic hallmark is lacking—the aesthetic consciousness out of which the inwardly powered ancient arts without exception emerged. It is precisely this consciousness which stands in close relationship with another world, making itself into a divided interpreter of that other world.

Nevertheless, this trend towards a would-be primitivism is hailed as the long-awaited revival of western art. It is so regarded not only in art circles, but among cultural sociologists. One of the most important cultural socio-logists of our time, F. S. C. Northrop, actually presents a weighty argument[1] in defence of the thesis that the crisis of western culture can be resolved through primitivism. His contention is that all eastern culture (especially that of China and India) is based on an aesthetically intuitive approach to knowledge, while western culture is based on an intellectually evolved theoretically systematic approach. The cleavage between East and West is the great problem of our time, and arises out of diametrically opposed, exclusive and equally one-sided culture-constructions. In order to achieve the necessary synthesis, the West—whose artistic creativity has been de-stroyed by intellectualism—must accord more place to the spontaneous, naive and aesthetically primitive world view of the East, with its unconscious, intuitive, irrational and mystical modes of thought, and the East must in its turn take over more of the theoretical-scientific and technological

1. See his *Meeting of East and West*, an inquiry concerning world understanding, New York, 1946. A summary of criticism of this argument is also to be found in Sorokin's *Social Philosophies*.

approach of the West. The revival of western culture, seen from this point of view, requires a *conscious* shift to *unconscious* primitivism.

Primitivism in art does indeed attempt to realize this inwardly contradictory self-conscious unconsciousness, contrived artlessness and sophisticated naivité. It has rendered the East in a western manner, achieving a hypermodern primitivism. It has shown itself ready to sacrifice both art and beauty at the altar of primitivism. But the miracle of Abraham and Isaac has not been repeated, for the faith was lacking. The blood-sacrifice has been carried out—and in vain. This western art did not provide a bridge for an encounter with the East, even as Kipling foresaw; rather, it lost itself and the consciousness of its own calling. It lost faith in itself, and gained instead an artistic inferiority complex which has eventually found confused expression in the testimonium paupertatis of image-flashed pouring out of the subconscious.

So these three counter-currents leading to modern art have the same negative result. The reversal from idealism to realism has broken off all communication between the artist and another realm. The artist is enclosed within this one narrow world of today and can no longer conceive an ideal world such as it truly ought to be, somewhere, sometime. Modern iconoclasm has made impossible the portrayal of this other world in an image. Todays' prevailing art banishes its symbolic representation and forbids its revelation in meaningful compositions. The turning to expressionism has only achieved a sophisticated anachronistic fixation in an infantile or primitive past, in conscious denial of the future. So all three contribute to the destruction of the positive idealistic image of the future, which is the heart and soul and life-blood of art. With mighty axes the roots of art are cut off: its aesthetic capacities of splitting space and time, and, via this indispensable instrumental process, its imaginative powers to create an inspiring world of the sublime.

D. A Permanent Crippling of Aesthetic Awareness?

This is then the sad story of the counter-movements thus far in art. I have, of course, made sweeping generalizations, as if the tangle of modern art formed a transparent and uniform pattern. The schematic ideal-typical approach has resulted in a certain amount of exaggeration, but in spite of admitted inadequacies I believe the general trends have been correctly delineated. But is it not after all possible to regard this self-disintegration as a "reculer pour mieux sauter"? I would like to hope that this is so. But there is one thing we must not shut our eyes to, and that is the possibly destructive effect of the cumulative retroaction possibly going beyond the point of a rebounding regeneration. The question is, for *how long* a negativistic and nihilistic practice of art can continue without destroying its own basis of artistic valuation, which is the aesthetic consciousness of the partici-pating, art-loving public. The degeneration in the transmission, i.e. the aesthetic representation, of images, and the perverted use or abuse of the artistic gift of sensitivity cannot in the long run fail to influence the indis-pensable integrity of the receiving stations—the human audience. Its receptive capacity must inevitably atrophy and decay.

The revolution in the value-system of art was not exactly a silent revolu-tion, but even so, it has taken the public by surprise. Historic works of "beaux arts" and "belles lettres", which have long served as classical models of exalted expressions of the eternal idea of pure beauty, are now for the most part denounced as cumbersome, old-fashioned, boring and ugly. Only the very newest can find grace as pure art, as long, that is, as this generation of art will remain in power: life-spans grow shorter and shorter as the modern tempo of life increases. It is shameful enough, that so many of the greatest artists in the history of human civilization ran too far ahead of their own times, were too "modern", and thus had to eat the bread of poverty and die in despised obscurity. It is equally shameful, that today's modern artist, if he only initiates a new direction, is immediately praised to the skies by a chorus of snobbish hangers-on, only to be dropped like a hot potato as soon as the art-hunters find a new quarry.

We must pity the artists of this mid-century generation, who now have every eye upon them and are the subjects of so much praise and serious analysis, while in another decade, if not sooner, their art will no longer be *the* art —or perhaps not even art at all. The sensational experimental "isms" of the art of even very recent decades are now practically forgotten, and have nothing to say to our time. Nevertheless, Sartre's oft-repeated cry that all must be "actual", "engagé" in the situation of our time, has become a valid code of art. The modern artist strives for the highest measure of actuality and originality, in order to be up-to-date. He sees only the present, which applauds him, and not the future, which will bury him because he has ignored it. The true work of art, that possesses eternal youth, reaches forth out of this time, and speaks in the language of the future. The larger the present looms in art, the more transitory the art, for then it must ebb with the hour and make way for the next wave, riding hard at its heels. This is especially true of our own century, in which the pounding of the steadily accelerating waves has already begun to breach the walls of the period.

The probability that the general level of art will continue to sink further, leads to the gnawing fear that the general level of taste may also deteriorate to the point where the occasional genius of genuine works of art, produced by isolated artists, may not be recognized or accepted, either by their own time or by succeeding generations.

II

We must sadly conclude that the future no longer speaks to us through art, or speaks only negatively, as the non-existent and the non-existable. If modern art no longer creates for future generations—will future generations be able to create art? Or are we on the brink of an era which will only be creative in science and technology?

E. Art as Component, Dominant and Determinant of Culture

Art is not only an important component, but equally a dominant and a determinant of culture. It has already been stated that art is an extremely sensitive barometer of the existing state of culture, as well as an indicator of probable future trends. This simile is inadequate, to the extent that in this case the future cultural trends are not only *prophesied*, but in part *effectuated* by art itself. This is accomplished, as we have already demonstrated, by means of its images and their ultimate meaning or intent. The intent of the image may to a certain extent be compared to the concept of the vector in science; that is, it not only gives magnitude but direction. The positive or negative symbolism of art contains a spiritual potential which co-determines the direction of cultural dynamics through its intensive influence on the human mind. A decadent, perverted or frustrated art is a massive hindrance to any further development of a culture. For it is more than a prophet of doom, it contributes to and must be answerable for that doom.

When modern art then devotes itself, with all the techniques at its disposal, to the representation of the prevailing cultural pessimism and existential conceptions of chaos, absurdity, bestiality, anxiety and despair, then it actually gives present-day culture a mighty push in the direction of dis-integration and destruction. Its sinister and suggestive images have in them all the power and the fury of an art transformed into a contradiction of itself. A despairing art can help reduce culture to a rubble-heap. [1]

A futureless defuturizing art is an important causal factor in the threatening decline of a dehumanized, futureless culture. Art is both *measure* and *matrix* of culture. It is at once the crystallization of a developing culture and the chrysalis of a coming culture. It could be said, "Das ist der Fluch der bösen Kunst, dass sie fortzeugend immer Böses muss gebären". *Degenerate art is not only the fruit of a culture in decline, but it engenders further decay.*

Unless... this vicious cycle can be broken in time. And it can! For in spite of all "modern art", there are even today in all fields individual artists of truly modern creative ability, whose work is charged with a positive symbolism concerning the future and breathes a vision of the future, and

---

1. This is to say that I am not convinced by the arguments of such authors as Sedlmayr and Holthausen that the path of spiritual suffering and despair, crisis and catastrophe, may automatically lead to hope, joy and rebirth after having hit the low-point.

there is still a special public that consciously appreciates this aesthetic-ethical testimony. It is a shrinking public, that stands staunch in its refusal to let Stravinsky dwarf Bach or Picasso overshadow Rembrandt. It is a public which defends the centuries-old ideals of classical beauty against the stream-lined hyper-modern idols.

Note on Modern Music and Poetry

Those who are acquainted with modern art are well aware that the various arts are closely interrelated and demonstrate striking similarities in develop-ment, especially with reference to the trend from impressionism to expres-sionism. Expressionism is now typically found in architecture, theatre, literature, music and poetry. We have chosen the plastic arts, and particular-ly the art of painting, as our main illustration because the numerous isms and trends are most clearly differentiated there, and because in my opinion nothing can throw a clearer light on the elimination of the functional essence of music and poetry, of the inharmonic tonality, than the banishment of spatio-temporal perspective from painting.

It makes little difference whether one dates the beginning of atonal *music* from the time of the last off-shoots of impressionism, or from its systematic development in the Vienna School of Schönberg and Alban Berg; neither does its further development in pluritonic and polyrhythmic composition (Stravinsky, Milhaud, Hindemith) and the exact location of this modern music have special significance in this context. For the musical layman the differences in style now appear to reside more in the personality of the composers than in clearly delineated trends (although such delineations can and have been made). For him, most modern music forms an amorphous whole, with degrees of modernity—that is of dissonance and unmelodious-ness—and this is true even for the progressive-minded. Paradoxically, the concepts "progressive" and "modern" here diverge. It is possible to be progressive-minded and nevertheless—or precisely for this reason—reject *this* modern art, considered as a whole. At the same time that one sym-pathises with the experimental striving for renewal on the part of a younger generation (as one sympathises with all striving for betterment which is future-oriented), one can nevertheless take an independently critical view and refuse to accept *this* result as betterment, even regarding it instead as a deadly danger for the future. [1]

1. Here we suggest only one possibility. A different sociological approach can also lead to approval. See for example the culturally optimistic appreciation of modern music by Andreas Liess, *Die Musik im Weltbild der Gegenwart*, Lindau, 1949. He uses different conceptual tools in his analysis, which lead to different results. He sees the beginning of a new renaissance in music, following alone the lines of a similar renaissance in the other arts which he feels to be already well under way.

There is scarcely any music being written today which is not "modern". In the sense that "modern" and "contemporary" are synonymous, this is, of course, a pleonasm. Bach, Beethoven, Berlioz, Brahms, Bruckner and Debussy also wrote modern music in *their* time, and as moderns were both reverenced and subject to indignity. I have already suggested that the modernity of our time is something more than a phenomenon of contemporaneity. In music, this modernism takes the form of a radical rebellion against *all* existing laws, forms and norms of style, harmony, metre, melody, tonality, instrumentation, and so on. The connection with the past is broken off in every respect, except with a past which is held to be archaic, chaotic and primitive. Apart from certain neo-romantic and neo-mystical trends, the greater part of modern music belongs to this genre which seeks renewal in total demolition, pandemonium and cacophony, without any original or imaginative creative power, and without positive symbolism. Nevertheless (or perhaps for just this reason), *this* modern a-musical or anti-musical music is chosen for performances, is praised to the skies by the critics (who move with the times), is proclaimed by a small clique as the only true music, and is thus gradually spread over the western world. There are few listeners in the musical audience who dare admit openly that this is neither music nor art, but rather a collection of uncomfortable and displeasing, ear-splitting sounds.

It does not dispose of the case to say that all the greatest composers suffered a similar abuse from their own contemporaries and that posterity will accord our modern composers their true position. For in former times it was the group of traditional conservatives, who were against anything new because it was new, who took up the battle stations. Now the line of resistance runs right through the progressive circles, and the issue is beauty or lack of it. Furthermore, the high tide of fashion favours precisely the most modern artists, and every contemporary artist who wishes to express himself in a neo-romantic, neo-classical or neo-religious style is subject to a social taboo. Where in former times the efforts at modernizing and renewal of musical genius had to struggle for recognition and forcibly break the bonds of the period, today the word "genius" is freely applied to all that is sensationally modern in composition, even when all melodious qualities are lacking. The glory of this modernity might well be of short duration, in an age of accelerated tempo of innovation, but its after-effects may cast a long-obscuring shadow.

If one considers this new-fashioned laboratory sound-product in a milder mood, as an experimental transitional stage to new paths in musical art and musical theory, and therefore suspends judgement, this can only be done on the basis of a faith in a dialectical, but unhistorical, development of art, which would make the beautiful spring forth out of the ugly. This is not quite impossible, but it is highly improbable, in view of the gradual under-mining of musical sensitivity through the progressive modernization of music.

This development is already apparent in the tremendous popularity of a degenerate form of originally melodious negro music, and in the great appeal of jazz, which has been said to operate more on the spinal column than on the spirit. By means of quasi-exotic and neo-primitive techniques, old folk music is distorted and abused, and gives expression to the spiritual poverty of our culture. In this, music lines itself up with the surrealistic arts, which well up out of the subconscious Freudian-Jungian individual or collective primal instincts. This is a regression which comes full circle, bringing culture back to nature; but not to the nature of the cave-man, who produced paintings of great beauty in his time—rather the nature of the lowest ape-man. Thus music, like the other arts, witnesses to the loss or destruction of a positive image of the future. It no longer seeks a way to the Other, but it echoes our chaotic times and in so doing sanctions them and influences them negatively.

If music is by its nature a field of imponderables, *poetry*, that other invisible and impalpable art, may provide a clearer view of these same trends. More-over, poetry's case is more accessible to the general public than that of the other arts (although painters and musicians have also often expressed their views and purposes in writing), because it is more given to explaining its intentions in detailed self-analysis. Probably no other group writes so much about poetry as modern poets themselves!

Poetry has at times been called "the art of arts". Aside from the question of whether it must be considered aesthetically the highest form of art, it can be said that it is the most spiritualized, in the sense that it expresses itself without the use of any material or instrument, but addresses itself directly to the human mind and imagination. It literally speaks in images, symbols and meanings. The poetic image is the "lustrous germ-cell" of all artistic images. Poetry paints, draws, sculptures, decorates, builds, dances, gestures and makes music; it has line, colour, sound and style; it is cha-racterized by rhythm, timbre, tempo; it presents its own image of har-mony and symmetry, of dimension and perspective. The art of poetry contains something of all the arts and yet it remains a distinct art. For thousands of years another and higher world has spoken to man specially, and often by preference, through its symbolic language. The pronounced predilection of the muses, of the immortal genius or of the evocation from the other world for *this* literary form of expression is known as poetic inspiration.

In the last half century poetry too has passed through the international

currents of surrealism and expressionism.[1] Let us state at the outset
that the intentions of modern poetry are for the most part pure enough
and can be fully appreciated. Modern poetry springs—like any renewing
artistic movement—from radical rebellion. From this point of view,
it has the same spiritual root and wells up out of the same split human
mind as, for example, the utopia. It is the protest of the revolted spirit
against all that is unjust, vulgar, superficial and hypocritical. It opposes the
dogmatism and conservatism of the existing order with all its vested interests
and false, parsimonious rigidity, whether this is represented by powdered
whigs or plunging necklines. It expresses the heart-felt protest of the artist
against a society which is wholly unworthy of man and in sharp conflict
with the idea of true humanity, with the highest values of the beautiful
which is also the true and the good, and so with all meaningful striving
for progress, peace, happiness and the full unfolding of life. His artistic
spirit seared by the two world wars, his sensitive imagination clutched by
fear of a third orgy of destruction, body and mind drawn into the vortex
of a mounting dehumanizing technocracy, the artist's protest is raised
against everything and everyone. His protest is against all fundamental norms
and forms, against all our spiritual heritage, against all authority of religion,
philosophy, science and also of art, against traditional rights and values,
dogmas, criteria, ideas, ideals and idols. A loud and vociferous protest it is,
a piercing cry or a thunderous roar, a long drawn-out lament or a heart-rend-
ing curse at all the world, including himself.

This protest of poetry, in itself so understandable, finds expression in an
explicit rejection of all existing poetic forms and images. Thus the protest is
not only against common usage in punctuation, syntax and symmetry, but
against rhyme, rhythm and metre, against ordered prosody and melodious
harmony, and above all against the coherent structure of a rationally or at
least intuitively comprehensible whole. In outward form, poetry has been
shredded into unrelated image-fragments, detached word-and-sound
combinations, a stream of vibrations which does not crystallize as a melody,
a series of image-flashes juxtaposed in deliberate disorder. Each separate
image is eloquent enough, but together they are a triumph of inarticulate-
ness, conveying no meaning.

But whatever may be the case in the other arts, in poetry it is quite impossible to impair existing modes of *expression* without seriously affecting
the *content*. Therefore the protest against the *form* of the poetic image inevitably turns into a protest against its intrinsic meaning and purport, its
message. This makes of modern poetry a pregnantly significant and sympto-

1. Examples from different countries: Ezra Pound, T. S. Eliot, André Breton, Paul
van Ostayen. The latter's work was recently reprinted in full, *i.e.* including expression-
istic typography.

matic keynote of the whole of contemporary art and culture, the *ideal-type* of unconscious and unintended self-destruction.

Modern poetry gives a series of instantaneous exposures, one after another, of the subconscious and of its associations and ceaselessly shifting representations, unfiltered and unretouched. The poem reproduces, without censorship or adornment, man's most intimate stirrings and promptings as purely natural or animal events. Modern poetry is not a *transcription* of the *other*, but a *description* of the *personal*. It does not come about through *ecstasy*, but through *introitus*. It is a combination of introversive self-gratification and spiritual exhibitionism.

It is true, of course, that every artist lays his soul bare in every work of art, even if this is done indirectly. The deliberate spiritual nakedness of modern poetry is certainly not in itself shameless or shocking. But it must be considered as corrupt and perverse to the extent that this turning oneself inside-out in public becomes a form of coquetry; it expresses poverty of spirit and insufficient artistic endowment. It may eventually appear that there are a few pure-bred artists among our modern poets—but unfortunately it is also true that almost any non-artist can pose as a modern poet. For modern poetry works with loose thoughts and associations, which are not organized intellectually or artistically, but have a subjective-arbitrary sequence. This is generally labelled child-like, bizarre, grotesque, irrational, etc. A charlatan with some flair and inventiveness for associations without rhyme or reason can serve up the same hors d'œuvre in a purely cerebral tour de force. He may even demonstrate more spirit and insight in his quasi-puerile or quasi-primitive imitation of the feeble-minded or of psychic unrestraint, in an ingenious blend of narcissism, neurosis, verbalism and snobbism. [1]

The "creating" of modern poetry requires nothing more than a well-developed sense for a senseless arrangement of words. [2] One can be a modern

1. In modern poetry the sharp distinction between artistic and artificial, modern art and the caprice of fashion, artistic expression and dilettant mannerism, and between spontaneously inspired creativity and standardized made-to-order literary production, has disappeared. It is precisely poetry, which *should* well up out of the deepest irrational layers of the mind; out of undecipherable spiritual processes, which can most easily and almost indetectably be imitated by the application of a purely rational technique which has no relationship to genuine artistry. Art with a capital "A" and art of the dimestore variety, artistic "possession" and impotence, true and false, imaginary and illusionary, the heart's blood and the brain's spidery webbing, inspiration and escapism —all this has broken adrift and become indiscriminately merged in utter confusion, a confusion which also reigns within artist's circles themselves.

2. Modern pictorial or musical composition still requires a foundation of technical mastery which is the prerogative, the special gift of a few gifted individuals and which they possess, whether one likes the result or not. Prokofiev can compose a Classical Symphony, Bartok can produce Roumanian Dances, Stravinsky can create a neo-

poet without any special preliminary study, spiritual maturing or unusual gifts, simply by virtue of one's own decision and announcement. No one can dispute or refute the matter. And every modern poem can—and indeed must—find recognition from one connoisseur or another. It must find this recognition because the logical extremes of modern poetry have deliberately sacrificed every essential and every positive criterion of the poetic art, and so every piece of writing that lacks these criteria is a poem. [1] The sanction of *non*-recognition is reserved for those symbolic representations which still retain a romantic-regressive and thus contra-natural meaning.

Here we arrive, it would seem, at the heart of modern poetry, and find that it is a typical sample of modern art at its most modern. There is no point in despising or ridiculing modern poetry (or any other form of modern art) as nonsense. For even should it deserve such an epithet, we would not then be doing it the justice that every honest artistic attempt at regeneration (apart from inevitable by-products and parasitic outgrowths) deserves, no matter how mistaken or downright dangerous it is considered to be. Modern poetry is not only a challenge, but is itself also an answer to a challenge of the times. Behind the negative there hides an eccentric and assiduous, if perhaps vain, seeking for the positive and for the deeper sense of the nonsensical. It is not so much its alien fruit as the *why* of its origin and continuing development which deserves our close and unprejudiced attention.

The "why" is already implicit in the terminology we have used above. For modern poetry of our time it is the *meaningless* which forms, now more than ever, the only natural, existential meaning. Conversely, the *meaningful* is unnatural, false and artificial. Genuine and honest art, according to this view, portrays reality as it basically *is* and as it is reflected in man's subconscious images and in the unchangeable conditions of existence: fear, suffering, evil, despair, madness, chaos and absurdity, death and destruction, fatalism and nihilism.

If modern poetry is nauseating, nonsensical and negative—this is the basic pattern of the modern image of the world, now for the first time coming to be fully recognized by the present, struggling generation. But at the very moment when modern poetry seems to have found a firm

classical choreography for the Ballet Russe, Respighi can write a Concerto Gregoriano, and many others can make use of classical or pre-classical forms, as most modern painters also can and have done.

1. With the ruling out of traditional forms and with the monstrous pact between art and any odd form which happens to emerge from the subconscious (or is artifically contrived in "imitation of nature"), we find ourselves in a situation where every portrayal of the uncontrollable unconscious must be automatically accepted on the basis of its pretensions to be and to promote an intrinsically equally uncontrollable art. The only check is a negative one, for the subconscious appears to know no checks and to be uncensored by reason.

foundation by this vindication of its existence as a reflection of *actuality* and *reality*, the poetic art as such is hurled from its pedestal by this very vindication. For this pedestal had placed poetry *above* its own time. Formerly, poetry spoke of and was inspired by an *other* time. It was not a duplication and reflection of the day-to-day stream of events, but history-in-the-becoming, its symbolic phrases pregnant with message and prophecy. Now, on the contrary, the age makes use of poetry in order to portray itself in endless repetition, and to celebrate itself in all its dubious uniqueness. And why not? In this view, the present age is the almighty, only possible and inevitable age which must be accepted, with good grace or bad grace. This age may well say with Caligula, "you may hate me, if you but fear me".

Along with existential philosophy, modern science and modern theology, modern poetry has let itself be captured by the present and nailed fast to the triumphal arch of the status quo. Initially it appeared, in its axiomatic reversal, its revolt against dogma and tradition and its heaven-storming assault against antiquated, fossil art-forms, to be following the revolutionary model of utopianism, but *this* avant-garde peters out in an actualism which is more conservative than the most rigid conservatism. Now we see an art gone out of its senses, feverishly embracing an age gone out of its senses, deathly afraid that in losing this it will lose the last remnant of itself. The *positive counter-part* of the utopia, always accompanying its destructive criticism, the *systematic and synthetic reconstruction*, the *perspective*, is lacking. Modern poetry is not anti-poetic because it depicts the ugly and the repulsive, but inasmuch and insofar as it contains that only and nothing more. It confines itself to the *anti*-human and knows nothing of the *super*-human. It sees *negation*, anchored in the present, as the only possible *position*. It can no longer see beyond its own time, much less offer any outlook to others. It drifts with the times, unheeding and uncaring, captivated by the reflection of its own contorted face in the time-stream.

In all the meaninglessness of the times which it so desperately glorifies, nothing finally appears so utterly meaningless as its own original rebellion, which has culminated in this servile and sterile poetic art, egocentrically contemplating its own navel. A nickel in the slot, and it will obediently deliver some current brand of image. The age has carefully distributed them over the compartments of the time-machine and each bears its familiar legend: anxiety, chaos, etc. This, ironically enough, is the new freedom imaginism has brought us. The sole meaning of the poetic image is now located in the hopeless present, after having been carefully purged of all unreal memories or imaginary expectations.

The work of some promising experimental poets does indeed contain many of the elements indispensable to true poetry: sensitivity to images and tone, playful fantasy, mastery of the use of words, creative emotions, a vibrant dynamism, magical suggestiveness, a realistic capacity for observation and a bold expressiveness. But other, equally essential elements are entirely lacking. For the modern poet is completely possessed by the demonic forces of this age; his inspiration is exclusively drawn from the drama of the actual situation, the irremediable human existence and the irrevocable death-sentence for Everyman.

So there is no way, and no way out; there is no other order of things, no direction, no directive, no values and no ideal; there is no purpose, no meaning, no redemption, liberation or purification; there is no prospect and there is no other future, but the shadowy bottomless abyss of Nothingness. If atonal poetry can offer nothing but nothingness and does not want to reflect anything but modern nihilism, the question finally arises whether it could not better become toneless and silent.

Chapter XXIV

SOCIO-CULTURAL DYNAMICS

> *The choice is no longer between Utopia and the pleasant ordered world that our fathers knew. The choice is between Utopia and Hell.*
>
> William Beveridge [1]
>
> *The construction of Utopias used to be despised as the foolish refuge of those who could not face the real world. But in our time social change has been so rapid, and so largely inspired by utopian aspirations, that it is more necessary than it used to be to consider the wisdom or unwisdom of dominant aspirations.*
>
> Bertrand Russell [2]

The field of knowledge which encompasses the organization of society, its social institutions, philosophies, forms and reforms, functions, roles and attitudes, movements and processes, is of the greatest significance for culture and vice versa. The fact that a sociology of culture has developed independently and that the difference between the "social sciences" and "cultural sciences" is often no longer maintained, is a sign of this.

The close interrelatedness of "society" and "culture" is, however, not only of a static nature, in the sense that a cross-section through any society or culture at any given moment will show an intricate network of connections between the two. It is above all a dynamic relationship of continuous interaction. Social and cultural patterns grow and develop and change in the course of time and mutually influence each other. Although these interdependencies have been recognized, the area of socio-cultural dynamics has remained largely unexplored. [3]

---

1. From a talk by Beveridge, quoted in his autobiographical *Power and Influence*, London, 1953, p. 355.
2. Bertrand Russell, *The Impact of Science on Society*, London, 1952, p. 85.
3. The chief pioneering work in this field has been done by Mannheim and Sorokin.

This is not the place to till this neglected marginal field, for a vast separate study would be needed. Our considerations will be strictly limited to three aspects only, namely capitalism, socialism and politics, and even so we will not do more than give a few relevant illustrations, chosen for their special significance for the *future*.

1. *Capitalism and Socialism*

There has been a veritable flood of literature concerning the rise and development of capitalism, both before and after the appearance of Sombart's standard works. There has also been a good deal about its gradual transformation and eventual decline. This latter, since the time of Marx, has been seen chiefly as a dialectical process of self-disintegration—a point of view which was greatly re-enforced by the crisis of the thirties. The dogmatic Marxist-Leninist doctrine has, of course, never relinquished this tenet and even maintained it as the official basis of Soviet international politics. But quite apart from this political background and entirely independent of the Russian dream of the coming collapse of capitalism, this doctrine has been subject to renewed economic and sociological analysis during and after the second world war, and powerful arguments to support it have again been presented. Two books stand out here as far above average in insight and foresight, in heretical-critical boldness, and in absolute independence of judgement. The one has remained largely unknown, the other book is familiar to everyone in the field. Both are written by versatile economists, who have emigrated from Austria to the U.S.A. We refer to Karl Polanyi and Joseph Schumpeter [1].

It would be like carrying coals to Newcastle to attempt here to describe again the self-destroying effects of capitalism, since Schumpeter has already done this so comprehensively and well. Nor do I know of any authoritative refutation of this argument. Therefore I would like to admit Schumpeter's magnificently composed analysis as our point of departure. Accepting his conclusions in the main, I will translate and reconstruct them into the categories and concepts made use of in this book

Vastly simplified, Schumpeter's general argument runs as follows: Capitalism is not destroyed by its failures, but by over-success. The bureaucratic

1. Karl Polanyi, *The Great Transformation*, New York, 1944. Joseph Schumpeter, *Capitalism, Socialism and Democracy*, New York, 1942.

Polanyi's outstanding contribution is his delineation of how the historical flowering of liberal capitalism in England, through and side by side with the first industrial revolution, already contained those explosive and dynamic forces of self-destruction which did not become fully evident until the twentieth century. Schumpeter, on the other hand, takes the present situation and observable trends as his point of departure. Each work complements the other to produce a historically adequate whole.

mammouth concerns, consisting of innumerable limited-liability and joint-stock companies with their salaried managers and their almost automatic, impersonal and mainly technologically propelled development—which is no longer primarily furthered by the private initiative and personal risk of adventurous and enterprising individuals—these concerns destroy the earlier unique position of new entrepreneurial combinations set up by profit-seeking capitalists. Capitalism itself undermines its own protective bulwark, the bourgeoisie; it attacks the position of the farmer, small business man, the middle class shopkeeper, trades and professions; above all, it devalues the function of the bourgeoisie as such in society. Its own extreme rationalism gives rise to a critical-rational attitude toward bourgeois values, which finally extends to the values of capitalism itself. It cancels or weakens the unique institutional conditions of private property, free competition and freedom of contract. Through its concentration and expansion it engenders an attitude which is increasingly hostile to itself. At the same time capitalism is not in a position to defend itself against these increasingly current, irrational and hostile attacks, supported by the influence of the organized trade-union movement and a discontented intelligentsia. It is precisely its hyper-rational, bourgeois and anti-heroic mentality which leaves it resistless. Capitalism not only fails to rouse itself to a manly and firm defense of the bourgeois framework of capitalistic civilization against all attackers, but even contributes to its own reshaping and the transition to a socialistic ("collectivist", in Schumpeter's terminology) social order.

The validity and force of Schumpeter's (and Polanyi's) analysis concerning the specific social-economic factors in the decline of capitalism will not be argued here. Suffice it to compare, on the social-psychological level, the operations of the capitalistic *image of the future* in the two periods—the former one of flowering, and the present one of decline. At this point Polanyi's historical study contributes more insight than Schumpeter's. Arguing from the development of the poor-laws of England, he shows how industrial capitalism in England was able to flourish thanks to a dominant and vigorous image of the future, an image which must itself in the end destroy the corroding effects of social disintegration coming in the train of economic industrialization. Numerous currents converged in this image of the future: liberalism, classical economics, biology, social Darwinism, the social philosophies of physicalism and mechanism, sociology (Spencer) and even theology.

All threads are drawn together in the ideas of the struggle for existence and the survival of the fittest, the harmony (established by a providential "hidden hand" or beneficently working natural law) between self-interest (particularly of the entrepreneur) and the general interest, and between free competition through the exercise of unbridled individual initiative and the common wealth. The economic mechanism of the market, provided it were functioning quite freely (laissez-faire), would lead automatically toward the optimum of prosperity and justice. Il mondo va da se. The evil of hunger, poverty and unemployment suffered by the working proletariat was not only unavoidable, but from the point of view of the general welfare it was a positive good. Seen from the large point of view, the exploiting capitalistic entrepreneurs who were enriching themselves by grinding the faces of the poor could look upon themselves as the nation's benefactors.

The capitalist-oriented [1] image of a future of unending progress and prosperity collapsed as much as a result of its social failure (Polanyi) as of its economic success (Schumpeter). It is true that there have been and are, also now, ultra-liberalist revivals on a theoretical level such as those of Ludwig von Mises, Friederich Hayek, Wilhelm Röpke, Lionel Robbins and John Jewkes. But even in neo-liberalism (especially as influenced by John Maynard Keynes) there is no longer this unconditional faith in a harmonious evolutionary development such as was symbolized in the earlier liberalist image of the future by the gold standard, maintained at the cost of so many human sacrifices all over the world. Today's entrepreneurs certainly do not adore any such golden calf. They mostly lack the necessary self-confidence to live for such an ultra-liberalist image of the future, much less die for it. This nineteenth-century image of laissez-faire belonging to an intellectual and industrial élite has been exhausted and made a hollow mockery by an unending series of shocks and crises and basic shifts in the world economy and social institutions. In spite of the lip-service it still receives in the United States because of its contribution to the development of the "American Creed", it has to all intents and purposes ceased to exist.

More and more social regulations have been instituted to restrain the hitherto unhampered pernicious effects of pure capitalism. Capitalism itself has met them with decreasing resistance, and finally has accepted them as inevitable, partly even as a matter of course. Some of these measures to check capitalistic excesses have contributed through their operation to the further weakening of the dominant liberalist image of the future. Not only the capitalistic image of the future, however, but in combination with other currents of the times they have in fact weakened every kind of image of the future. Schumpeter correctly singles out two phenomena which reflect this impairment of the essence of capitalism: the decrease in the average size of the

---

1. It is not necessary for our purposes to make the distinction between economic liberalism and industrial capitalism.

family, and the decrease in accumulation of capital through individual saving. A good deal of attention had of course already been given by others to both these phenomena. And it is certainly true that both—formation of family and formation of capital—are intimately related to the expectations for the future which men cherish. The number of children and the number of bankbooks speak, each in its own way, the language of *anticipation*. As far as I know, however, no one has attempted systematically to relate these specific anticipations to the *general*, cultural image of the future. It would be of great interest to study the relationship of these various anticipations in the total framework of different societies and cultures. Here, however, we will give only the outlines of such an approach in the framework of Western European culture. Our purpose is to make clear how the action of and the reaction to capitalism reveal *the same regression* which we have observed in other areas of culture: a literal reactionary driving back of the *future*, accompanied by an exclusive concentration on and consolidation of the *present*.

Let us first consider the decline in the average size of the family in the West. Originally the size of the family wavered between the two poles of a trustful faith in Providence and the wisdom, derived from bitter daily experience, of unnatural abstention (Malthus). For the proletariat children were formerly assets which helped to balance the budget; for the developing industries they were necessary factory fodder, for the military nation, indispensable cannon fodder, and for the Church, so many more souls to be saved. A large family was both necessary and good, also in view of the high rate of infant or child mortality, contributed to by early industrial capitalism. Now, on the contrary, the leveling of income and property, of monetary holdings, has led to the levelling of *time*. This levelling of time has worked out, as I will try to show, into a reduction of family-size and indirectly also through a smaller time-distance not only between the oldest and youngest child of the average family, but also between parents and children, both generations nowadays for a large part living in one and the same present.

Taxation and inheritance laws leave no prospect for those who are well off to make future capital provisions for a large number of children; at the most they can provide for one or just a few. Social regulations and cultural pressure have eliminated the possibility of children being economic assets for the less-well off. Rather, each additional child, particularly for the middle class, may mean at least a social and cultural down-grading of the family standard of living. This is even becoming increasingly true of the farm population, as its children are participating more and more in the urban community and because of mechanization are finding less and less work to do on the farm. Limiting the number of children increases their opportunities, as well as those of their parents, for the good life here and now. This is true not only for the traditional head of the house and lord of creation, the man, but also for his socially and sexually emancipated partner in marriage—thanks to the improved position of the "weaker" sex. "Das ewig-weibliche" has in the space of scarcely half a century moved with our present here-and-now-culture to become the moment-ridden feminine. Some western countries are already falling below the net reproduction rate, and are thus faced with stationary or decreasing populations. Other countries which continue to have an over-all increase, face a qualitative decline in the population because differential fertility operates in a dysgenic direction.

In the upper and middle income groups, among the white-collar workers, business men, the professions and the intellectual and artistic élite, and even skilled labour, the childless household is no longer uncommon, and the one or two-child family predominates. [1] The continuing increase—with ups and downs—of the divorce rate changes the traditional family-unit-pattern insofar as it is coupled with the disappearance of marriage-for-life, and makes it rather into a temporal, contractual relationship between part-time bachelors with as few bonds as possible in the form of children, and maximum guarantees for full individual self-realization. [2] Parents and children, adults and young people, live their lives in the present and for themselves, not as responsible stewards for posterity, nor in concern for a life after this life. The future is no more than the lengthening shadow of the present. [3]

These phenomena are closely related to the other point mentioned above concerning the accumulation of capital through sober living and thrift, More than ever before the accent falls upon enjoyment of this earthly life, regarded not as a temporary transitional stage but as the only true reality. This carpe-diem attitude is reflected in the emphasis on satisfaction of material wants and raising the "minimum" standard of living through ever-increasing consumption. Hygiene, comfort and luxury have become

1. In recent times there have been signs—in several Western-European countries and also in the U.S.—that some of these groups are tending towards larger families. It is too early to be able to discern a definite shift, but this phenomenon deserves close attention.

2. Not all marriages or all divorces participate in this trend, which rather represents an ideal-typical simplification, for the purpose of rough comparison between historical periods. Of course, this problem is much more complex. Some observers for example prefer to interpret the high divorce-rate quite differently, as being a healing process which in the end will contribute to the strengthening of marriage as such.

3. It is obviously possible to take widely different points of view concerning these developments, within the frame of reference of the sociology of the family. See for example recent studies by Agier, Burgess, König, Mead, Schelsky, Zimmerman and Parsons. It is our intention by the introduction of the concept "image of the future" to develop a more objective criterion for the testing of various optimistic and pessimistic valuations.

available to the masses through industrial technology and mass production. A revolution at the expense of individual saving habits has taken place in favour of mass consumption, mass recreation, sport, travel, play and every form of short-lived escapism made available by the mass-media. The traditional private saving has been replaced to a significant degree by compulsory mass saving through social security regulations and diversified voluntary types of insurance (life, sickness, education, indemnity, pension) which stretch no farther than to cover relatively immediate and foreseeable needs of any kind including those of old age. [1] Thus, *to the farthest extent possible, the future is already laid down as of to-day.* [2]

There is an unmistakable shift in our time from the uncertainties of chance imposed by the mobility and motoric power of the capitalistic adventure, towards a protective security of existence from cradle to grave. It is a shift from an independent position to a contractual, steady and salaried appointment; from bold ventures to insurance policies; from an irregular and highly variable income to a fixed income with constant purchasing power (according to a sliding scale, following the price index), with stability and security. In short, there is a noticeable shift from a future which—in spite of the general increase of national prosperity—would still remain materially insecure for large groups of the population, to a present which if not care-free is at least economically stable. For the maintenance of this present restrictions or even hardships are generally preferred to a speculation on future riches.

Add to this the fact that independent entrepreneurs are more and more giving way to salaried directors and holders of preferred stock, and that the dynamic philosophy of expansion by leaps and bounds through daring risk-taking is making way for one of consolidation by a solid step-by-step, almost mechanical development based on technological research, experimental testing and market and opinion surveys, also ensured by patents, monopolies, cartel organizations and chains covering whole continents, or sustained by huge government orders (both civil and military). Consider further that industry is often protected by high tariff walls and a cordon of trade restrictions, as well as through registered trade marks and well-advertised, price-fixed brand-name products. Again, reflect that the

1. It is now even possible to buy insurance protection against too many rainy days on a vacation trip.
2. These shifts have many aspects and must not only be judged from one point of view. There is for example the idea of consumption and dis-saving as an economic necessity for the sake of investment and expansion of production generally accepted since the writings of Keynes on this subject. There is also the point of view that social progress is best served by social security regulations which compel saving, and which may be considered as collective savings which offset the decline in individual savings.

relationship between employers and employees is largely regulated by collective contracts drawn up at the discretion of industrial and trade organizations, sometimes under government supervision, and, finally, that contemporary government regulation seeks through a more or less planned economy to stabilize the business cycle and achieve as full employment as possible.

The original capitalistic "Wirtschaftsgeist" was driven by the daring anticipation and bold imagination of foolhardy, adventurous and even unscrupulous enterprisers. Egocentric and heroic to a degree it was intent on the conquest of the future at any price for the sake of gain, ruthlessly exploiting men, women and children like beasts, but at the same time gambling its own total existence. This spirit has now turned into conscientious concern for the preservation of the present and the status quo of vested interests in the midst of a rapidly changing world and an ever accelerated tempo of life. This is not only true of the entrepreneurial interests in the narrower sense of the word, but also of the proletariat which so suddenly found itself hurled up from the lowest status to the top of the social hierarchy, thanks to the influence of its unions and their representatives or advocates in the legislative and executive branches.

The tremendous potential of the liberal laissez-faire image of the future, capitalism's source of energy, has evaporated. At the same time the idea of capitalism as such is drastically weakened and rapidly atrophying. The process of self-disintegration is now quite real, taking place through auto-destruction at the core of the idealistic image of the future. Without it, capitalism is no longer viable, and has already lost its future. This age is the age of neo-mercantilism, statism, interventionism, syndicalism, corporationism and mixed forms of central planning. Is this to say that the capitalistic image of the future is being succeeded by a socialistic image of the future? Schumpeter suggests the unavoidable transition from a capitalistic to a socialistic social order. This does not necessarily mean the same thing as the replacement of one *image of the future* by another—it can indeed mean the opposite.

If only for this reason I cannot at this point follow Schumpeter's brilliant and suggestive argument concerning socialism any further. All the less in that he defines socialism from a purely formal, technical-institutional point of view, as being synonymous with collectivism and communism, therefore as that social system in which there is centralized control over production and the means of production. Instead, with reference to the future of socialism, I find its external form less relevant than the basic idea which underlies its changing content. This is the idea of a totally other, humanly worthy and just society, proceeding from a radical break with the existing order which is not recognized as absolute and invariant. It is the idea of a basic re-ordering of society as a conceivable possibility, to be achieved by the collective and consistent use of human power.

My remarks on this subject must necessarily be scanty, although I have written extensively about it elsewhere. [1] I see socialism in the same light as capitalism, as a *social movement, moved by the spiritual force of a positive image of the future*. In capitalism, the image is one of a self-unfolding evolution toward a harmonious social equilibrium and the optimum welfare of the commonwealth. In socialism, especially pre- and post-Marxian socialism, it is a revolutionary image of a systematic intervention in the existing state of affairs to bring about a new ideal order, in which every man will have a reasonable and just chance to achieve a socially worthy existence and all men, everywhere, will be able to participate in a humanly worthy society. Both images of the future are *utopian*. Equally utopian is Marxism, wavering as it does between the two poles of thought, accepting on the one hand the automatic evolutionary development maintained by liberalism (though with the opposite outcome in mind!) and on the other hand sharpening up to a finer edge than ever before the tool of direct exertion of human power —the class struggle, with its accompanying national and international organization for revolution. But whatever concrete form the positive image takes on at different times and in different currents of thought, it is above all its representation and anticipation of the *future* which inspires and moves man.

No movement in the history of human civilization, including social movements, has ever literally *moved* the course of events without a radiating image of the future. Whenever a movement has magnetized men, whenever it has inspired them, at times to the point of ecstatic transport, this has been the source of its life and élan, of the high-powered energy with which it was charged. The spiritual capacity of any movement (and every movement with any power of emotional dynamics is essentially a spiritual movement, whether its goals be spiritual or material) can be measured—not in horsepowers or ampères, but in the qualitative intensity of the radiation and in the heat of its spiritual ardour and enthusiasm, emanating from its idealistic image of the future.

We have tried to demonstrate in our historical survey that each movement and socio-cultural trend has derived its effectiveness from its particular projection of the future, and that these projections have pushed and pulled the ongoing stream of events towards the future they foreshadowed. We have concluded that these images of the future have to a greater or lesser

1. Dr. Polak's articles on this subject, in Dutch journals, are unfortunately not easily available to the American reader (Translator's Note).

degree determined coming *reality* in advance through their *ideality* (insofar as other counter-forces have not intervened). In other words, the history of the past is to a great extent the history of images of the future, and the unfolding future has always been for a large part contained in the images of the future which have preceded it.

On the other hand, we have also come to the conclusion that any once-powerful historical movement which no longer possesses any genuine image of the future and does not inspire a direct of indirect influence-optimistic faith in the possible realization of that image, faces spiritual decay. This is all the more true of social movements that are oriented to the earthly sphere of human society, which is open to public control and daily experience. We have argued, therefore, that any historical movement which concentrates on the present must ultimately peter out in a stagnant pool; as a living and therefore moving idea, it can have no future.

This hypothetical point of view finds striking confirmation in the historical development of western socialism. (Because of the homogeneity of the fundamental ideas of the underlying socialist image of the future, we are lumping widely diverse manifestations of socialism in different countries and at different times together under one label.) This development in fact provides an almost classical illustration of our thesis Socialism, in its ups and downs, from its one spiritual origin to its present-day differentiated materializations, runs a course almost painfully parallel to the general course of socio-cultural development from utopia to counter-utopia, from a coming other and better world to the inescapable reality of this unchangeable existence.

The utopian vision of man and society on earth is without any doubt, in my opinion, the chief source and root of socialism; not only of that first bold and pioneering current of thought, called utopian socialism, but of *all* socialism. We have already discussed how "scientific" Marxism, through its complete secularization of eschatology, contained this same utopian image of the future, however strongly it denied this, and derived its tremendous and revolutionary influence precisely from this utopian source. History, which takes delight in perverting the best human intentions, has once more heartlessly amused itself at the expense of idealistic socialism. It has played two mean tricks the consequences of which could be fatal for the future, both of socialism and of the entire western culture.

The reader will remember that Marx and his followers resisted the non-revolutionary reformist socialism with tooth and nail, despising it as "utopian" and bourgeois socialism. In the end, they succeeded in destroying true utopian socialism, at least in the West. There it developed, instead, into a typical . . . bourgeois socialism! The Marxian brand, on the other hand, would result, according to the official doctrine, in an earthly paradise of a classless and stateless society of workers. Such a society is supposed to have been realized, especially in the East, with the help of the revolution for which the system provides. [1]

In the following I would like to discuss briefly some phases and forms of western socialism. [2] It must be understood that I refer to socialism in its broadest sense as a general spiritual current and social-political movement, without any specific Western-European country in mind unless it is specifically mentioned.

This socialism, in every phase of its development, was charged with the dynamic of the future, and was co-determining for the future, as long as it contained and brought forth a positively resonant and galvanic image of the future of an idealistic-utopian nature; that is, so long as it gave a decisive answer to the question "Where to?", taken up by a swelling self-confident chorus of "There!". It was vital as long as it functioned as the chosen image-bearer and pathfinder toward the new dawn of the future, in much the same way as the anticipation of the coming of the Messiah upheld and led the Jewish people through their disconsolate pilgrimage over the face of the earth from the old Canaan to the New Israel. It was alive as long as it could with visionary conviction depict the future as the totally other: completely different from, radically breaking with the existing order, a "revaluing of all values" in which the oppressed will rule, the possessors are dispossessed, the unjust judges judged, the downtrodden receive equality, men become brothers instead of wolves, and a realm of peace and joy replaces the unworthy pariah-state which sapped the life-blood from a pauperized proletariat.

Utopism was the great growth-hormone in the development toward present-day socialism. I would certainly not maintain that this utopism has worked in an exclusively beneficial manner or always influenced the growth-

1. This new society is chiefly to be recognized by its heightened class conflicts, its despotic moloch, the State, and the absolute control which a tiny minority, through political party-machinery, exercises over the total population. Also by a production system which makes slave labourers of millions and throws them into concentration camps from which death is the only liberation.

2. Let it be said with conviction that in the practical carrying out of Leninism and Stalinism all utopian ideals for humanity (including those of the Marxists themselves) have been deliberately crushed, so that the result has been a fearsome, tragically perfect counter-utopia. Not enough can be done to strenghten mental and moral resistance to this monstrosity. But I must strongly protest against the suggestion, often implied in the forms of this resistance, that such anti-humanitarian degeneration is logically and intrinsically part of all utopian striving as such. On the contrary, I am convinced that if the nations of the West had taken the approximation of utopian goals more seriously, the Stalinist caricature would not have been able to spread so tempestuously over the world of the East.

process towards a well-balanced state; only that it has continuously provided a highly effective dynamic power for the socialist movement. And socialist utopias also have of necessity had to relinquish certain aspects or elements, either because of changes in the social structure or because certain ideas later proved to be immature or ill-considered. But as long as the socialistic utopia was retained as an idea and its outward form was adapted to the onward-moving times, its potential energy remained undiminished.

The socialism of the last half-century has like Monsieur Jourdain unwittingly spoken the prose of utopism. The ripe fruits of modern socialistic political action, such as full employment, social security, government regulation to protect the poor, the weak and the workers, public health programs and a just distribution of incomes, are for a large part the harvest of the seed sowed by utopism. The realistic success and spread of these socialistic policies in the last decades are simply unthinkable without the centuries-long careful preparation and slow reshaping of thought by means of utopian ideas and the detailed development of ideal images of the future.

The utopists of former times constructed an *other* world, existing only in their mind and imagination, but thus they made possible the modern *real* world (deviant in so many respects both from their former world and from their exalted visions) in which we live, with its fundamentally reconstructed social pattern. This causal relationship between the unreal ideas of former ages and the rock-hard reality of the present, however this proud and stiff-necked generation may ignore it, is in my opinion one that cannot be denied. The social utopia was always the spiritual vanguard and conditio sine qua non of the social policies and programs of action, which materialize only much later. The relationship is not only the chronological one of seed to harvest. It is also the psychological relationship of tension between cease-less struggling with no apparent results and a confident waiting till the winds blow fair and the time is ripe. Where now are the utopias and utopian ideas which are preparing the way for far-reaching changes in the direction of a socialistic image of man and society? Are they giving direction and purpose to current socialist striving for the future? In fact, can we even say that the concept of a radical break with the existing order as possible and desirable is still alive? Or is this now considered as a dangerous illusion? Does that highly-charged tension between the real and the ideal, that sharp spur to ceaseless and utmost effort still persist?

It looks as though the social proletariat and the idea of socialism (connected with the former) have changed places: the proletariat has risen, the idea of the totally other has sunk. This scissors-like motion is threatening to pinch off the fundamental idea of socialism.

Although one could hardly say that socialism is currently in a state of decline, signs which point in this direction are not lacking. The most striking symptom is the undermining of the former utopian image of the future, the lineaments of which are almost entirely absent from modern socialism. The all-important question, which encompasses the future fate of socialism and culture, is: will the progressive dismantling of the image of the future lead in the long run to suicide, or will a rebirth prove possible?

The answer depends to a significant extent on the current situation of modern socialism (which need not be considered as a coherent unity) and the interpretation one gives of its essential nature and of the impression its present conduct is going to make on the future. This implies that every answer will contain a large element of subjective evaluation, and that ideal-typical generalizations cannot be avoided in the limited scope of this chapter. In spite of these recognized difficulties, or perhaps because of them, we will attempt to deal with this subject matter not in terms of personal political preferences, but on a more objective level, within our cultural-sociological frame of reference. Using our now-familiar conceptual tools, we will see by analyzing the projections of modern socialism that it no longer offers its specific promising image of the future, but little more than a reflection of the general image of the present time.

It is amazing that the fact apparently continues to go unnoticed that capitalism and socialism both, in spite of opposing ideologies, are demonstrating a similar curve of development (and one which coincides with the general cultural trends) through their loss of the undergirding perspective utopism. The rejoicing of socialism over the death of capitalism is premature. Once again extremes meet. Socialism was the answer to the challenge of capitalism, and remarkably enough the answer was given almost the same form as the original challenge. The outward similarities between capitalism and socialism are as striking as the resemblances between grandfather and grandson. They are even exactly alike in the matter of size and gigantic growth, modern equipment and concentrated power potential. Socialism itself was irresistibly drawn into the same stream of fundamental social changes initiated by industrial capitalism, and it was therefore predestined in its turn to re-enforce this structural revolution and thereby compelled dialectically to weaken its own basic idea. Should we carry Schumpeter's train of thought to its logical conclusion? Do both movements face a similar fate through sheer excess of success?

Once eyes have been opened to this remarkable coincidence of opposites, many parallels become evident—of which we will mention only a few. *Formerly* the liberalist evolutionary image of unhampered automatic progress led to a capitalistic concentration of economic life in extensive monopolistic organizations, to combines, trusts, cartels, chains, holding companies, etc. *Now* the socialistic revolutionary image of systematic intervention has led to similar patterns of vast social-economic organizations, political fronts, majority combines, labour unions and every other kind of mechanism or technique to pervade and control society and industry. *There* a metamorphosis of independent entrepreneurs into many-headed megalo-concerns, *here* a metamorphosis of socialistic pioneers into massive administrative bodies. The capitalistic apparatus now has its executive managers, salaried directors and anonymous stockholders—mute and inconsequential—and the socialist party-affiliations have their political functionaries, union officials, autocratic leaders of mass organizations and their anonymous army of members. At the company's annual stockholders' meeting a small clique approves of the management profit-report; at the party convention the prearranged decisions are unanimously acclaimed according to program in assiduous imitation of the juridical-formalistic democracy of liberal capitalism. And on and on.

Just as the classic liberal doctrine led to capitalistic crystallizations of monopolistic competition and to concentrations of power which impaired free enterprise and frustrated its own original ideal, so utopian socialism, in compulsive response, moved into a socialist party machinery and power politics which can in the end prove equally frustrating to its ideal. The combined effects of the technical revolution and increasing government regulation (which socialism itself has furthered) imperatively enforce a further elaboration and expansion of the socialistic apparatus. What will be the effect of a mammoth party (including integrated labour unions and a complex network of communication), a party which wields real political power, on the future of the socialist movement which gave it birth? As it is, these developments are for the greater part applauded or at any rate accepted, even though a growing sense of the dangers of the present situation breaks through and there have been a few rebellious attempts at taking initiative.

Let us assume, for the sake of argument, that challenge and response, at least in regard to form and size, do indeed display one and the same structure for the two opposing movements; what does this demonstrate? Does this in any sense reduce the tremendous difference of content, ideology and program, between capitalism and socialism? Is this difference not rather sharpened now that the protagonists can meet each other with equal weapons and equal forces at their disposal? Furthermore, just because one giant proves in the end to have feet of clay, must the same fate necessarily befall the other? Arguments and counter-arguments can be brought to bear on this question, and it is clear that the phenomenon of coinciding development is not in itself decisive for the ultimate outcome; it only points to possible further developments.

The possiblities of further development stem not from the nature of socialism as such but from the nature of any large political party which includes from one to three quarters of the total population. Obviously a nascent socialism, not yet possessed of an extensive party machinery, had a more critical eye for such developments than the flourishing socialism of the present day. At that time, however, the large political parties with their machinations and aspirations and with their anti-socialist point of view, formed a fine target for the fire of the growing socialist opposition. But gradually it has become clear that the development of a powerful political machinery is indispensable to the realization of socialistic ideals. Now comes the test of social growth and maturity, as in the life of the individual man: first we see the growing child, brimming over with criticism for the older generation—then the full-grown man, now himself responsible for the new lives he has begotten, and on the defense against a rebellious younger generation.

The question of whether the rapid political growth of socialism and its series of conquests may have to be considered as a process of triumph and tragedy ought first to be considered as a theoretical question, related to the modern phenomenon of party-structure as such. In a way this is reversing the approach taken earlier by the political sociologist Robert Michels. In his well-known 1910 study, *Zur Soziologie des Parteiwesens*, he offers hypotheses which he illustrates with examples from the typical development of the German socialist party of his time. This party, the S.P.D., gave him the basis for his "ehernes Gesetz der Oligarchie", the law of necessary development of all large parties, including the social-democratic party, toward an ultimately oligarchal form of administration. I begin instead with a general view based on a nearly half-century-longer experience of the evolution of political party-systems, and only afterwards consider whether the, or a socialist party holds a unique and deviating position in the total social and political structure.

One can argue with Michels in retrospect, both concerning the strength of his argument with reference to the S.P.D. and the stringency of his formulations; one can also question his dramatic presentation of the trends toward oligarchal development and its dangers. Nevertheless, from an objective point of view it must be admitted that his general prediction concerning the anti-democratic implications inherent in the building up of large and powerful political parties is correct. These tendencies, whether deliberately pursued or not, are certainly present. There is room for differences, however, in the evaluation of the amount of intrinsic harm done by these shortcomings in any specific situation and also of the possible consequences of such outgrowths or even excesses for western democracy. But let us, in discussing the present structural phase, first resume Michels' general argument, though in a somewhat modernized, less stringent form to suit the contemporary intellectual climate. The modern observer, who has witnessed the socialist "breakthrough" of an earlier social structure, has less sympathy with "iron laws of nature" as applied to society.

It can be said then, that at the present time any large political party, whatever its colour, creed or national background, can not do without a well-oiled, smoothly-running party machinery if it wants to exert any influence in the political arena. This in turn presupposes strict party discipline extending to all branches of the party. The smooth functioning of a large party thus unavoidably leads to a far-reaching shift of accent: the highest value is no longer placed on personal inspiration, progressive orientation, individual views and originality; unconditional trust, blind loyalty, acclamation and conformity on command and pliant obedience are prized instead. The party thus takes on the character of a well-drilled army or a strict ecclesiastical hierarchy grounded in authority. Therefore a large party cannot welcome independent, critical and perhaps heretical thinkers. It prefers steady, unimaginative and colourless mediocrities in responsible positions, who will think as little as possible, walk their appointed treadmill in the appointed manner, and feel happiest doing routine work of a limited scope.

Independent and comprehensive thinking steps outside the bounds of this uniform cadre, and can therefore as a rule not be tolerated. Minds that excel are apt to exceed the standard political requirements. Thick skin is preferred to a sensitive mind, post-boys to pioneers, and a dead level of obedience to spirited rebellion. Gradually, and at least in part in spite of itself, every large party is driven toward a measure of bureaucracy, the disciplinary maintenance of party-lines and party-decisions, and at least in some respects to a totalitarian oligarchy, in the process of ruthless competition with other parties. At its best an oligarchical form of administration may be conducted by carefully selected, conscientious and highly skilled specialists, but it will also by its very nature inevitably exercise a rather frightening attraction on less capable, power-hungry "managers" who not infrequently owe their positions to this very poverty of spirit and narrowness of mind. Great parties which have fought for self-government of the masses and who succeeded thanks to these masses, can hardly practise this principle internally in their present stage of growth. They are driven along the road of rigid centralization and progressive concentration of power in the hands of the administration as over against the mass of their own members.

In general, the above holds true more or less for every major party. Changes in the social structure seem to have made this development almost inevitable; the mechanization of culture is reflected in the mechanization of political and social organization. By the same token every movement which engages in political activity becomes enmeshed in party politics, which in its turn is dominated by pressure groups and spheres of influence of various kinds. Particularly, once a party attains to numerical majority in the legislative bodies of the nation and assumes the responsibility of government, the portals to its inner sanctum are willy-nilly thrown open and the temple veil of idealism and high convictions rent again and again under the onslaught of an opportunism and tactical compromise demanded by the realities of government administration. The external pressure of ballot box and lobby comes increasingly to supplant the inward pressure of conviction as the party attempts to build up its power in order to implement those convictions. In this process of striving and counter-striving, ideals are submerged under the exigencies of Real-Politik. Each time anew the question must then arise: how long can these infringements on a party's principles be tolerated? At what point must the line be drawn between a "yes" for what is just barely acceptable and a "no" that may no longer responsibly be suppressed? A survey of actual party behaviour indicates a gradual dulling of the social conscience and a tendency to accede to the so-called exigencies of circumstance—or what is interpreted as such.

All this is of course not new, although rather more strongly expressed than may be pleasant to those who are honestly struggling to fulfil their difficult political task. Moreover, in this respect all parties of any kind have been sifted through the same coarse sieve, even while each thinks of itself as better than the next. The question poses itself as to whether the socialist parties as such can justifiably claim to be an exception to the general rule. It is with considerable regret that I am forced to conclude that they cannot. This is not to say that I agree with Michels in seeing the rise of these socialist parties as the classical model for the typical tendencies of party growth as such—only that I am as little inclined to see it as an exception as I am to see it as a prototype. What *is* exceptional about socialism is that it, of all parties, can *least* tolerate these typical characteristics of a modern large party without irreparable damage to its essential nature.

The machinery of socialism is increasingly (and to a considerable extent unwillingly) approximating a historical counterpart of liberal capitalism. Its many-facetted structure bears the imprint of the age: mechanical, materialistic and mass-minded. The irony of fate has willed that socialism, sprung from a vision of the liberation and elevation of the worker as a human being, must now because of its modern large-scale organizational apparatus, sell man's dignity short. The collectivity which has swallowed up the worker has changed labels. Before it was the proletariat, the army of the workers; now it is mass-organization, mass-media and social mass-structures. [1] Power is dependent on large numbers for support and substance, but it cannot bother about the human individuality of adherents and constituents.

The high-and-mighty leaders of the masses have also changed labels. Formerly they were not infrequently tyrannical rulers and regents from the upper classes, the land-owners, entrepreneurs, the big business-men and property-holders, the aristocratic representatives of a birthright or moneyed élite. Now they are specialists who have arisen from the ranks of the workers in democratic fashion: managers, magistrates and administrators. The process always begins with the demand for participation, and ends in a struggle for domination—although it may be in a spirit of enlightened despotism. Plus ça change, plus ça reste la même chose. The power and abuse of power of the hated capitalist have now both been transferred, at least in potential, to the collective body with its army of anonymous employees and officials and its hierarchical caste system. And again too much power, which eludes public inspection, is concentrated at both top and bottom of this bureaucratic pyramid towering over the impersonal masses.

Political ascendency and moral decline often appear in the relationship of cause and effect. The human factors of both leaders and led are thus equally stinted. Here too general political trends seem to apply and are indeed observable in their opening stages in contemporary socialism.

If it can be said that the socialist movement is becoming bourgeois, narrowed down to parochial party politics, the paradox must be kept in mind that this is happening precisely through excluding the individual as an *active bourgeois*, a burger or citizen. [2] Instead, he becomes a small cog in the gigantic machinery of automated politics, which cannot be otherwise organized if it is to function efficiently in these times of technical development. As the spirit of the petty bourgeoisie spreads, individuals grow dispirited, losing their enterprising spirit as responsible members of society. Increasing passivity and even apathy go hand in hand in the modern state and the modern party. They are the two sides of one coin: a conservative fixation of the status quo, and the enfeeblement of a progressive striving towards a status ad quem. The fundamental difference, the essential *time*-difference between ends and means is gradually obliterated. The means loom so large in the modern eye, glued to the here-now, that they obscure

1. Goetz Briefs has written on this in *Zwischen Kapitalismus und Syndikalismus*, Berne, 1952. A second interesting document on the same subject is Joseph Goldstein's *The Government of British Trade Unions*, A Study of Apathy and the Democratic Process in the Transport and General Workers Union, London, 1952.
2. His individual vote is needed at the ballots certainly, but in a system of proportional voting no individual vote will have any real influence on the results.

the ends, reaching into the future and far-away. Cultivated conformity and sterile intolerance are coming to dominate over creative freedom, re-shaping the present into something radically different.

The greater the original idealistic and revolutionary impetus of socialism, the graver the reaction can be in political reality. A victorious movement loses its freedom of movement and dynamic power. "Un socialiste ministre n'est pas un ministre socialiste".[1] How far can realistic political conduct deviate from ideal principles? The answer varies in various situations, but it can descend to the very bottom of the scale. Socialist policy can travel the whole way back, albeit slowly and with the brakes on: radical, firmly-principled, forward-striving, responsible, moderate, realistic, middle-of-the-road, conservative—and finally—dogmatic. With scarcely noticeable transitions socialism inclines toward a recognition of the existing powers: the throne, the altar, the army and commerce. In the process it makes considerable gains, but also irrevocable losses. In learning to bridge the gap between its radical ideals and reality the basic drive to reformation is attenuated into a series of little pushes toward minor social improvements. Finally the pushes themselves grow weaker and stop altogether; the party is now a part of the traditional order, and pledged to maintain and defend that order and its own position within it.

In portraying this political transformation-process as a retrograde movement retreating from a future new order, to be created according to an ideal image, into the acceptance of the exising order, I do not mean to imply that this represents only regression and no progress at all. Obviously this more realistic and well-balanced political attitude has resulted in much positive good that could not otherwise have been achieved, or at least not in the current age. The problem is always one of weighing up opposing and in part imponderable values, of comparing non-comparable entities, balancing indirect anticipations against direct results, long-range visions against short-term accomplishments and abstract principle against concrete reality. Each position has its own undeniable merits and a logical line of reasoning which supports its own point of view and rejects opposed points of view. We are not faced here with simple alternatives of good or evil, for or against. We are rather faced with extremely complex, interrelated, mutually conflicting and essentially problematic basic questions of man and society.

Is the achievement of important social gains on the material level worth the

1. This is an inevitable generalization which of course does not mean to say that there have not been and are not still genuinely socialistic cabinet ministers in several European countries who persistently try to swim against the current of our moment-ridden time.

sacrifice of certain—perhaps crucial—spiritual values? How heavily does tangible progress in the direction of greater efficiency and responsibility in government, raising the standard of living of the lowest classes and making social provision for the weak and underprivileged, weigh against the loss of "unreal" illusions concerning the future? In order to achieve a right balance of socialist policy, all these aspects and more would have to be considered. We are here not concerned with historical valuation, but with assessing chances for future development. However high a value one places on the very respectable sum of socialist achievements from the past up to and including the present, on the favorable net result of all plus and minus, one may nevertheless entertain a negative or at least less hopeful expectation with reference to *future* developments. And even the most firmly convinced socialist must thoughtfully ask himself where the recent developments will lead socialism itself.

Modern socialism has made a conscious choice between orthodox Marxism and reformism, meeting the age-old dilemma between timeless ideals and current problems by replacing the prophetic with a more pragmatic approach. Simultaneously with the programmatic restriction of the number of possible or desirable changes in the established order, comes a deliberate narrowing of the range of vision and field of interest. Saying "yes" to the existing order inclines men to say "no" to revolutionary visions of renewal such as formerly emanated from socialism as a matter of course. Again, modern socialist policy can scarcely avoid the pressure of the actual situation, which must needs enter into any and every political activity. Although socialism once drew life from its compelling vision of a far but approaching future, its battle-station in the political arena compels it to keep near prospects in sight, even to the point of becoming near-sighted. This leaves it prey to a policy of "muddling through" in regard to vital long-term tasks. Socialism has learned the ancient political lesson that restoration is more easily assimilated than renovation.

The greater the success socialism achieves in the parliamentary and governmental sphere, and the more it becomes absorbed in this, the less it can retain its independence against the forces dominating the actual situation in political reality which form the common basis for all political parties in that these forces keep them all within the same limits of what can be achieved here and now. And so socialism, revolutionary in its European origins, very gradually and seemingly of its own free will, grows moderate with maturity and wisdom, and under the burdens of practical responsibility develops a dispassionate and realistic policy which is more *political* than *socialist*.

Is this unfair? I think not, in that the present *policy* which socialism is carrying out is not being judged as such, but rather an attempt is being made to evaluate the eventual implications for the future of socialism itself. On this latter point, scientific analysis and critical objectivity are more useful than enthusiastic approbation of everything that currently comes under the label of socialist politics. A socialist policy which has undergone a practical transformation into politically feasible policy can certainly be valued for its very real achievements on a national and international scale, at the same time that it might possibly draw severe criticism from a specifically socialist point of view. The political and socialist points of view do not necessarily run parallel, and may even in the long run clash.

Also it must be remembered that we are here attempting to capture in outline a process which is now only in its first stages, not to give a static description of one specific situation. Vaguely disquieting phenomena and premonitions of trends which cannot be clearly discerned in the kaleidoscopic shifting of events, are already allowed for in our view—and must be, where the problem is a timely recognition of the most probable outcome in a force-field of rapidly-changing social dynamics. This view contains a preview of a potential self-destruction of socialism. A similar preview of the self-destruction of capitalism, offered during its heyday, was considered nonsense even long after the somber Marxian prognosis, and it is only in the last two decades that symptoms of its decline are becoming more visible.

Therefore it is neither academic nor premature to ask, what now remains of the original, vital socialist idea? Does it really mean anything more to the great majority of its nominal adherents than a somewhat hollow-sounding phraseology concerning justice, solidarity and democracy, which no longer springs from a living, deeply felt human experience? Many see the extension of political power, combined with material welfare and social security for the workers, as representing in essence the realization of the socialist *idea*. How strong would the former socialistic ethos and pathos appear, the fiery faith in its principles and ideals, the unswerving pursuit of a new world in the face of all obstacles, according to a clearly perceived vision of the future, if one could measure their inner strength today? What kind of spiritual, intellectual or emotional motivation really moves the socialist movement today?

Or can this question be asked? Keeping in mind the old Dutch saying that the road is better than the inn, it is certainly reasonable to point out that the very fact of partial realization of old ideals through political channels must inevitably diminish their dynamic power in equal measure. Of course, when one is speaking of *those* ideals! But are there not plenty of other, unfulfilled and far-reaching ideals, particularly in connection with the social changes which have now taken place, which may equally be called socialist? The social problems and challenges which face society have not diminished; at the most they have shifted to new ground, and in part they have intensified. If we compare future prospects today with the future as it looked when socialism was first coming into its own, the outlook appears definitely less favourable. The challenge from the future to our generation is more compelling than ever before. Therefore this retreat from the future and the outspoken preference of modern socialism for the reality of the present must have deeper reasons than the per se significant fact of realization of older dreams. This surprisingly great change which has taken place in comparison with the former eager striving of socialism indicates a profound spiritual change which cannot be characteristic of socialism alone, but must be anchored in a deeper layer of modern thought. If even socialism, which was always intrinsically utopian and futuristic, is indeed subject to this uniquely contemporary delimitation of perspective and scope of activity, then the question arises whether socialism has not paid too high a price for political domination of an age which is now turn dominating it.

The socialist party too is increasingly developing the apparently inevitable political tendency to view international events through nationalist reducing-glasses. The circle of comradeship grows narrower, which means in practice that the basic differences between socialistic and non-socialistic politicians and partisans is disappearing. What does it mean to the average western socialist in his daily life (apart from specific occasions when such matters receive his momentary well-meaning attention) that two thirds of mankind does not even approach the minimum desirable standard of living according to western standards, either on a material or cultural plane? What does it matter to him that outside his own national boundaries countless millions live in the grip of a bloody terror, cut off from the world, helpless under the humanity-destroying regimes of communism or fascism? What cares he, in his inmost soul, that trapped minorities and "inferior" races are subjected to gruesome oppression and a systematic extermination of all "different" beliefs and convictions? Does he ever see the "displaced persons", uprooted and pushed into endless pilgrimages by the world's quarrels, as persons? Does that suffering rob him of sleep by night and of breath by day? Does it make him seeth with indignation, and recoil with contempt from the contrasting pettiness of quibbling coteries who pursue only their own self-interest? In the last analysis, is he ready to throw everything else aside, strip to the waist, and fight with all his might for a radical social transformation which will make a new world for all peoples? To put the question in this way is, alas, to answer it.

Instead, if I am not mistaken, the socialist movement is showing the symptoms of slow but steady ageing and slackening as a reaction to the increasingly bourgeois atmosphere of levelling and normalization of its party. *Ageing*, in that its ideas and images of the future are ceasing to attract the younger generation of our time. Where are the ideas that point out a new course of action and a new social order to the young people? In fact, as a teacher I am struck by the poverty of thinking about the future among the student groups, at least in my own country. In this new generation, which forms the hope of every nation, even a hopeful attitude towards their own personal future is often lacking. *Slackening* is painfully evident in the fact that socialism, once the pioneer of social dynamics, is now in certain important respects limping painfully behind the course of events.

The movement has in part become preoccupied with a laborious adaptation to the accelerated course of events, and in part it partakes of the automatism which is a reflex of the tremendous mechanization of our western culture. If modern socialism wishes to remain *modern*, it must go with the *times*. History has amply demonstrated that the same must apply to its image of the future. But modern socialism does something more than move with its own time in the usual historical sense: it moves with *this* time, which is to say with the breach in time, and is thus part and parcel of the crisis of our culture.

To put it clearly and bluntly, socialism too—tu quoque Brutus!—moves exactly like the spirit of the times, as we have observed it in religion, philosophy, science, humanism and art. Socialism too has turned resolutely towards the *present*. It is not only going along with the times but is surrendering to them and letting itself be immured in the restricted here and now. Socialism too is becoming pervaded by realities and actualities and topicalities. *It is no longer socialism that moves the times, but rather the times that move socialism.* Philosophically, socialism too has accepted that the world is evil and cannot be changed, and it is now convinced that it must restrict the scope of its aspirations and no longer envisage changing the world and human relations. In the process, it is subsiding into a mild neo-socialism, industrious apprentice to neo-liberal social engineering,[1] satisfied to move step by step and from moment to moment in an ever-lengthening present. Even where progressive socialism does have long-term paper plans they rarely consist of more than extrapolations of existing trends, and do not go much beyond what the masses are already prepared to accept.

This is the state in which we find socialism in the midst of this period of serious decline of our culture. It is a part of this decline. It even contributes

1. This is also true of England, where the realization of the "welfare state" has left the labour party empty of new constructive ideas for the future.

to it. Where the measure of cultural decline is the extent of the weakening of positive images of the future, it scarcely needs to be emphasized how serious the collapse of the socialist image of the future is. It is serious for the future of socialism itself, of course, and even more so for the future of the already undermined western culture, which now has one more crucial support pulled out from under it.

The only meaningful use which socialism could make of its hard-won political power is to stand in the forefront of the struggle—which has now reached a critical stage—for the preservation of a humanly worthy western culture. The image of man and society which incorporates the spiritual values of the personal and social fulfilment of man, an image inherent to socialism from of old, should play a major role in fighting the threat of progressive cultural devaluation and dehumanisation. This is a threat which socialism in its present mechanistic and organization-minded stage of development is not equipped to deal with, and on the contrary is even in part responsible for. The diminished power of the specifically socialistic perspective also diminishes the general prospects for western culture. These effects recoil on socialism itself, interwoven as it is with the Christian humanist values of our culture. Socialism's worst enemy is its own cultural blindness and deafness.

Is not the impersonal, passive structure of mass organization and mass opinion-formation basically anti-cultural, and thus in conflict with the image of man, society and culture contained in the earlier democratic-socialist ideal? Does this mass culture still give sufficient opportunity for the development of individual character and of a creative minority of "personalities" who provide the essential spiritual nourishment for any living society? Does it still have a humanitarian orientation to the relation between man and man, or only a functional orientation to classes, parties and the power structure? Furthermore, is it not so that socialism in the very fact of its large-scale organization and concentration of power bears the imprint of modern culture and in turn re-enforces it, without questioning whether this influence will not in the long run by crushing their common human core threaten the goals of both?

Socialists too are men, men of these times and this generation, products and producers of modern culture (or un-culture). One can scarcely blame them for conforming to the general thought and behaviour of their own mid-twentieth century, saturated as it is with existentialism and materialism, if not with negativism and nihilism. Indeed, humanly speaking they are not to blame; they fail only as *socialists*. Formerly, socialists were by definition non-conformists, [1] crusaders for a new society with a new culture.

1. Even today, however, the dying race of non-conformists can to a considerable extent

They may have erred in the choice of means and possibilities available to imperfect man in a limited space of time, and incorrectly assessed science and history; but they stood for and strove for, in their humanly imperfect way, one unchanging goal: the approach to another, higher and better human community for all men on earth, self-determination of destiny by man, and the banishment of all oppression, injustice, suffering and inhumanity.

The gigantic quantitative growth of socialism has blinded almost everyone, and especially the insiders, to the qualitative decline in the character and content of the movement. In a number of countries—not in all—this growth has been accompanied by a substantial lessening of the material want and injustice which still predominate in great parts of the world. But a new kind of want and new injustices have arisen. Living in the age of anxiety, man is now experiencing spiritual and cultural want. Our western culture and its spiritual inheritance of human values, its humanity and humanism, is considered to be in a serious crisis. The mass "unman" appears on the stage, and the chilly mentality of scepticism and cynicism, passivity and nihilism, creeps upon us like an ice age, crushing the spirit of socialism.

How is socialism reacting to this? Is it fighting these possibly fatal developments through a redoubled striving toward an ideal image of the future based on an entirely different image of man? On the contrary, it considers such an image of the future as incapable of fulfilment, an illusion which can only beget frustration. It does not say: The socialist movement has alas failed to realize its earlier image of the future, and needs both more time and more strength in order to do this. Rather, it says: The image of the future of our predecessors has failed, and could not but fail; we must banish it as a false notion. Even while giving lip service to older norms of liberty, fraternity, peace and justice, socialism has lost the courage to make a projection of the society in which these values could be realized, or at least approached through a clear statement of the necessary conditions for this realization. Asserting that the socialist utopia attempted to make angels out of men through false romantic promises, the modern socialist is so determined to avoid falling in the trap of any such misleading myths that he will end by impotently standing by and watching men turn once more into brutish animals. Or, even worse perhaps, into smooth automatons. The mechanization of culture and the mechanization of socialism go hand in

find a congenial home in the existing socialist parties. Only, they will no longer represent an average type of party member, but an unorthodox minority which the organization persistently tries to bring into line; they arouse irritation, rather than reverence. Nevertheless they represent a continuation of the pure strain of socialism, and it is to them that we must look for leadership in regenerating the movement and for cutting a new channel for a more vigorous political current.

hand. Both are in the long run as impossible as they are unnatural. They conflict with the nature of true culture and with the nature of true socialism.

In my opinion (speaking both as a socialist and as a cultural sociologist), this cutting down of every inspiring image of the future means the cutting of the navel cord which binds man to another and better world. The socialist complicity in the iconoclasm of images of the future will in the end, in spite of all its good intentions, draw the fury of the storm down on its own future. In so casually risking its future, it also invites being later on thrown out of the coming present.

The large and solid voting block which socialism has achieved in some countries would seem to belie this prediction. But whatever one may think of symbolic imagery, the image of the fallen colossus with the feet of clay is as much a historical reality as the dying off of the prehistoric dinosaurs. It is a paradoxical fact that in history the development of outward power and of inner spiritual force often move in opposite directions. In politics also it is true that one may gain the whole world and lose one's soul. And while we are dealing with images, the shooting star which blazes its glory across the heavens may fall to earth as a tiny meteorite of inert stone.

Unfortunately, it is almost impossible for the leaders of those socialist parties which have now reached hitherto unknown heights of power, to believe in any signs of inward decay, and to see any further ahead than their own time. Nor are they willing to glance backwards into history to be reminded of the collapse of other powerful movements through inward deterioration. They will not even examine closely the development of socialism itself. They may ignore present warnings, including that of the above analysis, but they cannot deny the lessons of history, which speak the same language and which confirm in the most realistic way the conclusions of our hypothetical argument. However, the present mood of adoration of realism, which refuses to dip into the future, is just as strongly resistant to the fateful events of the past.

Looking backward briefly, we may first consider the sad story of the socialist party in Germany, the famous Sozial-demokratische Partei Deutschlands. The S.P.D. at its zenith and in its fall provides a classical model for the course of development which has been outlined above, turning out to be both different and worse than Michels had foreseen. Not only did this party surrender its enormous and hard-won power (and thus its future) in the course of a few decades and without a blow, but as a result of this it also had a pernicious influence on the political situations which gave rise to the two world wars; its role even extends into the unfortunate development of the third, cold war of our time. In every decisive period, before and during 1914, in the years 1918-20 and in the period 1925 to 1933, it failed spectacularly and completely. It failed through short-sighted hand-to-mouth policies which were at the time defended as being highly realistic. These policies were no longer guided, however, by a principled and idealistic long-term image of the future which had the power to say "no" to the so-called requirements of present necessity.

It was not the disillusionment of the voters over the lack of fulfilment —or even the apparent impossibility of fulfilment—of the old socialist image of the future that was responsible for this catastrophe. Not the image of the future, but the party was at fault. In spite of the external façade of power, the party was inwardly rotting away, from the very lack of striving for the fulfilment of that original image of the future. The socialists were denying their ideals and becoming alienated from their own basic image of the future at the precise time when other political parties were hammering on the voters' doors with competing images of the future. They turned away from what had been the very backbone of their movement at the time when they needed it most.

The S.P.D. became more and more a completely "moment-ridden" party. It accepted the existing order, including itself, uncritically and without a firm dedication to renewing progress. It was destroyed in and by the present it accepted, and pulled the socialist movement with it toward the grave. [1] Through persistent near-sightedness and finally through cowardly submission or panicky flight, it paved the way for the domination of a national-socialism obsessed with the idea of a Pan-Germanic world of the future, thus dealing a heavy blow to the future of European culture.

In the second place a few words must be said here concerning the development of communism, with reference to its world-wide significance and its meaning for socialism. We will not concern ourselves with its original development straight from the Communist Manifesto, which was the source of modern socialism too, nor with the relationship of western socialism to the Russian Revolution. We will rather focus on the spread of communism over the world after the first world war, and its accelerated growth after the second world war.

Here again socialism must carry a heavy load of responsibility—albeit most certainly not alone. This holds whether one considers communism

---

1. Cf. "Ein Mann geht seinen Weg", Berlin, 1952, a collection of articles in honour of Julius Leber, the prominent German socialist, who unfortunately did not survive the last war. It also contains an article Leber himself wrote in 1933 when he was in prison, "Gedanken zum Verbot der deutschen Sozialdemokratie".

in respect to the world-wide turbulence it has brought about (China, South-east Asia, North Africa, Indonesia), or the reactionary tides that have set in, in the name of anti-communism, to choke off all progressive thinking (the American counterpart of this would be McCarthyism), or whether one simply looks at the injurious splintering effect it has had on the political allegiances of the workers (as in France). Just as socialism responded to the challenge of capitalism, so communism is now swarming over the world in response to the challenge of socialism. Where modern socialism has no image of the future to offer, or at most a pale anemic one, communism offers a lusty and glorified image of the future that has magnetic appeal for millions of people. However one may judge the validity and value of the communist image, it in any case represents a kind of over-compensation and counter-image evoked by our own vacuum. Once more inaction has turned out to be a kind of action, in that our very lack of an image of the future has indirectly assisted in the creation of the communist image of the future. We are in the position of having returned to us something which we have *not* given.

This is one more demonstration of the fact that the childlike and eternal longing for human fulfilment in another and better future is basic to man's mental structure. From the social-psychological point of view we see the demonstrable impossibility of the artificial maintenance of a vacuum. As soon as socialism lets go off its image of the future as outmoded, then another social movement will eagerly push its way into the empty space with its image. It is not possible to choose between having an image of the future and not having one, but only between this image or that, between a genuine or a delusive one, or quite simply between a good image or a bad one. If the socialist parties do not take sides on this issue, then they must share the blame for the wrong choice and all its consequences, and for their own impotence in the face of the flood-tide of communism.

Let this then be enough to suggest a tentative conclusion concerning the future of socialism, in the form of a question: Can we justifiable believe in a future for socialism (as an idea and as a movement) when socialism itself scarcely seems to believe any longer in a coming socialist society and culture (however this might be described)?[1] There can be little doubt that the socialist consciousness, originally unfolding in such strength, was mainly spurred by rebellion against the quietism of liberal optimistic philosophy and the detestable exploitation by capitalistic industrialism. Neither can it be doubted that this "protestant" social consciousness has weakened considerably in our generation.

1. Is it not significant that many parties based on socialist premises no longer use the adjective "socialist" in their titles?

The more we have nearly all become *socialists*, the less we become *socialistic*. As the formerly exploited workers have climbed up the social ladder step by step, the socialistic idea has climbed down in the same measured pace. The more stringently their just demands are anchored in the *present* through social legislation and a policy of government intervention, the further away a socialistic future recedes into the haze of the scholar's study or the realm of fable. And when the socialist image of the future has finally succeeded in removing itself beyond time by becoming relegated to the mythical land of make-believe, or to the fantasy of unstrung bookworms, it will not be socialism, nor the times, which will be blamed, but the image or the future itself!

This mental and psychological reversal of socialism which could at a given moment mutate to the opposite extreme of anti-socialism, can be seen most clearly with respect to (a) the prevailing forces of the time, (b) the spatially limited character of its aspirations, and (c) the new scientific and operational pragmatism of its approach.

(a) The association with the realities of political activity takes a high toll of idealistic and socialistic principles. All politics are by necessity predominantly pragmatic and opportunistic. The differences between socialist politics and the politics of other parties begin to disappear and the programs of the various parties begin to converge. As the material wealth of a nation increases we can even see how the present becomes a uniting factor which brings about a community of interests between formerly antithetical forces. Again and again we see neo-socialism and neo-liberalism approach each other for the peaceful carrying out of a realistic policy. [1]

I refer here in particular to anti-futurism, adopted in varying degrees by reactionaries, ultra-liberals, conservatives and anti-progressives of diverse plumage; we have already encountered this in our discussion of Hayek, Toynbee, Popper and others. They all plead, each with their own nuances, for the restoration of an ancient regime, or for the maintenance of the status quo, or, in the most moderate form, for what might be labelled a stationary continuity, immobilized movement, progress with the brakes on. In this cautious, sedate, respectable company, if present trends continue, a settled, replete socialism will feel itself increasingly at home. In order to protect its extensive vested interests it gravitates more and more into the sphere of conservative thought, and will be increasingly caught in the meshes of the

---

1. I do not protest this unavoidable realism, but the overstepping of limits in this respect—limits which cannot easily be defined. I protest the slackening of the struggle for the ideal in the face of the necessity to accept the real, so that the drive toward social change is lost. It is difficult indeed to steer between the Scylla of too much, and the Charybdis of too little, political realism.

existing order. Triumphantly captured by the present as its finest trophy, socialism is becoming socialized.

(b) Having started out to nationalize production and the means of production, it has itself in the meantime also become more or less nationalized. The spectacles of modern socialism have already for some purposes been exchanged for local brands of patriotically tinted diminishing-glass spectacles; when possible, they are fitted out with thick horn rims and blinders which protect against too strong a glare from the world around them, or at least dim it substantially even when it presses close. The Fichtean nationalistic anti-utopia, which exchanges the categories of time to those of space, has sowed its bad spatial seed in socialism too and choked off its message of a new aeon in time. The national element, in its narrow connections with autarchical, isolationistic, imperialistic and even militaristic currents, has made its imprint on nearly all contemporary socialist parties; the idea of an international socialism has been nearly eradicated or at least pushed into the background. Wars come and go over the nations which profess socialism, and each think their kind of socialism the only right kind. World federalism is nowhere in sight, and even European integration is not regarded as an evident "must" by all countries with socialist governments; it is not infrequently the socialists who throw up the biggest obstacles to such a unification.

(c) Finally, once "wild" socialism has been tamed and its sharp claws clipped and manicured so that it can appear in the polite society of conservatism and nationalism, what then remains as typically socialist? What *is* socialism? If I am not mistaken, it is now inclined to deal with the social situation in an operational and rational manner and once more (since Marx) takes pride in being "scientific". After all, the times use science for their every purpose, so why should not socialism? No matter if Marx failed because he attempted to replace utopian socialism by a scientific approach— another scientific method may prove more successful now. And even if no immediate success is obtained, this approach will at least deliver us for good and all from romantic illusions, myths, castles in the air and idle day dreams. Clad in more sober garb, it will be able to attack the problems of the day with greater efficiency. But—lest we forget!—science is neutral, and its results will suit socialists as well as non-socialists; thus the dividing lines between political parties become even more blurred.

The same is true for the scientific method of prognosis which socialism makes use of in planning for step-by-step progress. For this only permits a short-term statistical extrapolation which can be calculated with reasonable certainty from present data. This restriction and prudent matter-of-factness means the banishment of all visionary synthesis and the outlawing of prophetic pronouncements concerning a future radical transformation of society. Socialism's far reach has shrunk to arm's-length. But has not this careful step-by-step policy won it a certain fame? The differences with other parties become those of degree, not of principle, and are determined by the limited number of degrees of freedom present in the alternatives computed by science for the very near future.

The picture we have just considered is a disappointing one, also for the author. Or is it really but a caricature? Would this make much difference? A *good* caricature too contains a good likeness and often can express the essential traits better than the most thorough analysis. It could be argued, on the other hand, that this is a *bad* caricature. It is quite true that many positive traits of modern socialism have been left out of the picture. What if we added them to embellish the portrait? There would still be but two possibilities: either there is no truth at all in what has been said above—then I would ask socialism to demonstrate to the world its positive image of the future, however vague the outlines; let it show us its ideal goal and its specific inspiring model of a new society, which is more than a pious collection of hollow sounds from an outdated past. Or there is some truth in our picture, however little—in that case let it be remembered that projections always give a general indication of the *possible outcome* of certain trends, and not a description of their actual stage of development at one particular moment. If the presence of the tendencies we have sketched is recognized and acknowledged, however embryonic their state may still be at this time, then the only thing of real importance is whether they will be allowed to develop further or whether they will be taken in hand.

My conclusion is threefold: (1) The above trends are at present unmistakably growing stronger and more clearly pronounced. (2) If this growth is allowed to continue in the same direction it may set in motion a process of inner deterioration, leaving only this growth as an outer shell. In other words, socialism will no longer be a movement, although it may still be the name of a political party and may still possess great power as the representative of large group-interests, but it will not have a future as an ideal moving power. (3) Therefore only the arising of strong spiritual counter-forces directed at a well-defined goal can save socialism from this mortification and infuse it with new life and movement towards a new future.

Just as we cannot measure exactly the force of the currently operating tendencies, neither can we at present assess the future influence of possible counter-forces. Even if they are now but invisibly present in the germ, they may gain greatly in intensity later. But of one thing we can be certain, and that is that to be effective any such counter-forces must have the driving power of one compelling and comprehensive idea behind them. Among the various favourable factors present now in potential, it is not at the moment possible to choose one and say that this may indeed be the effective counter-force. One could point out the development of the unorthodox critical-idealistic opposition within the English Labour Party, the independent left wing opposed to the party's burocracy but so far remaining within the party hierarchy. There is also the realization—not entirely lost and occasionally quite lively—that there are *human beings* in other parts of the world, that our planet does not consist only of a large number of diverse national and racial groups, but that it is the home of mankind. Other interesting developments could be mentioned. But however valuable in themselves, these phenomena could scarcely be labelled uniquely socialist. It is not impossible that some time the left wing of the British Labour Party may split off into an independent party (whether freshly labelled or not) without this representing a primarily socialist movement. The purposeful striving for the unity of mankind can become manifest in other groupings, such as of pacifism or world federalism, without their being specifically socialist.

Socialism, whether as movement or counter-movement fired by a dynamic idea about the future, has only a future *as socialism* as long as its striving is recognizable as the fruit of a genuinely living socialistic *consciousness*, that is a deep-rooted drive towards social reformation based on the conviction that man can by his own ceaseless efforts realize or at least approximate an ideal society on earth. It has a future if, after a temporary waning period, it can be reborn in the white heat of a new vision of a totally other future, breaching the existing, predominantly individualistic order and breaking through to an all-encompassing renewal of the social order for all men and peoples on earth.

Of course socialism can pretend no monopoly on the means of approaching such a goal (and *approaching* is all that it will ever be). Other ways, with other names, may be as good or better. But if socialism cannot or will not project a course of its own, leading into the future—after having pioneered for so long—then in that sense it loses not only its traditional leadership in this direction but also its own unique significance and raison d'être. No hot tears need be shed, however, *if* other movements take up its utopian task of systematic reconstruction. Ultimately it does not matter *who* does it, or under which flag, but only *what* is done. But the chances of this changing of the guard seem very slim indeed at the moment. There is certainly no lack of interest from certain sides, which would gladly take over from socialism, but this is generally not motivated by pure idealism. The deliberately misleading images of the future hovering at the background of socialism rather aim at a usurpation of power and at a machiavellian exploitation of the people. It seems as if we have to choose between *no* images of the future and *false* images of the future, and western culture teeters back and forth between ominous reefs, threatened with being either immersed or dashed to pieces.

Is this development indeed inevitable? Here one can answer with conviction: "no!" But is it probable? This is a question no one can answer with certainty, but current trends do point in this direction. Personally I will continue to put my faith in the fundamental socialist idea, albeit at times against my own better judgement; I believe in the possibility of a timely rebirth, through the critical and creative efforts of a few far-seeing but mostly ridiculed individuals, of its exalted image of the future in a new world-wide form which will command authority and enthusiasm.

It is an encouraging sign that there is not a little unrest in the socialist parties and branch organizations of our time. Voices can be heard both among the leaders and the led, which express concern over certain aspects of current and expected developments. These small splinters may build up into wedges to chock the down-hill movement; they may become idealistic levers that can raise drooping socialism to new heights, giving it the courage and strength of idealistic vision to dominate the prevailing iron hand of realism and make the daring leap into the unknown future.

2. Politics and Culture

It should not be inferred from the above that special grievances can be nursed against the socialist parties or socialist politics. Socialist party politics are no better and no worse than party politics in general. At the most they lead to greater disillusion and frustration to the extent that they had given rise to higher expectations. But on the whole they reflect current practices in all parties, and therefore these need not receive special attention.

If the present-day condition of socialism seems to represent a great reversal and denial of its heritage and its goals, it must not be forgotten that this reversal fits neatly into the framework of modern culture, and is part of a greater social change. The position may be taken that this fact either lightens or increases the load of responsibility which socialism must take for the reversal. But socialism can never be given sole responsibility for what clearly is a general political regression from and reaction against the exaggerated progress-optimism of an earlier generation, nor for the spiritual hangover from two destructive world wars which have led to a general revulsion against all ill-founded idealism.

Let us not passively sit and cry over the spilled milk of the last half century.

Not much can be said without lapsing into platitudes, though platitudes are not necessarily untrue. But I will not repeat the endless litany of the ways in which the leadership of the century fell short (a wisdom after the fact, [1] by the hopeless failings and failures of our statesmen, by their often incredibly misjudging the future course of events, and by being totally inadequate to the heavy demands made upon them. Nor will I repeat the old complaint that the most able people in a country do not go into politics, but leave this to men of ambitious mediocrity. Even less will I maintain that things were very much better in earlier times. Nor, finally, will I attempt to play the role of sidewalk-superintendent of history and say that things would have gone so much better if only . . . For here again we will mainly concentrate on the present and the future. And again I will confine myself to broad outlines and let the reader himself fill in the details, from observations amply available to him.

I will therefore pass over most efforts of recent decades to capture political events in a scientific net, as being irrelevant to our frame of reference. I am somewhat acquainted with the extensive analytic literature in this field. [2] It is all extremely interesting and several of these studies throw some light on certain general aspects of politics as such. But they are all inclined, through excessive sophistication and originality, to obscure the most fundamental starting-point: the all too human narrow-mindedness, pettiness and small-ness of soul of people in general and the dismaying lack of wisdom of government leaders in particular.

The quintessence of all knowledge of politics is still expressed, in my opinion, in the sceptical adagium, ascribed to Oxenstierna (1641), and which can be read out of or into any unbiased description of historical events: "an nescis, mi fili, quantilla prudentia regatur orbis" ("don't you know, my son, with how very little wisdom the world is being governed"). This definition of human shortcomings should be just a little more specific, for it is a shortcoming indeed, a missing of the mark through too short an aim

1. But not always *after* the fact! See for example Dr. Edward Benes' *Mémoirs*, Allen & Unwin, London, tr. 1954, which for a large part consist of unheeded warnings and previsions.

2. For example, the attempt to build up a special science of politics (Laski in England, Lasswell in America), the development of psycho-analysis and socio-analysis of political ideologies and movements, progressing from the older mass-psychology (Le Bon, McDougall) to depth-psychology (from Freud to Van der Hoop and Franz Alexander), the social-typological approach (Jaensch, Fromm, Karen Horney, Lawrence Frank, Kurt Lewin, Kardiner), the sociological approach (Sorel, Pareto, Mannheim), the social-empirical method (recent studies by Allport and Klineberg on prejudice, those of Horkheimer, Adorno, Frenkel, Levinson, Sanford, Christie, Jahoda *et. al.* on the authoritarian personality), and so on. Recently the novelist Koestler has published a study of political neuroses, in which the political "libido" forms the basis of constructions of abnormality similar to the Freudian sexual libido.

or even through complete blindness for the real-ideal target lying beyond the existential present. This kind of flatness is characterized by a complete lack of insight and perception, by denseness and hollow ideals. There is no perspicacity and no imagination, only cold sober—realism and stony conservatism in respect to social changes. Deliberate mediocrity and over-cautious short-sightedness are the order of this workaday moment. There is no tension, no intense desire or concern for a better future, no idealistically intent ethos. All spiritual dimensions of height, depth and width have shrunk. And this distorted attitude is more and more coming to be considered as normal—although realism in politics has not precluded components by any means.

Illuminating in regard to this type of outlook is the symptomatically titled *Politik ohne Wunschbilder. Die konservative Aufgabe unserer Zeit,* by Mühlenfeld. [1] Apart from the apparently inescapable German Preoccupation with self-exculpation ("wir haben es nicht gewollt und nicht gewusst") in reference to national-socialism—supposed to be the offspring of the union of liberalism and socialism—it contains a double plea, for *politics without images of the future,* and for *conservative thinking.*

This book makes a ponderous plea for exactly those things which we have picked out as responsible for the short-circuit in socialism. Politics (like science) should turn away from the "Sollen" ("ought") and confine itself exclusively to the "Sein" ("existent"). It should purge itself of every progressive idea and ideal, and of every emotional movement such as humanitarianism or utopism. Revolutionary dynamics are to be replaced by static continuity or conservative revolution. All the misery in the world is due to the boundless irrational drives let loose by headstrong ideologies. Human happiness can only be achieved through the preservation of the status quo or by step-by-step improvements dictated entirely by the facts of the given situation.

There is no need to follow this argument in detail. It is a matter of evaluation pure and simple. By taking all the *negative* elements of our analysis of socialism and providing them with *plus* signs, we get the positively rationalized sanction for the conservative trend in all modern politics. Thus the stamp of approval is given to the shift toward realism and actualism, spatial *and* temporal limitation, and an anti-idealistic, a-cultural mentality, a burocratic-conservative approach to the material questions of the day, and the exchange of guiding principles and norms for a pragmatic-opportunistic mode of dealing with situations according to circumstances.

1. Dr. Hans Mühlenfeld was one of the early members of the German "Bundestag", and ambassador from West-Germany to the Netherlands at the time that this work appeared. It was published in Munich in 1952.

The question is whether this argument for a pure "Real-Politik" is really a challenge to achieve a desirable state of affairs or simply an ideal-typical rationalization of the actual state of affairs. In my opinion, practice has outstripped theory and this is in fact a description of our current situation, as in the case of socialism. There is also other evidence for this point of view.

It can be suggested, for example, that too little attention has been paid to the consequences of the so-called "managerial revolution" for the form and structure of politics. There is little doubt that a new managerial caste is developing which is providing leadership in key places in the governmental machinery, assuming top positions in industry, and now gradually extending its power to political parties. These managers are the prototypes of narrow specialism and inch-by-inch social engineering. The specialist with blinders on has difficulty in focussing on the far horizon, as experience has taught us. Conservative thinking flourishes in the managers' burocracy; its careful systematic approach is death to fundamental structural renewal, its sober, insensitive and slow realism chokes off all vision, fantasy and creativity.

The top leaders of government are coming increasingly from the ranks of the managers, and therefore assume the style of top managers. While the turbulent tempo of social change and the kinds of far-reaching decision it requires, make higher demands than ever before on responsible government officials, these leaders themselves reflect a very limited horizon and a lack of mental mobility, if not real poverty of spirit—of course related to the general, all pervading Zeitgeist. It is certainly not my intention to place all the blame for the evils of our times in the laps of the managers, but only to emphasize an aspect of our situation that has received insufficient notice. I will pass over other better-known aspects such as the growing influence of a technological and empirical scientific approach, the emergence of organized pressure groups, the expansion of government regulation and intervention, the rampant growth of social-economic and fiscal problems, the scramble towards industrialization, and so on. They all share in common the effect of concentrating government attention increasingly on the changing face of the present situation. "Gouverner ce n'est pas prévoir", one might say. If anyone thinks this an exaggeration, let him examine well current domestic and foreign policy. It is not at all unusual any longer for a statesman completely to retract, verbally or in writing, former position, on even the most essential points, and within a rather short period of time. His "here I stand" may shift locus with lightning rapidity, and our times move so fast that most of us do not even notice it.

From the point of view of domestic policy, within western lands, both socialist and capitalist images of the future have spent their force. Various blends of freedom and regulation have evolved, of state-capitalism or state-socialism, which may or may not be served with a sauce of neo-mercantile corporative economy. For the most part the workers are little less conservative than the entrepreneurs, and they often combine with them for a short-sighted oppression of the unorganized in-between groups, including the intelligentsia (part of which is thus driven either to the extreme right or the extreme left). The bitter class struggle of an earlier day is fortunately over, but its valuable aspect of building up long-range visions in both parties to the struggle has been lost; we have instead a weighing of small competing, short-range interests and a dearth of creative leadership. These two increasingly visionless interest groups cause an equal loss of vision in the leadership of governments, which they come to control more and more via their political machineries.

That modern foreign policy suffers from the same evils need scarcely be documented. In former centuries three great powers carried out long-range foreign policies, although they were predominantly spatially oriented and suffered from all the faults of this orientation: the British Empire, the Russian Czardom, and the Vatican. Dreams of future world domination after the decline of fascism and national-socialism are still cherished by pan-Slavic and pan-Asiatic groups, and carefully fostered by the communism which prevails there. Over against this, the western powers have little more to offer than ephemeral and changeable policies, arrived at in daily full disagreement. The times of a Jaurès, Rathenau, Masaryk, Smuts, Wilson and Roosevelt are over. At the same time that social changes are giving rise to problems of a world-wide nature that will affect the entire future of mankind for a long time to come, we are producing leaders who are immature and irresolute, unable to see ahead and so preoccupied with blind gropings in the dark that they miss the decisive action that might have been taken. Statesmen after the second war are making the same fatal blunders and displaying the same lack of vision as after the first world war. They fail to see the foreseeable, and do not heed the warnings of those who do see it. The historian of the 21st century, if he is indeed able to write freely then, would surely award a booby-prize to this age. With the greatest good will he would have difficulty in ascertaining any clear-cut vision in this century, except in the negative.

It is easy enough to scorn the endless petty rituals of diplomacy, the parties, banquets, notes, speeches and the so-called secrets. What is, however, much more serious is the mediocre or weak staffing of the foreign service at all levels and in all countries, great or small. [1] Exceptions can

1. Bertrand Russell found in high officials of the British Foreign Office an "ignorance unsurpassed except by their conceit" (The Impact of Science on Society, p. 51). This complaint is naturally neither new nor confined to England. We are again reminded

always be found to every rule, but it would be difficult to maintain that the finest flowers of the land are to be found in the foreign service; this, in spite of the fact that men like Keynes and Toynbee put in their stint in this service before they became well-known. Diplomatic functionaries above all men must be able to think broadly, in terms of time-spans and space far beyond the national borders of the present, and yet they are as confined to the boundaries of time and space and the moment as the rolling presses of the daily newspaper. They live as spiritually hand-to-mouth as the rest of us, and are perpetually surprised by the events of the day after tomorrow, which they had not foreseen. The only long-range planning to be found is in the field of economic development and applied social engineering (the Marshall Plan, the Schuman Plan for coal and steel, the European Union of Payments or Common Market, and so on). Or in such organizations as the European Defense Community or NATO, born of the fear of communist aggression. But while there is an abundance of fragmentary and partial plans, a comprehensive common plan which offers a genuine perspective on the future of western culture is lacking.

Foreign policy has also become a parochial moment-ridden policy, [1] bobbing on the patriotic currents of the fatherland. "Man glaubt zu schieben und wird geschoben." Government leaders (and who could imagine world leaders?) are pushed and driven and the people are pushed and driven. They are driven by the fearful shadow of a third world war, as if this were the work of some demonic superhuman power instead of the work of men and their governments.

There is, however, one more area within the field of political affairs . . . except that it is *not*. Therefore very little can be said about it, and yet it is of vital interest. I refer to a genuinely positive cultural policy. In the present force-field of socio-cultural dynamics this ought to be a crucial factor in terms of long-run effects. Our class of managers, half-barbarians that they are, lack the necessary perception and breadth of vision to develop such a policy. Measured by economic outlay and in terms of the population as a whole, there is indeed in some respects more culture-consciousness and more political activity on this behalf than would earlier have been acceptable or possible. But in the face of our present need, it is not enough by any means, it is too unsystematic and not sufficiently constructive. One can look for little help in the solution of our present culture-crisis from politics, im-

of Oxenstierna's words (cited above) of over 300 years ago. But in our day the consequences of a lack of understanding are much graver than ever before.

1. Point Four represents a promising exception, and there are also other long-range plans worked out by and for international organizations; the problem is that of political implementation.

mersed as it is in day-to-day material problems. Politics and politicians fail to realize that both owe their very being to ideas and to trail blazing spiritual currents, mostly utopian currents, out of history. Universal suffrage, parliamentary democracy, separation of the three powers (legislative, executive, judiciary), government intervention, constitutional and codified law, social legislation, budgetary control, taxation, all have their sources in the daring idealistic conceptions of earlier ages. A recognition of this debt to the creative thinkers of western culture would not be amiss. The continuation and defence of this culture is a life-and-death matter for western politics too. But even while western politics and culture may in the future die together, they are certainly not at present living together, at least not without grave discord. Only when expenditures have to be cut, a sudden interest in culture arises and its relatively small items on the budget are curtailed. If however, representatives of cultural interests make an appeal to political bodies, the tabu against "state culture" is piously invoked with deprecatory gestures. But what remained of the world-states of antiquity, once their culture had fallen into decline?

The cultural blindness of modern politics is on the whole so great that with all due allowance for progress made it may be said as of old: he whom the gods would destroy they first strike with blindness. The politicians and political managers of today are for the most part equally prisoners of the Zeitgeist, whether they stand in the ranks of the conservatives or the progressives. They have no eye for the dire need that our culture is in, or for the threat of future destruction which hangs over it and over themselves. One may wonder at this, become angry, or sink into saddened regret. But it would be far better, even if the task holds little enough promise, to work for the change which survival demands by tirelessly knocking at every door to demand a hearing. And to continue, while there is still time, to sound the tocsin. This too might be called ... politics!

II

NEW PERSPECTIVES: CULTURE-CRISIS ILLUMINATED IN THE PRISM OF THE IMAGE OF THE FUTURE

> *For here we have no lasting city, but we seek the city which is to come.*
>
> Hebrews 13:14

1. *Toward a New Diagnosis and Therapy of Culture*

We have now come to the last temporary resting-place in our long wanderings through the hills and valleys of human culture. We have covered too much ground too hastily, and can scarcely claim to a thorough knowledge of the terrain. And yet, as we look back over our route we cannot fail to see both system and pattern in the complex workings of the civilizations we have traversed. The pattern unfolds in a panorama that includes not only a view of the past, but a view of the future, if only in silhouette. Ignoring the details and following only the main outlines, it is possible to see proscopically right through this world into the Other behind it. The numerous little pieces of the jigsaw puzzle of culture do indeed fit together without forcing. The result is an intricate and subtly-patterned cultural mosaic. The many-coloured fragments adhere and produce a stereoscopic three-dimensional projection of Western culture: one world in the foreground, The Other in the background.

We have observed again and again, almost to the point of monotony, how the same developments are taking place in every area of Western culture. Whether we examine philosophy or art, Christian religion or humanism, sociology or socialism, we are faced with the same abrupt break in historic trend-lines in Western culture. The same sort of paralysis has set in everywhere; backs are turned to all positive visions of the future and feeble hands clutch at the crumbling structures of the chaotic present.

There is no escaping the symptoms of this frantic effort of man to wall himself up in the present. We meet them at every turn. The clinging to a favorite brand of existentialism and the reigning spirit of realism, which perceives empirical reality as the *only* and *unchangeable* reality, has as its counterpart the refusal to recognize the existence of The Other. First attacking dualism and the doctrine of the ideal, a powerful trend in modern philosophy proceeds to sterilize the future *and* the power to imagine the future, in both eschatology and utopism. This implies a marked tendency towards almost complete negativism and even nihilism, a retrogression from infinity to zero. The élite has as it were purposefully abandoned all purposeful thinking about the future, except in negative, anti-utopian terms, with the inevitable result that positive visions of the future in out present mass-culture are undergoing progressive decay.

In the end, all separate and apparently autonomous streams of culture merge into one torrential, rushing river: highly abstract philosophy together with the most opportunistic practical politics; the science of build-. ing and the science of biology; the science of spending and the science of psychology; music and the mechanism of the market; they all converge where the river banks of the Mighty Present loom high. These towering banks shut off all possibility of meandering currents exploring new river beds. There is no longer any way out from the Here and Now.

Culture is *more* than the sum of its competent parts. There is a great difference of opinion as to what culture as a total concept does mean. In connection with our present problem, however, it is irrelevant, or at least of minor importance, just how one does define culture. If we consider culture as any kind of stylistically harmonious totality of human behaviour, then that total equally with its component parts bears the peculiar brand-mark of the present. One can argue that all culture of any historical period bears the mark of its own present. This is of course true. All culture is in a certain sense a child of its own time. But our time is *completely swallowed up* in the present. It will not and cannot be more than a perpetually pro-longed instantaneous exposure, not bothering to differentiate itself from its outdated yesterday or to visualize a totally different tomorrow. Our culture shows a compulsion to conform to *that which is*, not because it is normal, or traditional, or particularly adequate, but because its snapshots bear the label Today. This represents the sickly narcissism of a civilization which sits motionless at the river-bank of time, spell-bound by its own image which it sees reflected there.

In this particular aspect it may equally be argued that a culture is *no* more than its component parts. Exactly the same process which has injured the imaginative and forwardthinking capacities of each individual facet of culture is at work on the whole; the course of development is completely analogues. One can speak with certainty of a general decay of positive and creative cultural awareness, reflecting an identical turn in each specific segment of culture.

This collapse can be observed in the violent swing of the pendulum, rapid even by modern tempi, from unbounded progress-optimism to a deeply pessimistic conviction concerning the inevitable decline of our culture. The general climate of opinion of the preceding century that there were no limits to the possibilities of cultural evolution has given way to the Freudian concept of "Civilization and its Discontent". *Activism of the will (influence-optimism)* and rational *positivism* have been transformed into *passivism of the will (influence-pessimism)* and irrational *negativism*. The heroic idea of transforming this world into a better one, either by the grace of God or by man's own efforts, has been replaced by a submissive resignation to life as it is, with none other in sight. This fixation on the tangible present is characteristic not only of various components of our culture, it is characteristic of the culture as a whole, regardless of how this complex might be further delineated after closer inspection.

Once we see that the same key fits individual cultural phenomena *and* the total structure of culture, and recognize that this key is made up of the three related parts, past, present and future, we get a new perspective of our own time. This perspective is radically different from that of the leading students of the sociology of culture of our day, however much their views may differ one from the other. This new insight applies not only to the history of culture-change that we can observe to have taken place in the past, but also to the dotted outlines of the unknown future. It not only offers a deviating diagnosis of past and present, but it may lead as well in the direction of a more meaningful and reliable future culture prognosis and therapy.

This new key which we offer, and which for brevity's sake we have labelled as the positive image of the future, should help to break the deadlock which existing theories now find themselves in through inability to handle the full complexity of the problems with which they deal.

We will first review under this heading the three chief functions which the concept of the image of the future has fulfilled in our analysis of culture so far, and then look into the possibility of its fulfilling a fourth, *synthetic* function. Before we are ready to take that last step, however, we will examine (in 2) those current theories of culture change which have gained the widest acceptance. The concluding section (3) of this work, which outlines the potential inherent in the final synthetic, regenerating function of the image of the future, will, we hope, leave the reader feeling that he or she has received a personal challenge to help build up a public image from his or her own store of private images.

To sum up: *in the first place* we found the positive image of the future at work in every instance of the flowering of a culture, thus explaining the hitherto mysterious phenomenon of why certain civilizations reached such great heights and left good seed which has remained culturally viable until our own times. In the same manner, we have seen weakened images of the future as a primary factor in the decay of cultures. The puzzling phenomenon of succeeding waves of cultural rise and fall has been taken up into the larger concept of the magnetic pull of the image of the future now exercising a positive, guiding effect, now ebbing to the zero point of weak and aimless drifting. The image of the future has been represented as itself subject (under the circumstances) [1] to an inherent dialectical movement between the poles or different configurations of optimism and pessimism.

In the second place, we attempted to measure the potential strength of a culture by measuring the intensity and energy of its dominant images of the future. These successive, periodically prevailing images were seen to act as a barometer indicating potential rise or fall of a culture. It was seen that this technique could put an end to the never-endings current discussion of whether or not we are at present experiencing a culture crisis. In the writer's opinion, the current negativizing of almost all previous positive and significant images of the future not only offers incontrovertible evidence that we are indeed in the middle of a culture crisis, but also indicates the extent and gravity of this crisis.

In the third place, the concept of the image of the future has put us in a position where we can move from diagnosis to prognosis. This is possible because of the intimate relationship we have discovered between image of the future and future. The more powerful the *image* of the future is, the more powerfully it acts in determining the actual future. This is true both for the positive and for the negative image of the future.

The image of the future can act not only as a barometer, but also as a regulative mechanism which alternately opens and shuts the dampers of the mighty furnace of culture. It not only indicates alternative choices and possibilities, but actively promotes certain choices and in effect puts them to work in determining the future. We realize, therefore, that the current degeneration of denaturation of positive images of the future not only demonstrates the existence of the present crisis, but announces what is to come. The prevailing negative images are already actively at work in undermining and eventually bringing about a general collapse of culture. The image of the future is then not only the mirror of the future and the source of prevailing ideas about the shape of things to come, it is also an active agent in the process of shaping this very future. A close examination

---

1. These circumstances, combined with endogenous and exogenous factors in each time-period, are further discussed in Chapters XVI and XVII. Inevitably this explanation, however much light it throws on the problem, is still incomplete, because it must leave prior circumstances unaccounted for, leading straight back to the inaccessibility of first causes.

of prevailing images, then, puts us in a position to forecast the actual future with a great measure of probability.

The author has ventured to state that any culture which finds itself in the condition of our present culture, turning aside from its own heritage of positive visions of the future, or which is instrumental in changing these positive visions into negative ones, *has* no future unless strong counter-forces are set in motion within the foreseeable future. In saying this we deviate from the positions taken by other culture-theorists, both of the pessimistic and optimistic variety. This view is not only of theoretical interest, however. It is of crucial importance for practical *policy*. It opens up new vistas for policy-makers, in the areas where they still have freedom of planning and action.

We have no intention of reviewing the complete current panorama of various insights regarding the future of our culture [1] in this final test of our theoretical framework. It may be helpful, nevertheless, to make a brief comparison with five main groups of cultural theories, according to their respective bodies of ideas and the resulting outcome therein prophesied.

2. *Untenable Principles of Cultural Prognosis*

A. Unconditional Cultural Pessimism

This school of thought sees the cultural process in terms of recurrent rise and fall, an inevitable phenomenon against which man's intervention is powerless. Western civilization is ultimately doomed when it reaches the end of its downswing. The following thinkers can be considered to belong to this group, although they vary widely in the significance they attach to the quasi-biological concept of a dying culture: Nietzsche, Spengler and Klages. [2] Our own position completely precludes such views, which are based on an unalterable determinism in regard to the future for in our conviction man is free as a matter of principle to determine his own future. However much one may argue back and forth about where the boundaries to man's freedom of action lie, the basic point is that *culture is the work of man*, not simply the work of impersonal forces.

The whole concept of the image of the future and its relationship to

1. A book which attempts to do just this is Sorokin's *Social Philosophies in an Age of Crisis*, which has already been cited. Sorokin's view differs from our own, however, and his review of existing theories is inevitably within the framework of his own position.
2. In Spengler's view every culture, once born, must without exception die again like man himself. In Nietzsche's view only Superman, coming to life through his evocation, might ultimately avert this fate. In Klages' view the end would be inevitable except in the rather improbable event of man yet giving precedence to the life-giving soul over his self-destructive mind.

succeeding waves of cultural optimism and pessimism, is irreconcilable with any idea of historical predestination. Even the idea of a divinely-ordained plan of human salvation was *operative* in history only to the extent that it was embodied in a man-made image of the future. On the other hand, certain thinkers (and we may take Spengler as our prototype) have themselves constructed negative images of the future which have actually contributed to the destruction of hitherto dominant positive images and therefore to the destruction of the culture itself. This is *not* simply an effect of writing down an idea; it can happen only of a succeeding generation of thinkers agrees to incorporate this idea into the current community of opinion regarding the future, as a free and responsible act. The influence of such ideas is not the result of their operating with the force of natural law. They have influence only because men choose to believe in them and integrate them into their visions of the future.

B. Conditional Cultural Pessimism

This second school of thought is also disposed to the idea of the inevitable course of history, but its adherents do not maintain this idea to the exclusion of any possibility of purposeful human intervention in the historical process. Extrapolating from historical trends, they see the threat of the decline of our culture, but they leave an escape hatch open. The majority of contemporary culture-specialists belong to this group, although they differ widely among themselves as to the location of the escape hatch and how man is to get to it. They unite only in agreeing that the passageway to it is so steep and narrow, and the opening so small, that the chance of escaping at the eleventh hour is very slight.

Whenever we examine the since qua non of this group of prophets of "doom unless . . ." we see that the necessary condition can only be fulfilled by a miracle or some exceedingly unlikely turn of events contrary to all existing trends. This frequently involves a romantic regression to some point in the historical past. There is considerable disagreement concerning the point at which the downswing of our civilization began. For Toynbee it began with the religious wars of the sixteenth and seventeenth centuries; for others it began in the nineteenth ventury, and for others again it is beginning at this very time. These differences of a few hundred years are irrelevant in a geological time-scale, but they are of crucial importance to man in his task of diagnosing his present situation and deciding upon remedial action. The further back the historian places the onset of decline, the more corrupt and degenerate our culture appears, the more radical and comprehensive the remedial measures must be, and the longer and harder the road is back to the peak of strength and vigour.

1. TOYNBEE

Let us consider Toynbee's brilliant investigations in this light. Of major importance in its own right, this work has unfortunately also achieved snob-appeal in the more popular circles of the pseudo-scientifically-minded. Its fashion there is well on the way to establishing a new aristotelian-type school of thought. This is especially true in regard to his views on the future of Western culture, which is the area in which he is most frequently cited—often incorrectly, and with a definite displacement of emphasis.[1] His *Study of History* was for many years an unfinished symphony that broke off just when it was about to sketch in the future course of events. His later *Civilization on Trial* covers less than the title suggests and throws no further light on the basic problem. Now, however, the long-awaited volumes VII to X of the Study of History have been published,[2] so we are able to discuss Toynbee's thinking as a reasonably completed whole.

One of the most striking aspects of Toynbee's position is that in an age of historians who consider God historically irrelevant he puts God back into history. In Toynbee's view, history is by definition "God revealing himself". He sees all civilizations as living and dying in cycles according to universal patterns and rhythms, but each dead civilization represents a bridge to a higher religion. Western civilization began its particular downward swing in the period of the religious wars of the sixteenth century, as mentioned above. Since then the West has been living in its "time of troubles". A time of troubles usually ends with the formation of a "universal state". This state and its civilization then decay because (1) the creative minority no longer gives timely or adequate responses to new social challenges and (2) the barbarians waiting outside ("the external proletariat") will easily conquer the dying civilization. This is the point where Toynbee left his readers at the end of Volume VI: late in the time of troubles, just short of the final development (and disintegration) of the universal state.

The concluding volumes minimize the impending catastrophe through their thesis that religion is not merely a guide or inspiration to civilization *but its very raison d'être*. He was formerly inclined to the view that religion serves mainly as a chrysalis for civilization. He now asserts that the higher religions do not exist to give birth to civilizations, but that civilizations exist to give birth to higher religions. "The birth of a civilization is a catastrophe if it is a regression from a previously established church, while

1. See the earlier discussion of Toynbee, Chapter XIV, p. 391 ff.
2. This was not true at the time of publication of the Dutch original of Dr. Polak's book, and this section has been expanded by the author specially for the English edition. (*Translator's note*)

the breakdown of a civilization is not a catastrophe if it is the overture to a church's birth"[1]. Civilizations must be the stepping-stones to higher religions.

Does this mean that Western civilization is doomed, with only the cold comfort that perhaps from its grave new religious life will sprout? Not necessarily, says Toynbee. Doom is no more automatic than progress. Everything depends on the development of the religion of the West, and its attitude towards the barbarism of Communism. Communism developed through the failure of Christianity in our post-Christian era. " 'Holy Russia' (is) a more rousing war cry than 'happy America' ".[2] The West must base its appeal on something more than freedom and prosperity; it must base its specific appeal on religion. Then, by turning of tables, the West might still win over communism. "The grace of God (might) bring about this miracle in ex-Christian hearts genuinely smitten with contrition . . .".[3] In this battle human dignity and freedom are great goods and mighty weapons only *if* dependent on eschatological religion, and not on primarily humanistic values. The only religion which can be effective in the battle, in Toynbee's view, is Christianity. His works are permeated with Christian symbolism and even Christian theology. But he scarcely represents present-day Christian orthodoxy or the Christian Churches. For example, he believes that all the "higher religions", i.e. Christianity, Islam, Buddhism and Hinduism are all separate but valid approaches to the City of God. The prophets of other religions are the precursors of Christ, and their sufferings are the "Stations of the Cross in anticipation of the Crucifixion".[4] Christianity is the "climax of a continuous upward movement of spiritual progress".[5] Toynbee thinks that "a twentieth century historian might venture to predict that Christianity's transfiguring effect on the world up to date would be outshone by its continuing operation in the future".[6] Still, Christianity is not the only religion. It has no monopoly of Divine Light. And yet the post-Christian West may be saved by Christianity. Not by the Christianity of the existing Christian churches, nor by a revived orthodox Christianity. It could be saved, however, by a Christianity acting as the vital agent in a blending of all the higher religions. Toynbee's message can be reduced to his own two-word device, "Amplexus expecta" (meaning:/while clinging/to the crucifix/wait). The West must "submit to the Law of God", cling to God, wait and pray. "In appealing to the Law

1. Toynbee, A Study of History VII, p. 526.
2. Ibid. IX, p. 584.
3. Ibid. VIII, p. 149.
4. Ibid. VII, p. 425.
5. Ibid. VII, p. 425.
6. Ibid. VIII, p. 627.

of God a human soul has to abandon certainty in order to embrace Hope and Fear" . . .[1] Then, by the grace of God, Western civilization may have a chance of miraculous survival.

The concept of rise and fall of civilizations takes on a somewhat different meaning in this context, with every dead civilization representing a step towards to the final transfiguration and triumph of the "highest" religion. Also, the old progress-optimism regarding culture, long since abandoned by the élite and masses alike, now crops up in the realm of religion as an area existing independently of, or even at the expense of culture. The Theodicy of Leibniz lives on exclusively in the religious sphere, abstracted from the general processes of socio-cultural dynamics. The latter, Toynbee still regards as subject to decline and decay, although serving the ends of religion in the process.

In my opinion this view rests on two premises which are completely counter to actual developments. The first concerns the autonomy of religion in relation to culture, in the sense that each can follow independent and even diametrically opposed lines of development. An examination of history reveals the most intimate connection between religious and cultural consciousness, and strikingly parallel developments of rise and fall in these areas. The second concerns the axiomatic assumption of a continued upward development of some form of Christianity in the face of a downward swing of the total culture of which it is a part and through which it first flourished. We have already shown that the general decline of Western culture is not only *mirrored* in a decline of religion, but in part *caused by* it. We have seen how the de-eschatologising of the religious image of the future, unmistakable indicator of the weakening of Western religious faith, has in itself threatened the actual future, by its contribution to the general decline in *all* cultural images of the future.

It can be said, and it is unquestionably true, that Toynbee's "way out" depends on an exclusive restoration of some modern version of the traditional Christian eschatological image of the future. That is the very thing that makes his solution rather dubious. It does not rest on any historically observable social processes or causalities. On the other hand, Toynbee makes the whole future of Western civilization depend on the restoration of this *one* image of the future, to the exclusion of all other possibilities, which he attacks and dismisses as pernicious futurism. We are then left in the situation that if divine providenec fails to intercede in the right way at the right time, our civilization is abandoned (by Toynbee!) to destruction, a bloody sacrifice on the altar of his particular religious conviction. Neither historical nor scientific considerations enter at this point. The sacrifice is made in the

1. Ibid. IX, p. 172.

hope that through the fall of our civilization religious faith will yet reach a higher level. This process will continue until a peaceful super-culture, symbolized in the concept of the Kingdom of God, is achieved.

When culture is thus degraded to a *means*, man loses the dignity and freedom of determining his own fate and once more becomes a pawn on the chessboard of higher powers. The future of our civilization then sinks into the background as a problem of only secondary importance. Its continued existence is subject to divine pleasure, its destruction can only serve the ultimate plans of Providence, and the whole matter is hardly man's affair at all!

Furthermore, we see here a fateful regression from *influence-optimism* to *essence-optimism*. The message: cling to God, wait and pray, goes counter to Toynbee's own more active system of challenge and response. He, himself, has shown that the challenge is always changing and that the adequate response should do so too. And now he pre-determines once and for all only one valid response to this everchanging challenge. Not only is it a fixed and passive response, it is an exclusive one, ruling out all answers and activities independent of religion. This is the more alarming as there is no clear sign of either a general revival of purely Christian faith or of a rising new universal, synthesizing faith. The objection, however, is not only that Toynbee rejects all constructive contributions to our cultural future if they cannot be labelled religious in his special sense of the word. It is that he loses all interest in the historical problem of culture and cultural control of the future particularly in the face of the possibility that future trends would be mainly humanistic or, like the American brand of Christianity, more directed towards social goals and community activity than towards the spiritual Kingdom of Heaven. European, American and Russian culture then become all alike and are all doomed in the end, perhaps in favour of some unknown religious force of the future. All the cultural forces which may work together for a responsible regeneration of culture are negated or subordinated to one specific concept of religion, thus reducing man anew to total insecurity and the ambiguity of "hope and fear". Our main objection is not to giving religion, and specifically Christianity, a crucial role in culture development, but to the narrow conception of the nature of that role. This modern version of theocracy is a tremendous step backwards in our cultural history: in this view man can only ressort to prayer and propitiation, unable directly to alter an unfavourable course of events by his own power. As a matter of principle, of course, no course of events can *be* unfavourable in Toynbee's deterministic system. Whatever is, is willed by God—a Toynbeean God who now at once seems to neglect many aspects of man that He in recent centuries supposedly took a great deal of interest in. The historian who himself has shown the danger of giving "archaic" responses to the challenges which proceeding time flings at each successive culture, is now proposing one of the most archaic solutions of all!

2. SCHWEITZER

It is of interest to consider Schweitzer's image of the future after that of Toynbee, as one which *is* specifically concerned with the fate of our own culture. He sees ethical values as the dynamic agents in the process of rise and fall of cultures, and looks particularly for the vitality of the attitude of reverence for all life in a culture. When this has a central place in social attitudes, the accompanying culture is vigorous. If it is absent, cultural suicide is immanent. This is the key to the decline of our own civilization. The process of decline can be halted, according to Schweitzer, if a new vital ethical foundation can be provided for our society. He points out that this cannot be done on the basis of our image of the empirical world, however, as the numerous decayed ruins of the ethical systems, which strew the floor of history, so eloquently testify. The world, we are able to perceive, is ethically neutral and provides no firm foothold for a system of belief which can stand in the face of the turmoil of day-to-day reality. An unshakable ethic can only be based on a new image of the world which chooses as its foundation the intuitively evident, inborn "will to live" of man. Built on such a foundation, a new system can be developed involving reverence for all life and a voluntaristic-ethical attitude towards the world; this will mean cultural advances as the mystical life-instinct is activated, and thus also is the *only* hope for civilization in the face of the threat of general cultural and social disorganization, Schweitzer asserts.

We are not concerned here with the particular ethical philosophy Schweitzer sets forth. The relating of cyclical movements of culture with one special ethical system, which Schweitzer does by postulation rather than demonstration, we need not discuss. It is scarcely a matter of argument that prevailing ethical systems play an important role in any culture, although opinions will differ as to how much weight should be given to ethics. But the value of the work is diminished by the fact that Schweitzer, like Toynbee, separates out his key factor (in this case ethics), and makes it an autonomous entity, independent of culture. The rise and fall of a culture, however, is the rise and fall of all parts of that culture, including the part known as ethics. It is pointless to abstract the course of development of ethics from the course of development of all the other cultural values with which it is inextricably connected. The general image of the world including the image of the future, can even less be abstracted from the dynamic processes of culture. The emphasis on the will-to-live and affirmative voluntarism of Schweitzer's ethics represents a special formulation of the positive image of the future, and as such presents a challenge to the currently dominating negative image of the future with its emphasis on existence-to-the-death.

Schweitzer's ideas concerning a possible revival of our culture can be characterized, partly in contrast to Toynbee's, as a plea for the revival of an unorthodox and undogmatic Christianity, humanistic in emphasis; a Christianity that replaces its specific eschatological image of the future by a broader mystical-metaphysical image of the future. Apart from the merits of this particular image of the future (and the merits of Schweitzer's own life, which harmonizes with his teachings) we are concerned with the idea of one specific image of the future being offered as a panacea, as the one absolutely universal and valid image, which man must take or leave. This monopolistic approach, however pure the motives behind it, runs the risk of cutting off other possible approaches. This is the more serious when the approach with monopolistic claims, shows little evidence of gaining general acceptance. It leaves us once more in the situation where the only salvation for a culture dying from exhaustion is expected from some kind of deus ex machina.

C. Cultural Optimism

We will pass over other ingenious cultural prescriptions, all with claims to exclusive validity, such as Northrop's suggestions for a mingling of Eastern and Western cultural elements, and give our attention to a third representative group of thinkers about the future of civilization. This is a group which rejects the notion of dying civilizations. Every civilization has enduring values which cannot die. All that can happen is that one *phase* of a culture can decline and a transition take place into a new cultural period with its own style and structure, perhaps even with a different geographic center. We are given the glad tidings that each new cultural period will establish itself on a higher level than the preceding one, until it too must give way to a still higher one.

1. SCHUBART

Schubart, Berdiaiev and Sorokin all belong to this group. The differences between them are not inconsiderable, but in this one respect they can be lumped together. Schubart, building on Danilevski and Spengler, postulates the existence of four alternative culture-types, and four accompanying types of human culture-bearers: the harmonic, heroic, ascetic and messianic. There are also four corresponding historical ages. In the last thousand years two culture-types have developed: the harmonic-gothic and the heroic-promethean. The last, which is now dominant, is doomed to death, and a new age, the Messianic-Johannine, is already peeping over the horizon. A new and higher culture is appearing through the work of a new type of man whose spiritual orientation is Eastern-Slavic and whose inspiration and strength come from Russia. Present wars and conflicts will end in a fruitful union, at a higher level, of Europe and Russia in a new and flourishing culture.

2. BERDIAIEV

Berdiaiev perceives three phases in the course of development of Western culture: barbarian, mediaeval-Christian and humanistic-secular. The last phase is already in process of dissolution and belongs more to the past than to the present. In the dialectical course of historical events, man's search for security and permanence inevitably leads to his self-destruction. In deep disillusionment over the withering away of the dreams which had taken shape during the Renaissance and the Revolution, man is now revolting in the direction of anti-humanistic and anti-secular ideologies. The time is ripe for history to take a new turn. Man is ready to step into the New Middle Ages, and through a new, genuine religiosity to exalt this degenerate technological civilization to a new high level where it can flourish again.

3. SOROKIN

Sorokin divides all cultures into three super-systems, labelled ideational, sensate and idealistic. The last is a blend of the first two. A cyclical succession of these types of their mixtures is going on for ever. Today's culture is purely worldly, and while it has amazing achievements to its credit, it has now reached the end of its tether, so to speak. It is decadent in every respect, and has sounded its own death knell. A new ideational or at least idealistic culture-phase stands at our very door, however. If we have but the wit to see it we can assist our age into this new phase and minimize the chaos and suffering of the transition period. Sorokin believes that the next new cultural flowering will take place chiefly in the region of the Pacific.

These very brief sketches have given a somewhat distorted view of the theories in question but are sufficient to indicate clearly that here again we are dealing with a kind of determinism. It is not a determinism which stands and weeps, but one which looks forward, past the antithesis, to a new synthesis. From this perspective, what appeared to be *decline* is only a *transition*. The Marxian dialectic, itself influenced by an older apocalyptic philosophy, has been strongly influential here. Evil is an indispensable preliminary to all good. History is progressing with endless turns and roundabouts *of its own accord* and this process can already be perceived by the initiated. The present crisis is part of a transitional catharsis. Our culture is not dying, it is only hard pressed for the moment and if it can become aware that it is actually undergoing a rejuvenation-cure it can work through this period swiftly and almost painlessly. Sorrow can turn to rejoicing. Culture is not dead, but sleepeth!

This solution to the problem of culture seems very comforting, at least at this critical moment, if one can accept this manner of analyzing the crisis out of existence. The disease now becomes a healthy indisposition as culture swings with a few violent jerks from one phase to another. The baby chick must peck its shell to pieces before it can emerge; the child of man is not born without travail (except in America: a sign of decadence or of progress?). This is nature's way. Cultural crises are thus reduced to a kind of natural phenomenon, with ascertainable rhythm, length and sequence of cycles, fluctuations, etc. The process is an automatic one, and phase follows phase for better or worse in a cycle containing three or four possible stages and styles, each set of stages bound to the life cycle of a particular culture. The same drama is played over and over again, only the geographical setting shifts from time to time over the face of the earth. This self-repeating solution is ultimately without comfort for man.

However, whether it is comforting or comfortless, both from the standpoint of our own culture and of all culture, need not concern us here. What is of prime importance is the fact that there is another school of thought which turns the future over to impersonal forces outside man's control. Man might just as well not bother about the condition of his time, because things will work out themselves. If this optimistic hypothesis should turn out to be wrong, however, we may find ourselves in the position of having permitted a seriously ill patient to die without lifting a finger to render medical aid. And the assumption of the immanent dawning at this very moment of a new and higher phase of culture is *hypothetical* in the extreme.

Sorokin finds support for the hypothesis in his discovery of the law of polarisation, according to which in periods of crisis the positive elements may become much more positive and the negative may become much more negative. In his view the positive forces will produce an ethical-religious renaissance (comparable to Spengler's "second religiosity" and Toynbee's notion of a "universal church"). This process will at the same time accelerate the disintegration of the existing phase of culture and create the basis for a new flowering of civilization as positive polarization is carried out.[1]

This "natural law" of culture is also extremely hypothetical, however.

---

1. It appears as if Sorokin, in spite of his sharp criticism of the decadent Americanism of today's ultra this-worldly culture, is himself possessed by the optimistic idealism concerning automatic progress embodied in the "American Creed". This positive image of the future, as has already been stated, must remain outside the scope of this work but will receive attention in a later study.

Our study has demonstrated not so much the increasing negativization of the negative, as the increasing reversal of positive into negative forces, with a triumphant nihilism winning the day. Concerning the phenomenon of positive polarization, whether in the form of a Messianic-Joannine Age or the onset of the New Middle Ages, one can only say that while there may be some visionary truth in these predictions, there are no verifiable indications of this to be found to any impressive degree at the present time. On the contrary, such predictions run counter to all the dominant trends of the time. They are essentially the personal expectations for the future of the writers who have expounded them, and may prove to be founded on nothing more than wishful thinking. While we are paying attention to them, precious time is going by. A too-sharply defined and unfounded prediction is barring the way to a change in public images of the future which may be more influential under the circumstances.

We will lay aside the questions of whether cultures as such in reality never completely decline and disappear; whether each succeeding stage is higher and more perfect than the last and whether there are indeed certain ideas, values and styles which never die, so that the best of Western culture will live on in a spiritually concentrated form forever. One can always pull such ideas out of history, provided that one first puts them in. In respect to this idea, at least, one can say that history perpetually repeats itself.

Such ideas can neither be proved nor disproved, since their absolute truth or un-truth will never be established within man's experience. I think it highly dangerous, however, to postulate invariants in the course of human history and to project them on to future developments. Ascribing immortality in a literal sense to any human achievements is a highly dubious proceeding. The idea of a culture which in essence never disappears is a beautiful one, but hardly verifiable in any scientific sense. It makes culture into an absolute and puts creative cultural awareness in the category of unimportant forces which can just as well be ignored. It lulls man into a false sense of security regarding his own future instead of roughly awakening him to the gravity of his plight. In short, this type of cultural optimism makes the one thing seem superfluous which is in fact indispensable to man's survival—the development of new and inspiring images of the future.

D. Cultural Indifference

Quite another point of view regarding culture is possible, and one that promises equally disastrous results. It does not arise among historians, but rather in othodox religious circles, although it receives considerable support from Toynbee's attitude. Certainly, this line of argument maintains, Western culture will decline, and perhaps disappear permanently from the historical scene, along with all its cherished treasures. *All* culture is transitory, perishable. Only one thing is eternal and imperishable, and that is the divinely-revealed truth of Christianity. Christianity should not therefore even try to bind its fate to that of any temporary temporal culture. It certainly does not make sense for Christianity to try to preserve at any price a culture which is already in a process of decline. It is not for Christianity to prop up that which is decayed and rotten. The collapse of this civilization, and possibly with it today's fossilized form of Christianity, may well fit into the plan of Divine Providence which is working for man's ultimate salvation in ways imponderable to man.

We have termed this view disastrous (although from a religious point of view it is perfectly tenable) because of its unavoidable consequences. It is disastrous for religion and culture alike. In our historical analysis we have tried to show that, however understandable this attempt to salvage religion by separating it from a dying culture may be, in the end the sacrifice of culture on the altar of religion is fruitless. Religion cannot be saved in this manner, for the same life's blood which flows through the body of culture flows through the body of its religion; their circulatory systems are intertwined. A condition of hardening of the arteries will equally affect both. In our opinion the future of Christianity is threatened equally with the future of Western civilization.

It will be even more outspoken, although at the risk of being misunderstood. While on the one hand it is possible, sociologically speaking, for Western culture to survive on the basis of a newly rejuvenated Christian-humanistic set of values concerning the future of man and his life on earth (such as has already been taught by a line of thinkers from Socrates to Jesus and from Joachim to Schweitzer) entirely *without* the ecclesiastical New-Testament dogmatism and ritual, on the other hand it is highly probable that this most recent theological and ecclesiastical form of a two-thousand-year-old Christianity will not be able to strike new roots in any *other* culture than that of the West. As I see it, the various forms of Christianity would be swallowed up by other religious or anti-religious movements if Western Civilization disappears and is replaced bij another culture, whether or not a predominantly Eastern one. This would be particularly true of those Christian sects which are primarily oriented toward the past and have nothing but an extinguished torch to pass on to their spiritual descendants.

Scientific speculation about the continued existence of Christianity beyond the life span of this or any other culture (for the religious man this is of course a God-given certainty) can find its only historical justification in the fact of the rise of Christianity amidst the ruins of the Roman Empire and the Hellenic civilization of Antiquity. *At that time* Christianity spread like wildfire in the face of all obstacles because of the power of its inspired and

ecstatic vision of the future which enabled its followers to break through
catacomb and cataclysm, through caesarism and collapsing culture, through
mass murder and martyrdom. *Now*, however, it must share the responsibility, along with other social forces, for the present state of decline of
our modern civilization. As an integral part of this civilization it suffers
from the same deadly illness, a loss of faith in its own positive image of the
future, or, what is worse, a compulsion to destroy what is left of that
positive image. It was just this religious, eschatological image of the future
which played such an important role in shaping not only Christianity,
but the whole of Western civilization. To postulate the survival of Christianity for all eternity is to speculate trustfully but without trust fund on the
Unknown. It also involves the sanctioning in advance of any situation in
which culture and religion may find themselves, including that of suicide.

E. Cultural Invariance

The last point of view regarding culture which we will discuss is clearly
related to cultural indifference, and has certainly exercised a strong influence on it. In the theory of cultural invariance the two extremes of Christian
theology and atheistic existential philosophy meet. The points of departure
for these two systems of thought are at opposite poles; one describes the
process of salvation, the other of damnation. According to a leading school
of existentialism, all culture is basically irrelevant. Man is doomed to exist
in a world which is fundamentally indifferent to him. No particular form of
civilization can alter this ultimate fact. One culture is as good (or bad) as
another and they all bring misery to man. The rise and fall of any one
culture can thus make no difference to suffering humanity.

The two theories coincide in the fact of separating culture from the
"basic reality" of history, which is in the one case labelled religion, in the
other philosophy. The phenomena which they describe are seen as absolute
and invariant, independent of all cultural forms, while in reality they
perspire the peculiar sweat of our own culture from every pore, and give
off the odour of its decay. The parallel can be carried even further. While
religion is busy emancipating itself from the cyclical movements of culture,
in an attempt at self-preservation, and asserting that the fall of our civilization will in the end serve the ultimate advance of Christianity, it is falling
deeper and deeper into the pit of cultural quietism—"whatever is, is best".
Since its expectations are bound up, not with any particular culture, but
with eternity, it can remain calm as cultures come and go, knowing that it
wil reach its goal in the end.

Existentialism, at least through some of its most prominent expounders,
sets no goal and envisages no final end. The world always was, is, and shall

be subject to the forces of evil. There is no salvation. Cultures may come and cultures may go, but man's sisyphean toil will go on for ever.

Thus we find influential representatives of orthodox Christianity and of ultra-modern existentialism staggering into the same bed, having both undergone the same self-inflicted operation of cutting themselves loose from the total dynamics of the cultural process. Far from being autonomous entities, they are pitiful victims of the cultural crisis, in their very sickness intensifying that crisis. The extremes of *essence-optimism* and *essence-pessimism* merge, rushing headlong away from the faith in the active human will which characterized the eighteenth and nineteenth centuries, into a pessimism of inactivity, apathy and resignation. Somewhere in the process the idea of human dignity and man's self-determination is lost. Civilization is left to its own fate.

These typical off-shoots of religion and philosophy, in thus deserting the sinking ship of civilization, announce to all the world that this civilization is of little worth and that its loss can make no real difference to man. They are abandoning their centuries-old comrade and ally just when she most needs them, and leaving her to drift rudderless on the sea of social dynamics. We have already seen that they may be spelling out their own doom in so doing, for these small life-boats, sturdy though they be, cannot long survive without the mother ship to come back to. Furthermore, in failing to fulfil their function of creating new and positive images of the future they must shoulder a large share of the responsibility for the failure of our civilization. In just those areas where they think to make the greatest contribution, through a rejuvenated and modernized (i.e., "realistic") theology and philosophy, they are serving the cause of Nietschean nihilism the best.

With regard to the five theories of cultural dynamics outlined above, it is not difficult to see how drastically they deviate from the point of view of this book. They can be briefly summarized, now, as follows:

1. There is practically nothing else man can do but accept that which natural law and destiny brings to pass.

2. There is nothing else man can do, unless a scheme or attitude particularly favoured by each writer in turn is, by some miracle generally adopted by or instilled in society.

3. There is nothing that man needs to do now; the current disturbance is a perfectly normal transitional phase, and the patient will feel better than ever when it is all over.

4. Even if there were something that could be done, man does not need to do it, because the cycles of cultural rise and fall serve only as springboards for the divinely-ordained upward climb of the Christian religion.

5. There is no point in doing anything, for this civilization is no more worth preserving than any other; they all bring the same amount of suffering to man.

All five attitudes are equally untenable. The real sickness of our civilization lies in the lack of belief in its future; in man's deliberate self-incapacitation and unwillingness to free himself from the bonds of the present, and in his refusal to allow himself to think anew and systematically about a radically different and better future.

We reject these views on the following grounds:

The first, because the transformation of faith in the future into lack of faith, whatever historical causes one may ascribe to this process, can never be the result of forces or laws operating from the *outside* on the human sphere of action. It results from a man-made social process, particularly in connection with man's thought about and behaviour in the face of the future, whether this thought and behaviour is religiously or humanistically oriented.

The second, because both the diagnoses and therapies are too one-sided and lack even an attempt at scientific impartiality. The remedies are all monopolistic, involving those writers' personally preferred images of the future to the exclusion of all *other* images regardless of their possibilities.

The third, because the true complexity of the problem is artificially analysed away, abnormality raised to the level of normality and the phenomenon of culture-crisis made into an automatic mechanism which will ensure the dawning of a new and better age. (The sad fate of similar economic visions concerning necessary catastrophes, of liberals and Marxists alike, should have taught us better.) This is the doctrine of supra-human and benign causation in a new form.

The fourth and fifth, because they both, each in their own way, are typically diseased products of the current situation and sacrifice completely faith in human power to reshape a good society. They not only countenance drifting with the times, but rejoice in it, as the only possible course to take in the present situation, thus exalting a serene and resigned amor fati.

3. How is a Revival of Culture Still Possible?

What *constructive* thoughts can be added to this *critical* review of existing trends of thought? Having cleared all hindrances out of the way, we are now ready, with the courage of despair, to dare the last great leap into the future. Let us assume for the sake of argument that it is indeed true that Western civilization has fallen into its present state mainly or largely because of the decline in its positive images of the future and that the breach in our times coincides with the iconoclasm of its images and an accompanying retreat into unimaginative realism. Let us further assume that it is also true that this negativization and iconoclasm, leading to an anti-dualistic destruction of the Other World and Time, and spreading cultural nihilism, would eventuate in cutting off Western civilization root and branch. If this connected survey, analysis and prediction is accepted in its essence as just and probable, then we must *now attempt to think backwards out of the future and draw the last logical consequence*. Our concept of the image of the future must now take on a fourth, therapeutic function which is also the ultimate justification for its existence.

Western civilization is not lost beyond the possibility of salvation, not yet irrevocably doomed to death, if we can find the right answer to the almost overwhelming challenge which the future offers to our own time, in the form of purposeful, vital and inspiring images of the future. These images must have the power to tear our civilization loose from the claws of the present and free it once more to think about and act for the future. The seed of these images becomes the life-blood of culture, and the transfiguration of our civilization waits upon the sowing of new seed.

This conclusion follows, as the redeeming synthesis, upon the foregoing analysis. It presupposes the possibility of a new spiritual wave in the stream of the times. It assumes that the old negativated images of the future can be welded anew into positive forms, and that right quickly. It further assumes that these reconstructed images can once more possess the minds of the Western peoples, both the élite and the masses, dominate the currents of science, philosophy and religion, and activate social movements and even politial parties. It presupposes, in short, a fundamental reversal? Is it a purely academic possibility, or is there still a realistic "fair chance" that this may happen?

It is certainly my intention, if time and circumstances permit, to deal further with this crucial question in another book.[1] At this point I can only indicate the general trend of my own thinking in rough outline. It is important neither to underestimate the difficulty of the problem nor to give up in advance on the assumption that it is unsolvable. We must first deal with the question of why a new swing of the pendulum in regard to images of the future cannot be taken for granted with an easy optimism. If history is indeed a long chain of dialectical movements, and is so often characterized by unexpected reversals and upheavals, why can we not assume that this particular reversal, a trend towards more optimistic images of the future will also take place in due course?

In the first place, it is not simply a question of any arbitrary reversal of trends at any random time. It is a question of the *right* reversal at the *right*

1. This intention has been partly carried out in two further Dutch books, the titles of which read in translation: *Hopeful Perspectives for the Future* (1957); *Automation, Industrial and Cultural Revolution* (1958).

time. Not only has the crisis of our civilization assumed grave proportions, but it has reached that critical stage where the *need for time* is the primary *need of the times*. There is not so much time left as we should like. The need for time pinches the more because the social sciences have not yet developed far enough to keep pace with the natural sciences and technology. They are racing their motors under pressure from the other sciences, but the nose of their vehicle is pointed towards an abyss.

Images of the future which are more than castles in the air and have the strength to dam up and divert in another direction the headlong rush to catastrophe of our age, are not so easily constructed. Least of all can one set the clock back by a romantic dreaming of *new Middle Ages*, a new primitive Christianity or any age of the dead and gone past, and simply restore positive images of the future out of the past to what they once were. No humanism can conjure up the classical Age of Antiquity again, nor can any rebirth make the Renaissance live again. The rivers of history flow without ceasing, and no society bathes twice in the same stream. All undulatory movements, even those which appear to be strictly cyclical, move forward in time though they may repeat their upward and downward motions. History does not repeat itself.

After the iconoclasm of the last half-century, the images of the future out of past centuries scarcely exist as such any longer, and could probably not be forced into new life. We may at this point recall what was said about the double charge which positive images of the future carry. First, they liberate the present so that it can move forward into the future. The images then sacrifice themselves to this liberated present in order to give it the dynamic power of movement. This dialectical process of charge and discharge can never be reversed. The battery is burned out, the power is gone. Images of the future contain no secret perpetum mobile. In influencing the times, they are in turn "used up" by the times. The changes which the images bring about in the society they work upon leave them gasping for breath as they try to keep up with a newly accelerated tempo of social life; in the end the images must give up and collapse, exhausted.

This is why it is not possible, except by a meaningless stroke of the pen on paper, to revive old images of the future. Neither is it possible, however, to pull casually out of a sleeve new images of the future, i.e. those which can really inspire and motivate a society. All this is perhaps obvious, and scarcely encouraging as we impartially review the numerous failures in the recent past to revive old images or set up new revolutionary images of the future.

These failures are fully explained when we realize that our contemporary culture disqualifies just those qualities, devalues just those values and makes, unthinkable just those thoughts and ideas which would be vitally necessary in giving new life to our culture. We refer to such things as the idealistic belief in the possibility of bringing about a new and better society on earth, confidence in man's collective capacity to do this out of his own power, and an unwavering faith in man's essential worth in spite of social cataclysms. There must be some basic certainty that, in spite of the current dehumanization of the increasingly mass-minded man, and in spite of the imperfections which stubbornly cling to the human race, some radical reversal of the existing order is possible. Not a reversal that will usher in a static age of perfection, but one that will make possible a considerably better world than man has known thus far.

If we reckon adequately with all the unfavourable conditions of our time and take their measure as accurately as we may, allowing for their existence as we assess every attempt to break through the general aversion to idealism and positive visions of any kind, we may then once more pose our question: is there still a real possibility for the maintenance and revival of our Western culture, in terms of a general spiritual rejuvenation and forward movement? Can an inspiring vision of the future for Western civilization still burst forth from our time?

We will not try to evade this question with the stoic wisdom, "point n'est besoin d'espérer pour entreprendre, ni de réussir pour persévérer" (It is not necessary to hope in order to try, nor is it necessary to succeed in order to persevere). Hopeful expectation, on the contrary, is essential in the formation of positive images of the future; this forms the basis for dogged perseverance in the face of unforeseen setbacks. Not only must the author of visions have this hopeful expectation deep in his own heart, but his audience must catch enough of it to be inspired with the necessary courage to overcome obstacles.

In good conscience we cannot give a categorically positive answer to the question we have raised. To the straightforward query: Do you yourself think a recovery of Western civilization is possible along the lines you have indicated? I can only answer: At the moment yes, certainly; but the time may come, even within the next half-century, when it *will no longer be possible*. The time *is* short, and therein lies our greatest handicap. We are fighting an unequal battle with time, because time has the most crucial weapon, the passing hours, on its own side. We are in a struggle in which the strongest power will win, and no special clemency will be shown to man.

How are we to weigh the relative strength of man against time? This is the crux of the problem. We must use the prevailing images of the future as a measuring instrument in order to calculate their own chances for survival, on the basis of whatever dynamic force is left in them. We have in fact already done this, and reached the conclusion that the spiritual

power of propulsion of today's positive images of the future has been
seriously undermined and weakened. The injury has been indentified from
a social-psychological point of view as a fading of the *purposeful awareness
of the future*, and its replacement by a narrowly delimited awareness of the
present. From a sociological point of view, it is a crippling of religious,
aesthetic, humanistic and idealistic awareness; in short, a general shrinking
of our creative cultural awareness.

This is our problem in a nutshell, for it is from this position of constricted
awareness of another and better future that the destructive trends of our
times are in danger of rushing forward with accelerated speed. Though
the damage may be serious, however, the downward rush has not yet
started, and the patient is not yet beyond recovery. Not *yet*.

It now remains to determine the extent of the damage caused by this
disease, this collective time-psychosis, so that we may know how much
time there is left to us. The situation in regard to permanent deterioration
versus the possibility of varying degrees of reparation is not the same in one
area of culture as in another. At the risk of appearing to contradict our
earlier remarks about the same life-blood running through all of cultures so
that no area can be autonomous, we must point out here that it is not at
all certain that each of those areas which have already reached a low point
will be able to regain former heights to the same degree. Conversely, our
argument that if a reversal in trends does not take place soon the whole of
our civilization will be doomed does not necessarily include every special
branch to the same extent or imply simultaneity of change.

If the general structure of Western civilization can indeed be maintained,
it is highly unlikely that it will be maintained unchanged from its present
state. The probability of change becomes instead a certainty when we turn
from the abstract statement that a recovery of our civilization is possible to
the concrete problem of the content of the new images of the future. Referring back for a moment to our earlier distinction between eschatological and
utopian images of the future, the pregnant problem is whether both types
can be brought to life again.

The eschatological image of the future is in the more serious trouble, in
my opinion. The situation is indeed a paradoxical one. Never has eschatology been the subject of so much writing and discussion as today, and
never has theology been so thoroughly de-eschatologized, never have
the expectations for the future Kingdom of Heaven of the community
of believers been so vague and contentless, especially as regards the
future of man himself. Nevertheless (or perhaps for this very reason?)
it is among the believers that one meets the greatest resistance to an
emphasis on the need for the reinstatement of positive images of the
future. "What a lot of silly talk about images of the future"! comes the

resentful chorus of orthodox Christians. "Don't you know that there is only *one* image of the future which is worthy of the name, one image which is valid for all eternity, and that this image is the *only* one which can possibly serve as the basis for a new flowering of Christian culture? All other images of the future are but the fruit of a godless and unholy futurism, the misleading illusion of utopism".

We will not repeat our earlier discussion on this point. This attitude is certainly understandable, and perfectly justified from the Christian point of view. But as a culture-sociologist I must strongly take issue with it, because it is a deliberate process of spiritual eye-shutting to the grave crisis we are in. The iconoclasts have in the end done the most damage to themselves! We cannot ignore the fact that the eschatological vision of the coming Kingdom is at one and the same time a source of security and a disappearing phenomenon. It no longer provides Christianity with its chief attractive force, as far as the outside world is concerned, nor is it the unmatched spiritual dynamic it once was for the religious community itself. To the extent that the eschatological vision does remain vital in certain small circles or in the religious convictions of some individuals, its basis has been narrowed down to the extent that no one can any longer pretend that this vision could possibly be *the* image of the future which can and will prevail for the whole of Western culture and save it from its present crisis.

We nevertheless find reflections of this more or less orthodox and dogmatic idea in thinkers such as Toynbee, Berdiaiev and Schubart. In less pronounced form, and amply clothed in ethical-humanistic garments, we also find it in Schweitzer and Sorokin. In direct opposition to these illustrious thinkers, I regret I must deny, on the basis of the foregoing analysis, that the weakened Christian vision of the future is at this moment in any condition to save our civilization. On the contrary, it is itself badly in need of salvation. It is, alas, threatened with inglorious extinction as an eschatology sans eschaton. Whether this eschatological image has the capacity and elasticity to rejuvenate itself and can in this way yet contribute to the preservation of our civilization is quite another question. However desirable such a turn of events might be, I personally doubt whether this could happen. Since I am not really qualified to judge, I am willing to state that I may be in error and give eschatology the benefit of the doubt. Even if it can regain its old position within the Christian religion, however, there is still the fact of creeping secularization, which has made deep inroads on Christianity that cannot be wiped out. Western culture is no longer *primarily* a Christian culture. Whether one rejoices or sorrows over this, the fact must be accepted. To make the fact of Christianization the ultimate condition for the continued existence of Western culture is the same as deliberately choosing to let Christianity be further weakened.

The Middle Ages, which had a thriving eschatological image of the future, will not return. Neither will the period of Revolution and Rationalism, when the utopian image had its hey-day. *Our age has turned against both images alike.* In this period of rejection and exile, those who are concerned for these images must let the accent fall on the unity which is present among their diversities. The warring brothers must swallow their differences in the face of the common enemy. The exclusive claims of the eschatological image have not lost their meaning, *within the religious sphere*, especially as these claims maintain themselves in the face of the pseudo-eschatology of modern myth and ideology. The utopian image is basically concerned with *another* sphere, the dynamically interacting human society on earth and its earth-bound goals. In a strongly secularized world the cultural task of the utopian image is more indispensable than ever—paradoxically enough, in part because it alone can in our time maintain the cultural base for religion. Eschatological and utopian visions, ultimately sprung from the same spiritual source and now threatened by the same social forces, must learn to *understand, tolerate* and *fulfil* one another.

The common threat which both face comes not only from within our culture, but from *outside* it. Culture, like nature, abhors a vacuum. Any internal disintegration which leaves such a vacuum attracts other forces which proceed to fill the empty spaces. The vacuum left by disappearing positive images of the future in our own time cannot long remain. The choice for modern man is no longer between this image of the future and that but between images of his own responsible choosing and images which are forced upon him by outside pressures. The empty void between today and tomorrow cannot withstand the magnetic pull of tomorrow, especially while a new kind of image of the future is flowing from Eastern Europe like white-hot lava over large parts of Asia and Africa, engulfing the minds of myriad masses of men. One may abhor this image as ungodly, inhuman and false both to religion and culture, but it is nevertheless an image of the future, however misleading and ultimately doomed to extinction it is considered to be. It is already exercising a tremendous attraction on certain circles in Western Europe. Only if and when the "Cold Peace" breaks out will this attraction really be felt to its full extent. There is an old saying "Once bitten, twice shy"! But alas, spreading paralysis has made Western civilization insensitive to the nips. It is hard to say whether the West at bay suffers most from apathy or from a lack of vision, but this decaying and divided house is hardly in good shape to meet the onslaught of new and virulent ideas from the East.

The urgency of having powerful and positive images of the future which will have mass appeal at the disposal of the West becomes ever more apparent. Between the eschatology and pseudo-eschatology of today lies a vast fallow field. If the eschatological image of the future can really be made to live again in all its old power, so much the better. If it cannot, as seems more likely, then we must pin our hopes for cultural survival on a blending of utopian and eschatological images, or even on predominantly utopian images. Christianity has as much at stake in supporting such images as does any part of our civilization. The task before us is to reawaken the almost dormant *awareness of the future* and to find the best nourishment for a starving *cultural awareness* and *creativity*. For Western Europe, this means finding its own way out, without resorting to a slavish imitation of either Russian or American patterns. For America, it means considerable soul-searching regarding the vitality of the American Dream, which has for so long been taken for granted. It is not too late to do this. Man has not yet been degraded to animal or machine. The new dehumanized species of homo, direfully predicted by some novelists and philosophers has not yet appeared, or at least not yet to be recognized as such.[1]

We cannot ignore the fact that a large-scale attack on broad fronts of Western civilization is already under way, however, and that some deep wedges have been driven into the lines of defense. Where Western man has been pushed the hardest his responses have not always been the most admirable, and there are points at which he appears to have abandoned his post altogether, escaping into whatever temporary havens he could find. Modern art has provided one such haven, attempting to retrain the eye and the ear to find beauty in ugliness and order in chaos. Religion has tried to divest itself of its transcendental character, and social democracy has tried to divest itself of its immanence: the one escaping the reality it is meant to preach, the other postponing the reality it is meant to approach. Philosophy has partly divorced itself from all knowledge of and seeking after the good and abandons man to present evil and eventual destruction. It has placed on the face of the future the granite mask of nothingness. Depth psychology endeavours to acquaint man with his bestial unconscious and leads him on to the next step of reconciliation with his own bestiality. Technology makes of man a slave; physically, as he tends the machines which dominate his life, and spiritually, as with increasing parasitism he consumes their soul-less products. The spirit of the times focuses all thinking on the realistic status quo, and carefully directs the dreamer away from reveries about the

1. Alfred Weber has written some interesting things about the "fourth man", a depersonalized robot-man, instrument of a burocratic terror-machine. The first three types of man in this scheme are, respectively Neanderthal Man (pre-homo sapiens); primitive man (who thinks in terms of myths and the irrational) and civilized man (rational and religious). See: *Kulturgeschichte als Kultursoziologie*, Munich, 1951, Chapter VII, "Kommt der vierte Mensch"? Also, *Der Dritte oder der vierte Mensch*, Munich, 1953.

idealistic status ad quem. And yet in spite of all this, one mighty fortress remains to man. His *capacity for dualism* has not yet atrophied, and thus the chief condition for construction of positive images of the future remains. The mental process of splitting reality continues, although frequently in inappropriate and grotesque ways.

Man knows better than ever, thanks to modern technology, how to create something different from day-to-day reality. But this type of creation no longer represents an ideal *tension* between present and future, but a strictly utilitarian *escape from tension* through a splitting of the present into two parts. We refer to daily life versus the modern dream-factories such as film, fiction and television, to all the sense-prickling, diversions for the eye and the ear, and to all products such as alcohol and drugs which elate the feelings, etc. These are all *diversions* in the truest sense of the word, diversions away from the future and the task of building visions.

But this same mental capacity can be used in another and higher way; it can serve the regeneration of culture. We are standing at what may be the last fork in the road, We can choose whether we will take the high road or the low road, and they don't both go to Scotland. If we take the low road and follow the vision of the negative utopia, the utopia upside-down, there can be only one end to the journey—the abyss of nothingness for our civilization. A new civilization may arise, Phoenix-like, from the ashes of the old, but there may be a long interim period of chaos and barbarism for man.

There is another, better choice. We can still choose to take the high road that leads to the Realm of the Future. In the face of such a choice, can we shrug our shoulders and say, "Après nous le déluge", or will we, each and every one, firmly put our foot on this high road and say in answer to the urgent voice of Time, "here I am, send me"?

We have striking evidence that the willingness and capacity for trying favourably to determine or influence man's own destiny have not disappeared. The fact that the Russian image of the future has commanded such a widespread following and elicited such remarkably dedicated, even if ill-fated, behaviour on the part of its disciples, including those *outside* Russia, indicates that man is still able to choose *and work for* a high and difficult goal. That the Russian vision may be based on some fundamental misunderstandings and illusions regarding social reality and in our view on undesirable objectives, which imply the denial of the dignity, freedom and individual rights of man and which must therefore eventually be shattered, does not entirely detract from the devoted service many men have given to this vision. Part of the European intelligentsia are even glad and willing to walk the road towards self-destruction to the bitter end on behalf of this vision. The whole tragedy of "Holy Russia" (and therefore of our modern world) is that her zeal could not serve a holy vision.

The evidence from America regarding the vitality of existing images of the future is somewhat mixed. The tragedy of "Happy America" is that it has not always impressed on the world a happy vision. The European observer on the whole sees a tremendous dynamic potential still active in this country, and at the same discovers what seems to be a dangerous social apathy. America is at present a land of extremes. The greatest visions, and most daring experimentation to the farthest limits of the human mind and the natural environment, exist side by side with the crassest materialism and preoccupation with a tomorrowless Now.

Although much of our thinking about the future today is inevitably in terms of choosing between the two alternative and bitterly competing images of the future which the East and the West have set before us, we must in the long run pass beyond these dichotomies which paint the future in black and white against the background of one or another national or imperial symbol. Neither Russia nor America, alone, can spawn the future. The image of the future, at its best, has always been *universal* in character, a vision to serve and foster the growth of all mankind. At a time when the lack of such a vision seems to be driving us to self-destruction, it is well to remember that one of the most potent and enduring visions in the history of man has been that of a thousand years' reign of peace. This is a vision which is never entirely absent from the hearts of every man and woman who come together to bear children and build a home. If the man leaves that home unfinished and the wife and child of his heart alone in order to go forth to war, as he has so often done in the past, it is only that he may in the end return and continue building in Peace. If the woman endures hardship bravely and finds ways to survive when there seems to be no hope of survival, it is only that the child of her womb may live to build a better world. The sparks of this universal vision lie in every human spirit in every land and clime, waiting to be enkindled by prophets who are not frightened by fences, walls and curtains and who will not rest until the world is Everyman's Garden. A vision of the future which falls short of this universality may indeed succeed in obliterating fences and walls, but at the cost of leaving the earth a barren smoking ruin instead of a garden. The same tool cannot serve simultaneously as sword and ploughshare, and the scope of the vision will determine the final use to which the tool is put. If our prophets are not far-sighted enough, we may perish through the inadequacy of our visions.

With Eastern Europe galloping at top speed after what seems to us largely a chimera, with Western Europe frozen into passive despair and America chasing her own tail in a rather confused state of mind, we can *still* take courage for the future, *for we know that the capacity to create and follow visions has not been lost*. We have already indicated that there are hopeful signs both in the Russia and in the America of today. We must look to what we have. Our first challenge is to examine the basic foundations of our existing visions, to analyze their contents, scope and direction. Analyzed in these terms, where did the upward striving Russians go astray and how far? Why are the traditionally full-speed-ahead Americans bogging down, or are they? These two questions lead straight into two major projects which social science must undertake, the theory and dynamics of image formation and propagation, and field studies of current images of the future in action. This book opens up these themes, but much remains to be done in both areas. The challenge is, moreover, for everyone, the intellectual, the artist and the layman alike.

For the social scientist, an adequate study of the image of the future, both theoretical and descriptive as in case studies of existing societies, means drawing on knowledge and techniques from every branch of social science and achieving a working integration of this knowledge. For other intellectuals, both "ivory tower" thinkers and those in positions of active leadership, for the social engineers of our society, from technically-trained people to business men and politicians, and for the artists, it means not only examination of their own visions, but an examination of their attitude *toward* visions. You who have provided mankind with its visions in the past, are you not now guilty of belittling all creative thinking about the future? Have not the adjectives "utopian" and "visionary" taken on a somewhat derogatory meaning? It was not always so. We need a new generation of Founding Fathers to father a new age—men of the same breed as that first generation of Americans, hard-headed visionaries who knew how to make dreams come true. We must rediscover the truths which they held to be self-evident and forge new dreams from them.

Perhaps we should ask whether we still have creative leadership in our democratic society. Or has the thinking élite (the very term inspires horror in the democratic mind) been absorbed into the passive mass-mind as a result of its own idealistic fraternization with it? The answer is no, certainly not yet. The very ideals which have prompted the fraternization can rescue both leaders and masses if *awareness* comes in time. The thinkers, leaders and creators of our age still have all the wealth of the uncensored past and the vast reservoir of the open future to draw upon in creating new visions, plus the opportunity to bring the great mass of the people into responsible partnership in fulfilling these visions. The same educational system and mass media which now threaten to deaden the mind of the average man can also be used to awaken it—if we *know* what we are doing.

If we can arouse our own creative leadership in time, are our ideals and values good enough for the task ahead? We must honestly confess that there are many shrivelled husks lying around in our culture—husks of once vital ideas which have somehow dried up. Existentialism has been busy sweeping up these husks in order to provide itself—and mankind—with a tidy if barren room. Though dead, there is living seed among them. If this is planted and tended, mankind will not go hungry at harvest time. If the sowing, tending and harvesting is *your* job, you will know it in your hart. Those capable and responsible should begin today; tomorrow may be too late.

It is the layman's responsibility to be aware of his own aspirations and those of the group to which he belongs. It is for him to choose the vision he will follow and to take the necessary steps to carry it out. Society offers him not just one role, but many. In the way he performs these roles, in the family, in the community, in his choices of vocation, he stands answerable for the vision he chooses. Because the old biblical truth is still the most modern truth: "When there is no vision, the people perish".

No man or woman can thus be exempted from taking up the challenge. Social scientists, intellectuals, artists, leaders and middle-men of every breed, and the Common Man (and Woman) to whom, after all, this Century belongs—we must all ask ourselves, "What is *my* vision of the future, and what am I doing about it"?

God forbid that we should end this book on a note of self-study! If Western civilization does go down irrevocably, the last figures to be seen above the flood waters will have pencil and notebook in hand, busily conducting an investigation of what is happening. No. We need to understand our ailing visions in order to know what to reject and what to accept in them, but all our study is only a preliminary clearing of the decks for the great act of purposeful, responsible recreation of images of a still glorious future which beckons if we have but the wisdom, courage and strength to break through the present and lift the veil of the future. All our self-study, like psycho-analysis, is only meaningful if it liberates us from our compulsion-ridden autodestructive behaviour as a society and frees us to choose our own destiny and build a new and better world.

To *choose* our vision we first have to *have* visions. Man has the capacity to dream finer dreams than he has ever succeeded in dreaming up to this moment. He has the capacity to build a finer society than he has ever succeeded in building. The poet, the painter, the musician have always known this, and so has the man of religion. The physical scientists know it too, and the social scientist, and the doctor of medicine and the doctor of the mind. Must we stay paralyzed by this self-awareness? Here lies a real, urgent challenge! There are among us even now dreamers and builders who are ready to step over the bounds of this passive self-awareness into the realm of free creativity. As they repeat the age-old process of splitting the atom of Time, the forces released through this temporal fission will set the Western world free from its over-long imprisonment in the Present. Man will once again move forward to meet his own vision of the Future, to "seek the city which is to come".

INDEX OF NAMES